MYSTICISM BUDDHIST AND CHRISTIAN

Nanzan Studies in Religion and Culture
James W. Heisig, General Editor

Heinrich Dumoulin, *Zen Buddhism: A History. Vol. 1, India and China*. Trans. James Heisig and Paul Knitter (New York: Macmillan, 1988, 1994)

Heinrich Dumoulin, *Zen Buddhism: A History. Vol. 2, Japan*. Trans. James Heisig and Paul Knitter (New York: Macmillan, 1989)

Frederick Franck, ed., *The Buddha Eye: An Anthology of the Kyoto School* (New York: Crossroad, 1982)

Frederick Franck, *To Be Human Against All Odds* (Berkeley: Asian Humanities Press, 1991)

James W. Heisig and John C. Maraldo, eds., *Rude Awakenings: Zen, the Kyoto School, and the Question of Nationalism* (Honolulu: University of Hawaii Press, 1995)

Winston L. King, *Death Was His Kōan: The Samurai-Zen of Suzuki Shōsan* (Berkeley: Asian Humanities Press, 1986)

Robert E. Morrell, *Early Kamakura Buddhism: A Minority Report* (Berkeley: Asian Humanities Press, 1987)

Nagao Gadjin, *The Foundational Standpoint of Mādhyamika Philosophy*. Trans. John Keenan (New York: SUNY Press , 1989)

Nishida Kitarō, *Intuition and Reflection in Self-Consciousness*. Trans. Valdo Viglielmo et al. (New York: SUNY Press, 1987)

Nishitani Keiji, *Nishida Kitarō* (Berkeley: University of California Press, 1991)

Nishitani Keiji, *Religion and Nothingness*. Trans. Jan Van Bragt (Berkeley: University of California Press, 1985)

Nishitani Keiji, *The Self-Overcoming of Nihilism*. Trans. Graham Parkes and Setsuko Aihara (New York: SUNY Press , 1990)

Paul L. Swanson, *Foundations of T'ien-T'ai Philosophy: The Flowering of the Two-Truths Theory in Chinese Buddhism* (Berkeley: Asian Humanities Press, 1989)

Takeuchi Yoshinori, *The Heart of Buddhism: In Search of the Timeless Spirit of Primitive Buddhism*. Trans. James Heisig (New York: Crossroad, 1983)

Tanabe Hajime, *Philosophy as Metanoetics*. Trans. Takeuchi Yoshinori et al. (Berkeley: University of California Press, 1987)

Taitetsu Unno, ed., *The Religious Philosophy of Nishitani Keiji: Encounter with Emptiness* (Berkeley: Asian Humanities Press, 1990)

Taitetsu Unno and James Heisig, eds., *The Religious Philosophy of Tanabe Hajime: The Metanoetic Imperative* (Berkeley: Asian Humanities Press, 1990)

Hans Waldenfels, *Absolute Nothingness: Foundations for a Buddhist-Christian Dialogue*. Trans. James Heisig (New York: Paulist Press, 1980)

Mysticism
Buddhist and Christian

Encounters with Jan van Ruusbroec

Paul Mommaers & Jan Van Bragt

CROSSROAD □ NEW YORK

1995
The Crossroad Publishing Company
370 Lexington Avenue, New York, NY 10017

Copyright © 1995 by the Nanzan Institute for Religion and Culture

Printed in the United States of America

Library of Congress Cataloging-in-Publication Data

Mommaers, Paul. 1935–
    Mysticism Buddhist and Christian : encounters with Jan van
Ruusbroec / by Paul Mommaers & Jan Van Bragt.
        p.   cm.
    Includes bibliographical references and index.
    ISBN 0-8245-1455-6
    1. Ruusbroec, Jan van, 1293–1381. 2. Mysticism—History—Middle
Ages, 600–1500. 3. Mysticism—Buddhism. 4. Christianity and
other religions—Buddhism. 5. Buddhism—Relations—Christianity.
I. Bragt, Jan Van. II. Title. III. Series.
BV5095.J3M63 1994
248.2'2–dc20   94-31692
                                                                              CIP

Contents

Foreword, by Jan Van Bragt   1

A Note on the Sources   7

PART ONE: THE NATURE OF MYSTICISM

1   Mystical Awareness, Mystical Texts   11
2   Buddhism and Mysticism   27
3   Mystical Objects, Mystical Marks   45
4   Buddhism and God   70

PART TWO: THE HUMAN AND THE TRANSCENDENT

5   Profiling the Human   99
6   A Buddhist View of the Human   121
7   Meeting the Divine Other   139
8   Mystically One with God   156
9   Union with the Transcendent Self in Buddhism   178

PART THREE: NATURAL MYSTICISM

10   Natural Mysticism: An Appreciation   211
11   Buddhism and Natural Mysticism   232
12   Natural Mysticism: A Critique   248
13   A Buddhist Critique of Natural Mysticism   268

Afterword, by Paul Mommaers   287

Index   293

Foreword

Jan Van Bragt

The central character of this book is the medieval Flemish mystic, Jan van Ruusbroec (1298–1381), a figure who greatly influenced European mystical literature and of whom it has been said that "in all probability...there has been no greater contemplative, and certainly...no greater mystical writer."[1] In the words of one of his English translators:

> Ruusbroec is universally regarded as the most important of the Flemish mystics and as one of the most outstanding of all the mystical writers who made the fourteenth century unique: Meister Eckhart, John Tauler, Henry Suso, Catherine of Siena, Bridget of Sweden, Julian of Norwich, Walter Hilton, Richard Rolle, and the author of *The Cloud of Unknowing....* [His] qualities led to him being called "Ruusbroec the Admirable" and "perhaps the very greatest of the mystics of the Church."[2]

Such high praise notwithstanding, Ruusbroec remains relatively unknown today outside of a small cluster of countries in western Europe. Explanations are not hard to come by. For one thing, he did not write in Latin, the lingua franca of his time, but in his local vernacular, Middle Dutch. This places his work in the literature of the Low Lands (the present-day Netherlands and the northern part of Belgium), whose internatinal influence was never very great in any case. For another, "Dutch" culture and literature had to contend with suppression in Belgium during the nineteenth century and only began to reassert themselves freely after the 1930s.

This is not to say that Ruusbroec has always been so little known outside of his own land. In earlier centuries, his works were widely published throughout the west of Europe. Besides the Middle Dutch texts, German and Latin translations quickly circulated throughout Flanders and neighboring countries. His masterpiece, *The Spiritual Espousals,* spread his name throughout the Low Lands and Germany to France, Italy, and even England.

[1] Cuthbert Butler, *Western Mysticism* (London: Constable and Company, 1927), 272–3.

[2] J. A. Wiseman in the Foreword to John Ruusbroec, *The Spiritual Espousals and Other Works.* Trans. by James A. Wiseman, O.S.B. (New York: Paulist Press, 1985), xvii.

1

Today no less than fourteen manuscripts of the original text remain, along with twenty-four codices of the two Latin translations made in the fourteenth century. No doubt the extensive attention that Ruusbroec's thought commanded owed a great deal to the superb Latin translation of Laurent Surius, first published in Köln in 1552, and again later in 1608 and 1692. This translation, together with the efforts of some of his better-known disciples, brought Ruusbroec's thought to the attention of the Spanish and French schools of mysticism, where it exercised considerable influence.

Nor was his influence limited to "professional" mystical milieus. Lay believers of all walks of life were touched by Ruusbroec's ideas, not least of all because of the impact he had on Thomas à Kempis's *Imitation of Christ*, a work long recognized as the standard handbook of the modern devotional life. His works were even read in certain pietistic Protestant groups in Germany. And perhaps still more surprising, a number of leading figures in contemporary French literature—among them J. K. Huysmans, Paul Valéry, André Gide, Paul Claudel, J. P. Jouve, and Roland Barthes—have expressed their admiration for the works of the Flemish mystic. No less a littérateur than the Nobel Prize-winning poet Maurice Maeterlinck produced an elegant French translation of *The Spiritual Espousals*.

Although his career coincided with the great upheavals that marked the wane of the Middle Ages, the life of Jan van Ruusbroec was largely uneventful. Born in the little village of Ruusbroec, after which he is named, he moved to the neighboring city of Brussels at the age of eleven. There he completed his philosophical and theological studies in preparation for the priesthood and was duly ordained in 1317. The first twenty-six years of his priestly life he spent serving as a chaplain at the St. Gudula Church in Brussels. Then, in 1343, his life took a decisive turn. Ruusbroec and two other priests left Brussels for Groenendael, a clearing in the forest of Soignes a few miles to the south, there to begin a contemplative life. In this small community, which was obliged by Church authorities to take on a traditional monastic rule but which seems to have been intended more as a kind of "ashram," Ruusbroec lived out the rest of his days in prayer and in spiritual direction. He died in 1381 at the age of eighty-eight.

Of his eleven mystical works,[3] five were written during the years in Brussels and six while in Groenendael. What moved this quiet, simple mystic

[3] The works written in the Brussels period, in chronological order, were *The Kingdom of Lovers, The Spiritual Espousals, The Sparkling Stone, The Four Temptations*, and *The Christian Faith*. During his years in Groenendael, Ruusbroec finished a treatise already begun in Brussels, *The Spiritual Tabernacle*, and composed the following works, again in chronological order: *The Seven Enclosures, A Mirror of Eternal Blessedness, The Seven Rungs in the Ladder of Spiritual Love, The Little Book of Clarification* (also called *The Little Book of Enlightenment*), and *The Twelve Beguines*.

to take up his pen and produce such a remarkable body of writings can only be surmised from those works themselves. It seems clear that Ruusbroec felt impelled to counter the influence of certain wayward spiritual movements in vogue at the time. Furthermore, he appears to have been appalled by what he saw as the "total lack of personal spiritual life" in the traditional and decadent Church around him. But perhaps most of all, Ruusbroec was simply responding to the request of those to whom he had given guidance that he put his thoughts down in writing.

This book aims, first, to draw the attention of the English-reading public to Ruusbroec's mystical doctrine, to that "majestic summa of Christian life in the spirit—at once daringly speculative and remarkably balanced."[4] But, as will be clear from the title, it has a second, interreligious goal: to engage Ruusbroec's mystical path in a "dialogue" with Buddhist contemplation. The seven chapters that expound and analyze Ruusbroec's mystical writings were authored by Paul Mommaers, a leading authority on Ruusbroec's thought. They are braided with six chapters of my own that chase after the echoes which I, as a Christian student of Eastern spirituality, hear reverberating in Buddhist contemplative thought.

In the sense that both authors are Christian, the partnership is not so much interreligious as intrareligious. Yet our collaboration is unthinkable except in the context of that broader, vital Buddhist-Christian dialogue that has shaped the vocation of many scholars of faith in recent years. If the genre of our work is new and the grammar of its discourse still in the rough, its materials are as old and as venerable as the diverse traditions it tries to weave together. While there can be no compromising the demands of scholarly conscience, the voices of religious belief in the present seem to be asking for more. I hesitate to offer this book as a response; it is really no more than a modest attempt to acknowledge those voices.

The contents are an intersection of two personal quests. For myself, a Catholic missionary in Japan for the past thirty-two years, Buddhism has been a challenge from the first moment I was introduced to it during my studies at Kyoto University (1965–1967). My mentor, himself a Buddhist priest, and the young Buddhist scholars that were my classmates, crystallized in me the paradox of Buddhism and Christianity that I have carried around with me as a kōan throughout my years in Japan: How can such a natural affinity in religiosity result in such an incurable disjunction in doctrine?

Then one day in February 1991, when I was at the University of Louvain delivering a brief course of lectures on Buddhism, I received a telephone call from a certain professor at the University of Antwerp asking for an appointment. I had no idea what was in store when Paul Mommaers came to

---

[4] Louis Dupré in the preface to John Ruusbroec, *The Spiritual Espousals and Other Works*, xi.

see me the first time. As a specialist in medieval mysticism and a member of the Ruusbroecgenootschap, he explained, he had long been intrigued by what he had seen of Hindu mysticism during a year's stay in India some years previously. His curiosity about Eastern spirituality, and especially Buddhist contemplation, had been piqued, and he felt that somehow it was important for him to pursue it before writing the book on Ruusbroec he had in mind.

As a result of this and subsequent conversations, the Nanzan Institute for Religion and Culture in Nagoya, of which I was director at the time, offered him a visiting scholarship for the following year. It was during the six months he spent with us in 1992 that the idea for this book materialized. In a series of seminars with the members of the Institute, Mommaers made a systematic presentation of Ruusbroec's mysticism, all the while soliciting from his audience possible parallels and contrasts with Buddhist thought. From these discussions, as well as from the time he devoted to reading Buddhist texts, Mommaers became ever more convinced of the connections between his own research and Buddhist contemplation. Meantime, as I expressed my own difficulties with Buddhist theory, he was often able to suggest parallels that Ruusbroec's mystical theory was grappling with.

In his final seminar, Mommaers laid out what he considered the most critical point of encounter between the fourteenth-century Flemish love mystic and the Buddhist path: the problem of "natural contemplation." Around it revolved the "three surprises" of his research. First, Ruusbroec goes to great lengths in nearly all of his works to do battle with an issue that few people even recognize as a problem, namely, the presence within Christianity of persons who claim to have experienced God without a leap of faith or the aid of divine grace. Second, for all his harsh criticism, Ruusbroec's assessment of the experience of these people is basically positive; for him theirs is a genuine path to God. And third, the similarities between the practices, attitudes, and reasoning of Western natural contemplatives and Eastern contemplatives are everywhere in evidence.

The lines of the triangle were drawn: on one side, Christian mysticism, as exemplified by Ruusbroec; on the second, the phenomenon of natural contemplation within the Christian tradition; and on the third, Buddhist mysticism. We were aware from the outset that this way of shaping the dialogue left out a good deal, not least of all the question of the diffusion of Eastern forms of meditation in Christian cultures. But our goal was simply to step into the space that the three lines of our concern had marked off in order to see what Buddhism and Christianity might have to say to each other.

The result of our work is a kind of diptych. The panel on the right (chapters 1, 3, 5, 7, 8, 10, and 12) depicts the thought of Ruusbroec and is intelligible on its own. The panel on the left (chapters 2, 4, 6, 9, 11, and 13), though painted in a quite different style, is intended as a contrast and commentary, and therefore cannot be expected to make sense on its own. If the shifting back and forth is dizzying at times, it is only because we have tried to resist blending and shading what belongs apart. The vertigo is very much a part of the dialogue; without it, we feel, the wider appreciation we seek for Ruusbroec's thought in East Asia can never take firm hold.

Mommaers's presentation consists of four parts. Chapters 1 and 3 analyze the general nature and characteristics of the mystical path. Chapter 5 fills in the view of the human that lies at the foundation of Ruusbroec's mysticism. The third and central part, chapters 7 and 8, outlines Ruusbroec's phenomenological description of his own mystical experiences. Finally, chapters 10 and 12 focus on Ruusbroec's confrontation with the natural mystics of his time.

The panel I have painted in the intervening chapters is something of an impressionistic reaction to this portrait of Ruusbroec. In the opening remarks to chapter 2, I shall have more to say of my overall intentions. Briefly, I have tried to pick up themes introduced by Mommaers and to highlight similarities and dissimilarities with Buddhist doctrine, always in the hope of shedding further light on Ruusbroec and on the relationship between Christian mysticism and Buddhist contemplation. Such a procedure inhibits to some extent a straightforward, sui generis presentation of Buddhist contemplation. At the same time, it has given me the occasion to touch on many, if not most, facets of the Buddhist tradition. In this sense, readers without a specialized knowledge of Buddhism should be able to navigate their way through the text and get a reasonably balanced idea of the nature of Buddhist teachings. Of course, I say this fully aware that I write of Buddhism as an outsider, sympathetic though I try to be. In the end, Christian thought from the Middle Ages viewed through a Buddhist lens held up to the eye of a contemporary Christian cannot but produce its share of misimpressions. Only further response from both Buddhist and Christian readers can correct these shortcomings and take the dialogue further than these first awkward steps.

Despite the concentration on a single Christian mystic, I am confident that our work has touched on a broad range of problems, universal in scope and timely in their positing. The nature of mysticism Christian and Buddhist, the relationship between religion and mysticism in general, the role of doctrine in mysticism, the providence of Eastern spiritual movements for Western cultures and religions—all these questions and more eddy throughout the course of these pages. If our work can provoke reactions from those attracted, whether academically or existentially, to the borderlands of Buddhism and Christianity, its chief aim will have been served.

It only remains for me to execute the pleasant duty of acknowledging the great debt of gratitude we have incurred in the process of writing this book. To begin with, we offer a heartfelt salute to all those, far too numerous to be named (and many who have already preceded us in death), whose guidance brought us to the crossroads at which this project was conceived. A special word of thanks is due to the president and senate of the University of Antwerp, who made Professor Mommaers's academic mission to Japan possible, and to Professor G. de Baere, director of the Ruusbroecgenootschap, who patiently read through the chapters on Ruusbroec and offered many valuable suggestions. Among those who lent their skills and support to the actual writing, our warmest thanks go first of all to James Heisig, director of the Nanzan Institute, without whose unflagging collaboration the entire adventure would have died in its infancy. He not only provided encouragement but devoted uncounted hours to hammering out the halting prose of two Flemings into balanced and readable English, not to mention the many other technical details involved in production. We are also in debt to the participants in the preparatory seminars for their many suggestions. In particular, we single out Paul Swanson, who on more than one occasion applied his scholarly expertise in Buddhism to our work to save it from unnecessary "heretical" interpolations. For their thoroughness and patience in seeing this book through more drafts than either of us care to remember, we thank our copy editors, Thomas Kirchner and Edmund Skrzypczak; and for their cheerful support and selfless work behind-the-scenes, our gratitude goes to the office staff of the Nanzan Institute. Finally, on behalf of both Paul Mommaers and myself, I would like to thank the Crossroad Publishing Company, and especially our kind and efficient editor Lynn M. Schmitt, for their enthusiasm in the project and for helping us bring it to term.

A Note on the Sources

An English translation of the collected writings of Jan van Ruusbroec, arranged synoptically with a critical edition of the original Middle Dutch and the sixteenth-century Latin edition by Syrius, has been in preparation since 1980. The complete *Opera omnia* will run to ten volumes, four of which are already in print:

> *Boecsken der verclaringhe* [The Little Book of Enlightenment]. *Opera omnia* I, ed. by G. de Baere, Introduced by P. Mommaers, trans. by P. Crowley and H. Rolfson (1981).

> *Vanden seven sloten* [The Seven Enclosures]. *Opera omnia* II, ed. with introduction by G. de Baere, trans. by H. Rolfson (1981).

> *Die geestelike brulocht* [The Spiritual Espousals]. ed. by J. Alaerts, with introduction by P. Mommaers, trans. by H. Rolfson under the direction of G. de Baere (1988).

> *Vanden blinkenden steen, Vanden vier becoringhen, Van den kerstenen ghelove, Brieven* [The Sparkling Stone, The Four Temptations, The Christian Faith, Letters].*Opera omnia* X, ed. by G. De Baere, T. Mertens, and H. Noë, with an introduction by T. Mertens and P. Mommaers; trans. by A. Lefevre (1991).

After the first two volumes were released (under joint publication by Lannoo of Tielt and Brill of Leiden), the entire project was taken over by Brepols in Turnhout, Belgium and published as part of the series Corpus Christianum. Even though the English redaction is somewhat uneven, this edition will be cited freely wherever possible. References refer to volume, part (where applicable), and line (e.g., *Opera omnia* III.b.255–6). A simple comma is used after the volume number to indicate introductory material or commentary (e.g. *Opera omnia* I, 27).

An excellent English translation of selected writings has appeared under the title:

> John Ruusbroec, *The Spiritual Espousals and Other Works*. Trans. with Introduction by James Wiseman, with a Preface by Louis Dupré. The Classics of Western Spirituality (Ramsey, N. J.: Paulist Press, 1985).

This edition is cited only when the *Opera omnia* does not include the section in question. References are to page number only (e. g. Wiseman, 123–4).

The only complete and thoroughly reliable edition of Ruusbroec's original texts has been published in four volumes:

Werken, naar het standaardhandschrift van Groenendaal uitgegeven door het Ruusbroec-genootschap te Antwerpen (Tielt: Lannoo, 1944–1948).

This will be cited only when no translation is available. References give volume, page, and line (e. g., *Werken* IV.204:12–8).

The writings of Hadewijch are cited in the following English translation:

Hadewijch, *The Complete Works,* trans. with an Introduction by Mother Columba Hart. Preface by Paul Mommaers. The Classics of Western Spirituality (Ramsey, N. J.: Paulist Press, 1980).

PART ONE

The Nature of Mysticism

1

Mystical Awareness, Mystical Texts

If the pages that follow are to focus on something called "mysticism," it is obvious that we should have some idea of what we are talking about, or at least what we are looking for. The problem is that there are a lot of books about mysticism circulating today—some scholarly, some popular—and they each seem to define the subject matter in a different way. But only, of course, after admitting the impossibility of pinning down in language what is finally "undefinable" or "inexplicable" or what have you. There is no way not to agree with the problem or with the solution. In a sense, the wider interreligious agenda of this particular volume complicates matters still further. As the demand for clarity of definition becomes stronger, so do the cautions against doctrinal provincialism. In the end, everything urges us to a simpler, more modest approach to the subject. Basically this approach rests on two guiding principles, which will be the matter of this opening chapter.

First, if we want to know what mysticism is, we should ask the mystics themselves. After all, it is there if anywhere that we can gain firsthand accounts and reflections about the subject. And where do we find these people? Unless one happens to be acquainted with a number of advanced and articulate living mystics, we have no choice but to approach them through the writings they have left behind.

Secondly, when we look at the actual texts of the mystics, two general traits emerge. On one hand, these people view themselves as possessed of a certain distinctive *awareness*. On the other, they try to *describe* that awareness. Thus mysticism consists in the descriptions of the particular states of awareness that we find in the writings of those who happen to be gifted with them.

To describe mysticism from the mystics' writings does not of course mean that this is all they wrote. Still, the core of their literary production, enough to account for its chief characteristics, is descriptive. This is why direct quotation figures so strongly in our account. The mystics' words and literary modes of expression are not meant merely to illustrate the direct sources from which the exposition has been constructed or to confirm the argument at its key points. They are the principal matter of the book, and it is in the way we approach these texts that its method will become apparent. To put it bluntly, to skip over the quotes is to miss the substance of mysticism, not to mention the pleasure of discovering it.

In direct deference to the aims of interreligious reflection, the mystical texts I shall work with come directly out of a single, concrete Western tradition. I restrict myself to the explicitly Christian and orthodox experience, drawing mainly on classic material, though in passing I shall touch on a broader Western scene. In thus limiting ourselves to the core of Christian mysticism, the possibility is opened for direct encounter with other forms of mysticism in their concrete expression, and the danger is averted of isolating "religion" from the varieties of actual, historical religious phenomena that are its lifeblood.

MYSTICAL AWARENESS

The one point highlighted by the mystics again and again is as simple as it is far-reaching, and it also helps loosen some of the knots that keep tangling up some very learned expositions. The point is this: what makes the mystic a mystic is simply a particular kind of awareness. The doors of perception are thrown open to something that is as new and unfamiliar to them as it is to the non-mystic.

In other words, mysticism is primarily a matter of consciousness. Something previously unknown and unexperienced is all of a sudden right there—*está allí*, as Teresa of Avila has it. This unanticipated presence is as vivid and real to the mystic's perceptive faculties as everyday experiences are, which is why they speak so often of being empowered to "see" or "touch" or "taste" what has so far been imperceptible.

The mystic uses the straightforward language of the senses with an ingenuity that is often disconcerting in the extreme, and one who would understand them had better get used to taking them at their word. To relax back into the contemporary habit of reading such texts as symbol or metaphor is to misread. The mystics, after all, write from experience and their experience gives them good reason for using the idiom of sense perception. What is more, they remain social beings, and that means that neither individually nor among themselves do they slip into a private language. The language they speak is human and, as with the rest of us, this means that it is primarily embodied in sensuality. This is why their expression remains rooted in plain French, English, Flemish, Spanish, and so forth.

The mystics are obviously out to convey not only the contents of their awareness but also its force and objectivity. This, too, drives them back to the language of the senses. Without it, what guarantee have they that their perceptions would not be transfigured into some kind of "spiritual" vision or "speculative" construct? And if they give themselves these guarantees, we can hardly assume a higher standpoint of "metaphorical" interpretation that claims to understand them better than they understood themselves. Time and again, as we shall see presently, body and senses are an indispensable part of mystical awareness. Unlike their spiritual interpreters, mystics are better suited to resist the temptation to *faire l'ange*, and that is a large part of what makes them mystics.

If we grant, then, that mysticism entails a particular awareness, does this mean that this enables the mystic to know something about God or Absolute Reality that is closed off to ordinary mortals? Though commentators on Christian mystical literature often make the mystics out to be guardians of an arcanum of transcendental information, this is hardly the way they themselves speak of the privilege of their state.

The gift of mystical experience does not imply an absolute, self-justifying state of consciousness, possessed of a unique object, yielding an uncommon knowledge, and impervious to ordinary criticism. The mystic simply knows in a distinct manner what it is open to all of us to know. The God known to the mystic is none other than the God that ordinary consciousness reaches by rational inference or belief.[1] Put the other way around, the One does not metamorphize, manifesting itself one way to the mystic, another way to the philosopher, and yet another way to the ordinary man or woman of faith. What is distinct about the God of the mystic is the felt presence of the divine as a datum touching human perceptive consciousness.

Thus the privileged gift of the mystic is not new information but a certain way of knowing. He or she does not know something "more" about God than theology or theodicy. This fact is confirmed on two fronts. First, mystics neither reject nor in any sense deprecate non-mystical ways to God. They may engage in debate with those who belittle their experiential way to the divine—and there has never been a dearth of champions of scholastic learning, common sense at the lowest common denominator, or activism to drag them into controversy—but they will not pass over the common religious heritage. Second, one need only comb the writings of the mystics with an eye to gleaning new knowledge about God to realize that the search for super-knowledge is doomed to frustration. The information they provide on this score is little more than a repetition of what is already familiar.

If the mystic's only claim to excellence is a particular awareness of God, it is little wonder that throughout the history of mystical writing the same

[1] This does not imply that the mystic stands above or outside of faith; nor does it imply any opposition between experience and faith. The mystic's faith is "enlightened," not done away with.

13

words keep repeating themselves again and again. Chief among them, of course, is *experience*. Bernard of Clairvaux (1090–1153), one of the great creative geniuses in Western mysticism,[2] sets the tone by stressing how his exposition of the *Song of Songs* flows from *experientia*:

> Only the touch of the Spirit can inspire a song like this, and only personal experience can unfold its meaning (*sola addiscit experientia*). Let those versed in the mystery revel in it; let all others burn with desire to attain to this experience rather than merely to learn about it (*non tam cognoscendi quam experiendi*).

Or again, his third sermon opens as follows:

> Today the text we are going to study is the book of our own experience (*legimus in libro experientiae*). You must therefore turn your attention inwards, each one must take note of his own particular awareness of the things I am about to discuss (*attendat conscientiam suam*).[3]

The fourteenth-century thinker Walter Hilton describes the mystic's specific gift by distinguishing between "reform in faith only" and reform "in faith and feeling." He further explains this *feeling* (which he also calls the "opening of the eyes of the spirit" and symbolizes by the Biblical "tasting of manna") as follows:

> This tasting of manna is an awareness of the life of grace, which comes from the opening of the soul's eyes. And this grace does not differ from the grace that an elect soul feels at the beginning of its conversion; it is the same grace but experienced in another way.... So the same grace that first turns men from sin...makes them perfect, and it is called an *awareness of the life of grace,* for he who has it is conscious of the grace within him.[4]

---

[2] Medieval mysticism—and love mysticism in particular—originates with Bernard. His notion of *experientia* has shaped the course of all subsequent mysticism. In *Medieval Humanism and Other Studies*, R. W. Southern says of Bernard that "he popularized the method of introspection.... He gave the whole exercise a new direction. He was not interested...in logic and analysis, but only in spiritual growth" (Oxford: Blackwell, 1970), 33–4.

[3] *The Works of Bernard of Clairvaux*, vol. 2, *Song of Songs I*, translated by K. Walsh, (Kalamazoo: Cistercian Publications, 1981), 6, 16.

[4] *The Scale of Perfection by Walter Hilton*, translated into modern English with an introduction and notes by Dom Gerard Sitwell (London: Burns & Oates, 1953), 153–4; 246, 277–8. The note accompanying the passage cited in the text is worth quoting: "Reform...means the reformation of the soul in the image of God...achieved essentially by the infusion of sanctifying grace at baptism. When this process takes place (as it generally does) with no further knowledge of God than that which is to be had through faith, Hilton calls it *reform in faith*. But when the restoration of the image of God in us has advanced so far as to be accompanied by some sort of

A few centuries later, Augustine Baker picks up on the word *feeling* to distinguish the mystic's awareness from common spiritual *knowledge*, and yet to stress the latter way as real and proper. Commenting upon "our nothingness," which figures so prominently in the *Cloud of Unknowing*, he writes:

> You must note that there is a great difference between the *knowledge* of our nothing and the *feeling* of our nothing. By a little consideration according to the light of natural reason or our faith, we may know our own nothing.... But this knowledge, although it be good and may help us to attain the feeling, is not the feeling. And many men have that knowledge, while very few have that feeling. Yea, the devil himself hath such a knowledge of his own nothing, but he hath not the feeling.[5]

John Ruusbroec gives us what is perhaps the most arresting formulation of the difference between the mystic and the non-mystic. When he takes up the question of the advanced mystical experience of "enjoyable unity" in *The Spiritual Espousals*, he suddenly states:

> All good persons have this, but how this is *(hoe dat dit es)* remains hidden from them all their lives, unless they are inner and empty of all creatures![6]

What distinguishes even the perfect mystic from any "good person" (by which Ruusbroec means any simple Christian) is the *how*. In his own case, this means that a relationship with God that already exists unfolds into a heightened datum of consciousness. Thus even though those who do not enter on the inner way—setting "their intention and their active inward impulse more on virtues and on outward modes"—actually "have" what the mystic "has," they yet lack the experiential knowledge. Of these Ruusbroec says "they possess One whom they do not know."[7]

In our own day we can find any number of texts straddling the borderlines of Christian mysticism, by conveying similar insights in much the same idiom. I would like to cite an instance of this from the *Writer's Diary* of Virginia Woolf. In trying to describe the particular state she has been in during a summer "retreat," she makes use of the terms *experience* and *consciousness* in a way entirely reminiscent of the medieval mystics. Mustering her

experimental knowledge of God beyond that of faith, he calls it *reform in feeling* or *in faith and feeling*."

[5] *The Cloud of Unknowing and Other Treatises by an English Mystic of the Fourteenth Century with a Commentary on the Cloud by Father Augustine Baker O.S.B.*, ed. by Abbot Justin McCann (London: Burns & Oates, 1952), 181.

[6] *Opera omnia* III.b.1482–4. My translation has adjusted "happens" into "is," which is the more literal.

[7] *Opera omnia* III.b.729–34.

extraordinary literary talents, she succeeds in evoking the perceptual nature of the way of knowing she "then" discovered. Note in particular the paradoxical connection she makes between "a thing I see" and "something abstract" and how, apparently still dissatisfied with her wording, she quickly restores the concreteness of that "something" by placing it "in the downs or sky":

> Often down here I have entered into a sanctuary; a nunnery; had a religious retreat; of great agony once; and always some terror; so afraid one is of loneliness; of seeing to the bottom of the vessel. That is one of the experiences I have had here in some Augusts; and got then to a consciousness of what I call "reality": a thing I see before me: something abstract; but residing in the downs or sky; beside which nothing matters; in which I shall rest and continue to exist. Reality I call it.[8]

William James, the first outstanding modern student of mysticism, was by his own admission not given to mystical states himself. To some extent, he opens himself here to the criticism of having allowed philosophical assumptions to bias his understanding of the phenomenon he was studying.[9] All of this does not alter the fact that in the opening years of this century James introduced the one method that gives the mystics their due. He let the original accounts speak for themselves and tried to base his conception of mysticism on the mystic's self-description. A few lines from *The Varieties of Religious Experience*, if only out of deference to the method we are pursuing here, seem relevant to our discussion:

> But the whole array of our instances leads to a conclusion something like this: It is as if there were in the human consciousness a *sense of reality, a feeling of objective presence, a perception* of what we may call "something there," more deep and more general than any of the "senses" by which the current psychology supposes existent realities to be originally revealed.[10]

To sum up, then, the mystics do not consider themselves singular creatures belonging to a class all of their own and apart from the rest of humanity, like a race of angelic griffins or spiritual centaurs. The mystics are as much

[8] Virginia Woolf, *A Writer's Diary* (London: Triad Grafton Books, 1978), 168–9.

[9] See N. Lash, *Easter in Ordinary:* Reflections on Human Experience and the Knowledge of God (Charlottesville: University Press of Virginia, 1988). Lash points out that "James' writings... embody a general account of experience...according to which...experience is systematically contrasted with thought" (16; 60f.) and also with institutions (46, 53). In that way James comes to identify personal experience with individual emotional states. Lash further lays bare James's Cartesian dualism (35–7).

[10] *The Varieties of Religious Experience: A Study in Human Nature* (London: Collins, 1968), 73.

part of the same "human nature" as the rest of us. Ruusbroec affirms on the very first page of *The Spiritual Espousals*:

This Bridegroom is Christ, and human nature is the bride whom God has made to the image and likeness of Himself.

It is only in and through common humanity—not some super-humanity—that mystics exist. What makes them stand out is that they have seen "how it is," and that makes them blossoms on the common trunk of human nature, not a species apart.

Defining mysticism as a matter of consciousness does not preclude us from recognizing it as a divine grace. It is only that mystical awareness is not what makes one pleasing to God. It in no sense supplants the fundamental category of "sanctifying grace" that is present equally and without bias in "every good person." When Christian tradition calls mysticism a grace, what is meant is that it is a (natural) gift given by God to aid the (supernatural) gift of the divine presence that is all of ours by birthright. *The Spiritual Espousals*, which we just cited, opens its exposition of the mystical life with these words:

There are three points necessary in order for one to see supernaturally in inner practice. The first is the light of God's grace in a higher mode than one can experience in an outward active life lacking inner zealousness.[11]

And a little further, Ruusbroec returns to this first point of "seeing supernaturally in inner practice," referring to it as

the interior illumination of God's grace. The grace of God in the soul is like a candle in a lantern or in a glass vessel: for it warms and illuminates and shines through the vessel, that is, the good person. And it reveals itself to the person who has it within, if he is observing himself in an inner manner....[12]

The mystics' description of their particularity as "only" an awareness, as "no more" than a perceptional gift or grace, helps us to clear up two questions. The first concerns the existential value of the consciousness the mystic is endowed with: Does the successful mystic consider mystical experience to be the greatest asset in life, to generate something in reality that would not otherwise be there? The answer is a definite No. Mystical consciousness, however greatly it be esteemed, is subordinate in the wider order of things that make up human nature. It is radically relative to a given that is more fundamental and of greater moment.

[11] *Opera omnia* III.b.21–4.
[12] *Opera omnia* III.b.121–5.

17

To anticipate the language we shall consider in greater detail in chapter 5, mystical experience may bring the "ground" or "essence" of the human to light, but it does not bring it into existence. It no more than uncovers what is hidden within each of us by virtue of our being born human beings. The mystical experience of one's relationship with God does not initiate the relationship or even mark its initiation. Mystical experience may enable one to savor that relationship, but in no sense is it a causal condition of that "living life, which joins together the created and the uncreated, both God and creatures."[13] Simply put, experience on its own is not the elemental force in the mystic's life. A state of consciousness, however "divine" or "absolute," is always and ever derivative of something more basic.

The same point is apparent in another common bias of mystical language. Ruusbroec speaks of the experience of God's "touching" as arousing the distinctively mystical level of awareness. The psychological experience of being touched is not the whole of mystical awareness, however. As the text of *The Spiritual Espousals* attests clearly, the joy and wonder of the "touching" lies rather in what it makes manifest: the presence of the divine in the human essence. This is what John of the Cross has in mind when, following the lead of Ruusbroec, he speaks of the *toque sustancial.*

The same bias is at work in the tendency of the mystics to speak of the "object" of their experience. Again, Ruusbroec:

> Even though the eyes be clear and the sight keen, clarity of sight without (its) lovely, delightful object (*voerworp*) brings little or no enjoyment or profit.[14]

The mystics themselves appear to be fascinated not by their own feeling but by *something* felt, by *someone* from without becoming present within. As a perceptual phenomenon, the mystical state no doubt testifies to a magnificent capacity of human consciousness. But this matters less to the mystic than who or what appears on the perceptual field. Consciousness is valuable not because of what it is but because of the other that it can experience as not identical with itself or at its own disposal.

It is altogether wrongheaded, then, to portray mysticism as a subjectivistic spiritual endeavor and the mystics as bursting at the seams with "feeling." Certain highly poetic, emotional, and sensuous utterances and images found in the writings of so-called "love mysticism" have tended to invite such misrepresentation. Underrating the realism of the authors themselves (their sense of substance and object), not a few commentators have concocted an opposition between "bridal" or "affective" mysticism on the one hand and

[13] *A Mirror of Eternal Blessedness;* Wiseman, 235.

[14] *Opera omnia* III.b.138–9.

"essential" or "speculative" mysticism on the other. The sooner such ideas are laid to their rest, the better.

As for love mysticism, a mere skim through the pages of the *Letters* or portions of the *Visions* of Hadewijch, the exponent of Flemish *minne-mystiek*, is enough to topple the subjectivist interpretation. The experience of *minne*—a very personal one and explicitly feminine at that—is not subjective in the sense of valuing and enjoying the emotion of love as such. For Hadewijch, *minne* as a movement of the soul is never detached from *minne* as the Other who causes it. To feel love is to meet the Beloved. And where the object of love is blurred by the emotion it arouses, the mystical beguine Hadewijch turns into the most penetrating soul-searcher, ruthlessly scrutinizing the joys and pains of love so as to relativize them to their object.

As for the misplaced opposition between "affective" and "essential" mysticism,[15] we need only consider the difficulty in classifying the texts of Ruusbroec. He is often referred to as "the great speculative mystic of the North," although the title of his undisputed magnum opus is *The Spiritual Espousals*. What is this champion of "essential" mysticism doing in the company of the love mystics, who, as theory has it, are enraptured in the "affective" means of mystical union? The opposition can only be sustained by doing grave injury to the texts themselves, and this fact invites us to a closer look at the distinctive genre in which the mystics have recorded their experiences.

MYSTICAL TEXTS

The core of the mystic's writing, as we have already remarked, is description. The genre is one of relation, in which the mystic is first and foremost a narrator. The aim of the description, obviously enough, will not be to portray publicly observable things. The accounts rather focus on, and to some extent evoke a sense of, phenomena that we are accustomed to classify as "spiritual" but which ultimately belong to the human world. At the same time, besides the records of mystical experience at our disposal, mystical experience itself is also a cultural fact. That means that the attempt to convey such an experience in writing must use a language that is intelligible but at the same time avoids the misunderstanding of being understood too easily. To read a mystical text as a theological, philosophical, or psychological treatise, or alternatively as a contribution to ethical, ascetical, or devotional literature, may make it easier to understand but is more likely to betray the aim of its author. The mystical author is not primarily engaged in arguing a point of view, analyzing an expe-

---

[15] See my introduction to *The Spiritual Espousals, Opera omnia* III, 17–18.

rience, or edifying public morals. If it is anything, the literary genre of the mystic is "phenomenological." Its native idiom is narrative, not archaeological or analytic. When a mystic puts pen to paper as a mystic, it is to unveil in language what has happened in the soul.[16]

True enough, mystical authors work at times with theological, anthropological, and other academic ideas. They may even, as is the case with Ruusbroec, expound them with some brilliance. But they do not do so *on the authority of their own experience*. Intellectual constructs are no more than a frame of reference, whose authority lies outside the text and outside the mystical awareness it is attempting to narrate. In the mode of narration, the mystic never leaves the cultural frame of the ordinary human being. In seeking a genuine expression of a particular experience, the mystic does what all of us need to do in order to remain anchored in our time and place, namely, to connect what is private with what is public, to construct a text of our lives in the context of general intelligibility.

So much for the literary genre of the mystic and the element of self-interest in the mystic's writing. As for the relationship to the reader, the one thing that mystical authors are agreed on is that it is absolutely impossible to transmit their experience to others, and they have no expectations of any readers trying to repeat it. Even if one is left free to, or invited to, follow an ascetical, moral, contemplative way that may possibly be indicated in the mystic's writing, there is no question of reenacting a mystical state. Indeed, can any one person's awareness or flash of insight *ever* be taken over by another? We may be able to borrow representations and concepts, the residue of perceptual acts, but not the actual perceptual experience itself.

The reason the mystic author has no intention of instructing the reader "how it is" to be "touched" by God or united with God is that the text is addressed primarily to those who are already gifted with at least some degree of mystical awareness. Note how Ruusbroec evokes the "measureless width of God's love" in *The Sparkling Stone*:

> In it we shall flow, and flow beyond ourselves in that unknown luxury that is the wealth and goodness of God, and in it we shall whirl and be whirled away in the glory of God forever.

And then he at once goes on to indicate his purpose as a writer, issuing a warning to his readers:

---

[16] *Soul* should not be taken here or elsewhere to refer to some precious spiritual thing hidden in the rudeness of matter. For the likes of Aquinas, Eckhart, and Nietzsche, it is the soul that envelops the body and not the other way round. We shall see later that John Ruusbroec and other mystics agree.

20

Look, in each one of all these likenesses I show his own being and his own practice to a contemplative man. But no one else will be able to understand this, since no one else can teach others the contemplative life.[17]

The same warning appears again and again at each stage of the mystical development. In taking up the "interior life" in *The Spiritual Espousals*, Ruusbroec observes similarly:

These are three comings of Christ in inner practice. We will now elucidate and explain each coming in particular. Now note with great care, for one who never experienced this will not understand it well.[18]

And at the beginning of the "contemplative life"—the highest level of mystical experience—the warning grows sterner still:

We are now going to explain and clarify these words [such as "the bridegroom cometh"] with respect to a superessential contemplation.... Few can arrive at this divine contemplation.... And therefore, no one will really thoroughly understand these remarks by means of any study or subtle consideration on one's own. For all the words and everything that one can learn and understand in a creaturely fashion is alien to, and far beneath, the truth that I have in mind. But he who is united with God and enlightened in this truth can understand the truth by (the truth) itself.... And therefore I desire each one who neither understands nor feels this in the enjoyable unity of his spirit not to be scandalized and leave things as they are.[19]

Hence the primary motive someone like Ruusbroec has in writing his descriptive accounts is that they be read by people who know from their own experience what he is talking about. He expects that at least part of the phenomena he is describing will be familiar. He verbalizes the conditions in which others may find themselves when similar experience befalls them. What the mystic writer has to offer the mystic reader is the measure of consolation that comes from knowing that one is not alone in what one is going through.

[17] *Opera omnia* X.112–17. In *The Seven Enclosures,* the pros and cons of language are presented as follows: "He shall understand the modeless essence of God, which is a modelessness, for it can be demonstrated neither by words nor by actions, by modes nor by signs nor by likenesses. It reveals itself, however, to the simple in-sight of the imageless mind. We may also set out signs and likenesses along the way, to prepare man to see the kingdom of God. Imagine in this way: as if you saw a glow of fire, immensely great, wherein all things were burnt away in a becalmed, glowing motionless fire" (*Opera omnia* II.788–94).

[18] *Opera omnia* III.b.178–81.

[19] *Opera omnia* III.c.19–33.

With a woman like Hadewijch, the intentions of the mystical author stand out in even sharper relief. She speaks as the "mistress" of a group of beguines, and as one who is very conscious of her spiritual authority. Recent studies of Hadewijch show that such apparently different works as the *Letters*, the *Visions*, and the *Poems in Stanzas* all share the common purpose of offering guidance on the way that leads from spiritual "infancy" to "adulthood." Evoking different moments of her own "adventure" with *minne*, she intends somehow to chart the variegated landscape of love mysticism.

Yet even in the case of Hadewijch, who explicitly aims at assisting those she addresses, the assumption is that these "friends" as she calls them have already received the gift of love-experience.[20] It is not something they receive from her because it is not hers to give. It is stated repeatedly that God alone plants the experience in the soul and makes it grow.[21] In the communication between Hadewijch and her readers, then, not two but three persons come onto the scene. Without the intervention of God, Hadewijch would have no grounds for contact with those who are reading her words.[22]

The implication would appear to be that one who is altogether lacking in mystical experience has no grounds for presuming to understand the first thing about a mystical text, let alone, as Ruusbroec says, to "really thoroughly understand." Is there to be no point of connection, ultimately, between the exceptional awareness of the mystic and the common states of the nonmystic?

In a letter to an unbelieving colleague, William James makes a few personal remarks about his reading of mystics. As we noted earlier, unlike many less reflective readers, James is well aware of the fact that he was not himself a mystic. He is further aware of an added hindrance specific to his own case: "I have grown so out of Christianity." His idea of disentangling (Christian) mystical experience from its (Christian) doctrine is not without serious problems.[23] And yet how clearly he lights the path for the non-mystic to the mystic's writing:

> I have no living sense of commerce with a God, I envy those who have, for I know the addition of such a sense would help me immensely. The Divine, for my *active* life, is limited to abstract concepts which, as ideals, interest and determine me, but do so but faintly, in comparison with what a feeling of God might effect, if I had one.... Now, although I am

[20] See for example Letter 2: 95–101.

[21] See the opening words of Letter 27.

[22] For further details on Hadewijch, see my *Hadewijch: Schrijfster Begijn Mystica* (Averbode: Altiora, 1989).

[23] See note 9 above.

so devoid of *Gottesbewusstsein* in the directer and stronger sense, yet there is *something in me* which *makes response* when I hear utterances made from that lead by others. I recognize a deeper voice. Something tells me, "thither *lies truth*." ...I have grown so out of Christianity that entanglement therewith on the part of a mystical utterance has to be abstracted from and overcome, before I can listen. Call this, if you like, my mystical *germ*. It is a very common germ.[24]

The non-mystic who sets out to read the mystic has thus first to learn to listen, to be open and attentive to what is being said about a particular phenomenon of experience. Concentrating on the doctrinal or ideological framework behind the description is to make oneself to that extent inattentive to the phenomenon as such. When James asserts "there is truth therein," what he means is not an ultimate, objective truth of logical inference or religious belief. *True* here means existentially authentic, and one does not need to be familiar with high mystical states oneself to recognize this as something that is possible for human beings. If the mystical authors themselves decline to assert that what they are describing applies only to their own particular case, how much more should their readers guard against the illusion that they in turn have been granted a special privilege of understanding by virtue of a mystical temperament or intuition. Let it be said again: the mystical authors have no intention of inspiring "pocket editions" of themselves but only of evoking something that belongs to our common "human condition."

Like James, Henri Bremond (1865–1933), a French student of mysticism, devoted himself tirelessly to the reading of mystical literature and in 1915 began publishing his monumental *Histoire littéraire du sentiment religieux en France depuis la guerre des religions jusqu'à nos jours*. But unlike James, Bremond was not only a confirmed Christian and practicing Catholic but a priest as well. Tormented by a dry, unfeeling response every time he tried to pray, he wrote in his *Diary* on 25 January 1898:

> My God, a thousand temptations to leave you and yet I want to stay. Time drags on, slower than ever. I am doing nothing, I am saying nothing. It is all for the best. In this sterile condition, I still praise you. And I confess that therein— seeing nothing, hearing nothing—I am better off than at Blondel's course.[25]

And four days later he adds:

[24] Quoted by Sven S. Hartman and Carl-Martin Edsman, eds., *Mysticism* (Stockholm: Almqvist & Wiksell, 1970), 18–19.

[25] I am borrowing here from A. Blanchet, *Henri Bremond, 1865–1904* (Paris: Aubier Montaigne, 1975).

Prayer bores me. I'd like to get away—to entertaining books or serious ones. Anything but prayer.

He even seems to feel guilt for his inability to pray since a child, wondering to himself, "Is it my fault that already from that time I hated to pray?"

On 11 July he writes, "Read with much joy and emotion the admirable life of Mrs. Hélyot." While browsing through the dusty library of the Jesuit house in Aix-en-Provence, Bremond's eye was caught by a collection of seventeenth-century works on spirituality, among them Grasset's *Vie de Madame Hélyot*. As he read, certain passages seemed to speak to him directly of his own condition. For example, when "the condition in which that holy lady sometimes found herself" is compared with the

> astonishment of finding oneself somewhere where there is no sky or earth or fire or water or light or color...or even any creature to keep one company, but only a wide desert and infinite emptiness, invisible and incomprehensible, eternal and immobile without any limitation, ...where one sees nothing, hears nothing, tastes nothing, is unable to touch anything or hold on to anything. One would there be suspended between being and not-being. In that condition...this saint sometimes found herself and there she saw God only...in the annihilation of all her ideas.

Two points in Bremond's account touch directly on the question of reading the mystics. First, he explains clearly what it was that led him to his indefatigable interest in mysticism and subsequent serious scholarly endeavors. In 1920 he wrote to Blondel that it was Gasset's volume "that gave me the idea to write my own thirty volumes." Second, some years earlier he tells us how he, as a non-mystic, approached reading the mystics:

> I don't think you have ever experienced prayer of quietness. Nor have I. But we are honest reporters, who interview the mystics—the grown-ups as well as those hardly out of the shell.

Bremond is exemplary not only in what he does but equally important in what he does not do. On one hand, he recognizes in Mme. Hélyot's desolations an experience similar to what he himself was going through. Recognizing this dry and unfeeling response to prayer as an oblique experience of "God alone," he was inspired to a love of mystical literature. On the other hand, Bremond does not identify himself with the mystic. He does not allow the similarity between what happens in Mme. Hélyot as an accomplished contemplative and what happens to him in poor and commonplace prayer to sow seeds of suspicion that he, too, was a mystic. He prefers his own dryness to such self-inflation. He is content to admire those with a higher experience without attempting to compete with them.

To sum up for a moment, we have seen that a mystical text is not to be read as a source of teaching. To delve into its obscurities like a miner with a headlamp strapped to one's forehead in search of some unattended fact or lesson is to demand something of the text that it does not have to give. What one *should* bring to the text is one's own experience of prayer or awareness of the presence of God, be it positive or negative. In closing the eye curious for objective information, one must open the inner, subjective eye that sees only what personal experience lights up. However unsure or vague, however secular or demythologized one's sense of God may be, this sense alone is the way to discovering what the mystical text is about. One must first tune one's ear to the key in which the mystic author is playing to enjoy it fully.

Admittedly, the literary testimonies of love mysticism lend themselves more easily to such an approach than some other type of mystical literature, since in reading them one can draw not only on one's sense of the presence of God but on one's broader experience of love. Not that the mystical experience of union in love with God is the same as being overwhelmed with love for another human person. Human love in whatever form—be it platonic, spiritual, erotic, or sexual—is not the same thing as divine love. One can never speak of God as a "person" in the same, direct sense as we speak of a human beloved. The give-and-take among human lovers is simply not there. In its place, the love play of the mystic, in its sweet and its bitter moments, relies continually on the initiative of the Other, just as the enjoyment of love is always a function of the overflowing richness of the Other.

To disallow the identity of human love and mystical love is not to ignore how much they have in common. Those who would reduce their actual, existential similarities to a mere coincidence of metaphors are guilty of just such ignorance. When the mystic, as a "spiritual" person, uses ordinary, understandable language, the intent is not to cloak something out of the ordinary. Nor do we, who are not quite so spiritual persons, get any closer to the mystical experience by metaphorical high-jumping over our ordinary means of expressing ourselves.[26]

The attitude we have argued for here is conscious of the difference between love mysticism and common experiences of love. While respecting the mystic's secret, it does not alienate the meaning of the mystic's language from what the non-mystic finds in it. It makes no attempt to sublimate the "lower" sentiments evoked in the idiom of love, but reveres the human love

---

[26] Is it not, for example, a striking feature of all the psychoanalytical commentaries on the phenomenon of mysticism that no sooner does the mystic speak of erotic enjoyment than her or his experience is *immediately* exposed as *evidently* not being a genuine experience of God? It is somehow too human, too embodied, for it possibly to be spiritual.

that is kept alive in love mysticism. In a word, it says: I do not grasp entirely what the mystic has experienced, and probably never will. I do not myself "feel" what their "desiring" and "enjoying" is all about. And yet, when I read their words something in me resonates, and that something is at least part of what the mystic is trying to communicate.

That having been said, we can now turn to a brief inventory of the chief traits of mystical awareness.

2

Buddhism and Mysticism

At this point the "dialogue of Ruusbroec with Buddhism" is supposed to begin. Since the idea itself of such a dialogue may strike the reader as rather fanciful and far-fetched, an introductory word on the meaningfulness of this exercise appears to be in order.

The expectation underlying the endeavor is that, through a comparison with the contemplative path of Buddhism, some supplementary light will be thrown on Ruusbroec's way of thinking and spiritual path; in other words, that the proper characteristics of Ruusbroec's Christian mysticism will be put into stronger relief than would be possible by a presentation solely within the Christian world of discourse. Conversely, it is also hoped that, by an investigation of the points of convergence with and divergence from Ruusbroec's thought, the nature, or some aspects, of the Buddhist path can be made clearer, at least for a Christian audience. Simply put, these investigations will thus consist of questions thrown at Ruusbroec by Buddhism and questions thrown at Buddhism by Ruusbroec. Such a dialogue, unfortunately, was impossible in Ruusbroec's own time but has become possible in today's "global village" as an encounter beyond geographical and historical boundaries.

Our scenario might be criticized for setting up a lopsided match: one Christian writer *versus* the whole Buddhist tradition. Ruusbroec's vision, however, no matter how original, is not a one-person stand but incorporates within itself a long Christian tradition; and, the Buddhist tradition, on the other hand, will be spoken for mostly by individual representatives of that tradition. But one more word must be said about Buddhism as it will appear in these pages. The Buddhist way is far from being monolithic; it shows a rich variety according to differing interpretations and adaptations to local cultures, without, however, losing a common configuration. In these pages every effort will be made, however, to make the remarks on Buddhism as universally applicable as possible to all the strands of that rich tradition. Still, the reader will soon notice that I focus primarily on the Buddhism with which, by force of circumstances, I am most familiar: Japanese Buddhism, and especially Zen Buddhism.

My project presupposes, of course, that there is a basic commonality between Christian mysticism and Buddhist contemplation; that, in a sense, both belong to the same *genus*. Indeed, little is gained by a comparison of rabbits and bottle openers. At first sight, however, Buddhism and Christianity are so different that many refuse to classify them both under the same category of "religion." The Chicago theologian, David Tracy, has expressed this as follows:

> A more "other" form of thought than Buddhist thought on God and self, on history and nature, on thought itself (including dialogical thought) would be difficult to conceive for Western Christians with our different strategies and categories of philosophical and theological thought.[1]

Spelled out briefly, this meant that, within the general category of religion, Buddhism and Christianity appear to occupy opposite poles: over against a religion of enlightenment, a religion of faith; on the one hand a religion of experience, on the other a religion of dogma; a religion of wisdom facing a religion of love; a religion centered on the human self over against a religion centered on God; on the one hand, a religion of introversion and equanimity and on the other, a religion of extraversion and desire.

It is, then, understandable that the Buddhist-Christian dialogue on the level of doctrine or theology, which got under way mainly after Vatican II, is fraught with formidable difficulties. This same dialogue, however, shows a rather surprising trait: namely, the central role mysticism plays in it. William Johnston points out the apparent reason for this:

> The Christian with some depth in prayer and experience of the things of God will find himself in wonderful sympathy with the monk who has practiced Buddhist meditation.... D. T. Suzuki and Thomas Merton found themselves in extraordinary harmony. Here, at the level of mysticism, East meets West. Here is the still point of the turning world.

And again:

> [The role of mysticism in Christianity] in modern times is enhanced because it brings Christianity into contact with non-Christian religions. Indeed, without mysticism, dialogue with many of these religions may well be impossible.[2]

And Thomas Merton himself testifies:

---

[1] David Tracy, *Dialogue with the Other* (Louvain: Peeters Press, 1990), 69.

[2] William Johnston, *The Still Point* (New York: Fordham University Press, 1970), 184, 131.

28

A little experience of such [contemplative] dialogue shows at once that this is precisely the most fruitful and the most rewarding level of ecumenical exchange. While on the level of philosophical and doctrinal formulations there may be tremendous obstacles to meet, it is often possible to come to a very frank, simple, and totally satisfying understanding in comparing notes on the contemplative life, its disciplines, its vagaries and its rewards.[3]

This point will come under further investigation later on, but it is easy enough to see the relevance of this surprising fact for the present undertaking. Firstly, in their respective contemplative paths, the religions under consideration appear, in some way, to transcend their doctrinal and ritual forms in the direction of a more "universal" level or realm, without—and this is important—rejecting or making abstraction of these forms. Secondly, Buddhism in particular is essentially a contemplative path and, as such, appears to recognize a kindred spirit in Christian mysticism. Thus, for example, in some remarks about Eckhart made by the great propagator of Zen in the West, Daisetz Suzuki, Thomas Merton recognizes "a kind of intuitive affinity for Christian mysticism."[4]

Thus far I have spoken about Christian mysticism in general, but what about Ruusbroec? Here it must first be remarked that Ruusbroec's mysticism is as yet not known in the Buddhist world and, consequently, has hitherto played no role in the Buddhist-Christian dialogue.[5] Let me confess at this point that my fondest hope behind the present project is that of "pulling" Ruusbroec into that dialogue because I am convinced that his thought and

---

[3] Thomas Merton, *Mystics and Zen Masters* (New York: Dell Publishing Co., 1980), 209.

[4] Thomas Merton, *Zen and the Birds of Appetite* (New York: New Directions, 1986), 57.

[5] This may be the moment to introduce the works that hitherto have been dedicated to the comparative study of Eastern and Western mysticism and that have been consulted for the present study. In chronological order:

Rudolf Otto, *Mysticism East and West: A Comparative Analysis of the Nature of Mysticism* (New York: Macmillan, 1932; German original, *West-Östliche Mystik*, 1926).

D. T. Suzuki, *Mysticism, Christian and Buddhist* (New York: Harper and Row, 1957).

Maurus Heinrichs, *Katholische Theologie und Asiatisches Denken* (Mainz: Matthias Grünewald, 1963).

Heinrich Dumoulin, *Östliche Meditation und Christliche Mystik* (Freiburg/München: Karl Alber, 1966).

Thomas Merton, *Mystics and Zen Masters* and *Zen and the Birds of Appetite*.

William Johnston, *The Still Point: Reflections on Zen and Christian Mysticism* (New York: Fordham University Press, 1970).

Hans Waldenfels, *An der Grenze des Denkbaren: Meditation Ost und West* (München: Kösel Verlag, 1988).

Of all these works, only Heinrich Dumoulin's pays serious attention to Ruusbroec's mysticism.

practice can play an irreplaceable role in the Buddhist-Christian dialogue. The precise "how" and "why" of this will have to become clear from the analyses made in the different chapters of this book but, at least provisionally, something can be said right now.

As already intimated, (Japanese) Buddhists engaged in the dialogue with Christianity spontaneously focus on Christian mysticism. In their statements, one can find references to St. Francis of Assisi and to the Spanish mystics, St. Teresa of Avila and St. John of the Cross, but the lion's share of their attention clearly goes to the "metaphysical mysticism" of Meister Eckhart. Buddhists seem to find in Eckhart's mystical writings something very akin to their own contemplative ideas and to recognize in them the possibility within Christianity, even within a Christianity they judge to be highly mythological, of a relatively pure mysticism of unity or emptiness. At the same time, they perceive this convergence as something unorthodox and clearly against the grain of official Christianity. In other words, Buddhists tend to consider Eckhart as a representative within Christianity of their own mystical path and thought—albeit one who, by his Christian roots, is kept from being totally consistent and going all the way in the right direction. Seen from the standpoint of the Buddhist-Christian dialogue, Eckhart is indeed an asset insofar as the feeling of affinity with Eckhart on the Buddhist side engenders a more general feeling of affinity with Christianity. But an Eckhart cut off from the Christian mainline and "pulled into the Buddhist camp" (Eckhart *captivus*) is no longer able to represent Christianity, nor can he constitute a challenge to Buddhist ideas, and this is unfortunate, since mutual challenge is the salt of the interreligious dialogue.

It is hoped, then, that Ruusbroec's mysticism can play a more fruitful role in the Buddhist-Christian dialogue. It is much more difficult, indeed, to disconnect Ruusbroec from the basic Christian doctrines (for example, the Trinity), and his finely honed balance and mutual dependency between unity and union, Wisdom (the cognitive) and Love (desire, the appetitive) constitute a decisive challenge to the dogmatically held Buddhist position of the indisputable superiority of compact unity (in Wisdom alone). I therefore beg to differ with Alois Haas (quoting Hans Urs von Balthasar) that, "From a Christian Eckhart, and probably only from him, the dialogue with Asia's metaphysical paths of salvation becomes possible."[6] Ruusbroec's challenge to Buddhist contemplative ideas even becomes very direct if Buddhist traits can be recognized in the picture Ruusbroec paints of what he calls "natural mysticism." Whether this is the case, or whether, on the contrary, Buddhism fun-

---

[6] Alois M. Haas, "Transzendenzerfahrung in der Auffassung der Deutschen Mystik," in Gerhard Oberhammer, ed., *Transzendenzerfahrung, Vollzugs-horizont des Heils* (Wien: Institut für Indologie der Universität Wien, 1978), 194.

damentally sides with Ruusbroec against that same natural mysticism will be the real focus of our investigation.

DOES IT MAKE SENSE TO SPEAK OF "BUDDHIST MYSTICISM?"

The first question we encounter on our path can be formulated as follows: Is the Buddhist contemplative path similar enough to Ruusbroec's mysticism for a comparison of the two to throw light on Ruusbroec's endeavor; and, conversely, can the category "mysticism" help us arrive at a deeper insight into Buddhism, or does it only confuse the issue further?

A first negative answer from Christian theologians of earlier days might have been: as the *fine fleur*, the full blossom of the life of faith and grace, true mysticism cannot be found outside Christianity. This position, however, can no longer be held as such in Catholic theology, since Vatican II has recognized the working of the Holy Spirit even beyond the boundaries of Christianity. Thus, given the universality of God's saving Will, "the universal availability of grace as the self-bestowal (*Selbst-mitteilung*) of God," Karl Rahner, for example, concludes that "the kind of mysticism, which is interpreted rightly as the proper experience of grace by Christian theology, can and must be found also outside institutional Christianity."[7] Since we may have to come back to this question in connection with Ruusbroec's judgment on so-called "natural contemplation," there is no need to say anything more at this point.

On the other hand, however, there also are Buddhists who refuse to apply the epithet "mystical" to Buddhism, or at least to their own brand of Buddhism. Thus, for example, the Japanese Buddhist philosopher, Nishitani Keiji, once declared: "Mysticism is an element common to both Christianity and Islam. Things are different, however, when it comes to Buddhism. The closest thing Buddhism has to offer may be the *myōkōnin* 妙好人 [believers in Pure Land Buddhism for whom Amida, the savior, becomes existential, experienced reality]."[8] One of Nishitani's disciples, Ueda Shizuteru, entitled an article in which he compares Eckhart and Zen "Zen Buddhism as Nonmysticism."[9] But the most famous pronouncement on the matter is from the pen of D. T. Suzuki, to whom we alluded earlier. Towards the end of his long life, and after he himself had written a book with the title *Mysticism, Christian and Buddhist*, Suzuki objected to Heinrich Dumoulin's

---

[7] Karl Rahner, "Transzendenzerfahrung aus katholisch-dogmatischer Sicht," in Oberhammer, *Transzendenzerfahrung*, 144–5.

[8] Nishitani Keiji, in *Soga Ryōjin taiwashū* (Tokyo: Yayoi Shobō, 1979), 69.

[9] Shizuteru Ueda, "Der Zen Buddhismus als 'Nicht-Mystik'," in: Guenter Schulz, *Transparente Welt* (Bern/Stuttgart: Verlag Hans Huber, 1965), 291–313.

qualification of Zen as "mystical": "Let it suffice to say here that Zen has nothing 'mystical' about it or in it. It is most plain, clear as the daylight, all out in the open with nothing hidden, dark, obscure, secret or mystifying in it."[10] In choosing to entitle the present book *Mysticism Buddhist and Christian*, we mean not only to acknowledge Suzuki's pioneering efforts but also to bring his final conclusions up again for review.

Below we shall have occasion to investigate what these Buddhist writers understand by "mysticism" when they refuse to apply the term to Buddhism, especially Zen. For the moment we shall simply thank them for two lessons they teach us and then go on to a more systematic enquiry into the relationship between Buddhism and mysticism.

The first lesson we learn here is that *mysticism* is evidently a very ambiguous or polysemic term and can thus evoke affirmations and negations, depending on the sense in which the term is understood. One would like a clear definition of the term. Unfortunately, however (as in the case of *religion*), a single definition covering all members in the group or covering the whole extension appears to be impossible. In other words, the reality called mysticism appears to be not monothetic but polythetic: one cannot require, when X and Y are both recognized as mysticism, that both would contain all the same elements, a, b, c, etc.; one can only demand "a certain amount of overlapping" of elements, sufficient to build a common intersubjective world of meaning.

Secondly, it is clear that Buddhists must refuse the advances of a partner who declares Buddhism to be mystical, when that partner thereby takes a particular form of mysticism (Christian mysticism, for example) as a model and insists on ascribing all the elements found in this model to Buddhism as well. That, however, is not what I intend to do here. When I set out to defend the thesis that Buddhism contains mysticism to a degree certainly not inferior to that of Christianity, I do indeed have Christian mysticism in mind as a model, but I only contend that Buddhism shows enough affinity to, or enough common elements with, that model to make the use of the term meaningful in our dialogue and useful for building a common platform of mutual understanding. I want it kept clearly in mind that, in both Buddhism and Christianity, the "common" mystical element is intrinsically "informed" or qualified by the totality of the religion wherein it lives and that these two religions are very different in character—a difference that D. T. Suzuki once described, albeit one-sidedly, this way:

> I would like to say that there are two types of mentality which fundamentally differ one from the other: (1) affective, personal and dualistic,

[10] Daisetz Suzuki, *The Eastern Buddhist* 1/1 (1965): 124.

and (2) nonaffective, nonpersonal and nondualistic. Zen belongs to the latter and Christianity naturally to the former.[11]

In confirmation of my thesis that Buddhism contains mysticism at least to the same degree as Christianity, the following phenomena can be adduced. First, as already mentioned in the opening paragraphs of this chapter, there is the sense of affinity Buddhists feel for Christian mysticism, for the mystical elements in a religion that they otherwise experience as very alien to their own. Second, as will be seen below, nearly all the questions broached in this book in order to clarify Ruusbroec's mysticism have their counterparts and are abundantly discussed in the Buddhist tradition. We can even go a step further: while these questions are rather marginal ones in Christian theology and are relegated to a side-branch called "Ascetical and Mystical Theology," in Buddhism they appear on center stage and are discussed even in the basic sacred scriptures, the sūtras. And third, insofar as it is intimately linked with the apophatic tradition of negative theology, Christian mysticism has much in common with the "tenacious process of negation" that pervades the whole of Buddhism, but especially Mahāyāna Buddhism.[12]

Before taking a closer look at the Buddhist tradition in search of its "mystical elements," I would like to introduce a few distinctions that might serve as guide posts.

The Mystical "State of Mind" and its "Objects"

When a state of mind, or a process of states of mind, is called "mystical," attention can be focused primarily either on the kind of consciousness itself or on the "object" intended by or supposed to be involved in that particular state of mind. The two evidently influence each other and cannot be separated, but the distinction may help our understanding. Thus, when it is said that mysticism is a "transcendent consciousness," the stress can fall either on "transcendent *consciousness*" or on "consciousness *of the Transcendent*."

In the former case we could speak of a "gnoseological transcendence." Here one thinks of a higher kind of experience or knowledge, beyond the everyday sensual and rational modes of knowing; or of a deeper level of consciousness, implying a descent into the core of the self. Thus, the *Dictionnaire de spiritualité* writes: "One calls 'mystical' that which goes beyond the

---

[11] D. T. Suzuki, in Thomas Merton, *Zen and the Birds of Appetite*, 133.

[12] Kees Bolle's comment on a fundamental common trait of this negational thinking is worth mentioning here: "In all these cases, the traditional concepts are forced to yield a higher reality, a vision the tradition supposedly intended but had not disclosed hitherto.... In all instances something higher and more powerful than what tradition allowed or was capable of understanding is posited as absolute." Cited in M. Eliade, ed., *The Encyclopedia of Religion* 5:295–6.

schemas of ordinary experience";[13] C. G. Jung (and also William James) declares that "mysticism involves a new, ordinarily unactuated consciousness"; and W. Johnston, after H. Dumoulin, speaks of a "vertical thinking" that goes down instead of going out like ordinary thinking and writes, for example: "Christian mystical experience, like Zen and psychoanalysis, cannot escape from the sense of profundity or 'going down'."[14]

In the latter case we seem to be obliged to speak of an ontological transcendence, of a transcendent "object" of the mystical experience, or again of the "presence" of the Other within mystical consciousness. The relationships between these two aspects of the term "transcendent consciousness" present us with delicate problems, but here I want to point out only the general Buddhist tendency to describe the highest state of consciousness as one wherein the discrimination of subject and object has disappeared.

With regard to the variety of "objects" of mystical experience, of which more will be said in the next chapter, the question arises as to the category Buddhist "mysticism" would belong to. The answer to this question will appear more concretely below, but for now I offer the following schema.

First of all, in Buddhism "mysticism of the person (human or divine) is at best only present *en mineur*, namely, in some presentations of the bodhisattva as pure Mercy-Love, totally identifying with all suffering living beings, and in some descriptions of the relationship between Amida and the believer in Pure Land Buddhism. It must be remarked, however, that in the theoretical reflections on these experiences, the "alterity" or otherness of the other person tends to be totally negated.

Second, "mysticism of the essence" or the "discovery of the untouchable depth within oneself" is, without any doubt, the central mode of Buddhist mysticism. It must then be remarked, however, that this "deepest self," "true self," or "original self" is essentially seen as free from all limitations, completely open to all reality, and one with the "All-One" that is the Real; and that, in East Asian Buddhism (the Chinese cultural sphere), mainly under the influence of Taoism, this often takes on the character of a veritable "nature mysticism."

THE BUDDHIST TRADITION

After this overly long introduction, it is time now to have a short look at the Buddhist tradition, in order to get an idea of the concrete shape of its mystical elements.

[13] *Dictionnaire de spiritualité* 10, col. 1893.

[14] W. Johnston, *The Still Point*, 49, 71.

Original Buddhism

Buddhism, no less than Christianity, is deeply "informed" by the life and experience of the Founder, who remains the supreme model. The paradigmatic event in Sakyamuni Buddha's life—in a sense comparable to the death and resurrection of Jesus in Christianity—is, without any doubt, the enlightenment experience under the bodhi tree. This event, wherein Sakyamuni is transformed into the Buddha (the "Enlightened One") and Buddhism finds its origin, cannot be explained in any rational way, but is constantly understood in the Buddhist tradition as, at the least, a "transcendent experience of true reality." From the very beginning, then, mental discipline, concentrated meditation, or "states of absorption" (*Versenkungszustände—dhyāna*) after the model of the Buddha himself, play a big role. Furthermore, the goal of the Buddhist path, Nirvana, is clearly presented as transcendent. It may be important to remark here, incidentally, that this Nirvana, although not described in any positive way as yet and not directly presented as a "substantial reality," is not seen as merely a subjective state of consciousness. This appears clearly, for example, in a crucial sermon of the Buddha, the *Udāna*: "There is an unborn, not become, not made, uncompounded; and were it not for this unborn...no escape could be shown for what is born, has become, is made, is compounded."[15] The path toward the goal is thus seen as "transcending the world" (*lokottara*) and consisting in "crossing over to the other shore." This is stressed, e.g., in a sermon by the Zen master, Abbot Obara:

> From the present illusory reality let us make the crossing to the shore of realization of Nirvana. Throughout Buddhism the idea is to cross from here to the beyond, to transfer our living from here to there. All Buddhism, Mahāyāna and Hīnayāna alike, has the notion of passing over. It is in Zen also.[16]

Still, the full reality of original Buddhism, as far as we can reconstruct it from the oldest texts, does not seem to be covered if we simply call it a "mystical path." In the oldest sūtras, the means of reaching the other shore is not presented as a direct experience of the transcendent reality (Nirvana) in absorption or ecstasy (*dhyāna*), but rather as the attainment of a clear and rational insight (*prajñā*) into the four Holy Truths preached by the Buddha—whereby, it is true, concentrated meditation can be a great, if perhaps not indispensable, help—while leading a good life. The ethical compo-

---

[15] *Udāna*, 81, as quoted in Sydney Spencer, *Mysticism in World Religion* (Gloucester, Mass.: Peter Smith, 1971), 78.

[16] As translated in Trevor Leggett, *The Tiger's Cave* (London: Routledge & Kegan Paul, 1977), 18.

35

nent of original Buddhism is beautifully expressed in an old didactic verse, called "Verse of Admonishment of the Seven Buddhas," which is still part of Buddhist liturgy today:

> Refrain from all evil actions
> Perform all good actions
> Purify your own heart
> This is the teaching of all the Buddhas.

Let us remark that the contemplative element appears here only in the third line. With this in mind, Stephan Beyer could write: "From the earliest disciples to the modern masters, Buddhism has set itself the goal of producing holy people."[17]

Of this oldest Buddhism we could say therefore that, although mental discipline-meditation is central, the main emphasis is ethical and rational.[18]

The Hīnayāna (the "Lesser Vehicle" or "the Old Buddhist School")

From early on the Buddhist movement split geographically into the school that flourished in the northwest of India, which used the Sanskrit language and is here called "The Sarvāstivādin"—and the Buddhism of the southeast, which used (and still uses) Pāli as its canonical language and soon spread to Sri Lanka, and from there to Burma, Thailand, Laos, Cambodia, etc.: "The Theravādin."

THE SARVĀSTIVĀDIN

The Sarvāstivādin still show strongly the original conviction that it is the (rational) insight into the four Holy Truths that destroys the passions, those causes of all human suffering, and thus leads to Nirvana. We could think here of Socrates, for whom too it was right knowledge that could put aright everything that is wrong in the human situation. This has sometimes been called a belief in the "magical power of cognition" or gnosis. Still, the Sarvāstivādin came to recognize that, in order to be able to eradicate the deepest passions, this knowledge must be "exercised," become bodily as it were, in meditation. It remains true, however, that the liberating insight is not yet seen as a cognition "which radically transcends all ordinary forms and contents of consciousness, as a consciousness of an essence that radically transcends all ordinary experience." In other words, liberating insight still shows "a rational-analytical, truly unmystical character."[19]

[17] Stephan Beyer, *The Buddhist Experience: Sources and Interpretations* (Encino, CA: Dickenson Publishing Co., 1974), 154.

[18] Cf. Spencer, *Mysticism in World Religion*, 75.

[19] Cf. Lambert Schmithausen, "Zum Struktur der erlösenden Erfahrung im Indischen

THE THERAVĀDIN

Briefly, we could say that a further step is made here in the direction of full-blown mysticism, namely, in the recognition of a sudden turnabout on the contemplative path: while initially the object of contemplation is the suffering and transiency in this world, at a certain moment one obtains a direct experience of Nirvana—moments of intuitive knowledge that have the unconditioned (Nirvana) itself as their object. Through this transmundane knowledge all factors that bind one to earthly existence are finally eradicated and liberation is obtained. Here we can speak in the fullest sense of an experience of the Transcendent as an ontological reality. On the other hand, however, the Theravādin have always maintained that, in order to be salutary, the supramundane experience in absorption or Quiet (*śamatha*) must go together (like a span of oxen) with exact analytical investigation (*vipaśyanā* or *prajñā*) of the real (the four Holy Truths). This fact has induced H. Dumoulin to write: "The peculiar mixture of rationality and mysticism might be the most surprising characteristic and astonishing paradox of Theravāda Buddhism."[20]

MAHĀYĀNA BUDDHISM (THE "GREATER VEHICLE")

Around the first century BCE a new trend developed within Buddhism which came to call itself the "Greater Vehicle." This is not the place to go into its characteristics or the different forms it took in history, but it may be useful to note that it is mainly this kind of Buddhism that spread to central Asia, China, Korea, Japan, and later to Tibet.

From its very beginning, Mahāyāna focuses much more directly on the supramundane object (which comes to be called, besides Nirvana, also Emptiness, Buddha-Nature, and *Tathatā* [suchness]), and on the suprarational and intuitive "transcendent Wisdom" (*prajñā-pāramitā*) wherein this object is experienced. It is this experiential knowledge of transcendent reality that is now seen as the real cause of liberation. Sydney Spencer can thus say: "The Mahāyāna is a religion of a definitely mystical type," and describe this new vision as follows:

> In the Mahāyāna it came to be believed that the knowledge or wisdom (bodhi) which is the essential quality of the historical teacher pertains to the heart of Reality itself. The Buddha-nature (buddhata) is the supreme Reality which underlies all things.

Or again:

Buddhismus," G. Oberhammer, ed., *Transzendenzerfahrung*, 100, 105.

[20] Heinrich Dumoulin, *Östliche Meditation und Christliche Mystik* (Freiburg/München: Karl Alber, 1966), 200.

The Mahāyāna brings with it a new understanding of Nirvana.... Nirvana is thus identified with ultimate Reality; it is the Buddha-nature, which is the essence of all things.[21]

Because they may be especially relevant to the theme of our investigations, I want to highlight two further traits of the Mahāyāna variety of Buddhism. To begin with, from my necessarily brief description above, it may still be sufficiently clear that a kind of "impersonal Wisdom" as it were in the prolongation of metaphysical speculation[22] became the central element in the Mahāyāna path of liberation. In Buddhist terminology, this could be called "right knowledge of the Dharma (true reality)." Still, even in Mahāyāna the central "prayer" of the faithful remains: "I seek refuge in the Buddha; I seek refuge in the Dharma; I seek refuge in the sangha" (the *sangha* being the monastic order founded by the Buddha as the centerpiece of his movement). This may indicate that personal devotion to the Buddha—who, all metaphysico-theological speculation notwithstanding, never totally loses his personal character—plays a bigger role in lived Buddhism than the theory would let on. In the same vein, it must be remarked that Compassion or Mercy-Love tends more and more to occupy center stage beside Wisdom. The ideal figure, then, is no longer the "Arhat," who wants to reach Nirvana as soon as possible by way of Wisdom, but the "Bodhisattva," who somehow puts off entering Nirvana out of compassion for his fellow-beings, for whose liberation he wants to continue working in this "vale of tears" (*samsāra*). In this connection, Wisdom and Mercy-Love are often seen to be, in fact, contradictory virtues. A rather classical formula expresses this in the words "Wisdom does not recognize any others; Compassion wants to save all others" (*recognizing others* being the work of our deluded discriminatory thinking, which is the cause of all our passions, while true supramundane Wisdom sees the unity and "emptiness" of all objects).

In the second place, Mahāyāna came to consider the rational and the ethical, two rather central elements in the older Buddhism, as basically illusory. Ethics is based, after all, on the discrimination of good and evil, and human acts performed with our ordinary consciousness, whether they be good or bad, all produce *karma*, which binds us to this earthly existence. The truly

[21] Spencer, *Mysticism in World Religion*, 68, 84; 90–1.

[22] Cf., e.g., Jacques Maritain's remark: "We are confronted here, indeed, with a metaphysical experience in the strongest sense of the word; and, from this point of view, the efforts of the contemplatives of the East truly appear as an endeavor to pursue the proper line of philosophical intellection beyond philosophy itself." *Œuvreres complètes*, vol. 7 (Fribourg, Suisse: Editions Universitaires, 1988), 183. The Japanese philosopher, Tanabe Hajime, then tried to pursue this ideal within the confines of philosophy. See his *Philosophy as Metanoetics* (Berkeley: University of California Press, 1986).

"holy man" is then not so much the one of high virtues (called *pāramitā* in Buddhism) as the "sage" whose transformed consciousness puts him/her beyond the sphere of ethics on the truly religious path. This can be interpreted as a (sometimes one-sided) radicalization of the insight that the uprooting of our evil passions cannot be effected by mere willful effort, but requires action on a deeper psychic level—an insight already present in Hīnayāna and equally stressed by the Christian tradition, as indicated by W. Johnston:

> Some mystical writers...declared that there were certain virtues that can *only* be acquired in the passivity of mystical prayer.... [And there is] the traditional doctrine that, whereas discursive prayer removes defects, mystical prayer removes the *roots* of these defects.[23]

The aim of this summary overview of the Buddhist tradition was to substantiate the thesis that Buddhism contains sufficient mystical elements to make a comparison with Ruusbroec worth our while. But the attentive reader will have noticed that I have, deliberately, overshot my goal and argued, in fact, that Buddhism, especially in its Mahāyāna form, is intrinsically or essentially mystical, is a "mystical religion": a religion that expects salvation from mystical states of consciousness. For a comparison with Ruusbroec, and especially with what he calls "natural contemplation," it is important to remark right now that Christianity, indeed, contains mysticism, but cannot be called a mystical religion in the same strong sense of the word, because salvation in Christianity is not as intimately linked with the mystical path. Let us listen to two authors who make this point very emphatically:

> Buddhism is essentially a mystical religion.... Christianity, on the other hand, ...is not essentially mystical.... For the Christian life can be lived in full vigor without any enlightenment.... In other words, mysticism as such has not been extolled by Christianity; it is always a way to, or an expression of, charity.[24]

> The significance of such an experience [a direct experience of a transcendent reality], though present, varies in importance. Christianity, especially in its reformed churches, attaches less significance to the element of experience than other faiths do. In Vedantic and Sāmkhya Hinduism, on the contrary, religion itself coincides with the kind of insight that can come only from mystical experience.... [And in

---

[23] W. Johnston, *The Still Point*, 130–1. See also Simone Weil's reflections on the necessity of "attention" in the struggle with the passions, for example in *L'attente de Dieu* (Paris: La Colombe, 1950), 85–97, and in *La pesanteur et la grâce* (Paris: Plon, 1984), 118–19.

[24] W. Johnston, *The Still Point*, 130–1.

Buddhism] once again we are confronted with a faith that from its origin is headed in a mystical direction.[25]

In chapter 1, the question "Do mystics think they have the monopoly of knowing God or the Ultimate?" was answered in the negative with regard to the Christian mystic: the mystic has a different, more experiential, way of knowing the same objects that the ordinary believer knows by faith in the Christian doctrine, presented by the Church from the treasury of the divine revelation. The answer in Buddhism, however, would rather be in the affirmative, since there the Ultimate or Absolute can only be really known by direct experience or knowledge of a transcendent level, and not by revelation from above (which is non-existent), nor by the ordinary human intellect (which is flawed by *avidyā*). Strictly speaking, the Ultimate in Buddhism is the Buddha's Enlightenment itself, a Wisdom wherein the content of knowledge is not distinct from the way of knowing. This "content" can thus not really be presented or reached apart from the "mystical" state of consciousness, but only in a reenactment (*Nachvollziehung*) of the Buddha's Enlightenment.[26] Still, of all the forms of Buddhism, it may be only Zen that (at least in its theory) adheres literally to this strict interpretation. In all other Buddhist schools, the doctrine preached (and thus objectified) by the Buddha, as the content of his Enlightenment and contained in the sūtras, plays an important role, out of the conviction that, without the merciful teaching of the Buddha, ordinary mortals would never have been able to gain that same knowledge. This is clearest in the Hīnayāna, with its stress on *prajñā*, clear insight into the four Holy Truths (considered as the core of the Buddha's teaching); but it continues even in the Mahāyāna, notwithstanding its nearly exclusive stress on *dhyāna* or *prajñā-pāramitā*.

We touch here on the perennial problem of the relationship between doctrine and experience, Word and Spirit, in religion. While mysticism is clearly centered on experience (without ever becoming totally independent of the word—doctrine or language), in religion in general the relationship and balance between the two is not so clear-cut. It cannot be doubted that religion, as a mere acceptance of a religious doctrine and compliance with prescribed practices without personal experience, soon becomes a "dead weight." What made Ruusbroec resign his chaplaincy in Brussels has been described as the consciousness "that his work as chaplain did not have much meaning: was not the daily work merely a bandage over a much-too-deep

---

[25] Louis Dupré, "Mysticism," in: Mircea Eliade, ed., *The Encyclopedia of Religion* (New York: Macmillan, 1988), 10:247, 249.

[26] Since this is considered to be a knowledge wherein subject and object coincide, or an "objectless consciousness," the Western concern for the "objectivity" of the experience, pointed out above (chapter 1, pages 17–18), cannot be detected in Buddhism.

wound, namely the interior shrivelling up of the faithful...their lack of religious experience?"[27] And do not today many people drift away from Christianity because it dawns on them that their own religion has been a dead weight for so long (and because the social constraints that kept them in the fold have fallen away)—with some of them turning to Eastern religions in the expectation of finding there authentic religious experience?

Thus, also for Christianity, experience is vital. "The heart of Catholicism is a living experience of unity in Christ which transcends all conceptual formulations."[28] Under the influence of Hindu mysticism, in the midst of which he was practicing his Christian spiritual path, Henri Le Saux, who came to call himself Abhishiktananda, became strongly convinced of this point and wrote:

> Anything about God or the Word in any religion which is not based on the deep I-experience is bound to be simple "notion," not existential. From that awakening to self comes the awakening to God—and we discover marvelously that Christ is simply this awakening on a degree of purity rarely if ever reached by man.[29]

Still, there is a basic difference on this point between Christianity and "mystical religions"—a difference that the same Thomas Merton formulates as follows:

> [In Buddhism] experience...is absolutely essential, the very heart of Buddhism. This is in a sense the exact opposite of the situation in Christianity. For Christianity begins with revelation....
>
> But the fact remains that for Christianity, a religion of the Word, the understanding of the statements which embody God's revelation of Himself remains a primary concern. Christian experience is a fruit of this understanding, a development of it, a deepening of it.[30]

That the difference is not an absolute one, however, has been intimated above. In a sense, Buddhist enlightenment, as presented by many Buddhist schools, could also be called "a fruit of the understanding of the four Holy Truths."

We could also indicate the difference between Christianity and "mystical religion" by saying that in the "mystical religions" the role of mysticism is

[27] P. Mommaers, Introduction to Jan Van Ruusbroec, *Opera omnia* I (Tielt: Lannoo, 1981), 22, 21.

[28] Thomas Merton, *Zen and the Birds of Appetite*, 39.

[29] H. Le Saux, Letter to Murray Rogers, 2 Sept. 1973, as quoted in James Wiseman, "Enveloped by Mystery," *NABEWD Bulletin* 45 (October 1992): 10.

[30] Thomas Merton, *Zen and the Birds of Appetite*, 39–40.

clear: it is the true factor of salvation, while in Christianity salvation is a question of faith, and the role of mysticism is extremely hard to define, especially since the contemplative path appears to form a kind of polarity with the demand of active charity, presented as the only requirement for salvation (cf. Matthew 25).[31]

But if, indeed, Buddhism is as strongly mystical as argued above, why then would some Buddhists, especially theoreticians of Zen, recognize mysticism in Christianity and not in Buddhism? It could be said, in general, that they must have a different "definition" of mysticism in mind than the one I have been working with. A number of elements seem to be relevant here.

To begin with, in their comparison with Christianity, these Buddhists, in fact, state that they find a well-defined special domain of mysticism in Christianity and not in their own religion—which, in a sense, is true enough but begs the question of whether their religion as a whole is mystical or not.[32]

Furthermore, Zen people, especially, insist that the "transcendent reality" experienced in enlightenment (satori) does not constitute "another world" (a "mysterium," as the word "mystical" itself seems to suggest) away from this one, but is totally immanent in this world, identical with the everyday world; that there is no "sacred world" apart from this profane world. On the other hand, they have the impression that mysticism (in its Christian variety) transports the mystic into a totally different and fantastic world (*ein Fortgerissensein zu einer phantastischen Weite*[33]), built up by the particular doctrines of the religion. In the same year (1965) that he denied that Zen is mysticism, D. T. Suzuki was asked about this denial by Winston King and on that occasion elaborated a bit more.

> *King:* ...You go on to say that there is nothing "mystical" or "hidden" about Zen, because it is direct and plain. Now I have been used to thinking of "mysticism" as fundamentally an immediate sense of direct experience of reality. It seems to me since the terms "direct or immediate experience of reality" would apply to Zen, that one may call it mystical.

[31] I have tried to come to grips with that difference in my "Tangenten an einem vollkommenen Kreis," in: Günter Stachel, ed., *Munen musō: Ungegenständliche Meditation* (Mainz: Matthias Grünewald, 1978), 378–96.

[32] In another context, Nishitani Keiji appears to think along these same lines: "It is now widely accepted in academic circles that mysticism is something universal that pervades the religious phenomenon all over the world. As to Buddhism, there is reason to think that Buddhism as a whole is mysticism. If this is so, we could also say that precisely this constitutes the peculiarity of Buddhism." Cited in Ueda Shizuteru, ed., ドイツ神秘主義研究 [A Study of German Mysticism] (Tokyo: Sōbunsha, 1982), 3–4.

[33] Shizuteru Ueda, "Der Zen Buddhismus als 'Nicht-Mystik'," 312.

Suzuki: If mysticism is defined as something immediate, without any medium, it's alright; but when it is understood to be something hidden "behind" what we actually see, then Zen is not mysticism

....

Yes, Zen differs from mysticism. In mystical experience there is something mystically experienced, that special experience which is something different from all ordinary experiences. But in Zen, ordinary experience itself is mystical experience.[34]

This difference, however, insofar as it really exists (and Zen is truly free of particular doctrines and does not speak of special experiences), is no sufficient reason to call the one mystical and the other not.

Finally, it may be considered that these Buddhists tend to take as essential to "mysticism" the very personal and often passionate character of Christian mysticism, nothing (or very little) of which they find in their own spiritual path, which they present as totally "cool" and purely cognitive ("metaphysical") in character. Again, however, this suffices to speak of a different kind of mysticism, but not of mysticism and non-mysticism as such.

Since these objections mostly come from the side of Zen Buddhism, and since Zen has a special place in these pages anyway, I may be allowed at this point to add a word on the relationship between mysticism and Zen in particular. It may be true that, for the enlightened ones themselves, their spiritual experience appears as having no other object than the everyday world. On the other hand, however, it remains true that the world that these enlightened ones speak of constitutes for the non-enlightened a transcendent reality, which they cannot possibly reach with their ordinary experience or reason.[35] An ingenuous testimony to this can be found in the record of the sixth Zen patriarch:

One day [after listening to Hui-neng's sermon]...Prefect Wei said: "I have heard what Your Holiness preached. It is really so deep that it is beyond our mind and speech...."[36]

Furthermore, it is hard to deny that, in light of what we have been saying about the mystical character of Buddhism in general, Zen appears as maybe

[34] "Conversations with D. T. Suzuki. Part II," *The Eastern Buddhist* 21/1 (1988): 96, 98.

[35] On this point, see for example Alois Haas, "Dichtung in christlicher Mystik und Zen-Buddhismus," *Zen Buddhism Today*, 9 (1992): 86–116. And for an expression with an unmistakable "mystical feel": "...full understanding can come to you only through an inexpressible mystery [and not through words or perception]. The approach to it is called the Gateway of the Stillness beyond all activity." Cited in John Blofeld, *The Zen Teaching of Huang Po*, 79.

[36] *The Diamond Sūtra and the Sūtra of Hui-neng.* Translated by A. F. Price and Wong Moulam (Boston: Shambala, 1990), 88.

the most mystical of all forms of Buddhism. It is so by the rejection of all forms and images, language and doctrine, on their contemplative path; by the exclusive concentration on *dhyāna* (absorption or "just sitting") with nearly total disregard of the counterbalancing element of rational analytical insight, as stressed in the more traditional forms of Buddhism under the titles of *prajñā* and *vipaśyanā*; and by their insistence on the sudden and immediate character of enlightenment. In regard to this last characteristic of Zen, the Belgian Buddhist scholar Hubert Durt remarks:

> In fact, one recognizes in this concern for immediacy the mystical exigency for the absolute and the one, which manifests itself by the abolition of space (all is in all) and of time (subitism, refusal of mediation, quietism).[37]

In the meantime, it is not impossible to consider Zen as a reaction against some forms of the Buddhist contemplative path, deemed to have become too complicated and *weltfremd* by an overly strong tie-up with an ever more subtle Buddhist doctrine.

[37] Hubert Durt, *Cahiers d'Extrême-Asie* 6 (1991–1992): 218. To this exigency of total unity, intrinsic to all mysticism, we shall have to come back below.

3

Mystical Objects, Mystical Marks

As we have seen in chapter 1, the mystics' own writings lead us to conclude that the distinctive feature of mysticism has something to do with a particular state of awareness. Of course, these texts tell us a good deal more than that about the stuff of which mystical consciousness is made. In describing their own inner states, the mystical authors will often tell us not only *how* they experience but also *what* they experience. We shall begin there.

THE "OBJECT" OF MYSTICAL AWARENESS

The first thing that strikes us about the "object" of mystical awareness is the lack of uniformity among different authors in naming it. Still, there is a kind of common essence that can be distilled out of these differences, which may be described as "ultimate Reality" or the "Absolute." For the mystic, the "thing" that is experienced cannot be relativized to any other "thing" in experience. It is incomparably more real than anything known before or since. It surpasses thought and desire—or perhaps better, no thought or desire is capable of surpassing it.

No sooner does one reach this conclusion than the stubborn fact of variety rears its head into the picture, bringing the transcendent back down to earth. And what variety there is! Let it be stated clearly at the outset: the mystics themselves would be the last ones to concede a single, common essence in mystical awareness.

In Western culture, which even today bears the unmistakable marks of Judaeo-Christian influence, the object of mystical awareness is most often experienced as the personal God who brings all things into being and beckons men and women everywhere to himself. But there are exceptions, many and remarkable, that deserve more than a passing glance.

Nature

A first group of mystics discover the Absolute as the ground of the natural world. For them, what lies outside the phenomenon of the human seems to become translucent of the one Reality that lies beneath and behind it. In addition to the passages from the diaries of Virginia Woolf cited in the opening chapter,[1] any number of examples are to be found in the pages of William James's *Varieties of Religious Experience*. To come still closer to our own day, we may cite a representative passage from the playwright Eugène Ionesco:

> In fact, I am unable to say what I want to say. I have had moments of certitude. I have gone through an experience of this. One day when I was seventeen years old I was walking in a country town, in June, in the morning. All of a sudden the world appeared transformed, in such a way that I was seized by an overflowing joy and I thought: Now, no matter what happens, I know. And I will always remember that moment and shall never again feel hopeless. I cannot relate to you what this was because it is unrelatable. It was as if there was a change in the appearance of the town itself, of the world, of the people. The sky seemed closer, almost palpable. The only words that can more or less define it are intensity, density, presence, light. But there is no definition possible. In any case, I told myself at that moment that I was sure. If anyone had asked me, "Sure of what?" I would not have known what to say. I was filled with a certitude, and I thought that I would never again be unhappy, and that in the worst moments I would remember this moment.[2]

The Human Essence

A second group of texts describes the experience of Reality as an insight into the core of the mystic's own person. Here it is not nature but the everyday self of the mystic that is illumined to reveal the unquestionable ground, the True Self. Jan van Ruusbroec refers to this experience as "finding one's own essence," and we will have more to say of this in later chapters. For the moment, we may turn again to modern literature.

R. C. Zaehner has argued that Marcel Proust "was content to note that another 'self,' a self that usually seems to be dead, was discovered below the ordinary experiencing ego, and that this self was concerned with experiences that transcended time and space." He cites, for instance, the well-known passage from *À la recherche du temps perdu* in which Proust describes an experience that occurred while eating a piece of cake:

---

[1] See above, page 16, note 8, and its accompanying quotation.

[2] An interview, cited in C. Chabanis, *Dieu existe-t-il? Non* (Paris: Fayard, 1973), 333–4. Ionesco gave another account of the same experience in *Journal en miettes* (Paris: Gallimard, 1973), 97–8.

But at the very moment when the mouthful mixed with the crumbs of the cake touched my palate, I shuddered, as I took note of the strange things that were going on inside me. An exquisite pleasure had invaded me, isolated with no idea of what its cause might be. Immediately it had made the vicissitudes of life indifferent, its disasters inoffensive, its brevity illusory—in much the same way as love operates, filling me with a precious essence: or rather this essence was not in me, it was me. I had ceased to feel mediocre, contingent, or mortal. Whence should this strong joy have come to me? I felt that it was connected with the taste of the tea and the cake, but that it transcended it infinitely and could not be of the same nature. Whence did it come? What did it mean? How to lay hold of it?[3]

In the light of what we shall have to say further on, we should note here that the true *I* of Proust—"this essence [that] was not in me, it was me"—appears as something absolute. As such it is revealed as not only different from but the very opposite of the everyday *I*, so much so as to render the latter "mediocre, contingent, mortal" by comparison. The same opposition comes to the fore in Virginia Woolf's *To the Lighthouse*, where one of her characters, Mrs. Ramsay, arrives at a self-discovery:

> For now she need not think about anybody. She could be herself, by herself. And that was what now she often felt the need of—to think. To be silent; to be alone. All the being and the doing, expansive, glittering, vocal, evaporated; and one shrunk, with a sense of solemnity, to being oneself, a wedge-edged core of darkness, something invisible to others. Although she continued to knit, and sat upright, it was thus that she felt herself; and this self having shed its attachments was free for the strangest adventures....There was freedom, there was peace, there was, most welcome of all, a summoning together, a resting on a platform of stability. Not as oneself did one find rest ever, in her experience (she accomplished here something dexterous with her needles), but as a wedge of darkness. Losing personality, one lost the fret, the hurry, the stir; and there rose to her lips always some exclamation of triumph over life when things came together in this peace, this rest, eternity.[4]

Over against the "wedge-shaped core of darkness" that is the domain of stability, peace, rest, and eternity, there is the "personality" with its futile fret, hurry, and stir. That the discovery of an unfathomable depth within oneself

[3] R. C. Zaehner, *Mysticism Sacred and Profane*, 2nd ed. (Oxford: Oxford University Press, 1967), 52–3, 59.

[4] V. Woolf, *To the Lighthouse* (London: Dent [Everyman's Library], 1977), 72–3.

47

should provoke such an exclamation of triumph over life is hardly to be won-dered at. What is curious is the writer's observation that in her triumph Mrs. Ramsay was able to continue her ordinary activities, accomplishing "some-thing dexterous with her needles."

The Man Without Qualities, the masterpiece of Robert Musil, also seems to take up this same mysticism of the deeper *I.* If the protagonist of the novel, Ulrich, is a man "without qualities," it is because he has experienced a different "state." While in that condition he is interiorly one, without self, awakened in a new and immediate way to everything about him. All qualities become relative and one loses one's grip on all attachments to concrete, everyday life. Ulrich's twin sister, Agathe, emerges as the personification of this state—as the Other that ordinarily lies hidden in Ulrich. The intertwining fate of the two twins raises the very question that has occupied mystics of all ages: how to integrate the two dimensions of the self, how to live a concrete human life in the light of the uncommon awareness of a different realm of experience.

The Human Other

In the third place, the Absolute or ultimate Reality may be seen to reside in the object of one's love. We have classic examples of this in Plato's *Symposium* and Dante's *Vita Nuova.* Even the *Sonnets* of Shakespeare seem to point towards the ultimacy of the beloved in this sense, as W. H. Auden suggests: "I think that the primary experience...out of which the sonnets to the friend spring was a mystical one."[5]

The Divine Other

We come now to a fourth "object" of mystical awareness: the Absolute as God, more particularly as the *personal* divine Other that we see in Christ-ianity. We may cite a passage here from Simone Weil, a Jew by birth who to the end refused baptism into Christianity to the end, despite her evangelical way of life and deeply Christian faith:

> I discovered the poem. It is called Love.[6] I learned it by heart. Often, at the culminating point of a violent headache, I make myself say it over, concentrating all my attention upon it and clinging with all my soul to the tenderness it enshrines. I used to think I was merely reciting it as a beautiful poem, but without my knowing it the recitation had the virtue of a prayer. It was during one of those recitations that, as I told you,

---

[5] William Shakespeare, *The Sonnets* (Toronto: The New American Library of Canada, 1965), xxix.

[6] By the seventeenth-century "metaphysical poet" George Herbert.

Christ himself came down and took possession of me (*Il m'a prise*).

In my arguments about the insolubility of the problem of God I had never foreseen the possibility of that, of a real contact, person to person, here below, between a human being and God. I had vaguely heard tell of things of this kind, but I had never believed in them. Moreover, in this sudden possession of me by Christ, neither my senses nor my imagination had any part; I only felt in the midst of my suffering the presence of a love, like that which one can read on a beloved face.... God in his mercy had prevented me from reading the mystics, so that it should be evident to me that I had not invented this absolutely unexpected contact. Yet, I still half refused, not my love but my intelligence.[7]

THE CHIEF MARKS OF MYSTICAL EXPERIENCE

Not only do the mystics specify *what* they understand the object of their special awareness to be, they also give us a rather clear idea of *how* they experience it. In particular, four chief marks of mystical awareness seem to emerge from their writings: passivity, immediacy, unity, and annihilation. True, they are more marked in Christian mystics of the West, but the authors cited above suggest a wider application. In any case, we shall devote the rest of this chapter to examining these four characteristics, again in the context of the mystical texts themselves.

Passivity

The first feature of the mystic's way of knowing is that it is *passive*. The word invites one of the commonest misunderstandings about the mystical states. To define the passivity of the mystical state as the simple antonym of ordinary activity suggests a kind of quietism or spiritual autism. Mystical literature presents a quite different picture, and we do well to pause to consider it at some length.

Mystics refer to the passive nature of their experience as a way of underscoring their inability to account for its origins. For this reason, the use of the passive tense is common in the texts. They speak of being "seized" (Ionesco), "invaded" (Proust), or "taken possession of" (Weil). From Plato and Plotinus to Ionesco and Weil, they speak further of something that happens of a sudden and without warning, as when Weil speaks of "this absolutely unexpected contact."

In fact a variety of linguistic devices—some of them ordinary, some of them quite extraordinary—are used to stress the absence of an intelligible

---

[7] Simone Weil, *Waiting for God* (New York: Harper and Row, 1973), 68–9.

causal link between the experience and what preceded it. (Proust's formulation here is particularly striking: the "exquisite pleasure" appears as something "isolated with no idea of what its cause might be.") The ability to perceive the Other is in no sense the outcome of a particular regime of discipline or training. However pure the psycho-religious state of the mystic-to-be, however intense the longing and arduous the effort aimed at spiritual perfection, there is no guarantee of passage from pre-mystical to mystical consciousness. The passage, which can be frightening in the extreme, is never taken to be the result of activity that preceded it.

What the mystic generally means by *activity* is what goes on in prayer. It is a comprehensive term for the efforts expended in the search for God such as meditation, speculation, expressions of longing, and the like. In fact, all inner movement is classified as the activity that will eventually yield, in mystical awareness, to passivity.

Of course, the mystic knows from the start that the inner life of the soul is not enough. The very act of giving oneself to the discipline of prayer seems to presuppose a virtuous attitude and a disposition to concrete action. Hence, as a rule, moral endeavor both precedes and follows spiritual activity. Or, to put the same thing in simple Christian terms, one cannot love God in one's heart without the practice of virtue in daily life. Hadewijch stresses again and again the point that a number of her mystical friends tended to forget:

> With the Humanity of God you must live here on earth, in the labors and sorrow of exile, while within your soul you love and rejoice with the omnipotent and eternal Divinity in sweet abandonment.[8]

Thus passivity means anything but forsaking action. Rather, the mystics assume that practice continues as before. Even where mystical awareness obliterates one's acts, it does not do away with action. The difference is subtle but not difficult.

When the mystical state brings inner movement to a halt so that one can no longer think of or desire "God" or "love," outer activity may become difficult in the extreme. But at no point, the mystics tell us, should one give up trying. The very difficulty of acting virtuously heightens the awareness of radical powerlessness that overtakes the contemplative. To forsake action would be to pretend that one is no longer an embodied being—a pretense that the mystics do not make. In devoting the first book of *The Spiritual Espousals* to the active life and the second to the interior life, Ruusbroec is not implying that one begins by acting and then, advancing to a higher stage of contemplation, shakes free of the bonds of activity. The advance is rather one of awakening to a different inner dynamism, not an initiation into abstrac-

---

[8] Letter 6:117–9.

tion unhindered by the things of life. Throughout his entire œuvre, as with Hadewijch, the insistence that mystical life requires a life of virtue echoes like a constant refrain:

> Therefore all secret friends of our Lord are faithful servants when the need arises. But the faithful servants are not all secret friends, for they do not know the requisite practice.[9]

His description of the interior life in *The Spiritual Espousals* opens with an almost naive reading of a familiar gospel parable:

> The prudent maiden, that is, a pure soul who has given up earthly things and who lives for God in virtues, has taken in the vessel of her heart the oil of charity and virtuous works, with the lamp of an unblemished conscience; but when Christ the Bridegroom tarries in consolation and in new influx of gifts, then the soul becomes drowsy, sleepy, and dull. In the middle of the night, that is, when one least expects and awaits it, a spiritual cry is produced in the soul: "See, the bridegroom cometh; go out to meet him."[10]

Ruusbroec sees here the impotence that overtakes one at the gates of the "higher way of knowing." The soul is doing everything it can to find the Bridegroom, but nothing "new" happens. Every effort is so spurned as to take away all hope of ever making contact with the object of one's desire. This is where passivity comes in. The expression "drowsy, sleepy, and dull" is not a mere rhetorical flourish, but describes a condition common to so many mystics: the utter boredom, even revulsion, that accompanies the transition from activity to passivity. And this transition takes place, he tells us, "when one least expects and awaits it."

These last words strike a chord with Simon Weil's experience recorded earlier. "In my arguments about the insolubility of the problem of God," she wrote, "I had never foreseen the possibility of…a real contact." She goes further, in a tone of almost pre-mystical agnosticism :

> I may say that never at any moment in my life have I "sought for God."…As soon as I reached adolescence I saw the problem of God as a problem of which the data could not be obtained here below…. So I left it alone.[11]

An even more telling proof of the unexpected and undeserved advent of divine Presence is to be found in mystical authors who insist that their

---

[9] *The Sparkling Stone, Opera omnia* X.318–20.

[10] *Opera omnia* III.b.1–7.

[11] *Waiting for God,* 62.

experience may befall someone who has not been leading an assiduous inner life. At a single stroke, this dispels the idea that the advance to mystical awareness follows a step-by-step itinerary of ascent. William of Saint Thierry, for example, writes:

> Sometimes also the affection of pure prayer and that good sweetness of sentiment do not have to be looked for but take the initiative. Without being asked or sought for, without any knocking, grace takes a man by surprise. It is as if one belonging to the servant class was welcomed to the table at which the sons of the family eat, when a soul that is still untrained and a beginner is taken up into the state of prayer which as a rule is given to the perfect.[12]

We find the same point in Ruusbroec:

> And he may also be at once enlightened at the very beginning of his conversion, if he would offer himself wholly to the will of God and would renounce all ownership of himself: everything rests on that. But afterwards he would have to go along the modes and the paths that were shown here previously, both in outward and inward life; and this would be easier for him than for another who goes upwards from below, for he would have more light than the other person.[13]

All of this leads us to wonder if, finally, there is anything to be done at all to prepare oneself for mystical awareness. If not, then is the whole of the first book of *The Spiritual Espousals* on the active life meant only for those who are destined never to achieve the heights of mystical experience? Or should we agree with the quietists that the best way to approach God for everyone is to set aside all our concerns with moral or religious practice?

The answer is simple but paradoxical. On one hand, no preparation, contemplative or otherwise, is a *sine qua non* for mystical awareness. On the other, the fact is that diligent practice generally precedes the mystical state. Taken together, the two suggest an attitude of being ready but without any sense of being deserving. One "awaits" without being "preoccupied" with the arrival:

---

[12] William of Saint Thierry (c. 1085–1149) is an important but neglected figure in Western mysticism. A native of Liege, Belgium who lived in France, he was friend, disciple, and teacher to Bernard of Clairvaux. His striking mystical themes—such as "love itself becoming knowledge" (*amor ipse notitia est*)—influenced Hadewijch and Ruusbroec. The passage cited in the text is from his masterpiece, *The Golden Epistle. See The Works of William of St Thierry*, vol. 4, trans. by Theodore Berkeley (Spencer, Mass.: Cistercian Publications, 1971), 72.

[13] *Opera omnia* III.b.829–35.

Whenever a person...dedicates himself to the honor of God...and seeks rest in God above all things, then, in humility, with patience, and in self-surrender, with confident hope, he should always await new riches and new gifts, always unconcerned whether God gives or does not give. Thus one creates a readiness and disposition for receiving the inward, yearning life. When the vessel is ready, noble liquor is poured into it.[14]

Before leaving this general account of passivity to consider its more advanced manifestations, two final points need to be made. First, it is clear that the mystic's arrival at passivity is the exact equivalent of what Christian doctrine calls "grace." As Ruusbroec tells us, the grace of God's presence is given to "all good persons,"[15] but the non-mystic feels it only as a matter of faith (which does not preclude religious sentiment as well) and responds in the practice of virtue. One believes that in doing good one is empowered by God, but as far as one knows it is all a matter of one's own effort. The non-mystic's consciousness is not radically changed by grace. It is still dominated, however subdued by the spirit of self-surrender, by the awareness of what *I* want or what *I* choose to do. The mystic, however, knows the arrival of grace not only in faith but in the "feel" of its contact. Consciousness is radically transfigured. The *I* who stood at the center of wanting and choosing to do fades away.

Second, if the mystical state is truly something out of the ordinary, then it is hardly surprising that full understanding of mystical passivity should escape the non-mystic. This does not mean the condition is so strange as to be entirely unintelligible. Anyone who has undertaken the discipline of prayer, who has devoted sustained effort at making contact with God, will sooner or later know the same feeling of powerlessness of which the mystics speak. When the most selfless and concentrated practice one is capable of generates new sentiments and insights into the interior life but fails to pro-duce the "presence" of the Other, when one's very achievements seem only to heighten the sense of failure, the non-mystic is not far from the passivity of the mystic. For when one fails in the search for God, it is not that one is left with absolutely nothing at all. The unfulfilled expectation, the object of one's desire, even if not present is not nothing. The emptiness is the silence of the Other that leaves open the possibility that something may yet happen, in the middle of the night, to make the soul wake up and cry out at last: "See, the bridegroom cometh."

Outside of prayer as well, the non-mystic appears to come to a sense of limits that approaches the mystic's passivity. Whenever one tries truly to

---

[14] *Opera omnia* III.b.81-7.

[15] See above, page 15, note 6, of chapter 1 and its accompanying citation.

know something—or more commonly, someone—different from oneself, there inevitably arises a point at which we have to "give in" and stop trying to "take in" the other. At the very moment one feels the limits of one's own powers, the *presence* of the other manifests itself most strongly. Here, too, the non-mystic can have a sense of why passivity is so important to the mystic. For the mystic, as we have seen, is also intent on the "object" of desire, but if that object were within the capacity of desire to control, it would no longer be the presence of a true "other" but merely an extension of the desiring self.

Passivity is not simply the negation of a causal link between pre-mystical and mystical experience that marks the first steps of the mystic. It is an enduring and ever deeper state that comes to take on new, more positive significance as mystical experience unfolds. In the first place, it is an awareness of the abundance of God. For the Christian mystic, the sense of divine otherness is not of something irretrievably distant. The God who "comes" is transcendent not because he is unreachable but because he is inexhaustible. The Absolute is not a static entity but Life in all its exuberance. Passivity is the mystic's way of experiencing this "all too much" of the divine Other. Its presence stimulates the faculties to outdo themselves. Our capacities fail us not by inactivity but by an exhilarating excess. As we will have more to say of this in chapter 7, suffice it here to include a single passage describing what happens to the mystic's reason when it has felt the divine "touch":

> Here reason and all created light fail to go further. For the divine brightness hovering above, which produces this touch, blinds all created sight in the encounter with it, because it is abysmal. And all understanding in created light here behaves like the eye of a bat in the brightness of the sun. Nevertheless, the spirit is ever anew compelled and aroused by God and by itself to sound the depths of this touch, and to know what God is, and what this touch is. And enlightened reason is ever anew asking whence this comes, and anew delving to pursue this honey-vein to its depths. But it knows as much about these things on the first day as it ever will. And this is why reason and all consideration say: "I do not know what it is."[16]

A further positive aspect of passivity is that God is felt to take over one's activity, or more accurately to enthuse it with his own vitality. At the premystical stage, inner and outer virtues were felt to spring from the human *I.* Now they are seen as having their source "in the wealth of God":

> The man who is sent by God down from these heights, into the world, is full of truth and rich in all virtues.... And he has a rich, mild foundation

[16] *Opera omnia*, III.b.1292–1301.

which is grounded in the wealth of God, and therefore he must always flow into all those who need him, for the living fountain of the holy Spirit is his wealth which cannot be exhausted. And he is a living, willing instrument of God with which God does what he wants, the way he wants.[17]

Im-mediacy

The second characteristic of mystical knowing is its *immediacy*. The word should not be taken in a chronological sense but rather as meaning "non-mediated." Hence Ruusbroec, for example, is fond of the terms *onghemiddelt, sonder middel*. The Middle Dutch word *middel* suggests something coming "between" that is at once a help and a hindrance. The French mystics of the seventeenth century translated "immediate" as *sans entre-deux*. In any case, the point is that in the mystical state one comes to know God directly; and the negative way being the most appropriate to express the uncommon fact to the common reader, the term "im-mediate" makes good sense.

Among the particular intermediaries the mystic has it in mind to deny here is the "image." Thus Flemish mystics speak of their experience as *onghebeelt* or "imageless," as in the following passage from Hadewijch:

All that comes into man's thought of (from, about) God, and all that he can understand of him and represent in any image, is not God. For if man could comprehend him and conceive of him with his senses and with his thoughts, God would be less than man, and man's love for him would soon run out.[18]

The passage needs pulling apart. Its opening sentence draws a contrast painfully familiar to the mystic. On the one hand, everything we make use of in order to know—concepts, insights, words, perceptions—is "image." On the other, something is present, something so inviolably *is*[19] that it cannot flow into an image or be caught in language. And that something is the reality of God. This does not mean that all images are to be discarded as useless or false, but only that they must not be elevated to a reality they can never have.

[17] *The Sparkling Stone, Opera omnia* X.781–8.

[18] Letter 12:31–8. The translation has been rendered more literal in the interest of the context.

[19] Letter 18:82–91. In a remarkable contrast drawn between the way of love and the way of reason, Hadewijch once again puts the word *is* at center stage: "Reason cannot see God except in what he is not; love rests not except in what he is. Reason has its secure paths, by which it proceeds. Love experiences failure, but failure advances it more than reason. Reason advances toward what God is, by means of what God is not. Love sets aside what God is not and rejoices that it fails in what God is."

The next sentence underlines the fragility of the image in the face of true reality. The graphic verb *comprehend* confirms the sense of clutching and clinging that the mystic sees in spiritual means aiming at what they cannot control. If what *is* were to hand itself over to human prehension, it would be "less than man." The relationship would deteriorate into a mere possession of the beloved, rejecting the unassailable otherness that love requires.

Three centuries after Hadewijch, we find another beguine, Claesinne van Nieuwlant, ruthlessly assaulting the deficiency of images. Before we read her words, we would do well to remember that they are the words of experience. They are not an exercise in aphasia or negative theology. Their aim is positive: to describe an extraordinary awareness of the transcendence of the divine Other. The presence is real and it is known as real. It is only that its conversion into thoughts and words compromises that reality. No sooner do I say to myself "I know God" than the presence recedes into the shadows. For Claesinne, not even the holiest of images will do when it comes to knowing God immediately. "Not the letter of holy Scripture nor the best of insights in it are able to enter into God, although Scripture does lead us to God." In their desire to "have God bare," as she puts it, the mystics

> desire to be free and empty of all images of this or that, of knowing, of realizing, of possessing, and to be without will or practice, so that God may make use of them. For where God is, there can be [only] nothing. They also desire that there be nothing in their insight or ideas, and that their activity be aimed at nothing, not the slightest thing, that would be a hindrance to God.

If knowing condenses God into "something" it turns the awareness of the Other into simple awareness of oneself:

> When one knows something of God, one knows oneself and not God.... Where nothing is known, there God is known. And this means that everything falls away so that one has nothing and knows nothing. Knowing cannot enter the realm of insight or ideas. These things are far too crude for it.[20]

Half a century later, Maria Petyt writes in a similar vein of learning to experience God without images. Like Claesinne she reminds us of something that our analysis of passivity, immediacy, and unitive knowing, might obscure: in the concrete, these characteristics overlap each other and rarely appear in the pure form of their critical definition. As long as one's experience is active, it will produce images; the passivity and immediateness of knowing

[20] Cited in Paul Mommaers, *Claesinne van Nieuwlant Samenspraak* (Nijmegen: B. Gottmer, 1985), 99, 79, 121.

depend on its being unitive. In addition, Maria Petyt introduces an interesting idea of "reflection" as a seeing that looks back on what one has seen:

> I am being taught to receive the divine light in a very passive way: to let it rise of itself, to enjoy it without the cooperation of the human mind or thoughts. Thoughts always play together with imagination, which immediately produces images.... The slightest thought or reflection of the human mind upon that light is too much, for it serves no useful purpose but only darkens the path to the light that appears. As long as one remains pure in mind and intention, as long as one does not give in to the workings of the faculties and intelligence, the soul goes on possessing that light in all its force and plenitude. But no sooner does one lapse than the light vanishes and once again the soul sees itself and creatures clearly.[21]

Hadewijch, Claesinne van Nieuwlant, and Maria Petyt make a good case for the need of the mystic to dispose of all images, and furthermore they show how one goes about doing so. Other mystical authors of importance have also tried to express in words the particular quality of mystical knowing that has arrived at perfection. For example, Catherine of Genoa writes:

> I see without my eyes, I understand without my intelligence, I perceive without any feeling, I taste without taste.... Of this seeing that is not a seeing there is nothing to be said or thought.... Behold, this is the whole of the bliss given to the blessed in heaven. And yet they do not possess it.... Even as I speak of these things, I reprove myself for my words and expressions: they are incorrect compared to what I (actually) feel—without any feeling—and to what does not let itself be comprehended.[22]

"I see without my eyes," says Catherine. This awareness of the confining effect of images is not limited to the mystics. A contemporary Dutch poet complains of the limitations of the ordinary mode of knowing one's beloved: "Separated from you by my own eyes...that I have to see you and cannot be you."[23] The American poet and novelist Sylvia Plath is said to have cried out, "Is there no way out of the mind?" Or again, in *The Man Without Qualities*, Robert Musil includes a suggestive dialogue between Agathe and her brother Ulrich:

[21] Translated from A. Deblaere, *De mystieke schrijfster Maria Petyt 1623–1677* (Gent: Secretarie der Academie, 1962), 386.

[22] Translated from P. Debongnie, *Catherine de Gênes: La grande dame du pur amour* (Bruges: Desclée de Brouwer, 1960), 35–6.

[23] M. Vasalis, *Vergezichten en Gezichten* (Amsterdam: Van Oorschot, 1966), 9.

"The normal state of affairs is that a herd of cattle means nothing to us but grazing beef. Or else it is something paintable with a background. Or it hardly registers at all. Herds of cattle beside mountain paths are simply part of the scenery, and what one experiences at the sight of them is something one would notice only if they were replaced by a big electric clock or a block of flats. Normally one wonders whether to get up or stay sitting there...; one looks to see whether there's a bull among them...: there are innumerable tiny intentions, worries, calculations and observations, and they form, as it were, the paper on which one has the picture of the cows. One isn't aware of the paper at all, one's aware only of the cows on it—"

"And suddenly the paper tears!" Agathe exclaimed. "Yes. That's to say: what tears is some tissue of habit in us. Then it's no longer something edible grazing there. No longer something paintable. Nothing blocks your way. You can't even form the word 'graze' anymore."[24]

The passages cited in the previous section give ample indication of how contemporary mystical writers treat imageless knowing. We recall Ionesco's simple way of putting it:

In any case, I told myself at that moment that I was sure. If anyone had asked me "Sure of what?" I would not have known what to say. I was filled with a certitude.

Or again, Simone Weil's description of the transition from reciting a poem to praying joins passivity to the disappearance of words ("images"):

I make myself say it over...and clinging with all my soul to the tenderness it enshrines. I used to think I was merely reciting it as a beautiful poem, but without my knowing it the recitation had the virtue of a prayer.

Accomplished mystics like Hadewijch and Catherine of Genoa testify to a freedom from "means," a knowing that is "im-mediate." Others, like Ionesco or Weil, recount moments of imageless experience. But one cannot help wondering about those who only get as far as the brink of freedom from images and only much later, if indeed ever at all, manage to take the final step out of the no-man's-land in which they have landed. Surely every step of the process by which the web of images is undone, and not just the final liberated state, deserves a hearing.

Before we do so, however, one further observation. In criticizing the images of the Bible, Claesinne van Nieuwlant reminds us that, after all, "Scripture *does* lead us to God." Unlike some of their commentators, the

---

[24] Robert Musil, *The Man Without Qualities* (London: Pan Books, 1982), vol. 3, 111–12.

mystics themselves are not so quick to dismiss the images that religion provides for ordinary "good people." While they themselves may encounter the divine without images, they are not blind to the fact that images, however mediate, are helpful for knowing God. The mystics do not see themselves as hoisted far above all words and concepts; nor do they engage in animated dispute with all received doctrine. We will return to this point later when we see how Ruusbroec insists on the importance of faith—in the existential sense of trusting God as well as in the dogmatic sense of "articles of faith"—at all the stages of the spiritual life.

In his *Spiritual Letters*, John Chapman has the following description of the initial undoing of the cage of images:

> You remember that I sent you a series of papers of theology—a theodicy—a theory of the world on the Christian hypothesis. *Now*, oddly, I can't say that any of that is my real spiritual life... It is my Faith—it leads me to God—it is most useful outside of prayer. But in prayer always—and out of prayer also—the mainspring of everything is wholly *irrational*, meaningless, inexpressible. "I want God"—and the word "God" has absolutely no meaning. I find so many in this positively absurd and obviously mystical condition; I suppose one "contemplates" without knowing it.... Of course it simplifies people's spiritual life into nothing but the desire of God's will. The whole object of life becomes to want nothing that is not God. *Only there is no reason for it.* The word "God" means *nothing*—which is, of course, theologically quite correct, since God is nothing that we can think or conceive.
>
> The time of prayer is passed in the act of wanting God. It is an idiotic state, and feels like the completest *waste of time*, until it gradually becomes more vivid. The strangest phenomenon is when we begin to wonder whether we mean anything at all, and if we are addressing anyone, or merely repeating mechanically a formula we do not mean. The word *God* seems to mean nothing.[25]

We may conclude our treatment of immediate experience by citing a particularly sharp passage of Ruusbroec's in which he suggests that ultimately the "images" that obstruct the encounter with the divine Other are in fact a result of one's "activity"—good, holy activity in both its inward and outward forms. Why is it, Ruusbroec asks, that some "friends" of God do not become his "sons," that is, do not reach the state of "unity"? He answers:

> They cannot pass through themselves or their works into an imageless bareness...for they are caught up with themselves and their works in the

---

[25] John Chapman, *Spiritual Letters* (London: Sheed and Ward, 1976), 248, 290.

manner of images and intermediaries (*verbeelt ende vermiddelt met hem selven ende met haren werken*).[26]

Unity

The third feature of mystical experience, *unity*, is also the most fundamental, lying at the roots of passivity and immediacy. For the mystic, knowing the divine means becoming one with a divine Other: in being one, one comes to know.

Mystical texts point out again and again that the divine "Object"—a term that, as we have seen, is anything but univocal—does not manifest itself as something so wonderful and so moving that the soul is only emotionally overpowered or flooded with profound insight; nor, conversely, as something so dark and overpowering that it only carves a deep, incurable wound in the heart and psyche of the experiencer. On the contrary, when the divine appears to one, it engages the whole person and not just a selection of one's faculties. Typically this means that, at least in the initial stages, one's whole being is taken possession of.

This kind of effective unifying presence is not restricted to explicitly Christian mystics. The awareness that Woolf, Ionesco, Proust, and others like them speak of is not that of Reality-at-a-distance, showering down new information or spiritual gifts on them. It is not as if there were some "thing" that convinces their reason or moves their emotions. Passively and immediately, they discover themselves as, in Woolf's words, being in something "in which I shall rest and continue to exist." This is also the sense of Ionesco's confession, "I was filled with a certitude, and I thought I would never again be unhappy." It is the same coincidence that we saw in Proust's comment, "This essence was not *in* me, it *was* me."

Clearly the unifying nature of mystical knowing is most apparent when Reality manifests itself as a Person and, what is more, as the Beloved who "comes." We see this in the way Weil speaks of her experience as a "contact"—"a real contact, person to person, here below, between a human being and God"—but goes on to specify it with the amorous expression "Il m'a prise": "Christ himself came down and took possession of me."

The word *contact* immediately calls to mind the use of the term *touch* in Ruusbroec (*gherinen*) and John of the Cross (*tocar*). Indeed, Christian mystics in general seem to have a special affection for the sense of touch. Ruusbroec was no doubt the first to give it a clearly defined mystical meaning. There is a revealing phrase in the writings of Hugh of Saint Victor that may have struck a chord in the Flemish master: "He comes in order that he

---

[26] *Opera omnia*, X.327–9.

may touch you, not in order that he may be seen by you."[27] Yet he was surely still more impressed by Hadewijch's use, however hesitant it was at the
time, of the term *gherinen*. In Letter 6 she comes close to presenting Love's
"touching" in the way Ruusbroec will later:

> But before Love thus bursts her dikes, and before she ravishes man out of
> himself and so touches him with herself that he is one spirit and one
> being with her and in her, he must offer (...).[28]

The mystics prefer to express their "knowing" as a "touching" rather than as
a "seeing," and certainly more than as solitary seeing that is isolated from the
other senses and modes of perception. Metaphors of sight would seem to be
more suitable, given that the perceptions of the eye are the clearest and
sharpest of all our sense deliverances. Sight has the superior ability to focus on
and differentiate its object, but as the word *ob-jectum* already suggests, there
is a price to be paid for this precision. To see something well, one must keep
it at a distance. The satisfaction and knowledge of visual perception carries
with it a certain frustration. As luminous and real as the experience may be,
sight does not allow for the immediate contact that takes place in touching.
Seeing falls short of possessing.[29]

This does not mean that the mystics do not make abundant use of visual
metaphors. The "eye of the soul" is almost commonplace. And is not the
height of mystical prayer usually called *contemplation*, a term that bears the
clear birthmarks of the term *theoria* from Greek philosophy? The language
the Church Fathers use to express awareness of God shows this predilection
for the "speculative" particularly well, but not without taking it a step further.
Gregory of Nyssa (ca. 335–395) is a good example here in the way he develops the (neo-)Platonic theme of "seeing God in the soul."[30] For Gregory, the
soul does not see God as an interior object, as though looking at something

---

[27] Quoted by L. Reypens in his study of Ruusbroec's *gherinen*, "Het Mystieke Gherinen," in
Ons Geestelijk Erf 22: 158–86. Hugh of Saint Victor (1096–1141) was, together with Richard of
Saint Victor (d. 1173), one of the most important figures of the Abbey of Saint Victor, near
Paris. Founded by a friend of Bernard of Clairvaux, Saint Victor was an influential community of
schooled canons of Saint Augustine who had quit their positions at the University of Paris in
search of enough quiet for contemplation and study.

[28] Letter 6:361–4.

[29] One of the most striking texts on this point appears in D. H. Lawrence's *Women in Love*:
"It was a travesty to look and to comprehend the man there. Darkness and silence must fall per-
fectly on her, then she could know mystically, in unrevealed touch" (Hardmondsworth:
Penguin, 1960), 359.

[30] See my article "Gregorius van Nyssa (ca. 335–ca 395): De mens is nooit voltooid," in H.
Berghs, ed., *Denkwijzen 4, Een inleiding in het denken van Plato, Aristoteles, Plotinus, Gregorius
van Nyssa* (Leuven: Acco, 1989), 93–120.

within. It sees God in the fact of God's "working" in the soul. It knows the cause by its effects.

From the middle ages on, the understanding of contemplation exemplified in Gregory's "seeing God in the soul" prevailed in Christian mysticism. In this regard, the love-mystics do not so much rule out the cognitive and speculative aspects of contemplation[31] as they relocate and enlarge on them. They understand the spiritual eye that has been given them as not belonging to a particular faculty of the soul (namely, the intellect), but as at the very core of the soul. In so doing, the "eye" moves from periphery to center and seeing is transformed from an intellectual awareness into a substantive one.

This is what Ruusbroec means by the "simple eye" (*die eenvuldeghe ooeghe*) which is said to open when one is able to "contemplate" (*scouwen*) mystically:

> this infinite resplendence so blinds the eyes of reason that they have to give way before this incomprehensible light. However, that simple eye which dwells above reason in the ground of our understanding is always open, contemplating with unhindered vision and gazing at the light with the light itself—eye to eye, mirror to mirror, image to image.[32]

The sense of *mirror* and *image* will be taken up in chapter 5. For now, further literary evidence may help to clarify things. In line with a tradition that goes back to the early history of Christianity, Ruusbroec adopts the image of the sun for God and Christ, but he does so to his own purpose. To begin with, the sun gives off a light that enables us to see things and to look for the source of their illumination. But the sun also provides the heat that brings things to life. In Ruusbroec's writing, this combination of light and heat is found at all the stages of spiritual growth. In the first book of *The Spiritual Espousals*, the beginner's soul is likened to a valley:

> When the sun shines its rays and its light into a deep valley…, the valley becomes lighter,… it becomes more heated and it becomes more fertile.[33]

The Spiritual Tabernacle speaks similarly:

---

[31] An important exception is Thomas Gallus (d. 1246) and his disciples. These "Dionysian Spirituals" interpreted the Areopagite to mean that the ultimate experience of the mystic consists in the "spark" or the "top" of his soul "being affected," which only brings about darkness.

[32] Wiseman, 238. See also the definition of the "simple eye" in *The Twelve Beguines* and the distinction between the "understanding eye" (which belongs to the intellectual faculty of the soul) and the "simple eye" (*Werken* IV.20:12–9, 22:5–11).

[33] *Opera omnia*, III.a.296–300.

The light and fire that come from God are given us together. First we feel the fire. And the fire of our loving leaves behind in us a clear knowing.[34]

We may also look at unitive knowing from a different angle. The texts speak of becoming one not only as "seeing" but also as "hearing" God. What is meant is something different from the ordinary visionary state where actual words are communicated.[35] Here, it is "in silence" (or in fruitive "rest") that one hears words that are "secret."[36] As Hadewijch puts it:

...you can rest with Saint John, who slept on Jesus's breast. And this is what they do who serve Love in liberty; they rest on that sweet, wise breast and see and hear hidden words—which are ineffable and unheard by men—through the sweet whisper of the Holy Spirit.[37]

In his *Commentary on the Song of Songs*, William of Saint Thierry has some striking remarks regarding those "hidden words."[38] First, in mystical union God in fact speaks only a single word—the Word that *is* God—and speaks it directly. This concentration and effectiveness, so unlike the discursive and

---

[34] *Werken* II.36:12–15.

[35] According to the large majority of mystics and to virtually all classic authors, visions—seeing and hearing things—are an epiphenomenon and do not belong to the state of union with God as such. Hadewijch, herself a visionary, makes a sharp distinction between being "in the spirit" and being "out of the spirit." The understandable sights and sounds of visions occur only in the first condition, not in the latter. In vision 6 (lines 74–91), she makes this quite clear: "In everything else I saw, I could understand that in the spirit.... But then wonder seized me...and through this wonder I came out of the spirit in which I had seen all I sought; and...I fell out of the spirit—from myself and all I had seen in him—and, wholly lost, fell upon the breast, the fruition, of his Nature, which is Love. There I remained, engulfed and lost, without any comprehension of other knowledge, or sight, or spiritual understanding, except to be one with him and to have fruition of this union. I remained in it less than half an hour. Then I was called back again in a spirit, and again I recognized and understood all reasoning as before." Ruusbroec, following closely Hadewijch's insight, quietly situates revelations and visions among the possible psychosomatic phenomena that may appear at the initial stages of mystical experience. See *The Spiritual Espousals, Opera omnia* III.b.471–90. Those who consider visions as essential to mystical experience should consult John of the Cross, *Subida del Monte Carmelo* II, *passim*.

[36] As is so often the case, this silence was first and brilliantly formulated by Saint Augustine. In the *Confessions* (IX.10.25), he enumerates the various things that have to be silenced in order for the Creator to speak. Among them there is, of course, *omnis lingua et omne signum*, all language and every sign.

[37] Letter 18:185–8.

[38] See note 12 concerning William of Saint Thierry. It is the end of the first Song of the *Expositio super Cantica Canticorum* that concerns us here. We quote from *Exposition on the Song of Songs*, translated by Mother Columba Hart, volume 2 of *The Works of William of St Thierry* (Spencer, Mass.: Cistercian Publications, 1970), 112–13.

instructive nature of our normal modes of discourse, can be stated simply: "There, one word comes to be."[39] The divine word appears by being realized in the soul. It is not a message whose meaning one has to work on or "decode," but a force to be experienced. In the act of being transformed, one understands. This is why William prefers to call that word the "voice of God."

> In this state of mind, words are of no avail, but the power of spiritual understanding and devout affections reduce them to one word—...God the Word who is coming to be in the Bride because he is working in her (*fit in Sponsa, in eo quod operatur in ea*). Nevertheless, "voice" is better than "word," for there is no distinction of syllables or formation by the tongue; it comes to be in the enlightened intellect by pure affection, while all the bodily senses and mental faculties are at rest and idle....

William goes on to explain what that efficient voice brings about. Where it resounds, it effects what it itself is. The word that the mystic hears is not a sign pointing to a referent outside of itself. This word *is* what it says. It is the speaking Speaker. The bridegroom does not send the bride a *locum tenens*. He is himself so very present, unrestrictedly and effectively, that the bride hears him im-mediately in being transformed by him. She does not perceive him by means of images; she knows him by becoming one with him—or, as Ruusbroec would say, by being touched by him.

> This voice is not heard except in the secrecy of silence. But where it is heard, where it takes effect, it takes effect not otherwise than according to its own nature.... And therefore, when he speaks to the Bride or in the Bride, he neither speaks nor works anything else and not otherwise than according to his own nature and his own manner of being; not speaking or working that he might be, but of himself working in her, so that she may be in him. And when he speaks to her, he speaks himself to her; and thus it is in himself that whatever he wills her to know, he makes known to her to whom he speaks....

There is a passage in Hadewijch on hearing the word of God that apparently moved Ruusbroec to borrow it from her. Note how the "touch" figures in each of their texts.

> [Love] cries with a loud voice, without stay or respite, in all the hearts of those who love: "Love ye Love!" This voice makes a noise so great, and so unheard of, that it sounds more fearful than thunder. This command is the chain with which Love fetters her prisoners, the sword with which

---

[39] This is the more literal translation of *ibi unum verbum fit*.

she wounds those she has touched (*haar ghereenne*)....[40]

[The holy Spirit] cries in us in a loud voice, without words: "Love ye Love, who from all eternity loves you!" His crying, that is an interior touching (*inwendegh gherinen*) in our spirit. The voice is more frightening than thunder. The flashes of lightning that come out of it open heaven up to us and show us Light and eternal Truth. The heat of his touching and his love is so intense as to totally consume us. His touching (*gherinen*) in our spirit cries incessantly: "Pay your debt, love ye Love, who from eternity has loved you!"[41]

The foregoing may help us better to understand the "ineffability" of the mystic's experience. If mystical knowing is not a matter of seeing or hearing signs but of being aware of one's own transformation, then there is indeed nothing to say. Or at least there is nothing intelligible that *can* be said. In a sense, the reason is obvious. One cannot undergo a change and in the process put oneself at the necessary distance from what is going on to talk about it. The popular explanation which has it that the mystic's verbal incapacity is caused by the "total darkness" of the ultimate Reality or the "complete loss of consciousness" sounds impressive enough, but it does not seem to accord with what the mystics themselves think of their being silenced. Note, for example, the following passage from Hadewijch evoking her highest state, "unity":

There the Father took the Son to himself with me and took me to himself with the Son. And in this Unity into which I was taken and where I was enlightened, I understood this Essence and knew it more clearly than, by speech, reason or sight, one can know anything that is knowable on earth.[42]

---

[40] Letter 20:103–11.

[41] *The Seven Rungs, Werken* III.268:8–17.

[42] Letter 17:105–11. In the passage from vision 6, quoted in note 35, Hadewijch does not say of the height of her experience of God—"when out of the spirit"—that there is nothing to be known there. She says "without any comprehension...except to be one with him." And these are words spoken by one blessed with a genius for linguistic expression and well aware of her gift. Her knowledge of Latin did not leave her with the feelings of inferiority typical in those who were restricted to the vernacular. "Words enough and Dutch enough can be found for all things on earth," she writes, "but I do not know any Dutch or any words that answer my purpose. Although I can express everything insofar as this is possible for a human being, no Dutch can be found for all I have said to you, since none exists to express these things, so far as I know" (Letter 17:114–22).

Annihilation

In the Christian tradition, the natural consequence of mystical union is a certain "loss of self." It is what Eckhart and the Rhineland mystics call *vernihten sin selbes*, or what Ruusbroec and the Flemish mystics equivalently call *vernieten sijns selfs*—"annihilating oneself." We will have occasion to look at this phenomenon more closely in chapter 8. For the moment, a few general observations will suffice.

To start with, it should be recalled that the mystics make a sharp distinction between the actual experience of becoming nothing and a speculative insight into the nothingness of all things and oneself. Baker's warning cited earlier[43] is a good example, but hardly atypical.

Secondly, the mystic's annihilation appears to be passive, in the sense that it is the consequence of being united with God and not a self-induced state. It is less an action than a *re*action, the "consuming" aspect of being transformed by an Other. When the mystics express "joy" at this annulment of their being, when they speak of the "sweetness" of that loss, they sound suspiciously morbid or at least inflated. But given the standpoint of an experience that moves from the Presence of the Other to the loss of self, their elation is by no means incomprehensible. Theirs is not a self-emptying undertaken in anticipation of being filled up again by something outside of themselves. Nor is it simple self-sacrifice undertaken in blind trust. They are first overwhelmed by an Other and as a result lose track of themselves. They disappear from their own consciousness because they are caught up in a living reality too different to be related to the ordinary self. Here is how a Carmelite nun (d. 1914) described her experience, connecting "presence" and "my own nothingness" in the mystical way:

> During prayer on the evening of the third day I entered the interior of my soul, and seemed to descend into the giddy depths of an abyss where I had the impression of being surrounded by limitless space. Then I felt the presence of the Blessed Trinity, realizing my own nothingness, which I understood better than ever before, and the knowledge was very sweet. The divine Immensity in which I was plunged and which filled me had the same sweetness.[44]

As to what precisely it is in the mystic that has to be annihilated, even a quick survey of the texts makes the answer plain. As we have seen, the root of all "means" and "images" is "oneself." Fundamentally, people are "caught up

[43] See chapter 1, note 5 and accompanying citation.

[44] Quoted by Dom Cuthbert Butler, *Western Mysticism* (London: Constable and Company, 1927), 16.

with themselves and their works."[45] To ask for this self to be "annihilated" might seem overly demanding. After all, if people are conscious of themselves, aware of their existence and what they are doing, this would seem all for the best. As Augustine said, the ability to "come across myself" is something distinctive to the human being.

The mystic does not repudiate this awareness. There is no claim that one loses all consciousness at the height of mystical experience.[46] The usual point is rather that self-awareness traps one in a kind of experiential cage in which consciousness is caught in self-consciousness. The mystic's interest lies in finding the cause of that confinement. And that cause is seen not to rest in the person as such, with its unique capacity for self-presence, but in the power to distort that capacity into preoccupation with oneself. There is a fundamental option involved in the use of consciousness.

Ruusbroec refers to the power to trap oneself in an interior hall of mirrors as *eyghentheit*, and to the one who gives in to that power as living *met eyghenscap*. These Middle Dutch words do not translate readily into modern English,[47] but in general they imply something to the effect of "own-ownership" "proprietary-property." They say, "This is mine." The point is not that one is in possession of something—in this case, one's own interiority—but that one possesses it in a particular manner. In *The Spiritual Espousals*, Ruusbroec criticizes certain contemplatives for "having come to possess themselves so firmly with ownership," like a proprietor.[48] And in *The Sparkling Stone* we see how even quite advanced contemplatives—the "friends"—can be caught up with themselves:

> But the friends possess their inner life in a self-conscious manner (*met eyghenscap*), because they choose clinging to God in love as the best and the very highest they can or they want to reach. And that is why they cannot pass through themselves or their works in an imageless bareness, for they are caught up with themselves and their works in the manner of images and intermediaries.... And even if they feel themselves raised up to God in a strong fire of love, they always keep their own self (*eyghenheit haers selfs*) and they are neither consumed nor burnt to nothing in the unity of love. And even if they always want to live in the service of God

[45] See note 26 above.

[46] As Ruusbroec says, it is not because the "touching" of God brings one "above reason" that one is "without reason." *Opera omnia* III.b.1273–4. We will return to this point in chapter 12, especially pages 253, notes 22, 23 and 25.

[47] The terms are closely connected to a fundamental concept of Ruusbroec's anthropology, *eyghendom*, which we will take up in chapter 5, pages 108–9.

[48] *Opera omnia* III.b.2502: *hebben hem selven so vaste beseten met eyghenheiden*. (I translate more literally here.)

and please him forever, they do not want to die in God to all self-consciousness of their spirit (*alre eyghenheit can gheeste niet sterven*) and live the life that is his.... The inner life of the friends of our Lord is an ascending practice of life in which they always want to remain in a self-conscious way (*met eyghenscape*).[49]

The critique of confinement in self-consciousness is not unique to the middle ages, let alone to the mystics. The term *personality*, for example, is often used today, in distinction to *person*, to refer to just such self-imposed limitation. Though not exactly synonymous with Ruusbroec's "ownership," there is a certain overlap here.

Virginia Woolf calls "personality" the hindrance she had to get rid of: "Not as oneself did one find rest ever...but as a wedge of darkness. Losing personality...."[50] Robert Musil describes "personality" as the way in which the adult, different from the child, becomes adult: "You think yourself entirely in possession of yourself." But, paradoxically enough, grown-ups appear to be alienated from themselves: "You'll always see yourself from outside, like an object.... You'll never get inside yourself." The cause of that estrangement masquerades as its remedy:

> Admittedly, we have managed to make up for this, as adults, by being able to think "I am" on every conceivable occasion, for what that may be worth. You see a motor-car, and in some shadowy way at the same time you also see "I am seeing a motor-car." You're in love or you're sad, and you see yourself being it. But in a full sense neither the motor-car nor your sadness nor your love, nor even yourself, is entirely there.... Everything you touch, right into your innermost self, is more or less petrified from the moment you have attained to being a "personality," and what's left over, enveloped in an out-and-out external existence, is a spectral misty thread of self-certainty and murky self-love. What has gone wrong? One has the feeling there's some process that could still be reversed![51]

Chapters 43 and 44 of the *Cloud of Unknowing* have been extremely influential on this question of self-annihilation. The thirteenth-century text speaks in strong and incisive language. The anonymous author makes it clear that there is a certain state of consciousness—a "knowing and feeling," or more precisely "a naked knowing and a feeling of thine own being"—that has to disappear. This awareness that one *is*, that one feels "not only what he

---

[49] *Opera omnia* X.325–54.

[50] See note 4 above and its corresponding quotation.

[51] Musil, *The Man Without Qualities*, 279.

is, but that he is," cannot be "destroyed" by one's own power. It needs to be taken away by an Other. And, most important of all, what has to disappear in mystical experience is not a person's being but a certain way of possessing it. The annihilation is not a total obliteration. "He desireth not to un-be."

> And therefore break down all knowing and feeling of all manner of creatures, but most busily of thyself. For on the knowing and the feeling of thyself hangeth the knowing and the feeling of all other creatures; for in regard of it, all other creatures be lightly forgotten.... Thou shall find, when thou hast forgotten all other creatures and all their works—yea! and also all thine own works—that there still remain yet after, betwixt thee and thy God, a naked knowing and a feeling of thine own being....
>
> But now thou askest me how thou mayest destroy this naked knowing and feeling of thine own being.... But to this I answer thee and I say, that without a special grace full freely given by God, and also a full according ableness on thy part to receive this grace, this naked knowing and feeling of thy being may in nowise be destroyed.... All men have matter of sorrow; but most specially he feeleth matter of sorrow that knoweth and feeleth that he is. All other sorrows in comparison with this be but as it were game to earnest. For he may make sorrow earnestly that knoweth and feeleth not only what he is, but that he is....
>
> And yet in all this sorrow he desireth not to un-be: for that were devil's madness and despite unto God. But he liketh right well to be; and he giveth full heartily thanks unto God for the worthiness and the gift of his being, although he desire unceasingly for to lack the knowing and the feeling of his being.[52]

---

[52] *The Cloud of Unknowing and Other Treatises by an English Mystic of the Fourteenth Century with a Commentary on the Cloud by Father Augustine Baker, O.S.B.*, ed. by Abbot Justin McCann (London: Burns & Oates, 1952), 60–1.

4

Buddhism and God

> And the mystic has encountered this God in the
> depths of his soul, as if he had discovered the primary
> and original state of his soul.
> — Jesús López-Gay, "Mysticism," in:
> *Dictionnaire de spiritualité* 10, col. 1895.

Having established, at least to my own satisfaction, that both Ruusbroec and great parts of Buddhism can be subsumed under the same category of mysticism, the road appears to be open to a fruitful comparison and interaction. However, no sooner have I said this than a new and seemingly insurmountable obstacle raises its head: How can there be anything in common between the mysticism of Ruusbroec, a mysticism that is totally focused on God, and Buddhism, a mysticism and worldview without God?

In the post-Christian West, a culture that for all its unbelief still lives from Christian notions, the idea appears to be widespread that Buddhism cannot be called a religion, because it does not entail belief in God. Is not "religion" essentially "Gottesdienst" (service of God): the living of a relationship with God? And is not atheism or "godlessness" its exact opposite? Indeed, our Western civilization is pervaded by an apparently clear-cut and noncreative tension between Judaeo-Christian theism, which ostensibly incorporates the totality of the Western spiritual tradition, and an atheism that, in its opposition to all that is Christian, cuts itself off from and rejects, together with the Christian God, all spirituality and mystery. We see here a polarization where both sides act as if they clearly knew what they were affirming or negating, as if they could tell you, at any given moment, precisely what "God" is (although Thomas Aquinas has boldly stated that we humans cannot know *what* God is, cannot distill or comprehend God's "essentia").[1]

---

[1] Winston King, a Christian theologian with several distinguished books on Buddhism to his name, formulates it as follows: "To the traditional Christian mind, however, the question of God's existence is often a matter of all or nothing: either there is a living personal God...or there

Ever since Buddhism was first introduced to the West, Buddhism has often been branded as atheism, by Western scholars of Buddhism as well as by Eastern Buddhists themselves—and this often for propagandistic reasons: atheism was "in" and Christian theism was deemed to be passé. A bigger misunderstanding, equivocation, or "swindle," however, is hard to imagine. The simple truth of the matter is that "godless Buddhism" may be said, in a sense, to stand somewhere between Judaeo-Christian theism and Western atheism, but one would have to add that it certainly stands nearer to theism than to atheism. To put it another way: an atheism that wants to reject all the implications of Christian theism cannot but negate, in the same breath, the greater part of what Buddhism stands for. Indeed, Buddhism believes in the "mystery" of human existence; only it refuses, for its own reasons, to call this mystery "God." One Zen follower, for example, expresses it this way:

> Zen followers (who have much in common with mystics of other faiths) do not use the term 'God', being wary of its dualistic and anthropomorphic implications. They prefer to talk of 'the Absolute' or 'the One Mind', for which they employ many synonyms according to the aspect to be emphasized in relation to something finite.[2]

It goes without saying that, if we want to express the common element of Buddhism and Christianity by saying that they are both religions—something that the science of religion has been doing for a long time already—we need a different "definition" of religion from the one given above. I have already indicated that a definition of religion in the strict sense is impossible to produce; thus, an "*ad hoc* definition," one wherein some striking common elements of the two religions under consideration are formulated, will have to do. For our purposes, then, we might define religion as "the belief that there is something supranatural (a Transcendent); that the natural situation of humanity is not the right one; and that the right situation can only be obtained by a new relationship to the Transcendent." In this case, the opposite of religion is not lack of belief in "the existence of God," but something

---

is only sheer mechanical process in the world, which leaves man...high, dry, and alone upon a cosmic beachhead into nowhere." *Buddhism and Christianity: Some Bridges of Understanding* (London: George Allen and Unwin, 1963), 34. With the help of Eastern spiritualities, some postmodern or New Wave people may be breaking through that massive dichotomy. For example, I recently came across the following remark: "Neither Daly nor Hampson [two representatives of a feminist 'New Spirituality'] want their rejection of the Christian God to imply their rejection of the spiritual dimension of life. What they want to reject is the idea that God is a personal being who transcends the world, and that divine revelation comes from without." Linda Woodhead, "Post-Christian Spiritualities," *Religion* 23 (1993): 169.

[2] Translator's Introduction in *The Zen Teaching of Huang Po: On the Transmission of Mind*, trans. by John Blofeld (New York: Grove Weidenfeld, 1958), 16.

that might loosely be indicated by the term "naturalism": the belief that there is nothing in existence beyond what we can ascertain by our natural faculties or, let us say, by positive science.

It is, of course, true that the detailed conceptions of these common elements are marked by profound mutual differences in the two religions—not sufficient, however, to undo the commonality or to make a "meeting" in mysticism impossible. A brief review of some of those elements that in Christianity are immediately associated with the idea of God and, on the one hand, negated in Western atheism but, on the other, "believed in" in Buddhism, may be of some help here. Buddhism believes in the unity and intelligibility of the universe: there is a "light" there that the human can discover and thereby be blessed; the universe is no pure coincidence or chaos, it is pervaded by a "law" (*dharma*), which is not merely a "natural law" ordering physical reality but a law equally governing human life in all its specificity. Human life is, then, not one of total and absurd liberty, but it has a finality or goal: the reaching of Nirvana; and human activity is subject to the strict law of *karma*: every human act necessarily produces its fitting "remuneration": according to its ethical quality, a good or bad effect, even in the physical order. And, finally, death is not the purely natural "full stop" of the individual's life; there is an all-important "beyond": rebirth according to one's karmic deserts or entry into Nirvana.

In the following, I shall focus on the first of the three common elements, namely the Transcendent, where the Christian God and the Buddhist "godless beyond" are brought together. There is no need to insist on the obvious and profound conceptual differences that separate the two religions here. To believe in God or not to believe in God makes a real difference after all, a profound and vital one; and it is important for us to come to a better understanding of that difference, since the two religions are deeply marked by it, while the mysticism they share in common may partly overcome it.

CONTRASTING VIEWS OF THE TRANSCENDENT

In what, then, does this difference consist? How is it lived, and how is it expressed? First, as to the expression, it is important to remark that both conceptions have been bolstered respectively by a very different, but equally heavy and culturally determined, metaphysical apparatus, and that, therefore, for an existential grasp and "for a proper dialogue, the metaphysical constructions on both the Christian and the Buddhist side need to be recalled to their phenomenological roots."[3]

[3] Joseph O'Leary, review article in: *Inter-Religio* 20 (1991):73.

Comparatively, and very roughly, speaking, it can be said that, from the time of the Greeks, Western speculation has been marked by "positivity" (being) and geared at "grounding" the world of everyday experience, while Eastern speculative thinking has been characterized by "negativity" (nothingness or emptiness), a way of thinking wherein the dialectical and the mystical never parted company, and geared at demonstrating the "unreality" of the objects of this-worldly experience (to "explain them away" as it were), for the sake of a higher and liberating vision. It is this fundamental difference in speculative attitude that is basically responsible for the difference in discourse about God. In this connection, a remark by a German theologian with a profound interest in Buddhism, Hans Waldenfels, is extremely important:

> Western man runs the risk of destroying the mystery positively in his aggressive desire to grasp and understand.... The obvious way (*Selbstverständlichkeit*) in which, in Christendom, the divine mystery is talked and written about fills whole libraries.... The East, on the other hand, runs the risk of destroying the mystery in a negative way. Eastern speculation often overlooks the fact that negations can also limit and thereby undo the possibilities of the mystery..., that negations can also be expressions of human arbitrary construction (*Eigenmächtigkeit*).[4]

To paraphrase this, I could say that the mystery of the universe and human life has confronted Westerners and Easterners alike with the "God problem," but that, for the greater part, their thinking has gone in opposite directions: in the West in the direction of an affirmative theology (only incidentally tempered by "negative theology"), in the East in the direction of an equally one-sided, negative speculation; and that the time may have come for these two ways of thinking to correct and transform one another. As a tentative approach to the extremely delicate question of what the idea of God, and conversely its negation, means in religion, I propose to investigate briefly, on the one hand, the objections that Buddhists adduce against theism and, on the other, the religious elements that I as a Christian sorely miss in the Buddhist religion that I so greatly admire.

Nearest to what we have been saying may be the Buddhist feeling that Christians always approach the mystery "from above," from God as an absolute and well-known given, and thereby get so strongly absorbed in that vertical relationship that they forget about other aspects of the mystery, especially the horizontal relationships of the self with other realities. My existence may or may not depend on a God, but it is important to recognize first that it is caused or conditioned by all other realities in the universe. This latter

---

[4] Hans Waldenfels, *An der Grenze des Denkbaren: Meditation Ost und West* (München: Kösel Verlag, 1988), 161.

insight, which is one of the mainstays of Buddhism, has been formalized in a doctrine called *pratītya-samutpāda*, which negates the independent existence of things and, instead, teaches their total interdependence and mutual "intersession" or indwelling. In certain respects, this doctrine has become a functional replacement of the idea of God in Buddhism.

The question will, of course, be whether this idea can satisfactorily play the religious role of the idea of God or not, but, for the moment, I want to remark only that I consider this Buddhist objection to be well-taken: indeed, we Christians often jump unwarrantedly over creatures in a direct flight to God, and the doctrine of *pratītya-samutpāda* is certainly an immensely fruitful religious idea.

The original motive behind Sakyamuni's negation of the powers of the God or gods of his Indian environment—and thus, of course, not directly of the Christian God— may well have been his refusal to entertain the idea of an arbitrary intervention of an extraneous agency into the methodic and relentless human effort toward liberation in Nirvana, which he advocated. Freedom from such intervention is intimated, for example in the following verse of the *Dhammapada*:

> Him I call indeed a Brāhmana who, after leaving all bondage to men, has risen above all bondage to the gods, and is free from all and every bondage.[5]

Here it may suffice to remark that the Christian idea of God also excludes such arbitrariness and would rather picture God as a secret "accomplice" in these efforts. (From the further developments of his doctrine, it may even be argued that the Buddha's notion of "Dharma" implied the idea of such a "complicity" on a higher level.)

But the brunt of the Buddhist onslaught on the idea of God—and the element that may be most relevant for mysticism—is directed against the "objectification" and substantialization or "reification" of the Transcendent, which the idea of God inevitably effects. "God" is then seen as a human image wherein the Transcendent is caught and set up in contrast to the human in an irreconcilable duality—which does not permit mystical unification. On a somewhat more popular level, this objection takes the form of a consideration that has often been addressed at me by ordinary Japanese Buddhists: "You Christians cannot dream of becoming God, or one with God, while we Buddhists can become the equal of the Buddha, a Buddha ourselves." Buddhist speculation itself prefers to define the Transcendent only negatively, and most centrally as "emptiness": total openness and pure

---

[5] *Dhammapada*, 417. F. X. Müller ed., *The Sacred Books of the East*, 10 (Delhi: Motilal Banarsidass, 1973), 93.

relation. The transcendence of the Transcendent is then called an "immanent transcendence" in a "non-dual" relationship with the world and the human self.

Again we cannot but concede that the idea of God carries all these dangers within itself and therefore needs the constant critique of a negative theology to remain religiously sound—an effort wherein Christianity can be helped very much by these Buddhist ideas, which echo and magnify the warnings of its own negative theology. On the other hand, however, it is impossible for us humans to build an existential relationship or take a religious attitude to the Transcendent totally without "image" or "embodiment" (according to Christianity, God himself has taken this into account in his self-expression in the incarnation of the "Word"); and in fact, the Buddhist "indetermination" on the speculative level often militates against its own religious impulses and even against its own viability for the ordinary mortal. Furthermore, the idea of God's "transcendent transcendence," "otherness," and "majesty"—God is standing infinitely above us—is responsible for some of the most beautiful traits of the Semitic religions, whose absence in (at least theoretical) Buddhism I feel as a privation: the jubilant praise of the divine perfections, the self-forgetting zeal for the "glory of God," and the total devotion to the "Lord," over against which one is painfully conscious, in basic humility, of one's own smallness and sinfulness.

In his study of different trends in Indian mysticism, Rudolf Otto considers the "Brahma-bhāva," a kind of theistic mysticism that puts all the stress on the nonduality of the self with God (Brahman), and comments, "Surely, the contrast in mood and the difference in experience is tremendous between the proud 'Brahmāsmi' ('I am the Brahman') on the one hand, and the Bhakta [devotional theist]'s humble, trustful submission to the God of personal theism on the other."[6] Otto then goes on to indicate that a balance is needed here: "A sense of exaltation is the complement of Christian humility, without which it is cant";[7] he further finds a good example of that balance in Meister Eckhart's bold phrase: "Ours to be God by grace as God is God by nature; but ours also to resign all that to God and to be as poor as when we were not."[8] Much Buddhist "theologizing" on the Transcendent and its relationship to the human self (especially in Zen, with its much repeated "the only Buddha is my self") shows sufficient affinity to this Brahma-bhāva (and this, it must be remarked, beyond the dichotomy of theism and atheism) for us to draw the lesson that Buddhist negative theory also needs a counterbalance in order to stay religiously sound.

[6] Rudolf Otto, *Mysticism East and West* (New York: Macmillan, 1970), 162.

[7] Otto, *Mysticism East and West*, 164.

[8] Otto, *Mysticism East and West*, 200.

In fact, Buddhist theory finds much of this counterbalance in lived Buddhism, with various concrete forms of devotion to the Buddha. In this respect, the most regrettable thing in the present situation might be that it is practically only the "cut flower" of theoretical Buddhism, without its existential, religious soil, that reaches our Western shores. Be that as it may, in view of the fact that I have singled out Zen speculation as particularly prone to "one-sidedness" on this point, I am glad to be able to present a "counterbalancing" example of lived Zen, culled from the same sermon by Abbot Obara that I have quoted already:

> The world of faith is to act entrusting all to Kannon [the Bodhisattva of Mercy]. Religion is not logic and all that. To entrust all to Kannon means to have merged self in the state of Kannon. By the power of myself I can do nothing, not even check one tear or one impulse to anger, but when I have pierced to the truth at the bottom of that self, the holy form of the Bodhisattva Kannon appears, which rescues the *I* into the absolute unconditioned.

And again:

> When the self seems merged in Kannon, enveloped in the power of absolute forgiveness which is Kannon, for the first time the heart becomes empty.[9]

The Buddhist objection that giving the Transcendent the name "God" amounts to catching it in an "image," to limiting it, and to putting it up as an over-against (*Gegen-stand*) or vis-à-vis, extends also, while taking on special nuances, to the idea of a "personal God." There can be no doubt that both Old and New Testaments present the relationship of God and human beings as an eminently personal one: partners in a covenant and a father-child relationship; and that God thereby appears as a "person," a "Thou," a reality endowed with the personal qualities of intelligence, feeling, and will.

In this connection, we may first pay attention to the Buddhist tendency that shows itself here, to bring "objective, isolated, being" and "person" in close proximity as objects of their critique. This may sound ironical to us, since in the Christian tradition the term "persona" was originally used, in connection with God, to express the total relationality and mutual indwelling (*perichoresis*) of the "Persons" of the Trinity—the idea in our Christian patrimony that comes nearest the central Buddhist notion of *pratītya-samutpāda*. And there is also the consideration, to which we shall have to return later, that, phenomenologically speaking, an interpersonal relationship is basically different from a relationship among "things" or "substances." On this point

---

[9] Trevor Leggett, *The Tiger's Cave* (London: Routledge & Kegan Paul, 1977), 36, 47.

we cannot fault the Buddhists alone. It is partly modern Western usage, with its conflation of "person" and "isolated individual," that is to blame for this confusion. We could even say that we owe the Buddhists a debt of gratitude for teaching Christians influenced by modern individualistic notions the necessity of "purifying" our idea of person when we apply it to God. Or, as Thomas Merton has it: "...the whole notion of personality, whether divine or human, will require considerable clarification before a real dialogue with the East can begin."[10] It is again Hans Waldenfels who beautifully evokes the pathos of the Eastern reaction against any association of the Transcendent with our modern substantialist and individualist conception of the person:

> No wonder that D. T. Suzuki and Radhakrishnan react allergically and vehemently, when the most valuable thing they possess and believe in is endangered. The fear of falling back from that radical openness-in-unity-with-everything, the fear of isolating the self anew by the affirmation-acceptance of another Thou and It, and thus of imperiling the possibility of a radical communication with all and everything, is greater than the fear of losing the little *I* and self.[11]

Indeed, no matter how great its other benefits, the idea of God as person can be religiously valuable only if, in the Person of God, our little *I* becomes opened to all and everything, and we can recognize in the Father that all humans are brothers. The theologian J. O'Leary, whom we cited earlier, uses Buddhist vocabulary to testify to the possibility and reality of this:

> Surely, [the address to God as "Thou," as in] the psalms, rather than being a barrier to the realization of emptiness, can open our minds to the suchness of things, the boundless openness of reality, in the contemplation of a world charged with the grandeur of God. To call God "Thou" has never been an obstacle to the awareness that "in him we live, move, and have our being" (Acts 17:28).[12]

On the other hand, however, I want to stress that it is precisely the personality of God that forms the basic characteristic of all real and "challenging" theism. In his study of Indian mysticism, Rudolf Otto makes it clear that the distinction between a spiritual path totally centered on the self (ātman) and an impersonal theism, which speaks of Brahman (God) at the limit of the ātman, is "paper-thin," and that ecstasy in an impersonal God and ecstasy in the soul or self are nearly synonymous: "When the Ātman has been found

---

[10] Thomas Merton, *Mystics and Zen Masters* (New York: Dell Publishing Co., 1980), 218.

[11] Hans Waldenfels, *An der Grenze* , 158–9.

[12] J. O'Leary (see note 3 above), 77.

there Brahman is reached. It is not easy to see what the Ātman would gain by being given the name of Brahman also."[13] God becomes a "living God," who makes a difference for the human, only when this God is endowed with the personal qualities of unforeseeable initiative and action, of will, and of love; when this God can call on the human as an "I" and respond to the human as a "Thou"; when this God not only "is" eternally but can "come" at any given moment. It is the loving exchange with such a God that is the true hallmark of theism.

As appears from the Obara quotation also, living Buddhism admits the personalistic element in its religiosity, in the form of devotion to the Buddhas and Bodhisattvas. Buddhists also call themselves "children of the Buddha," and the Buddha is said to love every living being as "his only child." Buddhist theory, however, admits this personal element only as an *upāya*, an "expedient means" that can lead to truth but in itself is not real and final truth. Herein it is in agreement with the Indian Advaita (non-dual) way of thinking, wherein "Bhakti, the entrusting of the human to the divine Thou, precedes the Jnāna, the enlightened negation of all differences. Bhakti is indeed a product of illusion, but it is at the same time the noblest means to liberation from illusion. Bhakti remains a means to Jnāna, its preliminary."[14] And insofar as he is identified with the Absolute or Transcendent, the Buddha is presented as totally impersonal Wisdom—and this even in the Pure Land school, which is reputed to evince the most personalist or "theistic" tendencies of all schools of Buddhism.

The same basic conviction manifests itself in the fact that, in Buddhist speculation, Mercy-Love is made subordinate to, and is finally reduced to, Wisdom, as non-duality of self and other. Since it may be important for our comparison of Buddhist and Christian mysticism, I want to underline this point, to which we shall return later, by a quotation from the American metaphysician, Charles Hartshorne:

> Like the Greeks, the Buddhists and many Hindus think there is something simply beyond love. The theist does not; he holds that social relatedness applies not only among the members of the cosmic society but also between any member and the cosmic whole or inclusive reality. The entirety becomes eminently personal.[15]

[13] Rudolf Otto, *Mysticism East and West*, 163.

[14] P. Schoonenberg, "Gott als Person und Gott als das unpersönlich Göttliche. Bhakti und Jnana," in: G. Oberhammer ed., *Transzendenzerfahrung, Vollzugs-horizont des Heils* (Wien: Institut für Indologie der Universität Wien, 1978), 218.

[15] Charles Hartshorne, "Theism in Asian and Western Thought," *Philosophy East and West* 28 (1978): 411.

Shorn of its specific Whiteheadian terminology, this idea could be reformulated as: for the theist, for whom God *is* love, the most basic character of being is intersubjectivity. Needless to say, this metaphysical underpinning of the primacy of love is not necessarily present in the mind of every theist. It can even be said that this vision is very little represented in Christian theology.

Intimately connected with this "personality" of the God of theism is his "ethical character." God is essentially "good." If God is called Being, it is in the understanding that "being and goodness are one" (*esse et bonum convertuntur*); if God is called "holy," it is not only in the sense of "sacred" or "numinous," but also in the sense of "ethically perfect" or just. The Buddhist objection here is that "good" is a polar quality, essentially relative to evil, and that the Transcendent must stand above all the polarities or dichotomies of our human understanding. A good expression of this Buddhist way of thinking is found in a dialogue of Huang Po cited earlier:

> When the Lotus opened and the universe lay disclosed, there arose the duality of Absolute and sentient world; or, rather, the Absolute appeared in two aspects which, taken together, comprise pure perfection. These aspects are unchanging reality and potential form. For sentient beings there are such pairs of opposites as becoming and cessation, together with all the others. Therefore, beware of clinging to one half of a pair.[16]

Metaphysically speaking, I find Buddhism to have the stronger position on this score, but it is precisely at this point that I find myself more convinced than ever that no matter how far religion and reason walk together, in the end religion transcends metaphysics and the realm of the rational ("logic and all that"). Indeed, the idea of a God who does not stand above the fray in beatific indifference but is personally involved in the struggle of good against evil, is immensely valuable, humanly and religiously speaking, although it may make metaphysical eyebrows frown. Mystical union with such a God then results in being sent back to the world to join the battle on God's behalf, by a holy life and an untiring struggle for justice. As we shall have occasion to show more fully later on, Buddhism also knows the idea of a "descent" or return to the world after the "ascent" to the mystical mountain or Transcendent, but it cannot provide the returnee with comparable credentials or a mission for ethical and social action.

Finally, there is one attribute of the Judaeo-Christian God that goes completely against the grain of the Buddhist path toward liberation. It is the idea of God, Creator of heaven and earth. Buddhism, of course, shares this rejection of the Creator-God with Western atheism, but it is important to

---

[16] *The Zen Teaching of Huang Po,* trans. by John Blofeld (New York: Grove Weidenfeld, 1958), 130.

remark that Buddhism bases its rejection on considerations that are the exact opposites of the atheistic ones. Western atheism has maintained that belief in a Creator-God takes away the "own" reality of this world and negates or totally relativizes the value of the things of this world and of human endeavors in it; in other words, that it leads to alienation from this world (*Weltfremdheit*). Buddhism, on the other hand, considers that the idea of creation by a good God leads to the conviction that this world is basically good; in other words, attaches to this world so much reality and value that the human being is inevitably induced to become attached to them. This is, of course, a fatal flaw in the eyes of Buddhism, which is all about total detachment as the only path to Nirvana, and which, in that perspective, presents the world as produced by the *avidyā* (darkness of ignorance) of the human mind in the grip of the passions, and thus as illusory "like the images in a dream or the visions evoked by a magician."

I cannot help but think that, of these judgments on the Creator-God by Western atheists and Buddhists, the Buddhist one is nearer the truth. It was, I believe, the German Christian philosopher, Joseph Pieper, who maintained that the positivity of the idea of "being" in our Western culture has its roots in the idea of creation. This idea, indeed, radically relativizes all the things of this world, but it basically affirms this world—along the lines of God himself, in the Genesis story, looking back on his handiwork at the end of a creative day and proclaiming: "It is good!" It is hard to overestimate the important bearing the creation idea has upon the relationship of religion with the everyday world of nature, culture, and society; let me here say only that it has permitted Christianity, strong Platonic and Manichean influences notwithstanding, to join in a spirituality of praise with Judaism and in a "celebration of life" in all its multiplicity and diversity with "primitive religions," while at the same time advocating a return to God from, and also through, God's creatures. A frank reflection of a Japanese Zen master and scholar may tell us more than anything else what exactly is at stake here: "When I am struck by the beauty of a rose, the idea of a neutral *pratītya-samutpāda* is clearly insufficient. At such a moment, only the idea of God fits the occasion."[17] As to the "rationality" of the idea of a Creator-God, a statement by the earlier cited metaphysician, Charles Hartshorne, will have to suffice:

> I believe that at its intuitive core (often partly betrayed by theologies) theism has an ultimate truth, a truth that properly relates unity and diversity, novelty and permanence, and causation...and creative freedom.[18]

[17] Kakuzen Suzuki, during a conversation in Tokyo, 19 June 1993.

[18] Charles Hartshorne, "Theism," 410.

MYSTICISM AND GOD

Up to this point, I have been trying to throw some light on the significance and role of the belief in God in religion. We have seen that, on the one hand, non-theistic religion is a real possibility and, on the other, belief in God entails deep, and in many cases beneficial, consequences—but not without real dangers. Let us focus for a moment on the idea of God in mysticism.

Given the Indian and Buddhist varieties of godless mysticism, we must conclude that mysticism is possible without the idea of God or consciousness of the presence of God. Not, however, without a (at the least, gnoseological) transcendence. H. Dumoulin, for instance, has the following observation:

> Eastern spirituality starts from the experience of the immanence of a divine holiness in the cosmos, and appears to shut itself off from the divine transcendence. Still, the negative theology of the Eastern mystics is pervaded by a truly passionate striving for the most absolute transcendence.[19]

It is clear then that, from our perspective, we cannot simply agree with T. J. Van Bavel when he defines mysticism as "direct consciousness of the presence of God,"[20] but should rather go along with L. Dupré's definition: "Any form of religious mysticism claims a direct contact with the Absolute. How it defines this Absolute depends on its particular outlook."[21] Furthermore, everything seems to indicate that we must go a step further and posit that belief in God, as we have tried to analyze it above, rather than being central in mysticism, creates serious problems for mysticism. Buddhists will maintain that "true mysticism," full unity with the divine, is not possible in theism; a Christian formulation might be that belief in a personal God stands in a dialectical (antithetical but not irreconcilable) relationship with mysticism. This "thesis" is, of course, congruent with what I have posited earlier: that Buddhism can be called a religion that is essentially mystical, while Christianity cannot. Let us briefly examine that dialectical relationship in two of its most evident points.

Immanence and Transcendence

As an attempt at, or experience of, unity with the divine, mysticism tends to put all the stress on the immanence of the divine or on the non-duality of

---

[19] H. Dumoulin, *Östliche Meditation und Christliche Mystik* (Freiburg/München: Karl Alber, 1966), 124.

[20] Cited in *Louvain Studies* 17 (1992): 411.

[21] L. Dupré, "Mysticism," in Mircea Eliade ed., *The Encyclopedia of Religion* (New York: Macmillan, 1988), 10: 250.

the "soul" and the Transcendent (as the Dumoulin observation makes clear). I have sufficiently indicated how, in Eastern mysticism, the transcendence of the Absolute tends to become tenuous or ambiguous, and the Transcendent tends to lose all its contours. From his long experience of Zen Buddhism, W. Johnston could write: "...some Zen masters seem to have a sense of a transcendent Being, while others have not."[22] A distinction that A. Haas makes in connection with "the basic concern of the German mystics" may be somewhat helpful at this point: "this double...transcendence, of the soul becoming interior to itself, and of the deity personally presenting and opening itself therein."[23] Applying a similar distinction to Buddhist mysticism, H. Dumoulin has written:

> For, notwithstanding the monism of identity, consistently maintained on the level of philosophy, there appears [in this Buddhism] a lower level of transcendence, insofar as Buddha-nature, although identical with the self, is experienced as transcending the world, which is subjected to the law of karma, and the empirical I.[24]

On the other hand, however, as intimated earlier, a personal God implies transcendence in a strong sense, a "transcendent transcendence." It is mainly on this point that Christian mysticism, which, as a true mysticism, is drawn to the immanence of God, becomes problematic, and many of its bolder statements on the unity of the soul with God tend to be judged as unorthodox by speculative theology. This characteristic is also the main reason why mysticism is looked at with suspicion by reformed Christianity. Thus, in the eyes of the champion of Protestant biblical orthodoxy, Karl Barth, mysticism did not do justice to the biblical "otherness" of God.

> [Barth's negative attitude towards mysticism] has to do with the exemplary function mysticism had in his thought.... At the hand of mysticism, he could clearly demonstrate that every theology, which neglects the vis-à-vis of God and the human (which is not the same as opposition), cannot in the end express the relationship between both in its full depth. While mysticism, according to Barth, basically underplays this moment of vis-à-vis, it cannot interpret the relationship of God and us humans in accordance with biblical revelation, and can therefore not constitute a true liberation for us humans.[25]

[22] W. Johnston, *The Still Point* (New York: Fordham University Press, 1970), 174.

[23] A. Haas, "Transzendenzerfahrung in der Auffassung der deutschen Mystik," in G. Oberhammer ed., *Transzendenzerfahrung*, 179–80.

[24] H. Dumoulin, *Östliche Meditation*, 260.

[25] R. T. Peters, *Tijdschrift voor Theologie*, 32 (1992): 422. For Ruusbroec's view on the apparent incompatibility between mysticism and personal theism, see Mommaers's Introduction

John Cobb nicely summarizes our problem in the following way:

> The features of Western mysticism which move furthest in the direction Buddhists advocate are just those that have been viewed with greatest discomfort by the vast majority of the Christian community. These features seem to arise historically more from the influence of Neoplatonism than from the Bible. They subordinate or annihilate the personal God and transcend the distinctions of right and wrong, better or worse. Thus, in finding a bridge of understanding between East and West, it is to the heresies of Christianity that the Buddhist turns rather than to its mainstream of faith in God.[26]

The Creature

Is the creature a "nothing" or a precious gift of God? In its passionate and exclusive aspiration for unity with the Transcendent, mysticism tends to consider, or rather experience, all this-worldly realities as having no real reality (as being "illusions") in the light of the only True Reality, or as obstacles and temptations on the path to the Transcendent, and thus of negative value. An ancient expression of this theme, which pervades all Buddhist literature, can be found in the *Dhammapada*:

> Look upon the world as a bubble, look upon it as a mirage: the king of death does not see him who thus looks down upon the world.[27]

Hindu and Buddhist religious philosophies mostly go along with these mystical evaluations and try to provide a logical underpinning for them— Hinduism in its view of all finite and multiple reality as *māyā* (not to be defined either as being or as non-being), and Buddhism in its thesis that all things are "empty," devoid of "self-nature."[28]

Christian theology, on the other hand, finds in the doctrine of creation a positive evaluation of the realities of this world: through God's self-bestowal, the creatures have their own true reality and are basically good. Still, many pronouncements about the things of this world by Christian mystics show a

to Jan van Ruusbroec, *Opera omnia* I, 27–8.

[26] David Tracy and John B. Cobb Jr., *Talking about God: Doing Theology in the Context of Modern Pluralism* (New York: Seabury Press, 1983), 63.

[27] *Dhammapada*, 170.

[28] Tanabe Hajime, the Japanese philospher to whom we alluded earlier, reacts against this kind of mystical theology, which he sees represented in his older contemporary, Nishida Kitarō: "It is necessary to avoid any attempt to interpret the Absolute contemplatively.... Mysticism does not allow us to regard what is relative as free and autonomous." *Philosophy as Metanoetics* (Berkeley: University of California Press, 1986), 80.

distinct similarity to the judgments of their Eastern brothers. Thus, for example, Rudolf Otto writes as follows about Eckhart's evaluation of the creature: "All the emphasis lies on the fact that as creature it is what God is not; it is the vain, unreal, non-essential"; and: "Eckhart...thereby approaches within a hair's breadth of Sankara's māyā doctrine."[29] Otto quotes one of Eckhart's strongest sayings:

> All that is created has no truth in itself. All creatures in so far as they are creatures as they "are in themselves" (*quoad sunt in et per se*) are not even illusion, they are "pure nothing."[30]

Once more theistic doctrine appears to militate against the innate tendencies of mysticism. Even more than in the case of immanence-transcendence, however, in the present case the apparent opposition may be softened—or explained away?—by the consideration that philosopher-theologians and mystics are speaking on different levels, are involved in different "language games," the former on the theoretical level of the ontological structure of reality and the latter on the practical level of the manner in which practitioners of the path should conduct themselves in the midst of things. Thus, even with regard to Buddhism, wherein it is often extremely hard to know on which of these two levels pronouncements are made, Thomas Merton feels entitled to write:

> This state of "enlightenment" then has nothing to do with the exclusion of external or material reality, and when it denies the "existence" of the empirical self and of external objects, this denial is not the denial of their *reality* (which is neither affirmed nor denied) but of their relevance insofar as they are isolated in their own forms.[31]

With regard to Christianity, where the two levels tend to be kept neatly apart, Jacques Maritain warns that "it would be a shame to exchange their languages by making use in the speculative order of formulas that are true for the practical order and vice versa."[32] Maritain elaborates:

> The real does not appear in the same light in both cases. The theologian declares that grace perfects nature and does not destroy it; the saint declares that grace requires us to make nature die to itself.... The saint has a right to despise created things.... The saint sees in practice that creatures are nothing in comparison with the One to whom he has given

[29] R. Otto, *Mysticism*, 105, 110.

[30] Otto, *Mysticism*, 110.

[31] Thomas Merton, *Mystics and Zen Masters*, 27.

[32] Jacques Maritain, *Le Paysan de la Garonne* (Paris: Desclée De Brouwer, 1966), 71.

his heart.... This is a lover's contempt for all that is not Love itself....
The theologian does not have this right; for the word contempt does not
have the same meaning in both cases.[33]

I consider this warning to be well-taken and very important to prevent
unnecessary confusion, but I do not believe that it eliminates our problem.
For I do not think that it would be a sound cultural or religious attitude to let
the two levels exist in simple parallelism or segregation, one from the other,
nor do I think that this is exactly what, in fact, happened in the history of
religions, or that the two levels would not have influenced each other. I have
already pointed out that the mystical view of things became an inspiration
and criterion for Eastern philosophies.[34] On the Christian side, there has been
a definite "inner penetration" of mysticism by the doctrine of creation in the
form of a "creation mysticism." Louis Dupré, for example, points out that, in
the history of Christian mysticism, the negative or "Pseudo-Dionysian"
trend, so strongly present in Eckhart, was not the only one that existed, but
that an evolution took place toward a "nature mysticism," partially by a more
universal view of the mystery of the divine incarnation (Dupré specifically
suggests there is an important difference on this point between Eckhart and
Ruusbroec).

> As the incarnational consciousness spread to all creation, divine tran-
> scendence ceased to imply a negation of the created world. Thenceforth
> God's presence has been found *within* rather than *beyond* creation.
> Precisely this immanentization of the divine accounts for the earthly
> quality of Christian love mysticism and for its followers' deep involve-
> ment with human cares and worldly concerns.[35]

The Mystic and the Ordinary Believer

Above I have been calling Buddhism, rather persistently, a "mystical religion." This, however, may not be the impression one gets after witnessing
the daily practice of Buddhism in temples (even Zen temples) and homes.
Indeed, what can be witnessed there is mainly a religion of faith, devotion,
prayers for this-worldly benefits, and external (also magical) practices. The
simplest way to explain this "contradiction" may be with the help of a term
that has been used to describe Thai Buddhism, but can be applied, *mutatis*

---

[33] Maritain, *Le Paysan de la Garonne*, 71–2.

[34] At this point we could bring up the much-discussed problem of what "Christian philosophy" might mean. Could it mean anything else but "a philosophy intrinsically imbued with
Christian spirituality?"

[35] L. Dupré, "Mysticism," 255.

mutandis, to all forms of Buddhism: Buddhism is a "double-decker religion."
The upper deck is the core or true reality of the movement, to which everything is supposed to be directed: the contemplative or mystical path to liberation from *samsāra*. This upper structure sits on top of and is carried by a
much larger lower deck, which, sociologically speaking, constitutes the bulk
of Buddhism as a religion but, ideally, has only a provisional status: it consists
of practices whereby one aims at acquiring merits in view of a future better
rebirth. The origin of this twofold structure lies in the fact that Sakyamuni
Buddha did not really found a "church," a religious assembly wherein people
of various capacities and degrees of fervor can equally and directly participate,
but a "monastic order" (*sangha*), an elite troop of people who left their
homes in order to follow the contemplative path in the footsteps of the
Buddha himself—an organization or institution with which "lay supporters"
soon associated themselves. But these lay followers never formed an organization as a community of believers; their coherence always lay in a common
adherence to the monastic order, in function of which—to use an overly
strong expression—they exist and believe. Theoretically, to be a Buddhist lay
believer basically means to live in the expectation that, sometime in the
future, one will also obtain a rebirth that will allow one to enter the monastic path toward liberation.

At this point, we meet two problematics that have been taken up already
in the context of Christian mysticism. About the first one, the "status" of the
mystic within the religious organization, it was said that Christian mystics are
considered by others, and consider themselves, as basically "ordinary people"
and not a class apart from other believers, since the latter have the same access
to saving grace as the mystics. Things are fundamentally different in
Buddhism. Here the "mystics"—the enlightened ones, who have reached the
mystical peak, and those on the contemplative path toward that peak—are
clearly set apart as, in a sense, the "only true Buddhists." In this connection
it could be said that Buddhism, which endeavors to do away with all
dichotomies and dualisms, suffers from a basic dualism, a gnoseological one:
that between the enlightened ones, who reach a deeper level of consciousness
and thus know the truth, and the ordinary mortals, who live their lives on
the everyday level of consciousness and thus are deluded. A few quotations
will illustrate the awareness of that difference in Buddhism.[36] For example,
the *Platform Sūtra* (the only Zen writing recognized as a "sūtra" or "word of
the Buddha") states:

[36] I borrowed this term from Schoonenberg, who attributes "a gnoseological form of dualism" to Hinduism. See his "Gott als Person," 217–18.

Those who awaken to this Dharma have awakened to the Dharma of *prajñā* and are practicing the *prajñā* practice. If you do not practice it you are an ordinary person; if you practice for one instant of thought, your (Dharma) body will be the same as the Buddha's.[37]

The ordinary man does not understand and from day to day receives the precepts of the three refuges. If he says he relies on the Buddha, where is the Buddha? If he doesn't see the Buddha, then he has nothing on which to rely. If he has nothing on which to rely, then what he says is deluded.[38]

And the Japanese Zen master and philosopher, Hisamatsu Shin'ichi, wrote: "...with the Awakening, being just an 'ordinary man' comes to an end" [through the complete resolution of the "ultimate antinomy" that constitutes ordinary man].[39] In his consciousness of the special status of the enlightened one, Hisamatsu also dared to declare: "I have no passions" and "I do not die," and, in line with this conviction, refused all funeral ceremonies.

Still, although in Buddhism "mystical consciousness" is the truly salvific factor, and the contemplative path is clearly institutionalized, Mahāyāna Buddhism, which postulates the inborn possibility of Enlightenment in ordinary people (in its theories of the "Buddha-womb" and Buddha-nature), can also put the stress on the basic equality of all people. Thus, for example, the same *Platform Sūtra* (in a different version) proclaims the following:

Learned Audience, the wisdom of enlightenment [*bodhiprajñā*] is inherent in everyone of us.... You should know that so far as buddha-nature is concerned, there is no difference between an enlightened man and an ignorant one. What makes the difference is that one realizes it, while the other is ignorant of it.[40]

This then appears to come very near to the Christian conception that mystic and non-mystic possess the same life of grace. Furthermore, there are, among the Zen masters, people who are keenly aware of the danger of a kind of arrogance that can easily accompany the consciousness of the enlightened one, and therefore insist that this consciousness must be overcome. To quote a few examples:

[37] P. B. Yampolsky, *The Platform Sūtra of the Sixth Patriarch* (New York: Columbia University Press, 1967), nr. 26, page 148.

[38] *The Platform Sūtra of the Sixth Patriarch*, nr. 23, pages 145–6.

[39] Hisamatsu Shin'ichi, *The Eastern Buddhist* 5/2 (1972):123–4.

[40] *The Diamond Sūtra and the Sūtra of Hui-neng*, trans. A. F. Price and Wong Mou-lam (Boston: Shambala, 1990), 79.

He who is puffed up by the slightest impression, "I am now enlightened," is no better than he was when under delusion.[41]

If someone is so conceited as to insist that he is enlightened but others are not, it is quite obvious that this person is not enlightened....[42]

If you would only rid yourselves of the concepts of ordinary and Enlightened, you would find that there is no other Buddha than the Buddha in your own mind.[43]

Our second problematic is that of the reason why many mystics feel compelled to communicate their experiences, and this naturally becomes the question of the role of the mystics in their religion. It is again significant that this complex of problems never became a "serious" topic of discussion in Christianity, while in Buddhist speculation it appears as a very important theologoumenon from early on, under the title of "The Silence of the Buddha."

The sūtras tell us how Sakyamuni, once enlightened, decided not to try to communicate his experience (to keep "silent"), since people would not be able to understand him anyway; but later yielded to the pleas of the gods, who entreated him: "Please, have mercy on the people and preach. It is true that many will not understand you, but there are people with less ignorance caused by passions, who from your words can get hints that set them too on the way to enlightenment."

This episode in the Buddha's life has remained one of the central topics of Buddhist "theology." In the course of history it received all kinds of interpretations, but two things appear to be rather commonly accepted. One, the Buddha could not directly communicate the full truth of his experience, and had to have recourse to *upāya* (expedient means, the instruments of compassion); and two, there are in people various degrees of receptivity to the Buddha's message (the "Dharma"), and the Buddha, in his compassionate wisdom, always adapted his teaching to the degree of receptivity of his actual audience.[44] It followed from this that the Buddha could teach the true Dharma only to an assembly of bodhisattvas, people who already stood on the threshold of enlightenment.

[41] *The Diamond Sūtra and the Sūtra of Hui-neng*, 119.

[42] Musō Sōseki, *Sun at Midnight* (San Francisco: North Point Press, 1989), 160.

[43] *The Zen Teaching of Huang Po*, 58.

[44] This accounts for the great differences in doctrine found in the various sūtras. From there, then, the problematics branch out into the ordering of the sūtras on a scale of greater or lesser proximity to the real truth, the distinction of different kinds of truth, the question of the possibility of language to express truth, etc. All this is mentioned here only to indicate how central the problem of the communication of transcendent experience really is in Buddhism.

All this appears to fit nicely with Ruusbroec's feeling unable to transfer to the reader his experience, and his intention to address primarily "those persons who are already gifted with...mystical awareness," and with his conviction that "all the words and everything that one can learn and understand in a creaturely fashion is alien to, and far beneath, the truth that I have in mind."[45] And as to the mystic's "intending to chart the variegated landscape of mysticism,"[46] Buddhist sacred writings abound in very detailed analyses of the "structure" of the contemplative path toward enlightenment. In these scholastic treatments, the "landscape" becomes more and more complicated, till one arrives at no less than 52 stages on the Bodhisattva Path.

Does this mean that there is an unbridgeable gap between mystics and ordinary people, and that the latter have no use for the former? Buddhism, like Christianity, evidently does not think so; on the contrary, it believes that there is in every human being (possibly with some exceptions, called *icchan-tika*—another important topic of Buddhist theology) something that resonates with the (not really understood) message of the mystics. This is in line with Bergson's remark: "It is not by chance, then, it is by reason of its very essence that true mysticism is exceptional. But when it does call, there is in the innermost being of most men the whisper of an echo."[47] In Buddhism, this "something" came to be interpreted as the "Buddha-womb" (*tathāgata-garbha*) or Buddha-nature, present in every sentient being but covered in most cases by a more or less thick layer of the "dust of the passions."

Here again we note that this question of the "usefulness" of the mystics, at best a marginal question in Christianity, occupies a much more central position, and is therefore the subject of vastly more scholarly investigation, in Buddhism. The main reason for this is, of course, that the message of the founder is seen as being of a "mystical nature"; and there is also the fact that, in Buddhism, the central path of contemplation is, as it were, institutionalized in the *sangha* or monastic order, so that the question also becomes one of the relationship between the *sangha* and the lay believers, and thus is also very important from a sociological standpoint.[48] There can be no doubt that the *sangha*—even more than the mystics or, on a larger scale, the religious orders in Christianity—represents for the faithful the living embodiment of,

---

[45] See above, pages 20–1.

[46] See above, page 22.

[47] H. Bergson, *The Two Sources of Morality and Religion* (Garden City: Doubleday, n.d.), 213–14.

[48] Monastic life is, of course, present in Christianity also, but in Christianity the monastic life does not have the same central position, and cannot as univocally be defined as "the path of contemplation." One indication of this is the birth in Christianity of the active (as opposed to contemplative) religious orders, something that is hard to imagine in Buddhism.

and testimony to, the reality of the things they believe in. The relationship of *sangha* and lay believers, already touched on above, is usually described as an "exchange of gifts": while the faithful support the *sangha* with their material gifts (Buddhist monks are essentially mendicants), the monks impart to the faithful the spiritual, and infinitely more valuable, gift of the "Dharma," the message of the Buddha, brought down to the level of the faithful.

THE CHARACTERISTICS OF LIBERATING KNOWLEDGE

Finally, I want to have a brief look at the presentation of contemplative knowledge or transcendent Wisdom in Buddhism, to see whether or not it shows any similarity with the "characteristics of mystical experience" described above, and if it does, to what extent.

First of all let me note that neither the term nor the category of "experience" appears in the old Buddhist texts. It is quite possible, then, that some of the nuances of the term as we use it today are not congruent with the Buddhist idea of liberating knowledge. This is certainly the case, for example, with experience as something "sensational." A Buddhist practitioner who would be after that kind of "experience" would certainly be severely reprimanded by the master.

Another thing to note is that in the two instances we may be dealing with a somewhat different kind of opposition. In Christianity one tends to distinguish the mystical kind of knowing from the ordinary "knowledge of faith." In Buddhism this also plays a role but, in general, the enlightened way of knowing is interpreted in a larger epistemological framework and contrasted with all "mundane" or "conventional" knowledge, the kind that we use to get along in the world. In spite of this, however, I can immediately add that, on this point also, the Buddhist views and concerns coincide for the greater part with those of the Christian mystics.

I imagine that a straightforward exposé of Buddhist liberating knowledge might better be structured differently, but, for the sake of comparison, I shall follow the headwords (and their order) used above[49] in the description of the characteristics of mystical experience.

Passive

Two questions arise here: In what sense is transcendent consciousness experienced as and considered to be passive? and, Is passivity considered to be a distinctive characteristic of the higher state of consciousness? For the sake of clarity, I am going to distinguish different connotations of the concept of

[49] See above, chapter 3, pages 49–69.

passivity. Right from the begining I must remark that in most Buddhism the presupposition is that "true reality" is only reached by the transcendent mode of knowledge and that, at least in Mahāyāna Buddhism, true knowledge is seen as "intuitive." This reminds one immediately of H. Dumoulin's remark: "Receptivity and passivity are essential traits of all intuitive cognition."[50]

"THE ABSENCE OF INTERFERING ACTIVITY"

In Buddhism, the higher mode of knowing is characterized very explicitly by the absence of the interfering activity of the subject, which makes our every-day knowledge essentially a deluded one. True knowledge is a faithful mirror of reality; it is to know things *as they are*, in their "suchness." The higher knowledge thus stops or eliminates:

— the biased viewpoint of the self-centered I, whereby all reality is dis-torted into a false perspective and the narrow "cage" of a subjective world is built up;

— the activity of senses and intellect, which, under the sway of the pas-sions, tranform reality by adding to or detracting from it (to begin with, adding the connotations "pleasurable" or "painful," good or bad);

— (especially in Mahāyāna) the cutting up of reality, which is essentially one and formless, by our discriminatory intellect into a multiplicity of forms and irrational oppositions.

"AN INSIGHT THAT IS NOT ACTIVELY BUILT UP BY A STEP-BY-STEP PROCESS"

Especially in Zen, enlightenment is presented as a sudden and unexpected breakthrough, which can befall or "overcome" one at any moment in the sys-tematic path of meditational practice. There is, then, no causal link between the efforts one has willfully put into the practice and enlightenment: the lat-ter is not the result of the former, and the former may not be lived as a means to the latter. A classical Zen story illustrates this point:

A Master saw a disciple who was very zealous in meditation.

The Master said: "Virtuous one, what is your aim in practicing *Zazen* (meditation)?

The disciple said: "My aim is to become a Buddha."

Then the Master picked up a tile and began to polish it on a stone in front of the hermitage.

The disciple said: "What is the Master doing?"

The Master said: "I am polishing this tile to make it a mirror."

The disciple said: "How can you make a mirror by polishing a tile?"

[50] H. Dumoulin, *Östliche Meditation*, 89.

The Master replied: "How can you make a Buddha by practicing *Zazen?*[51]

Dōgen, the most illustrious of all Japanese Zen masters, may be the one who elaborated this idea most thoroughly. He insistently warns people "to practice without any quest from your own mind, even as to obtain the result by this practice";[52] and, in order to do away with any idea of a causal link between the two, he presents practice and enlightenment as inseparable: "To think practice and enlightenment are not one is an heretical view. In the Buddha Dharma, practice and realization are identical."[53] Many motifs, which we cannot go into here, are involved in this position by Dōgen, but one of them is certainly that he wants to avoid presenting enlightenment as the fruit of one's own activity or practice.[54] In this respect it is significant that, in the long-running opposition in Japan between "self-power" and "Other-Power" (the latter represented by Amidism or Pure Land Buddhism), Zen is often seen by others as the clearest representative of self-power, but Zen refuses to recognize this epithet for itself and argues for the non-duality of self-power and Other-Power, apparently agreeing with the declaration of Japan's foremost philosopher, Nishida Kitarō: "Essentially, there can be no religion of self-power. This is indeed a contradictory concept."[55]

By the time of Dōgen (13th century), Buddhist speculation on this issue had been sharply honed through a long theological debate, not only in Japan, but also in India and Tibet, between the "subitists" and the "gradualists." This is not the place to present the elements of this debate,[56] but it may be relevant to our problematics to mention the central argument of the gradualists: If one sees enlightenment as a sudden and unprovoked happening, one comes to neglect practice and arrives at quietism.[57]

---

[51] Quoted from Thomas Merton, *Mystics and Zen Masters*, 20.

[52] *Record of Things Heard*, trans. by Thomas Cleary (Boulder: Prajna Press, 1980), 144.

[53] Dōgen, *Bendōwa*; translation from: *The Eastern Buddhist* 4/1 (1971): 144.

[54] "The Teaching of Huang Po," in C. Humphreys, *The Wisdom of Buddhism* (London: Curzon Press, 1979), 192. Carl Bielefeldt characterizes what is happening here as "collapsing the path and its goal and...asserting a transcendental plane of religion beyond the causal laws governing human spiritual works." ("No-Mind and Sudden Awakening," in R. Buswell and R. Gimello, *Paths to Liberation* (Honolulu: University of Hawaii Press, 1992), 501.

[55] Nishida Kitarō, *Last Writings*, trans. by D. A. Dilworth (Honolulu: University of Hawaii Press, 1987), 80.

[56] For a thorough investigation of one important phase of the discussion, see: David S. Ruegg, *Buddha-nature, Mind and the Problem of Gradualism in a Comparative Perspective* (London: School of Oriental and African Studies, 1989). See also Paul Demiéville, *Le concile de Lhasa* (Paris: Collège de France, 1952).

[57] We shall encounter these problematics again in connection with the problem of quietism,

"THE CONSCIOUSNESS THAT ANOTHER DYNAMISM TAKES OVER"

The idea of a dynamism different from the desires and will-power of the *I* is also well documented in Buddhist texts. From a certain moment on, the bodhisattva's activity is described as "effortless," and East Asian Buddhists tend to characterize all activity on this higher level, together with the Taoists, as "activity of non-activity" or as "natural": flowing from, and in complete harmony with, the dynamics of the deeper self and of nature, without any arbitrary interference by the human subject. And, at least in Zen, the idea of the turning-point is also clearly present: the experience of the total impotence of the *I* in what is called the "Great Doubt" or the "Great Death."

"OVERPOWERED BY THE OTHER"

There is, finally, the connotation of passivity indicated by expressions such as "letting oneself be overpowered by a foreign force" or "the experience of the presence of an 'other'"—often symbolized as a "touch" or "voice." In general it can be said that Buddhist writings on mysticism shy away from such positive affirmations. This can truly be, or can be interpreted as, either leaving the mystery open-ended out of honesty and awe, or limiting the experienced mystery because of an intellectual theory that, in principle, rejects all real "otherness." A good example of an open-ended expression may be the following:

> Without effort on my part
> The Buddha-nature manifests itself.
> This is due neither to the instruction of my teacher
> Nor to any attainment of my own.[58]

The former line of interpretation is clearly followed by Thomas Merton when he writes:

> The importance of this Zen intuition of reality is, in my opinion as a Catholic, its metaphysical honesty. It refuses to make a claim to any special revelation or to a mystical light, and yet when it is followed on, in line with its own vast and open perspectives, it is certainly compatible with a revelation of inscrutable freedom, love, and grace.[59]

Thus, in the description of the enlightenment experience, some Zen people will only speak of the discovery of the true self, which is different from but not really other than the I, while others will feel prompted to speak of "rest-

which will be taken up in chapter 13.

[58] *The Diamond Sūtra and the Sūtra of Hui-neng*, 135.

[59] Thomas Merton, *Mystics and Zen Masters*, 254.

ing in the hand of the Buddha." The "vast and open perspectives" of living Zen must certainly be recognized. It is all the more regrettable, therefore, that these are not always recognizable in Zen theory, which often hardens into an emptiness ideology or, as Thomas Merton himself has it, shows signs of the "'pantheist' ideological crust which so easily forms around the Oriental type of inwardness."[60]

At this point it must of course be remembered that, in Christianity, the mystic's passivity is, as it were, only the radicalization and becoming experiential of a life of faith, consciously lived by the grace of the Other, God, while in the path of the ordinary Buddhist faithful there is no such clear recognition of the hand of another.

Immediate

Immediacy is so evidently a characteristic of Buddhist higher knowledge (again, especially in Mahāyāna) that I can be extremely brief here. As already mentioned, immediacy is a characteristic of all intuitive cognition. Furthermore, Buddhism likes to describe the transcendent way of knowing as "imageless" (formless) and even "objectless," a consciousness wherein the dichotomy of subject and object has disappeared, a knowledge by identification. To express this immediacy, Buddhism, like Christian mysticism, preferentially uses the language of sense perception, most of all that of seeing, even though seeing might be the most objectifying of all the senses. This immediate knowledge or "pure experience" is then usually (although not always explicitly) conceived of as being prior to and beyond language, which is a "medium" of human convention.

Unitive

At this point, the problematics that announced themselves when we talked about transcendence and passivity appear to come to a head, and things become extremely delicate. We shall see these problematics fully at work in a later chapter, and I shall therefore limit myself here to a preparatory note.

If "unitive" is defined as "having to do with, or being intimately associated with, unity or union," Buddhist enlightenment and Christian mystical experience alike can be called unitive without the slightest trace of hesitation. Indeed, on the phenomenological level, Buddhist and Christian expressions show a great similarity on this point. When it comes to the interpretation of the experience (which in turn influences the experience itself), however, we could say that we are faced with two poles. On the one hand, "unitive" will refer to an awakening to an original unity, which had been adventitiously

[60] Thomas Merton, *Mystics and Zen Masters*, 253.

broken or hidden by a false consciousness. On the other hand, it will be understood as an actual unification (effecting a union) of two realities that stand in a relationship of real otherness to one another. In the first case, "unitive" denotes a simple "opening up," a return to an original or pure consciousness, a "consciousness that has not fallen into self-consciousness, separateness, and spectatorship."[61] D. T. Suzuki once expressed it this way:

> ...to *unite* with something may not be quite right. This something itself, when you realize you *are* that "something" which you thought to be *different* from yourself, higher and superior perhaps; when you go through that experience you find that you are it (i. e., that "something"). That's what Zen emphasizes.[62]

In the second case, one will speak, for example, as above, of "an effective presence that unifies" or can say that "the unifying nature of mystical knowing is highlighted especially when Reality manifests itself as a Person."[63]

Annihilating

The same polarity haunts the term "annihilating," only this time from the perspective of the *terminus a quo* rather than of the *terminus ad quem*. The element common to Buddhist and Christian contemplatives is the consciousness of an upheaval, a breakthrough, whereby something in the subject has to "give," to break, or to be annihilated. But this annihilation, painful as it may be at the moment, is not experienced as a loss or sacrifice but, on the contrary, as an immeasurable gain. What is broken or annihilated is therefore considered to be a negative element, an obstacle or "cage." Thus, Buddhists could make their own versions of expressions used in the previous chapter such as "losing track of oneself" or "being plunged into the divine immensity."[64]

But, when it comes to speculative interpretation—where the question is asked: What exactly is annihilated?—the ways part again. The Buddhist answer is simple and straightforward (this does not necessarily mean unproblematic): What is annihilated is the "I," the individuality, the "person" (seen as synonym of the individual). On the other hand, the Christian, who values the person, is obliged to formulate a delicate distinction—as was carefully done above. What is annihilated is not "the person as such, with its unique capacity of self-presence," but the distorted "preoccupation with oneself."[65]

[61] Thomas Merton, *Mystics and Zen Masters*, 245.

[62] "Conversations with D. T. Suzuki. Part II," 96.

[63] See above page 60.

[64] See above page 66.

[65] See above page 67.

We shall have to return to this problem in chapter 6.

One final remark may be in order here: on the highest levels of the Buddhist contemplative path, "annihilation" shows one more aspect, and the simplest way to indicate this aspect is by means of the Zen saying, "If you meet the Buddha, kill the Buddha." Indeed, in the Buddhist view, real unity with the Absolute implies a leaving behind of, or dying to, all religiosity that involves form or image, object, otherness, personal relationship. In Christian terms, this would mean: going beyond the personal God, the Trinity, and Christ. But these questions will be taken up later.

PART TWO

The Human and
the Transcendent

5

Profiling the Human

Earlier chapters have painted in broad outline a picture of the world of mysticism to which Ruusbroec belongs. Their working assumption has been that mysticism shows itself to us—readers and researchers alike—primarily in texts written by the mystics themselves. On their own accounts, their basic intention in writing is to *describe* the specific kind of *awareness* that has come to them. This in turn affects the way we approach the texts they have left behind. For if the mystic's own genre is descriptive of experiences or inner states, then the modern reader may well have to begin by letting go of the critical bias of looking in the first place for explanation and theory. Perhaps only by unlearning some of our attachment to studiousness can we come to somehow taste and see what these men and women have known.

In chapter 3 our focus shifted from the basic stuff of mysticism to the two interconnected questions of *what* these people experience and *how* they experience it. This led us to distinguish an assortment of possible "objects" of the experience and a constellation of four more or less common "qualities" of the experience: passivity, im-mediacy, unity, and annihilation.

It is time now to take a finer brush to this general portrait of mysticism and also to add some color to our canvas. For this purpose, I shall concentrate my remarks on the fourteenth-century figure of Jan van Ruusbroec, whose writings offer us a rich and highly original source for better understanding the state of mystical awareness. Like all creative genius, Ruusbroec' does not drop into history like a bolt out of the blue, but neither does his genius set him off from our times like a solitary figure stalking an unfamiliar landscape. The experience he sets to words is both embedded in a particular tradition and congenial to a wide variety of people from his age down to our own. It is in the delicate balance between the synchronic and the diachronic that we must move from here on.

Ruusbroec has a keen interest, as we remarked in passing earlier, in common objective knowledge.[1] His writings show him from the first a rigorous theologian who was well-informed in matters of cosmology and social struc-

---

[1] See above, pages 16–17.

ture.[2] He also has a distinctive view of the human. In each of these disciplines, the "common" and "objective" nature of the knowing resides in their attempt to lay out the facts of reality *as they are*—the whole, the parts that make it up, and the structure that they share in common. Just how this approach fares when it comes to descriptions of mystical awareness we shall see in the seventh chapter. For the present, it is important to note that Ruusbroec's view of the human aims at nothing less than knowledge of human *nature*. This preoccupation with the universally applicable structure of the human is one that he shared with his contemporary medievals, as they had with centuries of Western philosophy.

More particularly, Ruusbroec locates himself squarely in the line of psychology that reaches from Augustine and his disciples down to the Rhineland mystics and their recovery of interest in Neoplatonism. At the same time, his achievement marks a milestone in its own right. For even as he works out of that tradition, he is reworking it into a distinctive synthesis that was to influence mystics after him for centuries to come.[3]

Still, let it be repeated here, all of his efforts at a meticulous exposition of human nature is no more than a prelude to a fuller, mystical way of seeing. His whole purpose is only to set the scene against which the greater drama is to be played out. One may liken it to building a house in anticipation of an unpredictable visitor:

> [God] comes into us from within outwards, and we come to him from without inwards.[4]

THE PROBLEM OF THE "I"

Aside from its importance for understanding the properly mystical side of Ruusbroec's writings, a consideration of his view of the human gives us the occasion to address another, rather more familiar issue—that of the *I*.

---

[2] His cosmology shows up, for instance, in the parallelism between the construction of human interiority and the external world: the four lower faculties correspond to the four elements (earth, water, air, and fire), while the three higher faculties mirror the three heavens. Or again, his awareness of social structures appears in his use of feudal structures as a metaphor for religious relationships.

[3] See L. Reypens, "Âme" in *Dictionnaire de Spiritualité* (Paris: Beauchesne, 1937), 1:453–5.

[4] *Opera omnia* III.b.1395–6. *Visiting* and *coming* are among Ruusbroec's favorite descriptive terms. One also recalls Augustine here: "And see, you were within and I was in the external world…" (*Confessions* X.38). Quotations of Augustine are cited from the translation of Henry Chadwick, *Confessions* (Oxford: Oxford University Press, 1991).

In common parlance, mystical experience is said to be a matter of the "life of the spirit" or "interiority." In this regard, Ruusbroec may be called an exponent of mystical "introversion" (a not unambiguous label, but we may pass over such subtleties for the time being). Indeed, contemplation as he understands it entails a "turning inwards" in order to experience the "ground" of one's being where union with God takes place. This radically foundational notion of *ground* looks to be more or less the equivalent of what we might call today the "deep self" or "true self."

It is in the faint recognition of that "more or less" that a critical question arises. For alive and well as it is as far as the commerce of everyday life is concerned, to the eye of the philosopher and social scientist of today the *I* has turned into a mere shadow of its former self. Its once unassailable reality seems to have come under assault from every quarter. Even if only out of courtesy to the age in which we think our thoughts, the enlightened reader can hardly let the talk of a ground of being pass by unquestioned.

If the gist of the problem of the *I* in the West today is fairly common knowledge by now, so is its principal alleged cause: Cartesianism. This is not to say that Descartes (1596–1650) bears the responsibility all on his own. The contribution of the nineteenth-century German idealists to the inflation of "subjectivity" is at least as great. Not that there have not been criticisms along the way, such as Hume's (1711–1774) frontal offensive against the Cartesian ego and Nietzsche's (1844–1900) unrelenting assault on the "subject" of Kant and Fichte and Hegel. Still, when all is said and done, it is Descartes' *Cogito, ergo sum* that ends up the chief culprit of the story as we tell it today. The Cartesian insight is not only a primordial anthropocentric oversight, but a logical error that has laid the foundations for most of the models of the human self that are being toppled over, one after the other, in our times.

The risk of trying to find a place for Ruusbroec's "ground" in the modern imagination is apparent. One thinks in the first place of the urgency with which Wittgenstein (1889–1951) campaigned against the Cartesian ego. At the same time, the picture of the self that survives Wittgenstein's dismantling of Descartes' notion is a balanced one. The reason is that his final aim was not to excoriate the soul from our view of the human and close the door on interiority once and for all. It was only the current isolationist views of the *I* and the related ideas about a direct, "privileged" contact with a hidden, autonomous self, unmediated by language and the things of life, beyond the pale of time and history and yet permanently accessible, that he targeted. As a result, Wittgenstein did not rule out the possibility of people becoming aware of a spiritual self and inner life.[5]

---

[5] For a brilliant presentation of Wittgenstein's critique of Cartesianism, see Fergus Kerr,

Anglo-American philosophers after Wittgenstein went further to close the door on the reality of human inwardness.[6] Reading their analysis of inner experience, one has the sense of watching the soul fade away like a mirage, leaving one to wonder how one could have been taken in by its reality in the first place. As Quine says, the once mysterious parasite, feeding itself on the public domain while parading itself as something irrevocably private, turns out to be no more than the "effect of certain 'surface irritations'"[7] on the human object. In like manner, Dennett and others have been persuading us that consciousness is best understood as "the program that runs on your brain's computer."[8]

Meantime, Continental philosophy has been waging its own war against the self. There the favorite target is the subject, which is seen as a kind of self-contained, purely spiritual amalgam of the abstract ego of Cartesianism and the absolute *I* of idealism. One thinks particularly of schools of thought like structuralism or deconstructionism, which, as Mark Taylor suggests, assault the self from opposite directions: "The former detemporalizes and the latter radically temporalizes the subject. Selfhood disintegrates either in systematic synchronicity or in fragmented diachronicity."[9]

On its native soil, then, the Western self seems to be under siege, but things do not stop there. Eastern voices have joined the offensive. In particular, the classical Buddhist rejection of a distinct, persisting spiritual core in human beings has found a new audience beyond the pale of those concerned with the contemplative benefits of its metaphors. A number of rigorous philosophers today have expressed their agreement with the doctrine of *anatta* (or *anātman*), no-self. Typical among them is Derek Parfit, who argues an admittedly "reductionist view" that the Western concept of the person is based on "self-interest"—a position with which he claims the Buddha would have agreed.[10]

Theology after Wittgenstein (Oxford: Blackwell, 1986). His position on self-awareness is defined as follows: "My mind cannot have moments of self-transparence, any more than I can designate objects in the world around me, unless I have been brought up in a tradition which is sustained by very many other practices besides these two relatively sophisticated ones" (73). A little further on Kerr stresses the point that, according to Wittgenstein, I do not have a "natural way of being directly in touch with my own inner life (by introspection), as if such possibilities were independent of my membership of a lifelong conversation" (74).

[6] Iris Murdoch's *The Sovereignty of Good* (London: Ark, 1985) offers a sharp critique of this tendency. She writes "while Wittgenstein remains sphinx-like in the background, others have hastened to draw further and more dubious moral and psychological conclusions" (15).

[7] For a number of striking quotations, see Kerr, *Theology after Wittgenstein*, 82.

[8] D. C. Dennett, *Consciousness Explained* (Hardmondsworth: Penguin Books, 1993), 430.

[9] Mark C. Taylor, *Deconstructing Theology* (New York: Crossroad, 1982), 7.

[10] *Reasons and Persons* (Oxford: Clarendon, 1984), 273. Later Parfit adds: "On one view, we

But now what of Ruusbroec's "ground"? To begin with, we would do well to remember that today's preoccupations with lifting the veil of illusion from the interior life is something that belongs to an age that is not Ruusbroec's. Neither did he inherit the kinds of problems we have with the *I*. Preceding Descartes by some three hundred years, he is not burdened with the duty of answering the questions of Cartesian and post-Cartesian thought. But there is to this historical happenstance a more positive side as well. By the very fact of not inheriting our questions about the *I*, Ruusbroec's view of the human can question our very questioning. On a number of important issues, the medieval mystic appears to step out of his age and address his modern and postmodern readers directly on the question of the *I*.

This is not the place to detail the kind of revisions such an encounter might provoke, but a word about its starting point would seem to be in order. Simply put, contemporary critical reflection on the human does not take into account the entirety of the Cartesian heritage. We generally leave out the early Descartes and pinnacle what is rather a later elaboration of his original intuition. On closer inspection, we see that the "thinking" that is meant in *I think, therefore I am* is not the intellectual exercise we suppose it to be, and that the "thing" that Descartes had in mind in *I am a thinking thing* is anything but an objective given. For Descartes *I think* refers to consciousness and *thing* refers to the wonder of spontaneous spiritual activity. The idea of someone being able to reflect inwards and lay hold of an *I* is out of the question.

It is interesting to note that this early Descartes is of unmistakably Augustinian descent, and in this sense drinks from the same wells as Ruusbroec. In any case, the early Descartes—and a fortiori Augustine—did not in fact hold those views that have become the privileged targets of modern criticism of the *I*: that the human *I* is a self-founding reality; that this *I* is a substance in the sense of a hidden, rather reified substratum underlying the manifest activities of the mind; and that the spiritual *I* is separated from the non-spiritual rest of the human.[11]

That having been said, we can turn our attention for the remainder of this chapter to Ruusbroec's view of the human.

---

are separately existing entities, distinct from our brain and bodies and our experiences, and entities whose existence must be all-or-nothing. The other view is the Reductionist View. And I claim that, of these, the second view is true. As Appendix J shows, Buddha would have agreed." The challenge to people in the West, he goes on, is to learn that "personal identity is not what matters" (280).

[11] As the fuller story would derail the train of argument in these pages, I intend to publish a fuller account before long in a separate article.

THE THREE CENTERS OF UNITY

There is no better place to begin than a passage from *The Spiritual Espousals* that speaks of three levels—or dynamic centers of "unity"—in the human individual. I quote it at length:

> Now note attentively: we find a triple unity in all people naturally.... The first and the highest unity is in God; for all creatures hang in this unity with (their) being, life, and subsistence; and if they should be cut off in this way from God, they would fall into nothingness and be annihilated. This unity is in us essentially by nature, whether we are good or evil, and it renders us neither holy nor blessed without our effort. We possess this unity in ourselves, and in fact, above ourselves, as a principle and support of our being and our life. A second union, or unity is also in us by nature, that is, the unity of the higher faculties, where they take their natural origin as to their activity: in the unity of the spirit or of the mind. This is the same unity which is hanging in God, but in the latter instance we understand it as active, and in the former as essential. Nevertheless, the spirit is totally within each unity, according to the entirety of its substance. We possess this unity in ourselves, above sensory perception, and from it come memory and intellect and will. In this unity, we call the soul "spirit." The third unity which is in us by nature is the domain of the bodily faculties in unity of the heart, the beginning and origin of the bodily life. The soul possesses this unity in the body and in the natural vigor of the heart; and from it flow all bodily activity and the five senses. Here the soul is therefore called "soul," since it...animates the body.... These three unions exist in us naturally as one life and as one kingdom. On the lowest (level), we are sensitive and animal; on the middle (level), we are rational and spiritual; on the highest (level), we are upheld essentially. And this is natural in all mankind.[12]

For Ruusbroec, then, human being is tripartite. Beginning from the lowest (that is, most exterior) level, one finds the "unity" of bodiliness, sensibility, mental life (feelings, inclinations, moods), and imagination. Here the soul is properly called soul because, as the then current Latin phrase had it, *anima animat*: the soul *is what animates* the body. At this level one is "sensible" and "animal." All the faculties proper to this part draw their vitality from one and the same source, what Ruusbroec calls the "unity of the heart."

The second level consists of the three spiritual faculties of memory, understanding, and will. Memory is also referred to as "mind," following the Augustinian idea that memory is the most basic of the spiritual faculties, that

---

[12] *Opera omnia* III.b.35–58.

which makes self-consciousness possible. Soul here is called "spirit," and the person is "reasonable" and "spiritual." The three spiritual faculties here all have their ground in one and the same dynamic center: the "unity of the spirit" or the "unity of the mind," often referred to simply as "the ground."

The third and highest (that is, most interior) level completes this second-level "unity of the spirit" by enhancing its reality. As an "active" reality at the second level, this unity feeds the diverse activity of the faculties. As an "essential" reality on the third level, it is *wesen* or "being."[13]

THE HUMAN ESSENCE

At this point we may turn our attention to a number of specific traits of the human for Ruusbroec that will aid us later in understanding his existential descriptions of the mystical state. We begin with the most important, if also the most easily overlooked.

Ruusbroec ends his description of the different levels of unity by stressing the absolute oneness of the human being. "These three unions exist in us naturally," he insists, "as one life and as one kingdom." Faced with the modern question "What am I?" he would no doubt affirm: I am forever and by nature these three unities together; whoever I may be, saint or sinner, mystic or not, I only exist as being at once "soul," "spirit," and "essence." In his view, any separation in reality of what can be differentiated for the conveniences of reason is simply out of the question.

> The soul is common (*ghemeyne*) in all its faculties and in the whole body and in all its members; and (it is) entirely in every member, for one cannot divide it, except by reason. For the higher and the lower faculties, spirit and soul, have distinction according to reason; nevertheless, by nature it is one.[14]

. [13] The terms "essence" (*wesen*) and "essential" (*weselijc*) have caused not a little misunderstanding. The Thomistic notion of *essentia* was often read into Ruusbroec's *wesen*, but recent semantic studies have shown that the Middle Dutch word must rather be understood here as "being" or "existence." Even today, the Dutch word *wezen* retains this existential meaning. For example, *iets in het wezen roepen* means "to call something into being," not "into essence." Or again, *hier is geen levend wezen* means "there is not a living soul here," not "no definite essence." It is not hard to imagine the confusion this ambiguity could bring to Christian theology when Ruusbroec writes, for instance, "And our created being (*wesen*) is suspended in the eternal being (*wesen*) and, with respect to its essential being (*na weselijcken sine*) it is one with it" (*The Spiritual Espousals, Opera omnia* III.c.117–19). Can a definite "essence" be suspended in a definite "Essence"? And if it could, would this not make Ruusbroec a pantheist? For a basic semantic study, see the doctoral dissertation of J. Alaerts, *La terminologie "essentielle" dans l'œuvrere de Jan van Ruusbroec (1293–1381)* (Lille, 1973).

[14] *Opera omnia* III.b.943–7.

Ruusbroec's description of mystical union with God offers such a good illustration of this basic human trait that it is hard to resist interjecting a sampling of his mystical expression here. At a very advanced stage of the "innermost life," says Ruusbroec, the mystic "comes into an enjoyable savor, and he possesses the divine being." One feels "filled with the abysmal bliss and richness of God" and

> out of this richness there flow forth, into the unity of the higher faculties, an embrace and a fullness of felt love. And out of this fullness of felt love there flows forth, into the heart and into the bodily faculties, a delightful, pervasive savor. And through these streams, one becomes internally immobile, losing control over oneself and all of one's activities. One knows and feels nothing in the innermost ground, in soul and in body, but an unusual clarity, together with an overall sense of wellbeing and an all-pervading savor.[15]

One feature of the highest level of unity merits singling out here. Initially Ruusbroec says that one's innermost part or essence (*wesen*) "is in God." But soon after he adds that "we possess this unity in ourselves, and yet above ourselves." Christian theology has no trouble making sense of the apparent paradox. The ontological core of the human being (the essence we possess *in ourselves*) is not self-sustaining but depends on God to hold it in existence (the essence we possess *above ourselves*). Thus the relation among the levels of unity is not that of a series of concentric circles revolving about an immobile core. The innermost depths are in no sense a secluded, compact essence. Rather, by its very nature the ground of the human is groundless. It is always and in each individual sheer openness to the most all-encompassing reality— God. Ruusbroec likens it to a desert:

> Our created being (*wesen*) is to be regarded as a wild and barren desert, in which God lives and reigns over us.[16]

Elsewhere he compares it to one abyss being solicited by a greater, divine Abyss. If one feels the imagination reel at such an image, it is not unintentional. For Ruusbroec the aim is clear: to expand the conventional understanding of human "essence" to the breaking point.

This essence is far from an isolated monad. From the very outset it is bonded to the divine. By nature, we *are* a ceaseless relationship with God. The life-giving finger of the Creator reaching out to touch Adam's outstretched finger in the unforgettable image Michelangelo left us in the Sistine chapel is our natural state. Ruusbroec himself expresses it as being perma-

---

[15] *Opera omnia* III.b.1886–95.

[16] *A Mirror of Eternal Blessedness*, Wiseman, 247.

nently "suspended in God" (*hanghet in gode*):

> This essential unity of our spirit with God does not exist by itself, but it abides in God, and it flows forth from God, and it hangs in God.... For this unity is in us by our bare nature. And were the creature ever to part from God, it would fall into a pure nothingness.... This is the nobility which we have by nature in the essential unity of our spirit, where it is naturally united with God.[17]

In contrast to Eckhart, Ruusbroec rarely refers to man's "essence" as the "spark" of the soul, but when he does it is in the context of this innate relationship to the divine. Thus:

> And mankind also has a natural fundamental inclination (*natuerlijc gront neyghen*) because of the spark of the soul (*vonke der zielen*).[18]

For Ruusbroec, then, the all-pervading, all-encompassing, irrevocably relational reality of God is by nature immanent in the human person. As the Middle Dutch *in-sine* expresses so well:

> ...the spirit, according to its innermost, most sublime part, ...is an eternal abode of God, which God possesses with eternal indwelling (*insine*).[19]

With God as the center of its own center, the human being is defined primarily in terms of relation, not in terms of some specific substratum of its own. In effect, Ruusbroec's *essence* points at a dynamic, fundamental inclination. The passage just cited ends appropriately:

> This is the nobility which we have by nature in the essential unity of our spirit, where it is naturally united with God (*natuerlijcke vereenicht met gode*).[20]

THE HUMAN PERSON

It may come as something of a surprise, if not even a bit of a disappointment, to the present-day post-Cartesian or Buddhist reader to learn that the self-sustaining substratum of a human essence is lacking in Ruusbroec's anthro-

[17] *Opera omnia* III.b.1426–34.

[18] *Opera omnia* III.a.103–4. For a different use of "spark of the soul," see *Werken* IV.34:33–35:1.

[19] *Opera omnia* III.b.1405–8.

[20] *Opera omnia* III.b.1432–3.

pology. Medieval conventions aside, one has to wonder what kind of "self" he conceived the human subject to be, if indeed any self at all. And if not, then one wants to ask the further question of how he can manage the idea of "letting go of oneself," which is supposed to be a necessary condition for union with God. Or perhaps there is some other kind of oneness with the divine qualitatively different from the natural state of union we are born into?

These questions drive us back for a closer look at the second level of unity, the "unity of the spirit." At first, the nonsystematic idea of the psyche as an organic unity is disconcerting, particularly in the light of the complex psychologies we have come to expect of the medievals. The irritation deepens when we see that this second-level unity does not point to another reality different from the essential unity of the spirit. It *is* the same unity, only manifest in a distinct way. Ruusbroec puts it in terms of a contrast that is central to his thought, that between the *weselijc* and the *werckelijc*:

> The unity of our spirit behaves (*houdet hare*)[21] in two manners, namely, essentially and actively (*weselijc ende werkelijc*). You should know that the spirit, according to (its) essential being (*na weselijcken sine*), receives the coming of [God] in (its) bare nature, without intermediary, and without cease.[22]

> In another mode, our spirit conducts itself (*houdet hem*)[23] actively (*werckelijc*) in this same unity, and it subsists in itself (*besteet bi hem selven*) as in its created personal being (*in sijn ghescapen persoenlijcke wesen*). This is the domain (*dat eyghendom*) of the higher faculties. And here is the beginning and the end of all creaturely activity.... Nevertheless, the unity does not act inasmuch as it is unity. But all the faculties of the soul, however they act, have all their strength and their potency from their domain (*in haren eyghendoeme*), that is, from the unity of the spirit, where it subsists in its personal being (*daer hi steet in sijn persoenlijcke wesen*).[24]

The logical conclusion is clear. For Ruusbroec the essence of being human consists in the irrevocable *fact* of the human spirit. The active mode of being is absolutely of a piece with the essential mode. There is no "deep" or "quiet" essence of the human at one remove from the "not so deep" and "restless" spirit. Everything that one does or that is done to one in the active

---

[21] Wiseman translates: "...the unity of our spirit exists in two ways, namely, as it is in its essential being and as it is in its activity" (117).

[22] *Opera omnia* III.b.1399–1402.

[23] Wiseman: "In this same unity our spirit also exists in a second way, namely, as in its activity" (118).

[24] *Opera omnia* III.b.1442–9.

mode of human being necessarily has an impact on the essential mode of human being.

The importance of this point—namely, the ontological identity of the highest and middle unities of the human, of essence and spirit—becomes apparent in Ruusbroec's description of the active mode of being. At first, one cannot help being struck by the word *persoenlijck* (personal).[25] On the one hand, the term begs for comparison with present-day ideas of "subject" and "subjectivity." On the other, it is obvious that there is none of the solitariness of the modern subject in Ruusbroec's usage. He associates the *personal* with two other terms: "domain" (*eyghendom*) and "created." *Eyghendom* is a rich-ly suggestive word that eludes easy translation into modern European lan-guages. *Domain* conveys the idea of a locus at which one is in possession of all of one's human resources. This is clearly an important part of Ruusbroec's sense here, as when he notes that

> all the faculties of the soul, however they act, have all their strength and their potency from their domain.

In any case, this ground or "originating source"[26] of one's every act seems to belong to one as an inalienable possession. On that ground, one is truly one-self—or in Ruusbroec's terminology "subsists in oneself" and "subsists in one's being." These latter expressions bring us to the second key term, *created*.

Theological subtleties aside, Ruusbroec uses the term *creation* to express the interplay of ontological dependence and independence. The idea of

[25] Ruusbroec uses the terms *person* and *personal* often. Note, for example, the following Christological passage: "The humanity of our Lord Jesus Christ does not subsist in itself (*heeft gheen bestaen op haer selven*), for it is not its own person (*en es niet haers selfs persoen*)—as is the case among all other human beings—but instead the Son of God is its hypostasis and form (*hare onderstant ende hare forme*)" (*A Mirror of Eternal Blessedness*, cited in Wiseman's translation, 242). For a similar passage on the Trinity, see below, page 119, note 60, and its corresponding citation in the text. In *The Spiritual Tabernacle* Ruusbroec speaks of the "hypostasis and its per-sonal being" (*onderstant ende persoenlecheit*) of the Eternal Word (*Werken* II.110:14).

[26] This is how Wiseman renders *eyghendom*. Ruusbroec himself paraphrases it as the "begin-ning and origin" (*Opera omnia* III.b.51). And the excellent Latin translation by Surius has *fun-dus ac origo*. The disadvantage of the term *domain* is that it suggests a unity of the spirit that is itself active or the locus of activity for an *I* with intelligence and will. For Ruusbroec the unity of the spirit is *me* but never *mine*. It is the source, not the river. As long as one avoids thinking of the domain as a private possession or as a theater of personal activity, there is no problem. Indeed, *The Sparkling Stone* even refers to God as our *eyghendom* but only in the sense that we have passed beyond the possibility of being possessive: "For if we possess God in immersion of loving—that is, lost to ourselves—God is our own and we are his own (*god onse eyghen ende wij sijn sijn eyghen*), and we sink away from ourselves forever, without return, in our possession that is God" (*in ons eyghendom dat god es*) (*Opera omnia* X.503–6). The point is important, and will reappear later in this book.

109

dependency was already present at the first level of unity, where the person is "suspended in God." Here it is rather the correlative idea of independence that comes to the fore. The second-level unity of the psyche, insofar as it is the source of one's activity, is the proper domain of the human. It is here that men and women have their own being, it is the locus of creativity where they "subsist in themselves."

It is also here that the term *personal* yields up its final secret. To be a "person" is to have one's own "domain" where one can be "creative." It is to exist independently, by nature, as a human being. God's free gift to us of grounding our human being "essentially" is so completely gratuitous and so completely given that it leaves us free to "be something different from God." To be a person, therefore, means that in self-subsisting activity I am myself, and that this independence is so real as to keep me forever in otherness from God:

> Further, we are someone different from God (*een ander van gode*) and cannot become one; we remain in otherness (*in anderheit*). That is where we subsist in ourselves (*daer wij staen in ons zelven*), each in one's own person (*yeghewelc in sinen eyghenen persone*).[27]

It will not have escaped the reader's attention that this final qualification of the "personal" lands us in a contradiction of some moment. For if "person" means that one subsists in oneself, on one's own home ground, does this not give the lie to the fact that that home ground was and remains forever a free "gift"? How can "being" elicit "I am"? How can the given of existence give rise to the possession of self-existence? By what magic act does the human person succeed in disposing of something that one is absolutely incapable of providing oneself with in the first place? Can a being that has been loaned to me ever truly be mine enough to allow me to speak of an *I*? Is not our very core as human beings to be "suspended in God," our inmost depths a "desert" and an "abyss"? Is not everything about us permeated by a gift of creation from without?

For Ruusbroec, humans, like all of God's creatures, are unalterably dependent. Moreover, the special power that lifts us above the rest of creation is not something that has been added on to our nature but rather very much an essential part of it. The human being qua being is a spiritual dynamism. Its capacity to be present to itself, to know, and to will are not attributes that it *has* but the essence that it *is*. The difference from the rest of creation is substantial[28] and it consists in this: that I am able consciously and

---

[27] *The Twelve Beguines, Werken* IV.30:28–31.

[28] I am using the term *substantial* here in its current sense, not in the sense of a Cartesian substance-substrate. Here again, the point is only to stress that the "unity of the spirit" is something truly real, an ontological "otherness."

freely to live out a life that has been given me by Life.[29]

The human creature has, we might say, the discretion to "use" the being it has received. In this sense it is self-existent, it is a person "subsisting in itself." For Ruusbroec the exercise of this spiritual power of mine eventually comes down to one fundamental option: I am free to open myself to the divine Person or not. This takes us beyond the frame of his account of the human, but the point is that human *being* is not some *thing* that provides the ground for human *doing* which is its epiphenomenon. In Ruusbroec's terms, the essential and active modes are absolutely interpenetrated with each other; in fact, they *are* one and the same being. Everything that takes place on the personal level actually defines the essence, and without that essence, "suspended in God," there is no person. We are—or rather, we become—what we do. *What* I am coincides with *who* I am.

One final point needs to be made regarding the unity of the spirit in its active mode. The term *active* would seem to suggest as a matter of course that one is *acting* in that mode. This is not Ruusbroec's meaning, for as we saw above, "the unity does not act inasmuch as it is unity." Terms like *dynamism, power*, and *capacity* are therefore a better choice than *acts, action*, and *activity*. Human activity is manifested in the concrete exercise of our higher faculties, but the source from which these faculties originate is not in any sense "at work."

In the end, we are led back to the image of the human we started with— "as one life and as one kingdom." The Neoplatonic opposition between rest and activity that has hampered many a reader from meeting Ruusbroec on his own ground, is clearly given the lie. Quite the opposite, the harmony of essence and existence we find in his view of the human provides the psychological basis for one of the most striking characteristics of his understanding of mystical experience. One life and one kingdom like the rest of us, the mystic is enabled to exist simultaneously in the essential and active modes.[30]

THE HUMAN SPIRIT

At this point we may return to the second level, the unity of the spirit insofar as "from it come memory and intellect and will." Here we see the "spirit" expressing itself in its faculties. We shall concentrate our remarks here on memory and will.

---

[29] One can hardly express this better than Bossuet: "Je suis mon maître entre les mains de Dieu" (I am my own master in the hands of God).

[30] We will return to this later when we take up the question of the "commoner" in chapter 8, pages 174–7.

Memory and Mind

Within Ruusbroec's explanation of the spiritual faculties, his idea of "memory" is the most likely to cause confusion. To begin with, there is the semantic peculiarity that the term *ghedachte* signifies both "mind" and "memory." The following descriptive passage from *The Spiritual Espousals* may help. In an advanced stage, Ruusbroec tells us, the mystic experiences "pure simplicity that shines in the spirit without distinction." That simplicity

> pervades all the faculties of the soul, the higher along with the lower, and it raises them above all multiplicity and busyness, and produces simplicity in this person.... Thus this person is exalted with respect to his memory.

The result of this mystical gift is quite impressive:

> So by means of this simple light...this person...finds himself...steadied and permeated and sustained in the unity of his spirit or of his mind.... Here he possesses the...unity of his spirit as his own dwelling and as the eternal (and) personal inheritance of himself (*sijns selfs eewighe persoenlijcke erfachticheit*).[31]

It is clear that the term *memory* here has not the meaning that prevails today of recovering past thoughts and perceptions. The sense of the past "coming back to me" did not exhaust for Ruusbroec the full meaning of memory.[32]

Something else is striking in the passage. In the final sentence, memory is associated with unity of the spirit and thus also with the personal. In particular, memory appears to be a faculty capable of generating important psychological states that are not directly familiar to us. What is the "simplicity" that God produces in the mystic by means of memory? What is the sense of being "steadied" that owes itself to memory? And most intriguing of all, what are we to make of memory's crowning achievement of enabling us to "possess" our own ground?

The term *possessing* in this context means something like enjoying. It is the simple awareness of who one is and what one has. The sense of "me" and "mine" invigorates what is already present as a given, namely the person or unity of spirit. Simply put, memory allows for self-presence, enabling one not just to *be* a person but to *exist* as a person, to actually "possess" oneself. By means of memory the human being comes into its own.[33]

---

[31] *Opera omnia* III.b.846–62.

[32] That Ruusbroec did not mean to exclude the common meaning of memory is clear, as we see in passages like the following: "From out of your memory, reach for the white book written in red letters, that is, the innocent life of our Lord Jesus Christ." *The Seven Enclosures, Opera omnia,* II.938–40.

[33] This touches on a distinguishing feature not only of Ruusbroec's mystical experience but

On this point, Ruusbroec is clearly indebted to Augustine, who was the first to understand memory in this deeper sense. The fourteenth-century mystic, like so many in the mystical tradition before and after him, expects his reader to be familiar with Augustine's ideas. This is not the place to try to meet Ruusbroec's expectations in full, but two critical elements in Augustine's inner journey seem worth recalling in the context of the discussion of memory.

First, memory integrates what is "inside."[34] It not only brings together diverse contents of consciousness, it also unifies a variety of interior acts. And it is in that act of the mind tying together its own acts in memory that the *I* appears as a living *I.* At that moment I no longer merely know my "self," but also am fully self-aware.

> There also I meet myself (*ipse mihi occurro*) and recall what I am, what I have done, and when and where and how I was affected when I did it.[35]

This helps explain how Augustine was able in the end to identify mind with memory. Without the power to be present to itself, there would be mind but not consciousness. The *I* would be there, but not myself, or in Augustine's Latin, an *ego* without an *ipse.* We could talk about an *I* but could not utter the word reflexively:

> Great is the power of memory,... a power of profound and infinite multiplicity.... And this is mind, this is myself (*et hoc est animus et hoc ipse ego sum*).[36]

Thus Augustine not only puts memory on a par with mind, but singles it out as providing the most striking characteristic of the human being, namely self-presence. Memory is for him the "seat" of mind:

> I entered into the very seat of my mind, which is located in my memory, since the mind also remembers itself (*sui quoque meminit animus*).[37]

It is perhaps clear enough now why Ruusbroec uses the same term for mind and memory. His esteem for memory consists in this: that it allows us to exist as "persons" who "possess" the unity of spirit. For him, memory is

apparently of Christian mysticism in general. The mystic does not experience the presence of God as debilitating or destroying one's own person, but as enhancing it.

[34] Augustine is well aware that this interior integrating is not perfect: "I myself cannot grasp the totality of what I am" and "I fly here and there.... But I never reach the end" (*Confessions* X.15.26).

[35] *Confessions* X.14.

[36] *Confessions* X.26.

[37] *Confessions* X.36.

primarily consciousness, and the mystic's "exalted" (*verhaven*) memory points at a higher degree of consciousness or, as he puts it, one is "set in a new state" (*gheset in een nuwe wesen*).[38]

Will and Desire

Though perhaps not as initially unfamiliar as Ruusbroec's idea of memory, his idea of will can also do with a brief explanation. In *The Realm of Lovers* he speaks of four lower faculties, those that belong to the level of the "heart." The second of them is the "appetitive faculty" (*de begherleke cracht*) which requires temperance

> to control and preserve desire (*die begherte*) from superfluity...so that it may never desire (*beghere*) unnecessary things and may not desire (*beghere*) too avidly the things that are necessary.[39]

There is nothing out of the ordinary here. Indeed, we rather expect a serious spiritual author to issue warnings about untempered desire. But the fact that Ruusbroec keeps the same word *begheren* for his mystical descriptions proper comes as a surprise.

The second book of *The Spiritual Espousals* is devoted to the mystical stage of prayer, or the "inner, exalted, yearning life" (*begheerlijcke leven*) as he calls it.[40] And how does one reach that mystical stage? Ruusbroec describes the transition in these terms:

> In this light [God] speaks to that man's longing (*begheerten*): "Come down quickly...." This hasty descent is nothing other than a flowing-down with longing (*met begherten*) and with love into the abyss of the Godhead, which no understanding can reach in created light. But where intellect remains outside, there longing and love go in (*daer gheet begheerte ende minne in*).[41]

In this second book one often finds a similar praise of appetite:

> There remain in us an eternal hunger and an eternal desirous turning-inwards with all the saints (*een eewich begherlijc inkeeren*).[42]

His expressions of censure against those who have strayed from the path of true contemplation use the same words. On the one hand he criticizes those

[38] *Opera omnia* III.b.858.

[39] *Werken* I.13:17–24.

[40] *Opera omnia* III.a.43–4.

[41] *Opera omnia* III.a.851–5. I return to this crucial passage in chapter 7, pages 148–9.

[42] *Opera omnia* III.b.1847–8.

who sink down into natural rest, and who [do not] seek God with yearning (*met begherten*)....

and on the other, those who

give satisfaction to nature according to their desires (*begherten*), in order that their emptiness of spirit may remain unhindered.[43]

Something peculiar seems to be going on here. Why is the translator forced to render the same terms *begheren* and *begherte* in modern terms of such varying connotations as "appetitive," "desire," "longing," and "yearning"?[44] Has Ruusbroec perhaps forsaken his usually studied use of language and conflated psychological data that he ought to have kept distinct? Granted, he does seem to distinguish a positive or "eternal" *begherte* from a negative or at least risky one. But he also seems to equate desire with love. And, perhaps most surprising of all, he puts a higher value on this desire than on the intellect for progress on the mystical path.

A closer look at Ruusbroec's ambiguity shows not only that it is deliberate but also that it helps locate his thinking within the vital movement of his age. In short, Ruusbroec is saying just what he means to say. Take the issue of the role of desire in the spiritual life. To begin with, the Christian scriptures— the first source of expression for the mystic—are replete with images of desire. Indeed, talk of "extinguishing desire" is all but completely alien to the biblical context.

Even a cursory look at the Old Testament will show that humans are seen there as imperfect, unfinished beings lacking the fullness of life that they want. And did not Jesus tell his listeners that his reason for coming was "that they may have life, and have it abundantly"?[45] At the same time, the biblical authors are well aware of how easily human desire can be distracted or perverted. Desire can turn in on itself and degenerate into lust and greed. Who can forget the story of Yahweh's beloved King David coveting (*begheren*) Bathsheba and arranging for her husband's murder to get what he desired (*begheren*)? Or again, one thinks of the greed of King Ahab, who has Naboth put to death so that he can take over a vineyard he had set his eyes on.[46]

---

[43] *Opera omnia* III.b.1999 and b.2116–17.

[44] One wonders if this might not be an instance of the embarrassment John Burnaby speaks of: "While no mystic feels the need to explain what he means by the love of God, the non-mystic constantly betrays a more or less embarrassed consciousness that the words cannot retain for him their natural significance." *Amor Dei: A Study of the Religion of St. Augustine* (London: Hodder and Stoughton, 1960), 6.

[45] John 10:10.

[46] 2 Samuel 11–12; 1 Kings 21.

But for all the infamy desire has caused, the Bible continues to hold it in esteem. According to Jesus, once one's heart has been purified there is no "unclean" desire. And Paul also believed that once the heart had turned to God, "the desires of the Spirit are against the flesh."[47] But there is more than just disinfecting desire. There is a dynamic in us that inclines us towards the fullness of life, as the words of the psalmist remind us:

> As a hart longs for flowing streams,
> So longs my soul for thee, O God, for the living God.[48]

This theme reaches full crescendo in the *Song of Songs,* and it is not without good reason that this text is the one most cherished and most commented on by the mystics. This same desire carries Jesus into his passion, as his parting words to his disciples tell us: "I have earnestly desired to eat this Passover with you before I suffer."[49] Echoing these words, Paul writes in a letter to the community in Philippi, "my desire is to depart and be with Christ."[50]

This same biblical reverence for desire lives on in the spiritual tradition, culminating in figures like Augustine and Gregory the Great. We will see it at work in Ruusbroec's own account of his mystical states. What is important to note here is only that the tradition in which he has located himself does not separate lower, natural, "appetitive" human functions from the higher, spiritual, "volitional" ones. There is one and only one basic desiring force. That's why Augustine quietly states "appetite may already be called will."[51]

In addition, there is a specific period in the tradition that reinforces Ruusbroec's broad idea of *begherte.* Love, of course, had been one of the most widely discussed and variously expressed topics of the twelfth century. It fascinated not only the troubadours but poets, philosophers, theologians, and spiritual masters of that "First Renaissance" as well. Among these latter, one point seems to have been held in common: human love is a single force, with no dichotomy for natural or supernatural, for carnal or spiritual, even for egocentric or altruistic aims. Eros and agapé are one and there is no question of a miraculous mutation of one into the other.[52]

---

[47] Matthew 15:18; Galatians 5:17.

[48] Psalm 42:1–2.

[49] Luke 22:15. Several mystics play on the ambiguity of the term *passion* to include suffering and strong, even dangerously strong, desire.

[50] Philippians 1:23.

[51] "Qui appetitus...voluntas iam dici potest." *De trinitate* I.X.XII.18.

[52] For an impressive and balanced treatment of the question of the two loves, see M. C. D'Arcy, *Lion and Unicorn: The Mind and Heart of Love. A Study in Eros and Agape* (London: Faber and Faber, 1946).

116

Bernard of Clairvaux, the most influential spiritual author of that period, also gives us the most striking texts regarding this one human love. The love of the human being for God, he tells us, originates in one's love for oneself. If another sort of love appears, it is not that one has been transplanted but only that a new shoot has appeared on the original tree. Purifying love does not entail abolishing natural love. Rather, the perfect lover—exemplified in the accomplished mystic—is the one who brings the original, innate force of desire to the realization of all its potential. The waters of desire and charity flow from the same source.

To sum up, once we recognize that Ruusbroec is not only embedded in the biblical and patristic tradition but is also a willing heir of the spiritual temper of the twelfth century, the significance of the term *begherte* is clear enough. And in that clarity, the same phrase resounds yet again: "one life and one kingdom."

METAPHORS OF THE UNION OF THE HUMAN AND THE DIVINE

By now it must seem as if Jan van Ruusbroec's view of human essence as "naturally" one with God has hauled us beyond the natural realm and into the supernatural. To look at this question a little more closely, we need to focus on two key metaphors that will figure again when we come to his mystical descriptions proper: mirror and image-and-likeness.

Mirror

Ruusbroec likes to characterize people as "mirrors" of God. Speaking of the essence of the human, for instance, he writes:

> And with respect to its created being, it undergoes without cease the impress of its eternal image, just like an untarnished mirror in which the image is constantly dwelling.[53]

A brief look at the wider context of the metaphor should help clarify Ruusbroec's meaning here.

The image is an old one that has been part of Christian tradition at least since patristic times.[54] Until the era of modern science, Plato's model of the perceptual process was dominant. According to it, both the eye that sees and the object that is seen emit a ray of light, and where the two rays intersect sight occurs. The image that is seen in a mirror is thus something "real" in the sense that it must emit a ray of light in order to become visible. What we

[53] *Opera omnia* III.b.1422–4.

[54] See my remarks in the Introduction to *The Spiritual Espousals, Opera omnia* III, 23–4.

today think of as mere optical illusion was, in Plato's theory of perception, held to be a substantial part of the mirror, imprinted there even before we see it.

For Ruusbroec, too, the eternal image (*beelde*) embedded in the mirror of human nature is not an ephemeral, ethereal phenomenon but something genuinely, ontologically real. It actually *is* in the mirror. Ruusbroec's deliberate description of the divine image as ceaselessly "impressed" (*indruc*) in us "passively" (*lidende*) underscores the point.

The metaphor of the mirror serves the mystical author to make two points concerning the "natural" relation between God and humans. First, the mirror of human nature cannot exist of itself or by itself; it has to be impressed by the image of God. Without the image, there is no mirror. And without the Creator, there is neither, for in producing the image he also makes the mirror. This is the sense of Ruusbroec's oft-repeated insistence that we are made "to the image" of God.

Second, the "impress" of the divine image on the human is not a permanent seal given once and for all. It is not a "thing" that belongs to the individual as a possession. This is not what Ruusbroec has in mind when he tells us that the image can never be lost. Nor does he mean that the human is part of God or a counterpart of God. As the mirror by its nature carries the image, so is the human person by nature the "abode" (*woninghe*) of God. The human spirit, in its innermost part, is forever visited with new arrivals and new effulgences of the divine, like an ongoing eternal birth.[55]

Image-and-Likeness

The metaphor of the mirror is used to express a fact of nature. All of us, saints or sinners, are related to God. To further specify this natural union, Ruusbroec draws on the biblical story of creation, which speaks of God making humans "in the image and likeness of himself" (Gen. 1:26).

Following patristic tradition, he maintains a distinction between image and likeness. Gregory of Nyssa, for example, had distinguished *eikoon* and *homoiosis* as two aspects of one and the same reality: *eikoon* (image) refers to the relationship with God as a static given; *homoiosis* (likeness), as the dynamic process of the ongoing realization of the *eikoon*.[56]

Against this background, Ruusbroec distinguishes image (*beelde*) and likeness (*ghelijckenisse*). Image, he tells us, expresses a presence of the divine so indelible that "we cannot lose the image nor the natural unity with God."[57] It is part of the "essential unity of our spirit":

[55] *Opera omnia* III.b.1405–9.

[56] Several other Church Fathers had more or less the same idea as Gregory. A striking example can be seen in Augustine's *De trinitate* XIV.IV.6.

[57] *Opera omnia* III.b.1453–4.

This essential unity of our spirit with God does not exist by itself.... It receives the impress of its eternal image passively, insofar as it is God-like but creature in itself. This is the nobility which we have by nature in the essential unity of our spirit where it is naturally united with God. This makes us neither holy nor blessed, for all persons, good and evil, have this within themselves, but this is certainly the first cause of all holiness and of all blessedness.[58]

Elsewhere he defines the image more precisely when he says of the "essential unity" of the human:

And here it is like unto the image of the supreme Threeness and Oneness to which it has been created.[59]

Clearly he sees the divine Trinity reflected in the three higher faculties of human nature flowing continually out of their one ground and back into it. The essence and the domain of the three human faculties of memory, understanding, and will correspond to the essence and the domain of the three Persons of the Trinity: Father, Son, and Spirit. Once more this shows Ruusbroec's conviction of the "naturalness" of the divine-human unity. The brilliant treatment of the resemblance of human nature with the divine Trinity in the *The Twelve Beguines* is particularly instructive here. Suffice it to quote only a few lines:

God's essence (*dat wesen Gods*) is empty, eternal beginning and end, a living support of everything that has been created. And the same essence (*wesen*)...is the domain of the Persons (*eyghendom der Persone*). And that domain is personhood and personal (*dat eyghendom es persoenlijcheit ende persoenlijc*) by three qualities: it is fatherly and sonly and...willing spirit-edness.... The Father is an eternal beginning of the Persons, and that beginning is essential and personal (*dat beghin is weselijc ende persoen-lijc*).[60]

According to Ruusbroec we all have a natural relation to the divine, indeed to the trinitarian nature of the divine. It is this relation that is expressed by the term *image*. By and large he uses *likeness* to indicate a relationship with God different from the one we have by virtue of being created in his image. Whereas *image* specifies the unalterable, structural link with God that lies in the essential (*weselijc*) mode of human being, *likeness* points to a contingent, living dynamic in our active (*werckelijc*) mode of being. Ruusbroec clearly

[58] *Opera omnia* III.b.1426–37.
[59] *Opera omnia* III.b.1421–3.
[60] *Werken* IV 62:6–34.

relates this likeness to what Christian tradition calls "grace":

> And he receives grace and a likeness to God in the domain of his faculties....[61]

The kind of relationship that takes place here is no longer natural or necessary; it depends on the free action of God and the free reaction of the human person.

Two points concerning likeness to God merit mention here. First, it is "alive." Again and again we see Ruusbroec using words like *life, living,* and *lively* to describe it, as in the remark:

> He wishes to make us be living and like unto Him...[62]

Whereas the general, natural likeness of the image belongs to our nature, the personal, supernatural likeness can as well "increase and grow" as it can remain unrealized or be lost. To be made in the likeness of God means that we are able to attune ourselves to the élan of the One who is ever "new."

Second, the free grace of likeness to God is not something separate from the natural image. The two are the warp and woof of the presence of the divine in the human. In the end, therefore, it is the supernatural union of two living "persons" that is the most fully natural one. In the end, being like unto God means enjoying the possession of the image of God in which we were created. No matter how elevated the state of mystical awareness to which one might arise, for Ruusbroec it never loses touch with this fundamental fact:

> One obtains and possesses supernaturally, in one's essential being, all that the spirit ever received there naturally.[63]

[61] *Opera omnia* III.b.1487.

[62] *Opera omnia* III.b.1456-7.

[63] *Opera omnia* III.b.1481-2.

6

A Buddhist View of the Human

The aim of this chapter is to investigate the commonalities and differences between Ruusbroec and Buddhist "mystics" in their respective views of the human, insofar as these appear to be relevant to the possibility and the nature of their respective mysticisms. The underlying idea is that mystical experience takes place within, and is interpreted according to, a particular view of the human reality, which is its horizon; and that mystical experience in turn contributes to the way human reality is experienced and interpreted within each particular culture. An insight into the Buddhist view of the human is thus needed for a real grasp of the particularities of Buddhist mysticism.

The fact that the phenomenon of mysticism is found in extremely different religions and cultures has been said to be one of the strongest indications of the unity of human nature beyond all cultural differences. However, our comparative study might at the same time impress upon us the complementary truth, that of the enormous differences in the ways the human being experiences itself in different cultures, and even within the same culture at different times. We shall then get a feeling for Buddhist mysticism only insofar as we can envisage the Buddhist view (or views) of the human as a real possibility within a "human nature" that we ourselves share. With respect to the differences within the same culture, I must repeat the point made earlier that Buddhism is certainly not a monolithic and unchanging "essence." Indeed, even the Buddhist view of the human has undergone a profound evolution in the course of Buddhist history—an evolution that I shall point out when (but only when) it seems important for our dialogue purposes.

The expectation in this chapter is, again, that this attention to Buddhist anthropologies, which are so different from Christian anthropologies, will enable us to look at Ruusbroec's mysticism from angles we would never have thought of if we had looked at his mysticism only from our own view of the human reality, which in turn may have more in common with, and at the same time differ more profoundly from, that of the medieval Christian, Ruusbroec, than we might think.

Before embarking on our investigation, three remarks may be in order. It could be said that "anthropology" is a category alien to the Buddhist way of thinking. Indeed, anthropology, in its exclusive focus on the human reality as such, is essentially "anthropocentric," and in its thinking Buddhism does not really work within this perspective. It is true that, between inner and outer reality, Buddhism focuses on inner reality (which, after all, is only experienced in the human being). Buddhist speculation, however, shows no interest in what we might call, from a modern perspective, the "full reality" of the human being, but only in those elements that are considered to be relevant to the path of liberation. To highlight the fact that Buddhism is not directly interested, for example, in the socio-political aspect of human existence, Kenneth Cragg compares the "foundational experiences" of Sakyamuni and Moses. He reminds us that the Buddha was motivated to start his religious quest by the "excursions from the four gates," whereby he is successively shocked by encounters with a sick person, with an old and decrepit person, and with a corpse. After saying that this experience determines the "focus on the lonely, physical experiences of frailty, decay and death" of "the Buddhist story," he continues:

> Sakyamuni took stock of human privacy and mortal flesh, of generic man in natural contingency and flux. Moses' venture from inside the Pharaonic palace confronted him with Hebraic man.... He was wrestling with ethnic identity and social injustice. He encountered humanity, not in the raw of mortal fate, but in the raw of slavery, oppression and political despair.... The point [here is] to underline the focus of Sakyamuni's awakening awareness on sheer human, personal finitude, all politics, society, culture and history apart.[1]

Moreover, Buddhist speculation does not consider the human being by itself but always as an element in the cosmos. Consequently, the Buddhist vision of the human cannot simply be culled from a Buddhist handbook of anthropology, but must be gathered from the extremely well-developed Buddhist treatises on contemplative psychology and from their cosmological and metaphysical speculations—a fact that does not make my task any lighter. It may be worth observing that, until recently, the situation was not so very different in our Western culture, where anthropology is also a newcomer that possibly owes its origin to the discovery of the historical and sociocultural adventure of humankind ("culture") as a distinct reality over against "nature"—something that was unknown in Buddhist and Western ancient and medieval cultures alike.

The second remark is connected with something I have already indicated: that generally Buddhist speculation, in its religious context, aims at

[1] Kenneth Cragg, *The Christ and the Faiths* (Philadelphia: The Westminster Press, 1987), 247–8.

"explaining things (and even Being itself) away" rather than explaining ("grounding") them. The same is true, most emphatically, in our present question. Buddhist "anthropology" is not geared toward "founding," or providing a unified conception of, the human phenomena, but, on the contrary, toward unmasking the falsity of the deluded experience of the ordinary person or, to use the modern term again, toward deconstructing all unity and continuity allegedly found in it. No wonder, then, that these ancient Oriental speculations show amazing similarities to the postmodern theories of the West mentioned above.[2] Still, there may be a fundamental difference between the two: while it can be said of these contemporary thinkers that "they assault the human interior" or "deny people all access to their own interior," Buddhism is all about exploration of one's own interior, on the basis of a belief in its accessibility and potentially complete perspicacity (Enlightenment). It could therefore be argued that the Buddha had a more optimistic idea of the human capacities than our contemporary philosophers do, or, conversely, that these philosophers paint the "fallen state" of humanity as more radical and irrevocable than even the Buddha would do.

Indeed, a central element of the Buddha's message is the possibility for the human being to overcome its deplorable situation and to reach the ideal state of Nirvana (the third Holy Truth). It is not directly clear, however, how this optimistic outlook is compatible with the dark picture of the human being's condition that is painted in the first two Holy Truths—a lack of clarity that, in later doctrine, will give rise to various new theories: an originally inherent Buddha-nature, "Original Enlightenment," etc. For in these initial declarations the human being appears as totally vitiated in all its capacities, including the senses, by a foundational self-centeredness, or as existing in a totally corrupt state. It is true that the remedy proposed is a radical one: a complete "deconstruction" of the self and its false consciousness.

Thirdly, it appears that we are faced with four different anthropologies, rather than two. Indeed, an earlier chapter has briefly explained how our modern, basically Cartesian, conception of the human subject or *I* is profoundly—and for the problem of mysticism, decisively—different from Ruusbroec's (basically Augustinian) image of the *I* or soul. And it will soon appear that, on the Eastern side too, not one but two anthropologies are at work. Indeed, the centerpiece of the Buddhist anthropology, namely the *anatta* or *anātman* (non-ego) theory, is elaborated in direct opposition to, and thus dependency on, the Hindu *ātman* thinking. It is therefore of primary importance that, in our comparative study, we avoid all confusion among these four conceptions of the human being, which, respectively, see the human being basically as "self," "soul," *ātman*, and *anātman*. To make

---

[2] See above, pages 101–2.

this immediately a little more concrete: the Buddha certainly negated the Hindu *ātman*, but that cannot be directly translated as "the Buddha negated the 'subject' or the 'soul'."

THE BASIC WORLDVIEW

I have said earlier that, in Buddhism, the human being is never considered apart from, but always as an element in, the cosmos, and that therefore cosmology and metaphysics become important sources for our knowledge of Buddhist anthropology, and that this could equally be said about medieval Christian scholastics. Still, it seems to me that there is also a profound—and, for our purposes, important—difference between the two. In the following I shall be bold enough to try to formulate this difference, at the risk of over-generalizing (and overshooting my competence). But let me first prepare the terrain by two short considerations.

In my long acquaintance with Buddhism, it has always struck me how little Buddhists—who, under the category of "Dharma," recognize sense and order in the universe and abhor the idea of "chance"—are plagued by the question as to where all this comes from. When asked about it by any Western observer, for whom this is apparently an important question, they will indulgently refer to the chain of "horizontal" (synchronic or diachronic) causality, the already mentioned *pratītya-samutpāda*. On the other hand, when it is argued that Christian mystics do not work with the Cartesian idea of an isolated and self-sufficient subject but with an "open" one, the opening that is meant is a "vertical" one: the relationship to the origin, God.

Such considerations tempt me to posit the following "thesis": the basic metaphysical question, as experienced by the Buddhists, is not the problem of the archè or ground of things and the world, but that of the one and the many, the individual and the totality (the All-One). What I am trying to say here comes very near to what John Cobb formulated as follows:

> When we turn to Buddhism we find explicit and insistent rejection of the questions to which the God of the Bible is the answer. According to Buddhists we must cease to reflect on why the world is, how it came into being, what sustains it in being, and to what end it is directed. We must concentrate all our attention on realizing *what* we and all things truly and ultimately are. The answer to that question, profoundly experienced and brilliantly articulated, is that the "what" of our existence is Nothingness.[3]

[3] David Tracy and John B. Cobb Jr., *Talking about God: Doing Theology in the Context of Modern Pluralism* (New York: Seabury Press, 1983), 67.

To illustrate again: Buddhists will agree with St. Augustine that the *I* is not the *terminus ad quem* of the contemplative introversion, but, while for Augustine this is experienced as "by going inward, I am drawn upward," Buddhists would rather say: "By going inward, I am drawn outward" (toward unity with all things). In other words, it can be said that both mysticisms have the common concern of doing away with the idea of the *I* as an isolated substance, but, while Christian mysticism insists that the "soul" *is* relation to God, Buddhist mysticism will say: I am nothing but relation to all things. Or again: Buddhists presuppose, as it were, an original unity with everything, cut up by the self-isolation of the ego, but are not concerned with the source of that unity. They do not feel the need of what Christian theology sometimes calls a "protology."

I sincerely believe that something like this basic difference in metaphysical sensibility exists between the two lines of mysticism, but, as always, reality does not completely follow the lines of our nice distinctions. Indeed, that the "vertical thinking" is not completely absent in Buddhism can be shown by the fact that, albeit in a rather late development, the "ground" for the unity with all things is sought in the Buddha-nature or "Cosmic Buddha" present in one's innermost self. Could it be that, after all, the human spirit does not rest till it finds the horizontal relationships founded in a vertical relationship?

A second characteristic of the Buddhist—and possibly, on a larger scale, of the Indian or even Oriental—worldview is, to put it rather crudely, the tendency to reduce all reality, and especially the human reality, to the cognitive, accompanied by a basic suspicion of the appetitive or conative. It can be said that, in Western speculation, rather much attention has been paid to the appetitive element of reality, which was conceived of as comprising a rational side: the volitional (will), and a sensual side: the emotional (feeling). We only have to remember the discussions in medieval scholasticism concerning the relative superiority of reason and will, not only in the human being but in reality as such (including God). And it could be considered that this attention to the conative betrays an appreciation of the dynamic aspect of Being. Thus, for instance, "desire" (to which we shall have to return later) was seen as breaking through the static borders that our discriminating intellect puts up between things.

The same cannot be said, I believe, about Eastern metaphysical speculation. Certainly in Buddhism, which calls itself a religion of Awakening or Wisdom, the scales appear to be heavily loaded in favor of the cognitive, and the appetitive side of the human being seems not to be recognized as originally and legitimately there, but rather to be interpreted as illusion, a "privation" of right knowledge, and condemned as "passion" (the cause of all suffering), which is to be eliminated by right knowledge. This point will prove important when we come to the difference in appreciation of the role of "desire" and "love" on the spiritual path. Here I only want to add that the supremacy of the cognitive on the metaphysical level shows itself most clearly in the difficulty that Buddhist theory has always experienced in assigning a proper role to Mercy-Love in the theoretical scheme of things, even at times when it was strongly stressed in Buddhist practice. The reason is, love certainly belongs to the conative and—with all due respect to Nygren's agapé—implies desire. As Bergson puts it: "If God *is* Love, we accept that creative emotion is prior to intellect."[4] In the Buddhist logic of emptiness, however, Mercy or Love has always tended to be reduced to Wisdom as "the insight into the non-duality of self and other."

It may seem strange that in Buddhism, with its enormous stress on relations at the expense of substances, the relationships among human beings do not appear to be especially thematized or given any special status. They seem to be treated on the same level as the relationships among things, whereby every own-reality of a thing, and thus every real relationship, signifies mutual limitation, negation, and separation. Every "other" then only appears as "object" over against the subject, and the I-Thou relationship is reduced to the subject-object opposition. In other words, Buddhist theory does not know the category of "intersubjectivity" and does not single out the interpersonal relationship as a relationship *sui generis*. This may come as less of a surprise when we reflect that even medieval academic theology did not thematize it as such, although—and this is important for later developments—it devoted special attention to the relationships among the Persons of the Trinity. Mystical theology may have been a forerunner on this point, so that it could be written about Ruusbroec, for example, that "at the basis of his theory lies a theology of the interpersonal."[5] For Buddhism, the lack of this special category—or of the idea of the "societal and ethical authenticity of persons in relationship"[6]—means that unity in love can only be interpreted as the erasure of the borders between things, the disappearance of the duality of the partners and of any real relationship between them, and that all mention of a personal relationship with God is immediately equated with "making God into an object." In this view, Love mysticism is not conceivable.

A text by the French philosopher Louis Lavelle may now form a fitting transition to my final remark on the Buddhist worldview:

[4] H. Bergson, *The Two Sources of Morality and Religion* (Garden City, N.Y.: Doubleday, n.d.), 252–3.

[5] Louis Dupré, Preface to *John Ruusbroec: The Spiritual Espousals and Other Works* (New York: Paulist Press, 1985), xiii.

[6] Cragg, *The Christ and the Faiths*, 308.

This is why, in true love, the lover and the loved are not two distinct beings, but each of them is the one and the other at the same time. Can one imagine a unity that is more active and more alive than this unity, wherein the duality does not cease being reborn but in order to abolish itself; a more perfect form of union than this one, which does not cease, at the same time, to be fulfilled and to transcend itself?[7]

I think that we find in this text a vision of unity that, if it does not fully cover Ruusbroec's idea of the mystical unity with God, at least comes very near it. What we now have to consider is the fact that the idea or ideal of unity at work in Buddhism's most influential theories, is a very different one. In that theory it has become a self-evident truth, a verity so undisputable that he who questions it only makes a laughingstock of himself, that the final ideal, the peak of intellectual, religious, and mystical perfection (all in one) is "absolute unity," wherein all division, duality, multiplicity, relation, and interaction have been perfectly and finally overcome. It is, then, equally self-evident that all religion that centers on devotion (*bhakti*) to a personal God, with the duality this implies, is at best a second-string affair, a useful *upāya* for beginners all right, but not yet the real thing; and that all personal or love mysticism is not the true mysticism. It must also be noted that recent Western academia and public opinion have, in their (partly justified, but one-sided) fascination with Eastern Wisdom, widely and uncritically swallowed this Buddhist position.

It may very well be that we are facing here the Gordian knot of the Buddhist-Christian dialogue and confrontation. And it can be said that, precisely on this point, Ruusbroec's mysticism constitutes the most direct, well-thought-through and, I feel, convincing challenge to the Buddhist worldview, and in particular to its "unity dogma." It may be further intimated that Ruusbroec's thought owes much of its strength in this matter to his confrontation with what he calls "natural contemplation." The issue of this confrontation could be expressed, for example, by a sentence in one of Mommaers's earlier publications: "What is to be considered as final Reality: Being that ultimately reduces everything to the same, or Love that does not cease provoking difference?"[8] And the criterion deciding the issue between the two might be: Which side is more "fully human"? Which side represents

---

[7] Louis Lavelle, *Conduite à l'égard d'autrui* (Paris: Albin Michel, 1957), 194. The wording here comes close to that of St. John of the Cross: "Thus each lives in the other, and the one is the other, and both are one through the transformation of love" (*Spiritual Canticle*, Stanza XI,6, as quoted in W. Johnston, *The Still Point* (New York: Fordham University Press, 1970), 76.

[8] P. Mommaers, "La transformation d'amour selon Marguerite Porete," *Ons Geestelijk Erf* 65 (1991): 90, note 7.

true "wholeness"? In the following pages I shall try to substantiate these bold claims a little bit by a few random considerations.

To begin with, the Buddhist view of unity is in perfect accord with two tendencies mentioned above: the non-recognition of the interpersonal ingredient of reality and the absolute supremacy of the cognitive. On the latter point, we may recall, the mystical and the rational are brought into close proximity in Buddhism (and most Eastern religions). It is hardly fortuitous that Westerners coming into contact with Buddhism are unsure at times whether it is a religion or a philosophy they are dealing with. The American theologian and ardent student of Buddhism, Langdon Gilkey, in a review of a book by one of his Buddhist dialogue partners, expreessed his amazement at the sheer bulk of metaphysical tenets a Buddhist is supposed to accept:

> As in verbal discussions with Buddhist thinkers, so here the initial surprise is the (to us) strangely dominant role that what seem to be philosophical (epistemological and metaphysical) judgments play in the religious existence of the Buddhist, or at least in Buddhist reflection on that existence.... Buddhism seems at first glance to be a religion based on a particular set of speculative metaphysical affirmations, and even Buddhist salvation seems dependent on intellectual agreement to these metaphysical doctrines.[9]

It could be argued that in the triad of philosophy-religion-mysticism, mysticism represents "a certain dimension of philosophy *and* of faith,"[10] and that Buddhism is nearer to being a mysticism in which the philosophical prevails over the religious, than it is to being a religion. In this context, something I have written long ago may bear repeating:

I know of three urges toward perfect unity in man:

1. The romantic-naturalistic one towards a "vital unity" (*Lebenseinheit*);
2. The rationalistic-philosophical one towards a rational unity: reason cannot really come to rest as long as it is left with two irreducible elements;
3. The mystical drive for perfect unity with the Absolute....

I only want to suggest here (presupposing that religion and mysticism are not one and the same thing) that none of these three urges in their purity, and not even the three combined, are sufficient to define religion.[11]

[9] Langdon Gilkey, "Masao Abe's *Zen and Western Thought*: A Review Article." Unpublished manuscript, 3–4.

[10] This is the thesis of H. Laux in "Mystique et philosophie," *Etudes* 378 (1993): 793.

[11] J. Van Bragt, "Notulae on Emptiness and Dialogue," *Japanese Religions* 4/4 (1966): 68.

I could now add that the Buddhist ideal of unity is a conflation of 2 and 3 (combining further, in East Asian Buddhism, with 1). I also want to suggest that Ruusbroec's idea of mystical unity might be a more intrinsically religious one; one wherein mysticism comes nearer to faith. I want to remark here, in passing, that the above may account for, or at least throw some light on, the Buddhist predilection for Meister Eckhart's mysticism—a mysticism that has been characterized as very metaphysical and showing a strong equation of God with Oneness.[12]

Secondly, we should return a moment to our earlier considerations on the idea of creation. It was pointed out there that this idea has been conducive to the recognition of the reality of the things of this world. It can be added now that the same idea is also responsible for the positive evaluation of the multiplicity of beings in Christianity (and Western culture)[13]—in contrast with some trends in Greek thought and, even more clearly, with the Indian tendency to declare all multiplicity to be illusion or *māyā* (in other words, the "monistic view"). Edward Conze testifies to this when he writes:

> It is on two points that the Eliatics and the Buddhists seem to be in close agreement. There is first of all the *Monism....* Plurality, or even duality, are constantly decried as the root of all falsehood.... At no time has there been a pluralistic tradition among the Buddhists.... A plurality of dharmas would never have been regarded as more than a provisional fact.[14]

And the Dutch theologian, Piet Schoonenberg, notes in this regard:

> One could ask oneself whether all monistic philosophies are not based on the fact that they view unity and multiplicity exclusively as opposites, and therefore cannot conceive of a unity enriched by multiplicity.[15]

[12] Cf. "[For Eckhart] Oneness and God are sacred, interchangeable terms, and it is difficult to say which has preference." Rudolf Otto, *Mysticism East and West* (New York: Macmillan, 1970), 87.

[13] One of the most beautiful texts in this regard may be found in The *Summa Theologiae* of Thomas Aquinas, Ia, qu. 47, a. 1: "Does the Plurality-Distinction of things have its origin in God?" St. Thomas answers affirmatively and writes: "For God put things into being in order to communicate his goodness to the creatures, and so that his goodness would be represented by them. And since his goodness could not be sufficiently represented by any one creature, He produces many and diverse creatures, so that, what is lacking in the one for the representation, would be supplemented by the other...."

[14] Edward Conze, "Contradictions in Buddhist Thought," in *Indianisme et Bouddhisme. Mélanges offerts à Mgr. Etienne Lamotte* (Louvain-la-Neuve: U. C. L. Institut Orientaliste, 1980), 49.

[15] P. Schoonenberg, "Gott als Person und Gott als das unpersönlich Göttliche: Bhakti und Jnana," in G. Oberhammer ed., *Transzendenzerfahrung, Vollzugshorizont des Heils* (Wien: Institut für Indologie der Universität Wien, 1978), 228.

Thirdly, the "absolute unity" trend in Buddhist theory is often considered to be most strongly represented by the "logic of emptiness" (*śūnyatā*), which came to the fore around the beginning of our era and found its eminent champion in Nāgārjuna (second century CE?). If by the *pratītya-samutpāda* idea the individual was freed from its isolation and presented as nothing but a crossroad of influences from everything in the universe (thus, as pure relation), in the emptiness theory the individual or "form" loses all "own-being" or "own-nature" (*svabhāva*), so that even the relationships can no longer be considered as real. "All form is Emptiness." At first sight, then, and also in the way that Buddhist theoreticians mostly use it, the logic of emptiness appears as a true monism or theory of "absolute Oneness."

However, and here we pass to our fourth consideration, there are many voices in Buddhism that proclaim that this kind of monistic oneness or absolute unity is not the true ideal of Buddhism, not the endpoint of the Buddhist path; voices that plead for what we might call, from the perspective of our present problematics, a more dialectical and living idea of unity. With direct regard to the logic of emptiness as just defined, one can speak of two different reactions within Buddhism. The first declares that Emptiness does not stand for a compact unity or monistic identity, which would simply do away with multiplicity, but instead represents a "golden mean" between unity and multiplicity: neither simply one nor simply multiple. Thus, for instance, Huang Po speaks of "the Great Void in which there is neither unity nor multiplicity— that Void which is not really void, that Symbol which is no symbol."[16]

These people will point out that the real formula of the emptiness doctrine is not the one-sided "form is emptiness," but the reciprocal "form is emptiness, emptiness is form": not simply not-two, but "not one, not two." Zen Patriarch Hui-neng, for instance, once used the following formulation:

> Bhikshu Fa-hai...asked the meaning of the well-known saying "What mind is, Buddha is." The patriarch replied, "To let not a passing thought rise up is 'mind.' To let not the coming thought be annihilated is Buddha. To manifest all kinds of phenomena is 'mind.' To be free from all forms...is Buddha."[17]

And Layman P'ang sang:

> Grasp emptiness, and emptiness is form;
> Grasp form, and form is impermanent.

[16] *The Zen Teaching of Huang Po*, trans. by John Blofeld (New York: Grove Weidenfeld, 1959), 123.

[17] *The Diamond Sūtra and the Sūtra of Hui-neng*, trans. by A. F. Price and Wong Mou-lam (Boston: Shambala, 1990), 110.

Emptiness and form are not mine—
Sitting erect, I see my native home.[18]

I believe that these people are right. Nevertheless, I want to repeat here what I have been saying many times in my long-running feud with the logic of emptiness: namely, that this is so delicate a position that it is nearly impossible to handle it rightly, and that in nearly all cases in which it is used by Buddhist theoreticians it becomes, in fact, "less a theory of non-duality than one of monistic identity."[19] Huang Po, for one, appears to be very conscious of this difficulty when he says, for example:

Ah, this Dharma of Thusness—until now so few people have come to understand it that it is written: "In this world, how few are they who lose their egos!"
    It is all because you take it upon yourself to talk of explaining Zen! As soon as the mouth is opened, evils spring forth. People either neglect the root and speak of the branches, or neglect the reality of the "illusory" world and speak only of Enlightenment.[20]

The second Buddhist reaction to the logic of emptiness is the following: Emptiness by itself is not a full expression of the true Buddhist ideal. It is a very important station on the Buddhist path, which must be gone through at all costs. However, Buddhism does not stop there, it essentially goes a step further, by which it becomes much more dialectical, complex, alive, and geared to everyday reality. This "one step further" then appears under many guises, of which I shall mention a few.

To begin with, there is the influential doctrine of T'ien-t'ai (a very speculative school of Chinese Buddhism, that originated in the sixth century CE), wherein the opposition of form (the provisional or conventional) and emptiness (the "real truth") is seen as thesis and antithesis, to be overcome in a final synthesis called "Middle." A similar attitude is taken by Kamalaśīla, an Indian Buddhist authority of the eighth century CE, who insists on the necessity of a conjunction of Emptiness with Means (*upāya*):

Now, when *śūnyatā* is thus correctly and indissolubly bonded with *upāya* [in a syzygy or yoke], it is known to Kamalaśīla as Emptiness endowed with all excellent modes.... This notion is contrasted with an isolated

---

[18] *The Recorded Sayings of Layman P'ang*, trans. by Ruth Fuller Sasaki et al. (New York/Tokyo: Weatherhill, 1971), 87.

[19] D. Ruegg, *Buddha-nature, Mind and the Problem of Gradualism in a Comparative Perspective* (London: School of Oriental and African Studies, 1989), 6.

[20] *The Zen Teaching of Huang Po*, 111–12 and 106.

emptiness, that is, an emptiness-method (*śūnyatānaya*) that makes of *śūnyatā* something that is a self-sufficient and independent principle....[21]

There is also the rather classical pictorial representation of the Zen path toward enlightenment, called "The Oxherding Pictures." In some older versions, it consisted of 8 drawings, the final one of which was an empty circle, the symbol of emptiness, wherein self and world have disappeared. This pictorial series developed further into what is now considered to be the authentic representation, in which two more pictures are added, wherein first nature and then the self make a new, transformed, appearance. An oft-repeated theme is, then, that the contemplative "ascent" to the peak of emptiness must be followed by a "descent" back into the world of forms, whereby the Wisdom obtained in the mountain must be applied in the world and, as it were, complemented by a knowledge of the "expedient means" necessary for this practical application.

The ascent is often presented as the path of Wisdom, and the descent as the path of Mercy or Love. This double path is fully realized in the ideal figure of the bodhisattva who embodies and unites in himself the "contradictory perfections of Wisdom and Mercy." The warning then is sometimes heard that simple abiding in emptiness is the worst thing of all. To quote D. Ruegg once again: "...an authoritative Sūtra has nevertheless warned that the dogmatic view of Emptiness (*śūnyatādṛṣṭi*) is even more dangerous than the individualist dogma (*pudgaladṛṣṭi*)."[22]

Finally, there is the Buddhist mystic and metaphysical poet, Saraha (dates unknown), for whom the experience of wholeness was decisive. He sang:

> He who clings to the Void
> And neglects Compassion,
> Does not reach the highest stage.
> But he who practices only Compassion
> Does not gain release from the toils of existence.
> He, however, who is strong in practice of both,
> Remains neither in *samsāra* nor in Nirvana.[23]

An authoritative interpreter of Saraha's thought points out that Saraha severely criticized Nāgārjuna's view for its "logical reductionism," and writes:

[21] As quoted in Ruegg, *Buddha-nature*, 184.

[22] Ruegg, *Buddha-nature*, 43.

[23] Quoted from C. Humphreys ed., *The Wisdom of Buddhism* (London/Dublin: Curzon Press, 1979), 220. Mommaers pointed out to me that this very much resembles Ruusbroec's presenting of two "opposing" elements that "do not hinder but fortify one another."

The idea of wholeness as process presupposes for Saraha a pervasive intelligence/spirituality (*Geistigkeit*) that keeps wholeness in any form from stagnating.... It does this by effecting a break in the symmetry of the original, undifferentiated continuum of being.... The break in symmetry is effected as a differentiation of wholeness, first into two, then into three."[24]

All this is saying, of course, that Buddhism cannot simply be identified as the path of emptiness or absolute unity, and that its true ideal is a much more complex fusion of unity and multiplicity. The same Ruegg, for example, concludes: "In many classical periods of the Buddhist tradition it is indeed precisely this co-ordination of polarities [*samatha* and *vipaśyanā*, Emptiness and Compassion, etc.] that constitutes the specific character of theory and praxis."[25] Still, it cannot be denied that the ideal of a "compact unity," free from all disturbing distinction and multiplicity, pervades much of Buddhist thinking, especially with regard to the conception of the peak experience, and that the idea of "emptiness" is often construed in that perspective. It looks very much as if the idea of "emptiness," while originally representing a quest for infinity or infinite "openness," has very often been put in the service of the drive for undifferentiated unity or "absolute totality."

THE BUDDHIST HUMAN BEING

In chapter 5, it has been explained that Ruusbroec works with a definite "structure" of the human being, which allows him to explain God's working in us. What "structure" of the human being do Buddhists have in mind? For the sake of comparison, the following points are, I think, relevant.

As an individual in the cosmos, the human being essentially appears under the general category of finite or conditioned being. Still, Buddhism has assigned a special place to the human being, to begin with, under the epithet "sentient being." Practically speaking, this category embraces the six forms of being in which the human can be reborn in a future life: from heavenly being to animal. Furthermore, within this category the human is assigned a central place and special prerogative: only as a human being is it possible to reach liberation, since only the human situation involves the right mixture of pleasure and pain to make one strive for liberation. One should, thus, be grateful for the fact of being born as a human and not postpone one's efforts towards liberation, for how can one know when the chance will come again? This theme is already present in the *Dhammapada*:

[24] Herbert Guenther, *Ecstatic Spontaneity* (Berkeley: Asian Humanities Press, 1993), 37–8.

[25] Ruegg, *Buddha-nature*, 10.

> Difficult is the attainment of the human state.
> Difficult the lives of mortals.
> Difficult is the hearing of dharma true.
> Difficult the appearance of Awakened ones.[26]

Buddhism shows a clear similarity to the Augustinian tradition in the recognition, all through its history, of the polarity of "interior man" and "exterior man," whereby the inner man (the "mind") is seen as the decisively important one for the spiritual path. It is by a descent into one's own interiority by progressive contemplative steps that Nirvana is reached. This trend is to be found on all levels of Buddhist doctrine and at all moments of its history. Herbert Guenther summarizes this as follows:

> From its very beginnings, in varying degrees of explicitness, Buddhism has insisted on the fact that mind or spirit is a dynamic principle lying at the very heart of a universe of which the human individual is an integral part. Indeed, for the Buddhist the pure intensity of mind is the very stuff of which the universe, and we in it, are made.[27]

Thus, for instance, this note is struck right at the beginning of the same *Dhammapada*:

> All that we are is the result of what we have thought: it is founded on our thoughts, it is made up of our thoughts.[28]

And Huang Po sounds this note with a final "Zen twist":

> Ordinary people look to their surroundings, while followers of the Way look to Mind, but the true Dharma is to forget them both.[29]

But when it comes to defining what is more interior and what more exterior, Buddhism does not come up with the Western clear distinction and partial opposition between the sensible (exterior) and the (more interior) intelligible, so that on this score it might be called less dualistic.

But the fundamental difference between the two conceptions of the human being has to do with the Buddhist "spiritual policy," indicated above, of "deconstructing" all putative unity and continuity. Applied to the human being, this deconstruction produces a picture that is strangely different from

---

[26] *Dhammapada*, nr. 182. The translation is taken from John Ross Carter and Mahinda Palihawadana, *Dhammapada: A New English Translation with the Pali Text* (Oxford: Oxford University Press, 1987), 243.

[27] Guenther, *Ecstatic Spontaneity*, 32.

[28] *Dhammapada*, nr. 1. *Sacred Books of the East*, X, 3.

[29] *The Zen Teaching of Huang Po*, 41.

that of Ruusbroec with its three "unities," the innermost one of which stands for a final unity. In the earliest Buddhist analysis (the five *skandha* or "heaps"), the human being is presented as a provisionally assembled conglomerate of material elements, perceptions, feelings, impulses, and ideas, all changing from moment to moment in a chaotic fashion "like monkeys in a tree." Thus, there is no structural unity, and, as well, no unifying positive dynamism. The only dynamism recognized is a negative one: that of the passions that drive us on and bind us ever more solidly to this painful existence in *samsāra*.

Later Buddhist speculation, however, will postulate a kind of unity in the human being under the name of "mind" or "consciousness." This happened mainly in the Yogācāra school, which arrived at "the identification of the entity regarded as the self with the 'mind'."[30] Eight (or even nine) levels of consciousness then come to be distinguished, of which the most superficial are the sense-connected ones, and the deepest the "store-consciousness," which contains all the "seeds" of an individual's existence.

As to the negation of continuity, this is pushed to absurd lengths by the early Buddhist theoreticians (the Abhidharma), who insist on the complete atomic momentariness of all beings and then try to measure the precise duration of each of these moments of origination and annihilation—a type of argument very reminiscent of the alleged medieval dispute about the number of angels that can sit on the top of a pin. But, in view of the fact that the Augustinian tradition looks for the human subjective continuity in the basic faculty of memory, a note on the role of memory in early Buddhism may be called for.[31] Memory first appears there in the description of the Enlightenment of the Buddha. This enlightenment is said to imply a total recollection of all former lives. This memory is, thus, part of the "light" that chases away all darkness of ignorance and delusion, makes one's own reality totally perspicacious, and brings the past within the grasp of the present. In the Abhidharma, however, memory became a problem precisely because it seems to imply a real continuity in the human being, and the "dissident" Pudgalavādin, who believed in the ontological existence of the *I* or person, used this as one of the arguments for their thesis.

This leads us to the core of the Buddha's negative anthropology: Sakyamuni declared all human existence to be suffering, impermanence, and

---

[30] "It is the mind which constitutes the subjective agency of practice: ...the purification of the mind is equivalent to the purification of oneself." Takasaki Jikidō, *An Introduction to Buddhism* (Tokyo, The Tōhō Gakkai, 1987), 200–1.

[31] For the conception of memory in Buddhism, see Janet Gyatso, ed., *In the Mirror of Memory: Reflections on Mindfulness and Remembrance in Indian and Tibetan Buddhism* (Albany: State University of New York Press, 1992).

anātman—which is translated variously as "non-ego," "no-self," or "no-soul." What exactly did the Buddha mean by this *anātman* doctrine? This question has been much discussed in the course of Buddhist history and given all kinds of interpretations. Yet, even supposing that after some time the inner Buddhist circle had become so used to this doctrine as to forget its shocking and revolutionary character, Buddhism's recent encounter with the Western *I* could not but make it into a topic of heated discussion anew. In fact, as could almost be predicted a priori, the interpretations are spread out between two poles. On the one hand is the conclusion that with this doctrine, the Buddha proclaimed the ontological non-existence of the ego; and on the other is the conclusion that the Buddha thereby strongly promoted the ethical ideal of selflessness, as supremely important for the spiritual path.

My intention here certainly is not to solve this question once and for all, or even to add one more opinion to the many that already exist, but merely to reflect on the relationship between the standpoint of Buddhism and the standpoint of Ruusbroec on this matter and the consequences this entails for their respective mystical doctrines. Let me only point out that both polar positions are highly improbable. On the one hand, the Buddha does not appear to be overly obsessed by ethical questions. He does not belabor human sinfulness, but rather human suffering. On the other hand, the Buddha often indicated that he is not interested in ontological questions. Preoccupation with them "profits not." (The eminent pragmatist speaking.)

That the ego with its self-isolating self-centeredness is enemy number one of all moral and spiritual life—and a fortiori of all mysticism, which strives for unity—is, I believe, recognized in all cultures, and we do not need a Buddha to come and tell us this. But it may have taken a Buddha to make this insight absolutely central, to pursue it in all its ramifications, and to draw the most radical conclusions from it. For the Buddha, the idea spreads far beyond the ethical. He associates the idea of the ego first of all with permanence, the human craving for a fixed foothold, for unchanging being; then he associates it with suffering: fixation on the ego is the cause of all suffering. This association is directly attested to in the sūtras, but it seems also clear that, in the Buddha's view, the ravages of self-centeredness also spread to the cognitive sphere: it is the basic cause of, or at least intimately connected with, all our human ignorance and delusion, the enemy of true wisdom. The cognitive faculty within a self-centered consciousness has no access to true reality. Thus the Buddha had to conclude that the supreme task of the spiritual path is to do away with the ego, not only in ethical conduct but in all the realms of the human reality, and therefore to do away with any attitude, emotion, impulse, or idea that could make us stick to it.

Our question then becomes: how far does Ruusbroec's spirituality share this same conviction? Is this also the all-important point for him, or does he have another priority? Or again, would there not be points wherein the Buddha would judge Ruusbroec's spiritual path as endangering that all-important spiritual strategy? Before we try to anwer these questions, we would do well to take another look at a view explicitly criticized by the Buddha: the Hindu idea of *ātman*. Needless to say, we are not interested here in this Hindu idea as such, nor in the various interpretations of it within Hinduism, but only in what the Buddha found objectionable in it. Within these parameters, then, we could say that the Hindu answer to the question "Who am I beyond all changing phenomena and momentary illusions?" is: "I am an eternal *ātman*, ultimately identical with Brahman, the all-encompassing divine." For the Buddhists, this amounts to positing in the human a transcending and unifying reality beyond, or substratum below, the phenomenal multiplicity of the human "conglomeration," providing the human being with a self-sufficient foundation, and making it into an eternal essence or substance that cannot and must not basically change.

I am not going to speculate on how far the modern Cartesian self goes in the direction of the Hindu *ātman*. Far more relevant and rewarding for us would be to have a second look at the picture of the *I* in Augustine and Ruusbroec, as presented above[32] and to verify how far they go along in "deconstructing" the human fixation on the ego. They certainly refuse to reduce the human totality to an unchanging "Wesen;" for them the *I* is no eternal possession, but a new gift at every moment; not a closed and static substance, but a living and active relation. We might conclude that the Christian *I* is a strongly relativized one, and undoubtedly escapes several of the objections the Buddha turned against the Hindu *ātman* idea. It remains, however, a "person" with an own-reality and dignity and thus open to the Buddhist critique of constituting a possible object of attachment. Buddhists wiil therefore say that the Christian negation of the *I* is not radical enough and Christianity "does not succeed in eradicating the deepest roots of the human self-centered ego."

Among the Buddhist thinkers who formulate this criticism of Christianity most explicitly, the contemporary Japanese philosopher Nishitani Keiji (1900–1990) merits special attention in this regard. He concedes that Christianity does away with the cruder forms of self-centeredness, but adds that it encourages a "self-centeredness *via* God": "Human self-centeredness is a permanent fixture in religions in the West; once negated, it reappears, as in the guise of God's chosen people."[33] In his search for the roots of this problem, Nishitani then indicates two more characteristics of Christianity. In

---

[32] See above, pages 113–14.

[33] K. Nishitani, *Religion and Nothingness* (Berkeley: University of California Press, 1982), 203.

the first one, he clearly associates himself with the earlier-mentioned suspicion of the appetitive aspect in reality. He ascribes, that is, the survival of self-centeredness to the priority of the will in Christianity's view of God, the human being, and the relationship between the two.

> I think that, in the Western view, the will is seen as the basic element of the human being. This appears especially strongly in Christianity. Therein lies a grave problem. The God of Christianity is very voluntaristic.... Everything falls under the dominion of the divine Will. Also the relationship of God and the human being is viewed as a relation of will to will.[34]

As a second root cause, then, he considers the fact that Christianity is, after all, a "religion of life," a view of reality wherein life is given a one-sided priority over death, while Buddhism is a "religion of life-death," wherein the two are always seen together in a "double exposure."[35]

I would surmise, perhaps a bit rashly, that Ruusbroec's answer to this critique would have been twofold:

> First, a human being can get rid of its self-centeredness only by losing itself in God. And second, my view may imply that danger, but this is more than compensated for by, and is burned up in, the fire of the living relationship with God that it allows.

Personally, I feel inclined to add that the Buddhist negative concentration on a substantial *ātman* itself runs the risk of the substantialization that it wants to avoid at all cost. This is along the line of a much bolder statement by the Buddhist scholar and sympathizer, Herbert Guenther, who wrote that the Buddhist negation of the own-reality of things, once turned into a dogma, ironically seems "to perpetuate the very reifying and dichotomizing tendencies of ordinary thought that Buddhism set out to overcome."[36] And I have the impression that Zen Master Huang Po would also agree with me—that is, if his Zen rhetoric ever permitted him to agree with an interlocutor:

> ...if you have the merest intention to indulge in conceptual thinking, your very intention will place you in the clutch of demons. Similarly, a conscious lack of such intention, or even a consciousness that you have *no* such intention, will be sufficient to deliver you into the demons' power.[37]

---

[34] 西谷啓治著作集 [Selected Writings of Nishitani Keiji] 17 (Tokyo: Sōbunsha, 1990), 26.

[35] Cf. especially Nishitani's "Science and Zen," *The Eastern Buddhist* I/1 (1965): 79–108.

[36] Guenther, *Ecstatic Spontaneity*, 28.

[37] *The Zen Teaching of Huang Po*, 104.

7

Meeting the Divine Other

With Ruusbroec's general map of the human psyche laid out before us, we are now ready to locate the mystical experience that transforms this common topography into a vivid inner landscape. This encounter of the human person with an Other who "comes from within outward" does not abolish or even rearrange the natural order of human being. If anything, it requires that one "possess" one's humanity in its entirety and put it at the disposition of the encounter. In other words, we are about to see what happens when the tripartite profile of the human discussed in chapter 5 arrives at "life to the full."

A passage from *The Seven Rungs* captures this transformation succinctly. Although some of the language will have to be clarified later, the main point should be clear enough. The context is Ruusbroec's treatment of a "game of love" in which the contemplative follows God into the idle essence of human being:

> Living unity with God is in our essence. It is not ours to comprehend, to attain, or to overtake. It plays itself right out of the hands of all our faculties and demands that we be wholly one with God without intermediary. But what it demands we cannot accomplish, and so we follow him into the idle being of our essence.[1]

The transition from the orderly description of the psyche to the unpredictable world of "mystical awareness" brings us at last to the experiential data that I defined at the outset as the heart of mysticism. Here the method of description works changes of its own on the style of the writer, and our commitment to honor the mystic's text obliges us us to look more closely at just what is going on. Before doing so, however, a few preliminary remarks seem in order to position this chapter within the ampler argument I am trying to present along the way.

In presenting a broad outline of mystical awareness in chapter 3, mention was made of the various "objects" that different mystics understand as the absolute focal point of their experience. Ruusbroec's descriptions will show

[1] *Werken* III.260:15–21.

him to be concerned with a "divine Other." Neither "nature" nor the "human other" figure in his accounts, though "human essence" will remain the locus at which one meets the Other. At the same time, the turn *inward* is not merely a negative turn *away* from the outer world but a positive contact with that very core of human nature that for other mystics is seen to be ultimate. The point is critical if we are to understand what distinguishes Ruusbroec from other mystics.

I also made mention in chapter 3 of four characteristics of the mystical way of knowing. The key terms I used there—passive, immediate, unitive, annihilating—will also show up in Ruusbroec's own descriptions, which would seem to encourage us to use those terms as a framework for presenting the material of this chapter. I shall not do so, however, and the reasons bring us to another distinctive feature of Ruusbroec's work.

In the context of a general characterization of the mystical knowing, the traits I singled out serve to set mystical awareness apart from ordinary awareness. They look at the mystic's experience from the outside, comparing the unfamiliar with the familiar: activity ceases and one becomes passive; instead of being full of oneself, one feels annihilated; the means we dispose of in order to manipulate the things of life fall away and knowing becomes immediate; the distinction between subject and object yields to a sense of union with the known. This is all correct as far as it goes.

When we shift to the context of Ruusbroec's descriptions, however, the viewpoint changes. There we are looking at the mystic's experience from within, where comparison is at best a distraction. The touchstone of understanding is no longer ordinary consciousness. The mystical state stands on its own and is described as such. The difference is considerable, and we should not be surprised at all if a new vocabulary were generated to emphasize that fact. Yet this is precisely what Ruusbroec does *not* do, and there lies what is perhaps his most original contribution to mystical literature.

For Ruusbroec, the reasons that the features and way of expression of pre-mystical knowing reappear in his accounts of the fully developed mystical state lie in his unshakable esteem for human nature. The mystic is not shuttled away to the clouds and back again, but remains planted on the native earth of ordinary humanity. The mystical state is special, exalted, "graced" because it enhances the essence of human life. It is *within* mystical experience that the mystic rediscovers the fullness of being a human person with all its attributes and faculties. In the pre-mystic state, one uses a variety of means to express "oneself" as a person and to address oneself to the Absolute. The passage then from non-mystical to mystical lets go of these means but does not obliterate them. They are alive and well, no longer as the *means* they once were but as *expressions* of a new experience. The tools of action become the discourse of reaction.

Let us try to put it another way, in terms of the distinction between "falling in love" and "being in love." When I fall in love, I undergo a kind of passage that makes me lose control of myself. Where I used to walk secure, one foot before the other, I am aware of being driven by something outside of myself. The state of being in love takes this a step further, to its natural conclusion. I am no longer the person I was before. It is not only my awareness but my every activity that changes. The transition arrives at a state of being, and with that the bittersweet torment of the passage yields to a heightened sense of being alive. I can of course fall back out of this state of being in love, just as the mystic can fall back into normal consciousness, but in any case as long as I am in that state I have not lost anything of my natural humanity. What we have in Ruusbroec is a description of being in mystical love.

RUUSBROEC'S STYLE

To approach the mystic's texts as the primary source of understanding what mysticism is does not mean shelling the husks and grinding down its unconventional grain to get to the pure germ of mystical awareness. Insofar as the texts are descriptive, their contents are of one substance with the style and flavor of their language. Moreover, insofar as the mystical author does not stop at description but goes a step further to order knowledge, it is important for the reader to know the difference and to get a sense of where the one flows into the other. In chapter 5, I focused on Ruusbroec's rational structuring of the psyche. We must now prepare for the distinctive style of expression of his mystical description.

General Structure

As a writer, Ruusbroec strikes the reader in the first place as a master architect. Each of his works is a carefully structured composition. We do not find descriptions strung together in loose chronological order, or ideas linked to one another by the mere association of ideas. Rather, the specific elements of the text are worked together in such a way as to unfold to the reader a greater picture. In this sense, his main intent is not to testify to his personal experiences but to shape those experiences into a more general, recognizable form. When we read his accounts of mystical states, then, it is important not to see them as stitched together end to end like a motley-colored quilt, but to follow the weave to the interlacing patterns that make up the larger tapestry of the practice of prayer.

Ruusbroec's artistry as a stylist shimmers in the pages of *The Spiritual Espousals*, but even a skim through *A Mirror of Eternal Blessedness* or the lengthy *Spiritual Tabernacle* shows the peculiar gift that was his. His clarity

141

of construction is all the more remarkable when we recall that he was primarily situated in a context of oral communication.[2] As odd as it may sound to modern ears, Ruusbroec wrote mainly to be listened to.

Against the background of so discriminating a style, the failure of disorder or disruptions in the structure of an argument stand out all the more, and this is surely the case with Ruusbroec, most significantly in his organizational masterpiece, *The Spiritual Espousals*.[3] To begin with, the reader soon notices that the same "thing" is being repeated again and again at each stage of the exposition. Each rung of the spiritual ladder is set neatly above the next, but the same descriptive model repeats itself without regard for the ascending construction.

This annoying repetition is aggravated by another more comprehensive disruption: Ruusbroec seems incapable of keeping to his original agenda and following his own schema. In the second book of *The Spiritual Espousals*, for example, he announces the topic of meeting God "with intermediary and without intermediary." One expects him to treat first the one and then the other in orderly succession. Instead, he keeps crossing back and forth from one to the other. Gradually, and after considerable irritation, it dawns on the reader that the mystical author is simply not able to constrain his description of mystical experience to the demands of systematic presentation, that he has no choice but to forfeit linear, logical order for a spiraling, repetitive one. In other words, the very disruption of the style signals a struggle with a phenomenon that refuses to cater to the demands of a rational framework.

Sentence Structure

From these comments on general structuring, we may look at the parallelism that Ruusbroec uses to design his sentences. His sentences frequently consist of two syntactically similar but semantically contrasting halves, occasionally linked by phonetic correspondence. To what are we to attribute this predilec-

---

[2] I refer here to an insight of Prof. F. Willaert, who points out that Ruusbroec's works were mainly meant to be "heard" and that he uses the oratory devices of the sermon. See F. Willaert, "Is Ruusbroec's 'Brulocht' literatuur?" in Th. Mertens, ed., *"Siet, de brudegom comt": Facetten van "Die geestelike Brulocht"* (Kampen: Kok, 1994). That is why the present-day reader is not as comfortable with the critical edition, where Ruusbroec's ordering devices are not visible, as with modern editions that are fitted out with titles, subtitles, and the like. Still, if one can *listen* to the text, one will not fail to hear the ordering that Ruusbroec imposes. In *A Mirror* he himself highlights his concern with clear structuring: "I have spoken of (the living life) already but did not clarify it sufficiently. Even though I did not proceed through this material in an orderly way, I was aware of that and did it on purpose. What I then left unsaid I will now fill in" (Wiseman, 243).

[3] For a more detailed presentation of this point, see my Introduction in Ruusbroec's *Opera omnia* III, 34–6.

tion for a kind of "balanced imbalance" between structure and sense? Is it his way of drawing attention to unusual insights? Or perhaps he means to underline the originality of an experience? In fact, the habit asserts itself mainly in his descriptions, but also in his theoretical passages. A few examples may help. *The Spiritual Espousals* speak of the mystical state in these terms:

> for he is wholly in God where he rests in enjoyment
> (*daer hi ghebrukelijcke rast*)
>
> and he is wholly in himself where he loves with works
> (*daer hi werckelijcke mint*).[4]

In *The Seven Rungs* the correspondence between a first and a second *daer* is replaced by *in den* and *in den*:

> Inasmuch as we work, we always fail; we cannot love God enough.
> (*In den werkene ghebreken wi altoes*)
>
> Inasmuch as we enjoy, we have enough: we are all we want.
> (*In den ghebrukene es ons gnoech*)[5]

The sense of *daer* connecting the two phrases is not always easy to render. In the first quotation, the translation by "where...where" can do, but what about the *daer...daer* in this passage from *The Sparkling Stone*?

> When the spirit burns in love it will find a distinction and an otherness...
> (*Daer die gheest berent in minnen...*)
>
> But when it is burnt up it is onefold and there is no distinction left.
> (*Maer daer hi verberent...*)[6]

The chronological "when" raises a question about the translation, for the simple reason that the introduction of succession disturbs the strict parallelism of Ruusbroec's sentence. The repetition of *daer* signifies equivalence and simultaneity, a balance we might normally express by repeating the phrase "in so far as."

A more thorough survey of the different devices Ruusbroec employs to combine syntactically phrases that contrast with each other semantically falls beyond the scope of these pages. Suffice it to note that the contrast is not

---

[4] *Opera omnia* III.b.1936–8. In *The Sparkling Stone* the same structure appears in the following passage: "And so we live completely in God, where we possess our bliss, and completely in ourselves, where we practice our love towards God" (*Opera omnia* X.485–7).

[5] *Werken* III.261:2–5. Here is, from the same work, an instance of the same sentence structure in a theological passage: "And thus God is, as to the Persons eternal work, and as to the Essence eternal idleness" (*in den Personen eewegh werc, ende, in den wesene eeweghe ledegheit*) (266:28).

[6] *Opera omnia* X.98–100.

meant to imply contradiction or mutual exclusion. Thus, contrasting *work-ing—enjoying* maintains a connection between them, but not a causal or chronological one. Working does not precede enjoyment (nor for that matter is one "burnt up" because one had previously been "burning").

Such stylistic peculiarities force themselves upon the reader too abruptly to be passed over. There is no way to the content of Ruusbroec's thought but through his style, and it is best to keep this in mind as we approach his descriptions of mystical awareness.

ORDERING PRAYER

Ruusbroec's way of structuring his writing and the significance of the disruptions that seem to deconstruct it, are at least in part a function of his developmental approach to his subject matter. His assumption is that one who engages seriously in the practice of prayer will pass through different stages. Taken earnestly, prayer becomes something living. So, too, the experience of God is always in process. Either it grows or it decays. In Ruusbroec's case, this "prayer life" has three phases which he calls active life, yearning life, and contemplating life. In examining his careful construction of these phases, we will also have occasion to see what are perhaps his best descriptions of two central themes of his mystical doctrine: meeting the Other and passing from non-mystical to mystical experience.

Before doing so, however, three observations need to be made. In the first place, the life of prayer is going to be presented as flowing smoothly through three principal and numerous secondary stages. This should not be taken as a temporal succession of moments that one must go through, and go through in proper order. In line with what we have seen of his style in general, one must always remain alert not only to the ordering that is going on but also to the breakdown in order. Like the rest of his works, *The Spiritual Espousals* was not intended as a manual for mountain climbers. The "ascent" is not a balanced rational activity but one that is continually relativized by the imbalance of passivity and letting go.[7]

In the second place, the word *active* in expressions like "active life" implies that one can exert oneself to come into contact with the divine Other. To some extent, of course, all spiritual discipline goes hand in hand with virtue and right action in the world. But the activity that dominates the "active life" is rather an *inner* activity. Ruusbroec's primary concern remains with the practice of prayer. And we must never think that for him prayer starts only in the "inner life" or—worse still—that the exercise of virtue

[7] See above, chapter 3, pages 51–2.

belongs only to the "active life."[8]

In the third place, something must be said of three connected but easily misunderstood terms: "grace," "supernatural," and "faith." The tenth chapter will present us an occasion to define them more accurately in the context of his ideas of "natural contemplation" and mysticism "without grace." Meantime, a working understanding is needed, if only to avoid tripping up on matters of secondary moment. In any case, it is characteristic of the mystic's writing that it can be read, and even savored, without belief in, or proper theological understanding, of the reality of divine grace.[9]

Briefly, then, *grace* refers to the effective intervention in one's spiritual life of divine forces that one becomes particularly aware of in contemplative prayer and in the mystical state. The term occasionally appears in the plural form, *graces*, which is often set in apposition to the term *gifts*. The sense is that the single effective presence of God differentiates itself into a multiplicity of stimuli on the different levels of the psyche, of which the contemplative gradually becomes aware. In any event, inasmuch as the intervention of grace is made by a divine Other, it is called *supernatural*, an ambiguous and somewhat disturbing use of language that we shall have to put up with for the time being. Finally, *faith* signifies one's existential and also doctrinal acceptance of God's gracious "coming" or "inworking," as Ruusbroec puts it.

With that, we may turn our attention to the three phases of the life of prayer.

The Active Life: Going out to Meet the Other

In the first phase of prayer life, one employs all of one's faculties, lower and higher, in the ordinary way. One focuses the senses, the heart, and the imagination on the contents of the Christian message. One recalls the life and passion of Jesus, stirs up images and feelings that inflame one's longing for God. In a word, this first phase is one of meditating and aspiring for a meeting with the divine Other. The intellect reasons about divine truth, the will submits itself to the divine will; the memory recollects the actions of mind and heart into a single desire that only God can satisfy.

At some point in the midst of this activity, one awakens to the realization that all this busyness does not end in real *contact* with the object of one's

---

[8] This question has also been touched upon above. Note in particular the striking text about the "secret friends" who always have to be "faithful servants." See chapter 3, note 9 and its corresponding quotation in the text, page 51.

[9] This does not mean that grace and faith do not matter, or matter only very little to Ruusbroec and to readers who wish fully to enjoy his account of meeting the divine Other. That is why it is a serious gap in our presentation of the Brabant mystic that the essential role Jesus Christ plays in his experience, and which he brings forth so beautifully, does not come out here.

aspirations. Without ever losing the assurance that one is always united to God in faith and trust, one senses the absence of a personal presence. There is no perceptual response, nothing to taste or see or feel, but only a collection of "images" of the Other. The more one strains to focus one's power on God alone, the more the images multiply and obstruct.

At this point one has reached the end of one's tether in the active life. One has gone out to meet the Other, but there is no Other in experience:

> ...he does not feel that he is resting in God above all virtues. And therefore he possesses One whom he does not know. For the One whom he seeks in virtues and in manifold modes, Him he possesses within himself, above intention and above virtues and above all modes.[10]

If one would go further and "elevate" oneself beyond this impasse, one must

> go in from the activities to their ultimate reason, and from the signs to the truth. Thus he becomes master over his works...and he enters the inner life.[11]

If one does not dare to take that step, then one remains forever an "outward person," as we read a few lines earlier.

The culmination of this initial stage is what Ruusbroec calls *ontmoet* or "meeting." Not only is this term the key to the entire *Espousals* from the first page to the last; it is the heart of the mystical experience he has described in some ten other works. Everything he has written, literally everything, hinges on this notion of meeting. We read in Book Two of *The Spiritual Espousals*:

> For all our inward spiritual seeing...and all our virtuous going-out...all tend toward the meeting and union with Christ our Bridegroom, for He is our eternal rest and the end and reward of all our labor.

He prepares his description with the general structure of meeting:

> You well know that every meeting is a gathering of two persons who come from diverse places which are opposed to and separate from each other.

And speaking of the encounter with Christ, he adds:

> Christ comes into us from within outwards, and we come to Him from without inwards. And therefore a spiritual meeting must take place here.[12]

---

[10] *Opera omnia* III.b.732–6.

[11] *Opera omnia* III.b.1602–5.

[12] *Opera omnia* III.b.1387–96.

Turning back to the concluding words of Book One, we see the underlying opposition that is assumed to exist between the soul and God:

> We should also rest upon the One and in the One whom we intend and love, more than upon all the messengers which He sends, namely, His gifts. The soul should also rest in God above all the enrichments and the presents that it can send by its messengers. The messengers of the soul are intention, love, and desire; these bear all good works and all virtuousness to God. Above all this, the soul should rest in its Beloved above all multiplicity.[13]

This opposition, however, is only a starting point. Its static simplicity ends when movement "from diverse places" begins. Each of the two partners of the encounter as well as the bond that will unite them is subject to change and differentiation. The soul's reality shows itself to be a manifold composed of "us" at the innermost level and, closer to the exterior, our "presents" and the "messengers" that bear them. The reality of the One is also complex insofar as it is expressed in a multiplicity of "gifts." And the relation that gathers soul and God together is composite insofar as it contains rest and intention. This latter point is worth pausing on for a moment. For Ruusbroec, one offers gifts in order to reach out to the other, but in so doing gives oneself *in* the gifts. Thus the soul that recognizes the gifts as having come from the divine Other must somehow get beyond the gifts to the giver, but at the same time receive the gifts as the self-expression of the One. This is why the "rest" of the recipient needs to recognize the "intention" behind them and also to return that intention by good works of one's own.

Ruusbroec's final description of the active life treats the transition from the non-mystical to the mystical way of prayer. It begins with a person at the height of active life and shows this same interplay of resting and intending:

> The person...who offers all his life and all his works to God's honor and to God's praise and is intent on God and loves Him above all things, will frequently be touched in his desire (*gherenen in sire begheerten*) to see, to know, to understand who this Bridegroom, Christ, is: for his sake He became man and labored in love until death...; (He gave) bodily sustenance, interior consolation and sweetness and countless gifts according to every mode they are needed. When a person considers this, he becomes overwhelmingly moved to see and to know Christ his Bridegroom as He is in Himself; even though he knows Him in His works, that, he thinks, is not sufficient.[14]

---

[13] *Opera omnia* III.a.809–14.

[14] *Opera omnia* III.a.826–36.

At the height of the active life, one is no longer satisfied with the intermediaries (the "gifts") that come between the soul and its intended. There wells up a yearning to break through to the Giver:

> Even though he knows Him in His works, that, he thinks, is not sufficient.

But what must the active person do when touched in desire? Ruusbroec signals a twofold path. First,

> he should do as the publican Zacchaeus did, who desired to see Jesus and who He was (*begheerde te siene wie hi ware*). He should run ahead of the whole crowd, that is, multiplicity of creatures; they make us little and short so that we cannot see God. And he should climb up the tree of faith.... This tree has twelve branches, namely, the twelve articles. The lowest ones speak of God's humanity.... The top of this tree speaks of the divinity, of threeness of Persons and of oneness of God's nature. It is to this oneness that a person should hold fast on the top of the tree.... Here comes Jesus, and sees that man and addresses him in the light of faith: (telling him) that He, according to His divinity, is incommensurable and incomprehensible, and inaccessible and unfathomable, and surpassing all created light and all finite comprehension. This is the highest knowledge of God that a person may have in the active life: that he recognize, in the light of faith, that God is incomprehensible and unknowable.[15]

The twelve articles of the Christian faith[16] are the guide for human intelligence to come as near as possible to God Himself. And what is the highest knowledge of God in the active life? That he is "incomprehensible and unknowable." The apophatic comment, needless to say, will not stay the pen of Ruusbroec from continuing to speak of the divine Other as Bridegroom. In any case, when desire has been touched, there is a second step involved:

> In this light Christ speaks to that man's longing (*begheerten*): "Come down quickly, for today I must dwell in thy house." This hasty descent is nothing else than a flowing-down with longing and with love (*met*

---

[15] *Opera omnia* III.a.836–51.

[16] The twelve articles of faith is the Nicaea-Constantinople *Symbolum*, that is, the Nicene Creed used as a confession of faith in the Catholic Mass to this day. That Jan van Ruusbroec, who can hardly be labeled a "minor mystic," attaches such importance to the doctrinal aspect of faith is all the more remarkable given that so many today are bent on insisting that the "great mystics" do not care for religious tenets or transcend them. For further details about Ruusbroec's view of faith, see my Introduction to *The Christian Faith*, in *Opera omnia* X.347–50, where it is also pointed out that the mystic retains faith in doctrine even after having reached the highest level of experience, namely the "life of contemplation."

begherten ende met minnen) in the abyss of the Godhead which no understanding can reach in created light. But where intellect remains outside, there longing and love go in. When the soul thus inclines itself with love and intention unto God above all that it understands, it is then that it rests and dwells in God and God in it.[17]

The opposition is suggestive: desire descends, intelligence ascends. The twofold dynamic of ascent and descent is central to Ruusbroec's description of mystical union. For the moment it is enough to keep the image as graphic as he intended it. Climbing upwards toward the divine Other I am under my own power and remain myself. Going down I lose myself. I "flow down," liquefied, as it were. Only in this way can I dare to enter into the unfamiliar "abyss." In Ruusbroec's arresting adage,

where intellect remains outside, there longing and love go in.

Ruusbroec dwells on this in more detail in describing the consequences of the mystical "touch":

...even though reason and intelligence fail in the face of the divine brightness and remain outside, before the door, nevertheless, the faculty of loving wishes to go further; for, like the understanding, it has been compelled and invited, but it is blind and it wants enjoyment; and enjoyment lies more in tasting and in feeling than in understanding. This is why love wants to move on, where intelligence remains outside.[18]

In this context, there is no better explanation than Hadewijch's image of the "two eyes" of the soul, reason and love:

Reason cannot see God except in what he is not; love rests not except in what he is. Reason has its secure paths, by which it proceeds. Love experiences failure (*ghebreken*), but failure advances it more than reason. Reason advances toward what God is, by means of what God is not. Love sets aside what God is not and rejoices that it fails (*ghebrect*) in what God is. Reason has more sense of moderation than love, but love has more sweetness of bliss than reason. These two, however, are of great mutual help one to the other; for reason instructs love, and love enlightens reason. When reason abandons itself to love's wish, and love consents to be forced and held within the bounds of reason, they can accomplish a very great work. This no one can learn except by experience.[19]

---

[17] *Opera omnia* III.a.851–7.

[18] *Opera omnia* III.b.1308–13.

[19] I will be borrowing here from my *Hadewijch. Schrijfster Begijn Mystica* (Averbode: Altiora,

When the soul looks at God, there is a twofold dynamic, or rather a casting of two different looks, a reasoning one and a desiring one. When the active, non-mystical person tries to see God, each of the spiritual eyes has its function to perform. The approach of God by means of reason is marked out as follows: "Reason cannot see God except in what he is not." The point of this sentence lies in the word *is*, which will appear five more times in this passage.[20] The person who, by the gift of charity, already participates in God's being, wants to fully experience what God is in himself. But between what God is and that which a human being may comprehend of him—may come to see with the eye of reason—there is a yawning gap that can never in this way be bridged.

The approach towards the Other through desire is said to "rejoice that it fails in what God is." The failure is not one of having done too little. Quite the contrary, in desiring the Other one is led to do too much. Without the inhibitions of reason, one advances so far in the direction of God as to become enchanted by what lies beyond one's grasp. The "failure" that drives one out of oneself is thus for Hadewijch and Ruusbroec a positive term. It is a moment of liberation that opens one to what lies beyond oneself and ushers in the "sweetness of bliss." Reason introduces moderation and brings with it the security of one step following the other in measured pace. It approaches the Other only inasmuch as comprehension allows. Love is so overwhelmed by what it cannot grasp that it trips over itself.

Only after explaining the normal progress of reason and love does Hadewijch indicate how they work in the mystic. In the early stages of prayer life, the two eyes of the soul see differently. Only later do they focus together so that "reason instructs love and love enlightens reason." Though love is more fundamental and its impetuosity more productive, this does not mean that reason is eliminated. Just as the opening of the second eye brings depth of perspective, so does reason insure that love is "kept within bounds."

When Ruusbroec speaks of love as "blind," he is hardly thinking in the cliché of modern usage. Love makes it possible to perceive the divine Other. It is blind only to the calculating eye of reason. Led by the blinded eye of love, reason finds its way to God. And with that, prayer has unfolded into a simple, unadorned longing for the Unknowable.

1989), 91–9. Hadewijch's passage appears in Letter 18:80–105, and is all the more significant as the Flemish beguine translated it herself from William of Saint Thierry's *Liber de natura et dignitate amoris*, albeit not without integrating it in her own description of mystical experience. The image of the "eye of the soul" is as ancient as Plato and Plotinos. Gregory of Nyssa has taken it over in his usual Christian-creative manner. See my article "Gregorius van Nyssa (ca. 335–ca. 395): De mens is nooit voltooid," in H. Berghs, ed., *Denkwijzen 4, Een inleiding in het denken van Plato, Aristoteles, Plotinus, Gregorius van Nyssa* (Leuven: Acco, 1989), 93–120.

[20] See chapter 3, page 55.

The Inner Life: Yearning for the Other

To "flow down into the abyss of the Godhead" inaugurates the second principal stage of the life of prayer. This "turning inwards"—or more precisely, the being-drawn-inwards—replaces the dynamic of activity with one of passivity. It is not a question of disciplined, self-induced introversion. As it is put in a passage cited earlier,[21] the soul is "drowsy, sleepy, and dull," and the call of the Bridegroom is heard "when one least expects and awaits it."

From here on in, it is God's "inworking" in the soul that does the most important work, including a heightened concentration of the psyche on all its levels:

> Out of this swift movement by God comes a...gathering of all the faculties within and without in unity of spirit, in the bond of love.[22]

Though touched at one's innermost core, one first senses at the surface the working of the Other "from within outwards":

> And God produces this spiritual stirring in us first of all, before all gifts; nevertheless, it is the very last thing to be properly recognized and savored by us.[23]

Ruusbroec distinguishes three phases in the life of yearning, three "comings of Christ," that are felt as ever deeper and more integrating states of awareness. Here the unfolding of the life of prayer shows its direct connection with the general psychological structure we saw in his profile of the human.

The first awareness of the Bridegroom's presence takes place in the lower faculties and in the "heart." The prayer that unfolds here remains affective in nature. Ruusbroec's masterly description of the "sensible" gifts that accompany these first mystical moments, corresponding to what we might call today a psychosomatic reaction, defies simple paraphrase. We may note only that this first phase culminates, paradoxically, in an experience of the Bridegroom's absence.[24]

---

[21] See above, page 55.

[22] *Opera omnia* III.b.128–30.

[23] *Opera omnia* III.b.1819–21.

[24] This is the experience that since John of the Cross has been known as the "night of the senses." Hadewijch refers to it in frequent and gripping descriptions of the "winter" that is a permanent feature of her experience. In Ruusbroec, who has the image of night and darkness, the same experience is present, but it does not occupy the same position of prominence. In addition to the image of the soul passing from the yearning to the contemplative life, there is its image as experiencing "darkness, bareness, and nothingness," which follows a bit later in the text of this chapter (page 154). For a moving description of spiritual abandonment, see Wiseman, 195–7.

The second visit of the Bridegroom engages the higher faculties. A single bright light streaming out of the hitherto unrecognized "fountain in the unity of spirit" floods the memory, the intellect, and the will until one becomes a single mass of desire. And this "inworking" in the spiritual faculties impels one further inwards in search of the source.

As one follows these three streams of light to their source, overcome by "burning love and the total impress of all faculties," one senses

an inward stirring, or touch (*gherinen*) of Christ by His divine brightness in the innermost (depths) of our spirit...the grace of God...is situated in the unity of our spirit like a fountain, and it wells in the same unity whence it arises, just like a living vein welling out of the living ground of God's richness, where neither fidelity nor grace can ever be wanting. And this is the touch which I mean. And the creature undergoes and suffers this touch, for here is the unification of the higher faculties in the unity of spirit, above the multiplicity of all virtues. And here, no one works but God alone....[25]

This is what Ruusbroec calls the opening of the "simple eye."[26] Intellect and will are brought together in their common home ground, the unity of spirit. They are no longer distinct faculties but work as a single receptivity. Ruusbroec's terminology is vividly passive here, but it is not a gift bestowed on faculties grown lax or idle:

In the unity of spirit, in which this vein wells, one is above activity and above reason, but not without reason; for the enlightened reason and especially the faculty of loving, feels this touch, and reason can neither comprehend nor understand the mode or manner, how or what this touch might be.[27]

The touch of the Other does not induce an incomprehensible paralysis. Rather, the spiritual faculties are excited to a greater activity than ever before. We have already seen what this means for reason.[28] Here is a composite picture of what Ruusbroec says happens to the will:

Here begins an eternal hunger which will never be filled. It is an inward avidity and craving on the part of the faculty of loving and of the created

[25] *Opera omnia* III.b.1260–72.

[26] *The Mirror* notes that the divine "resplendence...so blinds the eyes of reason that they have to give way before this incomprehensible light. However, that simple eye which dwells above reason in the ground of our understanding is always open" (Wiseman, 238; see also 244).

[27] *Opera omnia* III.b.1273–7.

[28] See above, page 54, note 16 and its corresponding text.

spirit for an uncreated good. And since the spirit desires enjoyment and it is compelled and invited thereto by God, it always wants to fulfill that (desire). See, here begins an eternal voracity and insatiable craving in an eternal failing.... God's inward stirring and touch make us hungry and make us crave, for the Spirit of God spurs our spirit: the oftener the touch, the stronger the hunger and the craving. And this is the life of love in its supreme activity.... God's touch in us insofar as we feel it, and our loving craving, are both creaturely, and therefore they can grow and increase as long as we live.[29]

But what exactly is the object of this gathering of the faculties? Not God in himself (this occurs only in the final stage, the "contemplative life"), but God as effectively present in the human "essence":

For this [touch] is a divine activity, and the origin and irruption of all grace and of all gifts and the last intermediary between God and the creature. Above this touch, in the still essence of the spirit, there hovers an incomprehensible brightness, and that is the supreme Trinity, from Whom this touch comes. There God lives and reigns in the spirit and the spirit in God.[30]

Thus does one follow the way inwards to its end. But this inward-turning is always accompanied by a movement in the opposite direction. For all of its emphasis on introversion, *The Spiritual Espousals* is replete with references to the mystic's being driven outwards, such as the following:

For those who are most simple are the most quiet and the most totally peaceful in themselves, and they are the most deeply sunken away in God, and they are the most utterly enlightened in understanding, and the most utterly manifold in good works, and the most utterly common in outflowing love.[31]

THE CONTEMPLATIVE LIFE: SEEING GOD WITH GOD

The experience of God in the life of yearning remains an inner event. The divine Other as such continues to elude the seeker. For Ruusbroec, a small number of mystics are able to go further to "a life of contemplating God in divine light, after the mode of God."[32]

[29] *Opera omnia* III.b.1314–39.

[30] *Opera omnia* III.b.1277–81.

[31] *Opera omnia* III.b.1767–71.

[32] *Opera omnia* III.b.1376–7.

How does the mystic who has come to the end of the yearning life proceed to the contemplative life? Once again, the passage begins with a sense of having reached one's limits and being left staring into an apparently empty abyss:

> And out of the unity of God shines forth a simple light in him, and this light shows him darkness, bareness, and nothingness.[33]

It is in this darkness, not a blindness but a temporary blinding, that the highest form of prayer can occur:

> In the abyss of this darkness in which the loving spirit has died to itself, there begin the revelation of God and eternal life.[34]

Here "the spirit is to contemplate God with God, without intermediary" and "God is apprehended and seen with God."[35] As in the first two phases of mystical experience, it is a question of awareness—"they see and feel and find," as Ruusbroec says.[36] The contemplative perceives being one with the Son of God who is coming to birth within. This indwelling of the Son is a light by which one can see anew:

> And without cease, [the simple being of his spirit] becomes the very brightness which it receives.[37]

and is also the reality that one sees by that light:

> transformed and at one with that same light by which they see and which they see.[38]

Here being is seeing. But as there is no son without a father, so the mystic who experiences "a new birth and a new enlightenment" also discovers something else:

> For we find indeed that the bosom of the Father is our own ground and our origin, in which we begin our life and our being.[39]

One is taken up experientially and full-aware into the inner life of God, in the "loving meeting" of Father, Son, and Spirit.

[33] *Opera omnia* III.b.1878–80.

[34] *Opera omnia* III.c.55–6.

[35] *Opera omnia* III.c.44, 93.

[36] *Opera omnia* III.c.149.

[37] *Opera omnia* III.c.63–4.

[38] *Opera omnia* III.c.156–7.

[39] *Opera omnia* III.c.136–7.

At the risk of repeating what has been stated already so often, I conclude my treatment of the life of prayer by observing that even in this most exceptional state, the mystic remains as human as ever:

And this is the noblest and most profitable contemplation to which one can come in this life. For in this contemplation, one remains sovereignly master of himself and free, and in each loving turning-inward, can grow in sublimity of life beyond all that one can understand. For he remains master of himself in inner practice and in virtues.[40]

[40] *Opera omnia* III.c.160–5.

8

Mystically One with God

In the preceding chapter I noted two features of Ruusbroec's writing: the occasional disruption of an otherwise orderly exposition by wandering thoughts that seem to move in a spiraling pattern, and the use of a parallelism consisting of syntactically equivalent but semantically contrasting elements. This latter will feature dominantly in our treatment of what it is to be mystically one with God.

"WORK AND REST ARE CONTRARIES"

The first thing that strikes the reader of Ruusbroec's accounts of mystical union is the sharp and persistent opposition he sets up between the elements that make it up. He never leaves any doubt about their distinction, nor does he ever confuse them one with the other. No matter how deeply he enters into analyzing the composition of the elements, he never compromises this radical duality. We do well to take seriously his choice of the term *contrary*. For example, in *The Sparkling Stone*, after affirming that the state of the accomplished mystic is "only one life," he goes on:

> But it is contrary and twofold according to experience (*contrarie ende tweevuldigh van ghevoelne*), for poor and rich, hungry and replete, working and at rest (*werkende ende ledich*), these are contraries indeed.[1]

The opposition could hardly be clearer. Everything Ruusbroec wrote illustrates this again and again. To cite only one more example, in book two of *The Spiritual Espousals*, the second element of being one, namely "rest," is taken up as it is experienced at the height of the "inner life":

> ...the spirit sinks away from itself into enjoyable rest (*ghebrukelijcker rasten*), for the rest is without mode and fathomless (*sonder wise ende sonder gront*). And we cannot know it but by itself, that is, by rest, for were we to know and understand it, then it would fall into mode and into mea-

[1] *Opera omnia* X.488–90.

sure (*in wisen ende in maten*), and then it could not suffice for us, but rest would become eternal unrest.[2]

Within this general pattern of contraries-in-opposition, we may distinguish three steps to the process of becoming mystically one: activity, transition, and rest. As we are about to enter into the most original aspect of Ruusbroec's exposition of prayer life, a word of caution is in order. Throughout the tightly-woven text of his rich and varied descriptive material runs the unmistakable golden thread of Ruusbroec's own experiential insights. For the sake of the argument being pursued in these pages, I shall have to content myself with a crude unravelling of the fabric of his writings. But even this will only finally have achieved its purpose if it persuades the reader to return to the original texts.

Working — Werken

The chief trait of the second stage of prayer life, as we saw, is a passivity that is not a blessed paralysis but an intensification of work in response to the felt "inworking" (*inwerken*) of God. From this stage on, the action of the contemplative is mainly a *re*action. For instance, the "first coming" of the divine "in the heart and in the unity of all the bodily faculties" sets up a clear opposition:

> For this coming stirs and acts in our lowest part....This impulse of God within gives and takes; it makes rich and poor, prosperous and blissful; it produces hope and despair; it makes heat and cold. The gifts and the activity which occur here in opposites are ineffable for any tongue.[3]

In Ruusbroec's view all this inner activity, from its most affective moments to its most spiritual, rests on the one fundamental event of the "touch." This touch, together with the reaction it provokes, is what Ruusbroec calls "union," *eeninghe*. It is the experience of one "meeting" the divine Person as the person one is. At the outset of *The Sparkling Stone*, Ruusbroec summarizes the "inner life" in three points. I cite the last of them:

> If man can raise himself up freely to his God in his inner practice, unhindered by images, and if he aims only at the honor of God, he shall taste the goodness of God and experience the true union with God inside (*eeninghe met gode*). And it is in such a union that the interior, spiritual life is perfected. For it is out of this union (*ute deser eeninghen*) that desire is always stirred and aroused anew to new inner works, and by working the spirit ascends to a new union (*in een nuwe vereenighen*). And in

[2] *Opera omnia* III.b.1862–65.

[3] *Opera omnia* III.b.148–53.

this way both activity and union are renewed again and again *(vernuwet werc ende eeninghe altoes)*.[4]

Rather than try to dissect Ruusbroec's description of union, we would do better to focus on his words and images. To begin with, one notices the dynamic involved in the word *eeninghe*. It is not a static condition but a process. This will become still more apparent when we come to the other aspect of being one, namely the actual "unity" or *eenicheit*.

Furthermore, one is struck by the repetitive use of the word *new*. There appears to be no end to the union. It is not a matter of a process that goes on forever and ever without any hope of succeeding, but of something that starts over again and again, each time more intensely than before. Union is not unfulfilled but rather incessantly fulfilled; it is not permanently frustrated but continually renewed. On more than one occasion Ruusbroec characterizes this by the image of the "embrace." For instance, in *The Mirror* we read:

> Insofar as we embrace and touch (*kussen ende gherinen*) each other, we feel a duality which does not allow us to remain in ourselves.[5]

Thus "union" implies both reciprocity and difference. Embracing is bliss, but always a "measured" bliss, limited by my ability to assimilate it. In *The Spiritual Tabernacle* Ruusbroec calls it

> a loving embracing (*minleec omhelsen*) at the height of our union (*eninghen*) between God and ourselves, with which our love and all our works are crowned. And this is the height in which our measured bliss consists.[6]

We may now turn to descriptive passages focused on this experience of *eeninghe*. A first passage, from *The Sparkling Stone*, speaks of the "friends of God" as impersonating union without achieving unity:

> But the friends possess their inner life in a self-conscious manner (*met eyghenscap*), because they choose clinging to God in love as the best and the very highest end they can or want to reach. And that is why they cannot pass through themselves or their works in an imageless bareness for they are caught up with themselves and their works in the manner of images and intermediaries. And even if they experience union (*eeninghe*)

---

[4] *Opera omnia* X.47–54.

[5] Wiseman, 240. In *The Spiritual Espousals* the same word appears in a trinitarian context: "For the Father gives Himself in the Son, and the Son in the Father, in an eternal (mutual) complacency and in a loving embrace.... And this is the active meeting of the Father and of the Son, in which we are lovingly embraced..." (*Opera omnia* III.c.200–6).

[6] *Werken* II.355:12–15. A few pages further it is said that enjoyable love is situated "beyond the loving embrace that is between us and God" (361:13–14).

with God as they cling to him in love, they will always find a distinction and an otherness between themselves and God within that union (*onderscheet ende anderheit inder eeninghen*). For they neither know nor love the simple passing over into bareness and modelessness. And therefore their highest inner life always remains bound by reason and manner.... And even if they feel themselves lifted up to God in a strong fire of love, they always keep their own self (*eyghenheit haers selfs*) and are not consumed or burnt to nothing in the unity of love (*in eenicheit der minnen*).[7]

I cannot dwell here on the semantic game that Ruusbroec is playing in his criticisms here,[8] but at least the relevant phrases bear singling out. The activity of the friends is spoken of as "standing upright," "clinging to God," "raised up to God," and "burning." The self-attachment that still prevails in their union shows up in his phrasing also: "in a self-conscious manner," "they choose," "caught up with themselves," "bound by reason and manner," and "keep their own self." And finally, the sense of an activity that drives a wedge between oneself and God is captured in the terms "intermediaries" and "a distinction and an otherness."

In *The Mirror*, Ruusbroec again focuses on union, which he describes significantly as a "living union." The following passage enlarges on the vocabulary of union by introducing the positive terms "active," "encounter," and "like God":

The living union (*levende eeninghe*) which we experience is active (*werkelec*) and is always being renewed between ourselves and God. Insofar as we embrace and touch each other, we feel a duality (*anderheit*) which does not allow us to remain in ourselves. Although we are above reason, we are not without reason and therefore feel we are both touching and being touched, loving and being loved, and always being renewed and returning to ourselves.... God's touch and our secret, interior striving constitute the last intermediary between ourselves and God, in which we become united (*vereenighen*) with him in a mutual encounter (*ontmoete*) in love.... We therefore always remain standing above reason in our very selfhood (*in ons selfheit*)—imageless, gazing, and striving in incomprehensible richness.

In our own works we always remain like God (*ghelijc*) in the purity of our spirit, for we feel that we are seeing and striving after someone who is different from ourselves (*in een Ander*). It is through this that we are like God (*ghelijc*). In God's works, on the other hand, we undergo

---

[7] *Opera omnia* X.325–38.

[8] See my Introduction to *The Sparkling Stone, Opera omnia* X.22 and notes 19–21.

the action of his Spirit and the transformation wrought by his resplendence and love. There we are above likeness (*boven ghelijc*).[9]

Let us linger for a moment on the expression "like (God)," *ghelijc*. The opposition between "like" and "one" figures frequently in Ruusbroec's phenomenology. We have also seen the importance of the notion of "likeness" (*ghelijckenisse*) in his portrait of the human.[10] Later we will meet the experience of being "like (God)" in his treatment of "natural contemplation." At this stage, the contemplative's active pursuit of "likeness" (unto God) belongs to a state of passivity. It is a *re*action to God's "exacting," *eysschen*:

> For the fruitful unity of God maintains itself above the unification of our faculties and always exacts from us likeness (*eyschet ghelijcheit*) in love and in virtues. And this is why we are touched, every moment anew, so that at every moment we may be newer and more (God)-like in virtues (*nuwer ende ghelijcker*).[11]

Clearly the demand that God makes is not a moral one. Eventually ethics will come into the picture, but it is far from being a matter of obligation from the start. There is no sense of a divine Other whispering mandates to one at prayer, who is then obligated to carry them out or undertake a program of moral self-improvement. If there is any demand being made, it is a function of the sheer presence of the Other as an efficacious "inworking." God's "coming" *is* God's demand. One who has been so touched by this Other can do nothing else than begin to resemble that Other. God's flow is also an ebb; the demand for likeness is part and parcel of the epiphany of the divine.

> This flowing of God always demands a flowing-back, for God is a flowing, ebbing sea, which flows without cease into all his beloved.... And He is ebbing back in again, drawing all those whom He has endowed.... And of some He demands more than they can do. For He shows Himself as so rich and so generous, and so fathomlessly good, and in this manifestation demands love and honor in proportion to His dignity.[12]

As something demanded by the Other, likeness is obviously integral to being one with the Other. And yet to be "like" carries with it the sense of something irremediably partial. It belongs to union, *eeninghe*, but can never of itself evolve naturally into unity, *eenicheit*.

[9] Wiseman, 240–1.

[10] See above, chapter 5, pages 118–20.

[11] *Opera omnia* III.b.1837–40.

[12] *Opera omnia* III.b.986–93.

For at this stage the saints always remain, in grace as well as in glory [in heaven and on earth] a likeness of God (*een ghelijc Goids*). Never can grace or glory be so great as to become incommensurable. And no one may possess unity unless it be with incommensurable love. That is why no likeness (*ghelijc*) can obtain it (unity) and yet remain likeness (*ghelijc bliven*).[13]

What keeps *likeness* from being *unity* is that it assimilates the reality of the other, reducing the difference by imitating it in one's own mode (*wise*). This means that unity will require that one break through one's own modes to become "modeless" (*wiseloes*). One would do wrong to see this as a simple criticism of egocentric manners. It is more radical. Whenever the experience of "being like" the other is part of an encounter of two persons, this experience implies consciousness of a duality, and it is this duality that unity requires one to let go of.

Of course, "perfect" likeness with God, in the sense of a complete assimilation of the divine, is an illusion. The Creator can never be imitated fully by any creature, nor can the love of the divine Person ever be confined within the modes of human love. This is why I said that when the object of "being like" is an absolute Other, one can continue to grow in likeness without end. It is in this incessant growing into this never-achieved likeness that the mystic experiences this divine transcendence as an inexhaustible richness.

I would like to conclude my treatment of the second stage of prayer with a suggestive passage from *The Spiritual Espousals*, where "union" is described as "like (God)." This will provide a natural bridge to the third stage in the description of being one with the divine Other.

And here (the spirit) is like unto God (*ghelijc gode*) through grace and divine love. And since it is (God)-like and it intends and loves God simply, above all gifts, the spirit does not allow itself to be satisfied with likeness (*ghelijcheit*), or with created brightness, for it has a fundamental natural and supernatural inclination towards the unfathomable being from which it has flowed forth. And the unity of the divine being is eternally drawing all likeness into its unity. And therefore the spirit sinks away from itself in enjoyment and floats away into God as in its eternal rest.... And likeness sinks away from itself every moment and dies in God, and becomes one with God and remains one.[14]

[13] *The Realm of Lovers, Werken* I.64:4–9.
[14] *Opera omnia* III.b.1692–1703.

Outdoing Oneself — Hem utewerken

Ruusbroec finds in the activity of the mystic something he calls *hem ute-werken*. Literally an "overworking" or "overdoing," *hem utewerken* describes what happens to the human spirit in crossing over from work to rest and enjoyment. The transition is not a mere shift from activity to inactivity, but an overexertion, a working oneself to the limits in which one so "outdoes oneself" that the subject of the work is in a sense no longer the subject of the rest.

In addition to the term *utewerken*, Ruusbroec also speaks of this transitional dynamic as a *faelgeren* (failing), *ghebreken* (falling short), and *ontbliven* (lacking in). Nuances aside, all these terms point to the same fact: that one is no match for what is being demanded. They each suggest in their own way the sense of an inner deficiency in the contemplative, who is likened to someone trying to gaze upon the sun. For when we try to "peer into the solar disk, our eyes must fail in their operation, and must passively receive the inshining of its rays."[15]

At this stage one is not only aware of the divine demand (*eysschen*), but of our inability to answer it. A passage cited earlier bears repeating here:

> And of some He demands (*eyschet*) more than they can do. For He shows Himself as so rich and generous and so fathomlessly good....[16]

Confronted with such an Other, the contemplative feels not only the limitations of being human but also a sense of "indebtedness." Further, this sense of obligation to return the grace is not moral in nature. Rather, the mystics understand it as a constitutive part of the bridge that leads to the experience of unity. In *The Spiritual Tabernacle*, Ruusbroec offers the following description of this debt:

> But in our activity (*in onsen werken*) we feel ourselves falling short and lacking (*ontblivende*) in all virtues.... For in its activity, love always remains unsated and unappeased, because she feels a debt greater than she is able to repay. Each new paying creates new debts. And love practiced with reason (*in redenen*) exacts more love and works of love than anybody is able to achieve.[17]

This movement back and forth between the gracious Other and the human soul is what brings about the decisive experiential step. As the movement grows in intensity, every payment only brings out more and more one's fail-

---

[15] *Opera omnia* III.b.1828–30.

[16] *Opera omnia* III.b.990–2.

[17] *Werken* II.288:28, 289:6.

ure to match the exigencies of divine Abundance. It is precisely here that the spirit is brought to *hem utewerken*, to "outdo itself." Its activity is strained to the limits and yet still further provoked, until at last the contemplative comes to feel "reduced to nothing in love "(*te nieute in minnen*):

> And the more inner and nobler (the spirit) is, the more quickly it must exhaust its activity (*hem uut werket*), being reduced to nothing in love (*te nieute in minnen*), and then it falls back into a new activity. And this is the life of heaven. The voracious spirit always imagines that it is eating and swallowing God, but by God's touch it is itself constantly being swallowed, and it fails in all its activity (*faliert in al sijn werken*), and itself becomes love (*wert selve minne*), above all activity.[18]

Ruusbroec calls all this restless readiness to exhaust oneself, "active love," *werkeleke minne*. Furthermore, in an obvious reference to the structure of the psyche, he speaks of the kind of love it prepares for as an "essential love" (*weseleke minne*) that is "above all activity." Thus the idea of outdoing oneself indicates a shift away from the activity of the psychological faculties to the unity of the spirit; away from the realm of reason and its modes to one of essence and modelessness. In *The Tabernacle* the change is described like this:

> You should also realize that there is a great difference between our sensible longing or desire, which always remains bound to reason (*in redene*), and the love of our spirit, which leads us beyond reason and unites us with God. For the inward love of our spirit—that is, modeless love (*minne-sonder-wise*) exhausting itself without end—makes a loveless spirit (*minneloes*)—that is, a spirit annihilated in love (*te nieute in minnen*). For in the passing over of outdoing oneself the spirit becomes love itself (*wert de geest selve-minne*)—that is, essential love (*weseleke minne*) in the ground of its unity.[19]

The more one reads of Ruusbroec, the more one recognizes him as a master at weaving different levels of description together. The phenomenological level (describing how two persons meet), the psychological level (describing where and how events occur in human consciousness), and the anthropological level (describing relations between the Creator and human beings), are interconnected in such a way as to shed light on each other. The interplay between active love and enjoyable love, between faculties and essence and the God who "is always in the essence of the soul,"[20] makes for a rich and vibrant tapestry.

[18] Opera omnia III.b.1364–9.

[19] *Werken* II.65:22–30.

[20] *Opera omnia* I.226–7.

Ruusbroec was particularly attracted to images of heat and fire. I cite two examples of this imagery—if indeed, it is only imagery. The first appears in *The Twelve Beguines*, where he likens the initial stage of being one to oil that foams and bubbles as it heats up, or to fresh coal that sparks and crackles when first thrown into the fire. So, too, does the contemplative's self-consciousness draw attention to what it is doing or what is being done to it. In describing the move to union and unity, Ruusbroec uses the same verb *verberren* in different forms to show distinction and relation:

> ...then the Holy spirit bestows on our spirit an eternal brilliance that is both light and fire. Our spirit becomes like oil bubbling in the fire of the love of God. So long as the oil is foaming and crackling and bubbling, there is still un-likeness (*onghelijc*). But when the fire has consumed and burned up all un-likeness (*al onghelijc verbernt hevet*), the oil becomes pure and hotter than hot, and it is still and immobile like the fire.... The greatest heat is there where our spirit is burning (*berrent*), and hotter than hot when it burns up (*verberrent*) and undergoes transformation by God. But where it has been burnt up (*verberrent es*) and is one spirit with God, there it is idle, essential love (*ledeghe weselijcke minne*).[21]

A second image comes from *The Sparkling Stone*:

> The eternal summoning inward by God's unity creates an eternal burning of love (*berren van minnen*) in the spirit. But where the spirit pays that debt continuously it is burnt up inside forever (*een eewich verberren*). For in the transformation of that unity all spirits fail (*falieren*) in their activity and they only feel a total burning up (*al verberen*) in the single unity of God. And no man can experience or possess this single unity of God if he does not stand before him in brightness unmeasurable and in love that is above reason and without manner. In this standing before God the spirit feels within itself an eternal burning in love (*berren in minnen*). And in that fire of love it finds neither beginning nor end and it feels itself one with that burning of love. The spirit always burns in itself (*berrende in hem selven*) for its love is eternal. And it always feels that it is burnt up in love (*verberrende in minnen*) for it is drawn into the transformation of God's unity. (Where) the spirit burns in love (*daer die gheest berrent in minnen*) it will find a distinction and an otherness between itself and God when it examines itself. But (where) it is burnt up (*daer hi verberent*) it is onefold and there is no distinction left.[22]

---

[21] *The Twelve Beguines, Werken* IV.102:25–103:8.

[22] *Opera omnia* X.87–100.

Two final passages may be cited to conclude the description of the contemplative's shifting from union to unity. In each, we see a reciprocity between the divine and the human partners. In the first, this relationship is expressed as a kind of vertical movement up and down. In the second, it is presented as a tete-à-tete of two persons at an equal level. The first text, from *The Seven Rungs*, reads:

> Our heavenly Father is voracious and generous.... He generously gives his grace, his gifts, and his presents, and he demands of everyone in particular that he responds with thanksgiving and with praising and with all good works.... But above all works and practice of virtues, our heavenly Father shows to his chosen beloved that he is not only voracious and generous in demanding and in giving, but that he is himself voracity and generosity, for he wants to give us himself and all he is, and he wants that we in return give ourselves with all we are.[23]

The second passage, no doubt a high point in the literary work of Ruusbroec, comes from *The Spiritual Espousals*:

> In this storm of love, two spirits contend: the Spirit of God and our spirit. God, through the Holy Spirit, inclines Himself towards us, and thereby we are touched in love (*in minnen gherenen*). And by God's operation and the faculty of loving, our spirit presses into and inclines itself towards God, and thereby God is touched (*wert god gherenen*). From these two, there arises the strife of love: in the depths of the encounter and in that innermost and most intense visit, each spirit is wounded the most by love. These two spirits...flash and shine each into the other, and each shows the other its face. This makes each spirit continually crave for the other with love. Each exacts of the other that which he is (*eyschet den anderen dat hi es*), and each offers and invites the other to that which he is (*dat hi es*). This makes the lovers flow away (into each other). God's touch and His gifts, our loving craving and our giving in return, keep love steadfast.
>
> This flowing out and flowing back cause the fountain of love to overflow. Thus God's touch and our love's craving become one single love. Here a person is so possessed by love that he must forget himself and God, and he knows nothing but love. Thus the spirit is burned up in the fire of love, and it goes so deeply into God's touch that it is overcome in all its craving and is reduced to nothing in all its acts (*gheet te niete in al sijn werken*); and it must exhaust all its activity (*werket hem ute*), and it becomes itself love (*wert selve minne*), above all devotedness,

[23] *The Seven Rungs, Werken* III.258:33–259:15.

and it possesses the innermost (core) of its created being, above all virtues, where all creaturely works begin and end. This is love in itself (*minne in haer selven*), foundation and ground of all virtues.[24]

"*Resting*" — *Rasten*

The term Ruusbroec most commonly employs to indicate the second aspect of being one is "resting." This is the stage at which the activity of "working" yields its expected result: rest in the Other. This state is spoken of alternatively as "enjoyment" (*ghebruken*), a term whose original flavor is that of a man and woman "possessing" each other.[25] Indeed, the term "possess" (*besitten*) is also used to express unity, as are "blessedness" (*salicheit*) and "satisfaction" (*satheit*). A passage from *The Seven Enclosures*, which serves almost as a glossary of Ruusbroec's vocabulary here, treats the highest enclosure, "which surpasses all enclosures," as

> above all activity (*werke*): a quieted rest in inactivity (*raste in ledicheiden*); above all holy living and practice of virtue: simple blessedness (*salicheit*); and above hunger and thirst, love and longing for God: eternal satiety (*sadheit*).[26]

A passage from *The Sparkling Stone* underlines the sense of "possession" and specifies its meaning:

> ...once we have gone out of ourselves and possess God (*gode besitten*) in immersion of loving. For if we possess God in immersion of loving, that is: lost to ourselves, God is our own (*es god onse eyghen*) and we are his own (*wij sijn sijn eyghen*) and we sink away from ourselves forever, with-

---

[24] *Opera omnia* III.b.1340–59. The paragraphing has been adjusted to indicate the crucial transition.

[25] Despite the more ethereal connotations of the word *enjoy*, even today it retains in some Flemish dialects the ancient meaning of sexual intercourse. Ruusbroec himself uses *ghebruken* in its first, sensory sense: "When one eats and drinks not from being hungry...but only in order to please and satisfy one's nature, then one feels an enjoyable sinking away (*ghebrukelec ontsinken*) in the food..."(*The Spiritual Tabernacle, Werken* II.214:19–23). The same observation applies to that very mystical term *gherinen*, "to touch." One of the ways in which unchastity is "fed" consists in "touching (*gherijnne*) in any manner unseemly." And the reason why is all but far-fetched: "For touching (*gherinen*) and all such things that heat a person most are always more grave and sinful than to see or to speak and other things that heat less and move less" (211:13, 23–26). Heat, as we have seen, plays an important part in the description of the mystic's experience. Again, it would be a mistake to spiritualize it altogether. In any case, our spiritual author does not go for abstraction: "And by means of the grace of God and our good will, we shall heat our inwardness towards God and good works, the way we have been lusty and hot in sins. And with this hot lust (*heter ghelost*) we shall come before God..." (242:24–8).

[26] *Opera omnia* II.615–18.

out return, in our possession that is God (*in ons eyghendoem dat god es*).[27]

At this point I would like to single out three other passages, each of which illustrates this second aspect of being one in its own way. In the first, we find the characteristic expression "above union with God in unity." This unity is viewed as the state that combines "blessedness" and "idleness" in an experience of "no difference." In unity, the person at prayer is

> in a state of eternal enjoyment—that is, above works and virtues in a state of blessed [idleness] (*een salegh ledegh sijn*), and above union with God in unity, where no one can work except God alone....There, however, we are above reason and also without reason in a state of clear knowing, in which we feel no difference (*gheen onderscheet*) between ourselves and God, for we have been breathed forth in his love above and beyond ourselves and all orders of being. There we have no demands or desires and we neither give nor take. There there is only a blessed and [idle] being (*een salegh ledegh wesen*), the crown and the essential reward of all holiness and virtue.[28]

The second passage returns to the images of burning coal and boiling oil. Here, unity is located in the process of love as the phase at which love is "appeased" and in which the experience of "no difference" is such that "nothing else can come in it."

> This unity (*eenicheit*) cannot be found or felt by any but those who outdo themselves (*utewerken*) to the point of love appeased.... Appeased love is above everything. It is occupied with itself and nothing else. It is the perfect enrichment of all the virtues. Glowing like burning coals, it is beyond the heat of burning and consumes all matter and all unlikeness by taking it into itself. It is itself the highest degree in love. In it there is neither coming nor going; nor does the passionate quest of love and virtue exist in it any longer. When oil has boiled, burning away and consuming all unlikeness, it is appeased, pure, fiery, and hotter than hot. Appeased love lives in God and God in it: nothing else can come in it.[29]

The third and final passage from *The Spiritual Tabernacle* has Ruusbroec asking "how in this life we can enjoy God and experience blessedness." His answer is that it is possible only by means of an "enjoyable love" situated "above the loving embracement which exists between ourselves and God." For him, this enjoyable love transcends all things. It is "without measure and

---

[27] *Opera omnia* X.502–6.

[28] Wiseman, 246.

[29] *Werken* IV.58:7–22.

without ground, situated above all practice of love." There follows his description of unity:

> Then the loving spirit flows out of itself and melts away in an essential enjoying (*weseleec ghebruken*). This melting away in love is without manner or mode or return, as is the nature of enjoyment. For the spirit dies to itself in God, that is, in a simple blissful experience. It is to be understood in terms of enjoyable love, which is ever moving beyond itself, and not as active love (*na werkeleker minnen*), which advances and retreats. Essential enjoying is a fundamental rest (*grontraste*) which can never again be moved.[30]

This brings us to a question whose full import will come into relief when I come to discuss Ruusbroec's idea of natural contemplation. As we have seen, differentiation is integral to his view of reality. God is a composite being, as are human beings and their human nature in general. In the passage from *The Mirror* just cited,[31] unity appears as a state characterized as "above and beyond ourselves and all orders of being." If the experience of unity implies an abolition of all distinction, and if this puts one in a state of "idleness," how could one still perceive differences? How could one enjoy full blessedness if one were still aware of the quantities and qualities that separate things one from the other? And how then can Ruusbroec reconcile his idea of unity as "beyond all orders" with his conviction that reality is essentially differentiated? Further in the same work he alludes to persons who, on receiving holy communion, pray to God:

> ...that I, in your life, might be able to rise above myself and above all particular forms and exercises to a state devoid of forms (*in onwisen*)— that is, to a state of formless love (*wiselooese Minne*) where you are your own beatitude (*salicheit*) and that of all the saints. It is there that I will find the fruit of all the sacraments, of all particular forms, and of all holiness.

The question of whether the contemplative should transcend concrete religious practice—and this applies in particular to the sacraments—is clearly critical for Christian mysticism. It is not primarily a matter of getting beyond the particular but of the suspicion that there is no need to return. At first sight, the prayer would seem to be Ruusbroec's own. His response to it is instructive:

[30] *Werken* II.360:33–361:29 *passim.*

[31] See note 28 and its corresponding citation.

However, we must seek this fruit in particular forms, in the sacraments, and in a holy life; only then will we find it in a state devoid of form and measure, in eternal and fathomless love. We will eternally remain within ourselves (*in ons-selven bliven*) and be blessed (*salegh sijn*) and well ordered in particular forms of glory, each of us in a special way according to the degree of our virtue and love, and we will blissfully enjoy God above ourselves (*boven ons-selven Gods ghebruken*) and live in him apart from particular forms and above ordered divisions, in that fathomless love which he is himself.[32]

In *The Spiritual Tabernacle* Ruusbroec takes up the same problem in a more graphic way, bringing out nicely the Brabant lifestyle:

And though each one be holy and blessed (*salich*) in oneself, ...the superessential blessedness (*salicheit*) they possess in common is a fathomless (*grondeloes*) abyss that can never be fathomed (*vergrunden*).... For each one's vessel is filled to the brim, though simple blessedness itself is ever overflowing and never completely dug out (*onversceepen*). We are hungry as we dig, and yet we are satisfied with the abundance we find in the superessence where we possess (*in overwesene daer wi besitten*). Hunger is not satisfied; satisfaction does not displace hunger.[33]

Ruusbroec occasionally goes into further detail regarding the phenomenology of the second aspect of being one. In *The Sparkling Stone* he points out three such details:

The first of these points is to rest in the one you enjoy (*rasten inden gheenen die men ghebruyct*). That is where the beloved is conquered by the beloved and the beloved is possessed by the beloved in bare, essential love, there the beloved has fallen into the beloved with affection (*lief in lief met liefden gevallen*) and each is utterly the other's in possession and in rest. There follows the second point and that is to fall asleep in God (*ontslapen in gode*): that is where the spirit sinks away from itself and knows not how or where. And there follows the last point man can put into words: that is where the spirit contemplates a darkness it cannot enter with its reason. And there it feels itself dead and lost and one with God without any difference (*sonder differencie*). And where it feels itself one with God, God himself is its peace, its enjoyment, and its rest.[34]

---

[32] Wiseman, 225.

[33] *Werken* II.362:16–26.

[34] *Opera omnia* X.765–74.

"LOVE WORKS AND RESTS IN A SINGLE NOW"

We have seen Ruusbroec's insistence on the composite nature of being one, and in particular on its contrasting elements of work and rest or union and unity. *The Twelve Beguines* sums it up this way:

> Unity in love (*eenheit in minnen*) cannot become otherness (*anderheit*), and otherness cannot become unity; thus they are both divided in one spirit.[35]

The final three words, *in one spirit*, stress the contrast and open us up to the next stage of uniting what is still divided.

No doubt Ruusbroec's descriptions of unity in dividedness represent a high point of his achievement as a mystical author. Fail as they might, his words seem to gain in significance through that very failure. As language is pressed to do everything it can, somehow it communicates the core of his original contemplative experience and the heart of his doctrine.

On the surface, there is little surprise for the modern reader in what Ruusbroec has to say. The progression from act to rest and from seeking to enjoyment are too reasonable to be very startling. But at the very moment that we find ourselves fighting to stifle a polite yawn, he makes an unexpected move, reversing the course of his analysis in an apparently self-contradictory way. While continuing to affirm that work is followed by rest, he lets us know that the "rest" he has in mind is something dynamic that stimulates activity; that unity, though different from union, somehow helps to bring the latter about. He sees the contraries as complementary elements in a living, organic whole.

Where is the enjoyment of unity for one engaged in the work of union? In Ruusbroec's case, it does not lie so much in a leap beyond as in a passing through. The "rest" of unity lies at the base of the "work" of union. The contemplative may not be initially aware of this fact, but it is ever there, awaiting discovery. A passage in *The Sparkling Stone* makes the point:

> And [the spirit] feels it has strayed in width and dwells in a knowing that is unknown, and it feels it has flown away from itself through the clinging [feeling] of union into unity (*dore dat aenclevende ghevoelen der eeninghen in eenicheit*) and through all dying into the living being of God. And there it feels itself to be one life with God.[36]

The idea of a hidden depth in unity, when it "reveals itself to the spirit as unfathomable," is echoed in *The Little Book*:

[35] *Werken* IV.198:27–30.
[36] *Opera omnia* X.68–72.

...he feels that the depth of his love (*sine minne in haren gronde*), there where it begins and ends, is enjoyable and fathomless.[37]

The Sparkling Stone also points to the open-ended nature of love's burning:

> In this standing before the spirit feels within itself an eternal burning in love. And in that fire of love it finds neither beginning nor end and it feels itself one with that burning of love.[38]

The inner bond between union and unity is not made clear only by showing how union opens up to unity, but also how unity relates back to union. This recalls a relationship we saw earlier between the different stages of becoming one, between union and desire:

> For it is out of this union that desire is always stirred anew (*van nuwes gherenen*) and aroused to new (*nuwen*) inner works, and by working the spirit ascends to a new union (*nuwe vereenighen*). And in this way both activity and union are renewed (*vernuwet*) again and again. And this renewal in action and union (*dit vernuwen in werken ende in eeninghen*) is the life spiritual.[39]

The almost obsessive repetition of words like *new, anew, renewal,* and particularly *to renew* (*vernuwen*) is typical of Ruusbroec. The verb form suggests best that it is not some "thing" or "quality" that is being added on from outside, but an intensification from within of activity already going on. The renewing of desire is the constant newness of life.

Perhaps Ruusbroec's most convincing description of desire being rekindled by union acting back upon it appears in *The Mirror.* The image of the glow of burning coals that calls forth an appeased love devouring everything into itself [40] reappears here:

> For its part, that infinite love which is God himself reigns in the purity of our spirit like the glow of burning coals. It sends forth brilliant, burning sparks which, in the fire of love, touch and inflame the heart and senses, the will and desires, and all the powers of the soul to a stormy transport of restless, formless love. These are the weapons with which we must do battle against the awesome, immense love of God, which strives to burn up and devour all living spirits [in itself]. Nevertheless God's love arms us with its own gifts.[41]

[37] *Opera omnia* I.214–6.

[38] *Opera omnia* X.94–6.

[39] *Opera omnia* X.51–4. See note 4 and corresponding text.

[40] See note 29 and corresponding text.

[41] Wiseman, 238.

When union works back on desire, it is itself stirred further by unity. Ruusbroec speaks of an "unmoved enjoyment" that influences union. In the following passage, the image of the "face"—so apparent and yet so evasive, so self-contained and yet so outgoing—is particularly suggestive:

> For although enjoyable possessing (*ghebrukeleec besitten*) remains always idle and unmoved, always burning away and melting away (*verberren ende versmelten*), it is ever renewed (*vernuwet altoes*) in the face of enjoying.... Ceaselessly it takes in and it tastes what the spirit has already obtained and possessed in enjoyable rest.[42]

Now this "enjoyable love" is presented as something that embraces "active love." Far from suppressing the "work" of the contemplative, it is a stimulus even to "perform all virtues":

> And the more one turns inward the more this simple enjoyable love (*ghebrukeleeke minne*) will envelop and transform (*overgaen*) active love (*werkeleeke minne*). It does not rob love of its activity (*wercs*), but returns it to ever new works and the performance of all virtues. The more one achieves enjoyment beyond oneself, the more virtuous one becomes in oneself.[43]

Clearly even after reaching the rest of enjoyment—or, rather, especially after that—the mystic's activity grows stronger and more vital.

For Ruusbroec, then, being one mystically is not a matter of stages following successively one after the other but of a circuitous, spiraling dynamism. He formulates it this way:

> For no one can enter into rest above activity unless he has first yearningly and actively loved. Therefore, the grace of God and our active love must precede and follow, that is, they must be practised before and afterwards. For without the works of love, we can neither merit nor attain God, nor preserve what we have obtained through the works of love.[44]

Despite all the descriptive accounts, it may still seem to the reader that the experience of unity creates a gaping abyss that separates it from union. Indeed, Ruusbroec himself often speaks of an abyssal state where "we feel nothing but losing our spirits and sinking away from ourselves without return in simple love unfathomable."[45] The phrase *without return* seems to suggest that the mystic's spirit is irretrievably "lost." If the spirit really abides in

[42] *Werken* II.362:1–6.
[43] *Werken* II.364:4–10.
[44] *Opera omnia* III.b.1922–6.
[45] *Opera omnia* X.498–500.

"modelessness," does this not imply liberation from all the fetters of activity? Ruusbroec answers these questions in *The Sparkling Stone*. Having described the experience of "possessing God completely," he draws attention to two characteristics of the mystic's consciousness of "practice." First, it is seen to be an ongoing activity that adheres to and follows the complete possession and immersion in love. Second, it is "modeless" and "without manner."[46] In a word, this practice is a re-action that is too stimulated by inexhaustible enjoyment to get stuck in particular habits or modes of activity. This is what Ruusbroec speaks of as the dying life of love or the "annihilating life"—in other words, an activity that continually transcends itself:

> This contemplation is always linked with a modeless practice, which is an annihilating life (*vernieutende leven*). For where we go out of ourselves into darkness and modelessness that is unfathomable, there shines the simple ray of God's brightness always, in which we are grounded and which draws us up out of ourselves into the superessential being and the immersion of love. And this immersion is always linked with and followed by a modeless practice of love, for love cannot be idle, but it wants to know and taste to the full the unfathomable richness that lives in its ground.[47]

In this way, the two aspects of being one come close to one another in the complex vitality of the highest state of the mystic. The final explanation for this lies not in the mystic but in the One who is the "object" of the experience. The coming of the divine Other is always twofold, because—and here I come to one of Ruusbroec's most notable expressions—"in each new now, God is born in us" (*in elcken nuwen nu*):

> Now, God beholds the dwelling and the resting-place which He has made with us and in us, that is, the unity and the likeness. And He wills to visit this unity without cease with a new coming of His sublime birth and with a rich outflowing of His fathomless love...and He would visit the likeness of our spirit with rich gifts so that we may become more (God-)like and more radiant in virtues.... And He wills that we should visit the unity and the likeness without cease with each work that we do. For in each new now, God is born in us.[48]

A little later he summarizes:

[46] *Opera omnia* X.478–9.

[47] *Opera omnia* X.457–64.

[48] *Opera omnia* III.b.1518–28.

For in one now (*in eenen nu*), in one instant (*in enen tide*), love acts and rests in its beloved. And the one is reinforced by the other. For the higher the love, the more the rest; and the more the rest, the more inner the love. For the one lives in the other. And he who loves not, rests not; and he who rests not, loves not.[49]

THE COMMONER

The portrait of the fully developed mystic Ruusbroec gives us is not that of someone seated on a mountain top or withdrawn deep into the interiority of the psyche. It is rather that of an integrated personality in whom all the different and contrasting elements of the mystical way are coordinated into one. The psychological distinction between faculties and essence, the anthropological distinction between likeness and image, the phenomenological difference between activity and rest, are all present and alive in the reality of a single life.

In his description of the "summit of the inner life"[50] that appears at the end of the second book of *The Spiritual Espousals*, Ruusbroec gives us what may be the key sentence of the entire work and an epitome of his mystical doctrine.[51] His phrasing is a brilliant piece of chiasmus that links the opposites:

Now understand: God comes without cease within us, with intermediary and without intermediary, and demands of us enjoyment and activity, and that the one should not be hindered by the other, but rather always be fortified.

This passage is immediately followed by a portrait of the inner person at the height of the spiritual life:

Therefore, the inner person possesses his life in these two modes, that is, in resting and in activity. And in each, he is whole and undivided (*in elcken es hi al ende onghedeilt*), for he is wholly (*al*) in God where he rests in enjoyment (*ghebrukelijcke rast*), and he is wholly (*al*) in himself, where he loves with works (*werkelijcke mint*). And he is admonished and bidden by God at every moment to renew both rest and activity (*beyde, raste ende werc, te vernuwene*).

[49] *Opera omnia* III.b.1709–13.

[50] *Opera omnia* III.b.1931–60.

[51] For a study in detail, see my article "Une phrase clef des Noces Spirituelles," in *Jan van Ruusbroec:The Sources, Content, and Sequels of his Mysticism*, ed. by P. Mommaers and N. De Paepe (Louvain: University Press, 1984), 100–23.

174

A similar picture is given in *The Sparkling Stone*, where Ruusbroec underscores his point by repeating the key word *gheheel*:

> And so we live completely in God (*gheheel in gode*), where we possess our bliss (*salicheit*), and completely in ourselves (*gheheel in ons selven*) where we practice our love towards God. And even if we live completely in God and completely in ourselves, yet it is only one life.[52]

Let us return for a moment to *The Spiritual Espousals* to see how Ruusbroec concludes his description of the summit of the inner life:

> For this just person has established a true life in the spirit—in rest and in activity—which shall abide eternally; but after this life, it shall pass over into a higher state. Thus the person is just and goes to God with inner love by eternal activity; and he goes into God with enjoyable inclination, by eternal rest; and he abides in God (*hi blivet in gode*) and yet, he goes out to all creatures in common love (*in ghemeynre minnen*), in virtues, and in justice. And this is the summit of the inner life.[53]

Two points deserve mention here. First, Ruusbroec uses the word *ghemeyn* (common) to represent the fully developed mystic. We met the term earlier when presenting Ruusbroec's view that "the soul is common (*ghemeyne*) in all its faculties and in the whole body and in all its members...."[54] The continuation of the passage just cited notes in a similar vein that "God is all and particular (*sonderlinghe*) to each one, and yet common to all creatures (*ghemeyne allen creatueren*)." The term *ghemeyn* is the opposite of *sonderlinc*, "particular" or "special." Applied to the love of the mystic, it implies not only a going out, but a going out without discrimination.

Second, we note the sequence "goes to God,... goes into God,... abides in God...goes out to" that is grounded in a constant abiding in God. Only in the experience of this complex dynamic does the fact of continually living in God make sense to the mystic. Ruusbroec makes the same point graphically in *The Seven Rungs*:

> Even if the spirit loses itself (*ontgheest wert*) and if its activity fails as it (at the moment) achieves enjoyment and blessedness, it is always renewed in grace, charity, and virtuousness. Thus the retreat into idle enjoyment (*ingaen in een ledegh ghebruken*) and the advance into good works (*uutgaen in goeden werken*) always remain united (*altoes gheeeneght bliven*) with God's Spirit. This is what I mean. For just as we blink our eyes open

---

[52] *Opera omnia* X.485–8.

[53] *Opera omnia* III.b.1955–60.

[54] *Opera omnia* III.b.943–4. See chapter 5, page 105.

and closed so quickly that we are not aware of it happening, so, too, we die in God and live from God, and yet always remain one with him (*bliven altoes een met Gode*). So, too, we shall advance into our sensitive life, and retreat with love and cling to God and remain one in God without moving (*ende in God gheeeneght bliven sonder beweeghen*).[55]

The humanity of the mystic is echoed in two further passages. In the first, Ruusbroec crowns his description of contemplatives by noting their utter ordinariness:

> For those who are the most simple are the most quiet and the most totally peaceful in themselves, and they are the most deeply sunken away in God, and they are the most utterly enlightened in understanding, and the most utterly manifold in good works, and the most utterly common in outflowing love.[56]

In the second passage, Ruusbroec closes his treatment of "the noblest and most profitable contemplation to which one can come in this life" with a reminder of the marvel of common humanity that shines forth in the mystic:

> For in this contemplation one remains sovereignly master of himself and free, and in each loving turning-inward, can grow in sublimity of life beyond all that one can understand. For he remains free and master of himself in inner practice and in virtues. And the gazing in the divine light holds him above all inner practice and above all virtues and above all merits.[57]

This stress on the commoner runs throughout Ruusbroec's work. Indeed, his very first book, *The Realm of Lovers*, ends with a description of the commoner.[58] A short passage in *The Sparkling Stone* sums up his position best:

> The man who is sent by God down from these heights, into the world, is full of truth and rich in all virtues. And he seeks nothing for himself but only the honor of the one who sent him, and therefore he is just and true

---

[55] *Werken* III.269:12–23.

[56] *Opera omnia* III.b.1767–71.

[57] *Opera omnia* III.c.161–5.

[58] *Werken* I.100:12–7: "Thus the commoner will be standing...between essence and faculties, that is, between enjoying and working." For a literal parallel with the holy Trinity, see 73:1–3. In *The Mirror* Ruusbroec formulates this as follows: "Their life and exercises therefore consist in turning inward to God and outward to themselves.... They stand in the middle of these two turnings, sometimes looking inward, sometimes outward, and are always in control of themselves and therefore able to turn either way whenever they want" (Wiseman, 224).

in all his actions. And he has a rich, mild foundation which is founded in the wealth of God, and therefore he must always flow into all those who need him, for the living fountain of the Holy Spirit is his wealth and cannot be exhausted. And he is a living, willing instrument of God.... And therefore he has a common life, for contemplation and action come just as readily to him and he is perfect in both. For no one can have this common life unless he is a contemplative man.[59]

[59] *Opera omnia* X.781–93.

9

Union with the Transcendent Self in Buddhism

In chapters 2 and 4, I argued that the Buddhist contemplative path and Christian mysticism have enough in common for both of them to be called by the same name of "mysticism" and for a meaningful comparison to be made between Ruusbroec's mysticism and various elements of the Buddhist path. In chapter 6, on the contrary, a short analysis of the profound differences in their respective views of the human may have prepared the reader for the discovery that, as an existential reality, the "same" turning-inward toward a higher consciousness and a deeper self is lived in a very different way in the two mysticisms. The present chapter, then, which reacts to Ruusbroec's concrete description of his mystical experience from a "Buddhist perspective," will try to describe that difference more concretely and analyze it more deeply—with the expectation that thereby the true character of both mysticisms will be highlighted in a more distinct way, and with the secret hope that, at the same time, a "family likeness" will show through.

Summarizing Ruusbroec's descriptions of the mystical life as it has been presented, our attention seems to be drawn to the following points:

1. Ruusbroec offers phenomenological descriptions of what "happens" on the mystical path, making use thereby of a distinctive style of expression;
2. Ruusbroec presents the mystical life as an evolution in different stages, and pays special attention to the point of departure, points of breakthrough, and the "high point";
3. At each and every step, even at its peak, the unity obtaining in the mystical life shows a complex, but organically integrated, structure;
4. For Ruusbroec, the whole process is lived as an encounter, an adventure of love, with a "divine Other."

In what follows these points will be taken up one by one. But before embarking on this task, I should make the honest confession that, at this point, I have been assailed by doubts about the soundness of our undertaking: is not Ruusbroec's mystical journey, as seen here in its concreteness, so "utterly Christian" as to make a confrontation with Buddhist contemplation totally irrelevant and senseless? After due consideration, however, I have personally come to the conclusion that the radical differences in concrete shape notwithstanding, an "extra illumination" of Ruusbroec's mysticism by data from the Buddhist tradition, and vice versa, is possible and worthwhile even at this phenomenological level, be it more by contrast than by parallelism. I begin in the hope that the reader will come to a similar conclusion at the end of this chapter.

BUDDHIST EVOCATION OF THE MYSTICAL PATH

Ideally speaking, I should be able to present in this chapter a Buddhist phenomenological description of the contemplative path that matches, in its own way, Ruusbroec's description. However, to the best of my knowledge—even after consulting several Buddhist scholars—comparable descriptions of the path as a whole appear not to exist in Buddhist literature. If this is true, we are immediately faced with the intriguing question: why this difference? As a tentative explanation of that surprising finding, I can only think of the following hypothesis.

The Christian mystic lives his/her path inward to the deeper reaches of the self as a real "drama," the ongoing "story" of an encounter, a developing love affair, with another person; an encounter wherein there are various happenings and unforeseeable developments, mostly provoked by the partner. The Buddhist contemplative, on the other hand, lives his/her endeavor as a solitary path, wherein all that happens, until the triumphant arrival, is a progressive dropping away of false perceptions and concomitant passions—nothing to "write home about" or to make a "story" of. We might also say that the Christian mystical experience becomes a story because therein all the faculties of the whole person, and especially the feelings, are involved—are not stories essentially about feelings?—while the Buddhist path is basically lived as a cognitive endeavor, the clarity of which makes the feelings fade away. Or again, if we adopt J. Maritain's definition of experience, we could say that the mystical path constitutes an "experience" in a stronger sense for the Christian than it does for the Buddhist. In connection with Christian mysticism Maritain wrote: "We have here indeed an experience, if the word experience means the knowledge of an object as present, wherein the soul undergoes an action exerted on it by the object, and perceives by reason of the 'passion' to which it is actually subjected."[1]

All this does not mean, of course, that Buddhists did not speak or write about the mystical path. Far from it. Buddhist writings about the contempla-

---

[1] J. Maritain, *Degrés du savoir. Œuvreres complètes* (Fribourg, Suisse: Editions Universitaires, 1988), 4:736.

tive path are legion and constitute a substantial part of Buddhist scripture. Only, it can be said that these writings approach the subject in a way and express themselves in a style very different from the writings of Ruusbroec. What do the Buddhist scriptures offer us? We shall have occasion to say something more specific about this in later sections but, if I may be so brash as to generalize at this point, the following might be said right from the beginning. Buddhist scriptures mostly offer detailed structural analyses of the path together with prescriptions about the attitudes to be taken at different stages along the path, rather than descriptions. And instead of focusing on the path, the Buddhist scriptures, especially the Mahāyāna ones, tend to focus on the peak experience and its cognitive contents. Autobiographical writings are, of course, more descriptive, but even these usually concentrate on the difficulties and drawbacks on the way, to end with a short evocation of the enlightenment experience.

THE STYLE OF BUDDHIST MYSTICAL WRITINGS

As to *the style* of the Buddhist writings—which is of course not uniform throughout that whole plethora of texts—I must limit myself to two observations in direct response to what has been said about Jan van Ruusbroec's use of language. First of all, Ruusbroec is certainly not alone in being incapable of sticking to the logical or architectural structure he has set up for the orderly expression of mystical experience. The same thing happens, not infrequently, in the Buddhist writings on the subject.

Secondly, as for the parallelism often found in Ruusbroec's sentences, this may be meaningfully compared with the paradoxes or antinomies that abound in the Zen use of language or "rhetoric." In such a comparison, the following contrast appears. Ruusbroec's paradoxical parallelisms are descriptive and constructive: indicating a structure that is not meant to be overcome. The Zen paradoxes, on the other hand, constitute a use of language that can be called strategic and deconstructive: meant to exacerbate the horns of the conceptual-linguistic dilemma in preparation for a breakthrough into an undifferentiated unity at a higher level of consciousness. Moreover, Ruusbroec's parallelism has been characterized as a "balanced imbalance."[2] There is indeed an imbalance between the two parts of Ruusbroec's parallel sentences, insofar as one part appears as "more intrinsically mystical" than the other; still, the two parts "balance," since together they form one structured whole. In the case of the Zen paradoxes, we would then have to speak of a "total imbalance": the negative part usually gets all the weight, and there is

[2] See chapter 7, page 143.

no question of solving the paradox by balancing the two elements.

With regard to the deconstructive strategy essential to the Zen rhetoric, the "Final Instructions" given by the sixth patriarch, Hui-neng, to his disciples are truly "instructive":

> Whenever a man puts a question to you, answer him in antonyms, so that a pair of opposites will be formed, such as *coming* and *going*. When the interdependence of the two is entirely done away with there would be, in the absolute sense, neither coming nor going.
>
> Whenever a question is put to you, answer it in the negative, if it is an affirmative one, and vice versa. If you are asked about an ordinary man, tell the inquirer something about a sage, and vice versa. From the correlation or interdependence of the two opposites the doctrine of the mean may be grasped.[3]

THE MAP OF THE BUDDHIST CONTEMPLATIVE LANDSCAPE

Buddhist contemplatives, as well as their Christian counterparts, have always tended to see the contemplative life as an evolution or process and to distinguish several stages in it. This is again an area in which I cannot even begin to present a full overview of the rich variety shown in Buddhism on the subject. I shall limit myself, therefore, to a brief evocation of three important models of structuralization of the contemplative life, found respectively in the oldest Buddhist texts, in Mahāyāna texts, and in Zen writings.

Of the three elements presented in the oldest texts as necessary to obtain Nirvana: *śīla* (ethico-ascetical endeavor), *dhyāna* (concentrated meditation, turning inwards), and *prajñā* (wisdom, insight), it is *dhyāna*, the "mystical element," that is most clearly divided into stages. There are then supposed to be eight *dhyāna*s or stages of trance (four "formed" and four "formless" ones), whereby consciousness distances itself gradually from all (attachment to) objects, or, as E. Conze has it, "the impact of sensory stimuli and our normal reactions to it are gradually transcended." One finally reaches a stage "where there is neither perception nor non-perception." But above and beyond that—and this is one of those breakdowns in neat classification that will lead to many later disputes—there is still the station of "cessation of perception and feelings, where one is said to touch Nirvana with one's body."[4] From this elementary description it is already clear enough that the evolution

---

[3] *The Diamond Sūtra and the Sūtra of Hui-neng*, trans. by A. F. Price and Wong Mou-lam (Boston: Shambala, 1990), 142, 144–5.

[4] Cf. E. Conze, *Buddhism: Its Essence and Development* (London: Faber and Faber, 1963), 100–1.

is seen here as going in the direction of withdrawal, negation, cessation of (at least the lower) faculties.

In Mahāyāna, the structuralization of the Buddhist path is most clearly represented by the *bodhisattva-bhūmi*s, the stages of spiritual progress of the bodhisattva. Disregarding later, much more complicated, systematizations, one can say that the classical number of these *bhūmi*s was ten—although the original number was probably seven; and that even in the systems of ten stages, the contents of each stage are described very differently depending on the sūtra or commentary wherein they appear. But, leaving all these complications aside, we shall concentrate on two characteristics of the *bodhisattva-bhūmi*s that have a bearing on our problematics. Since now we have to do with the "growth process" of a being whose aim it is not simply to "disappear in Nirvana" through pure wisdom but to use its acquired wisdom in merciful activity for others, the stages can no longer go unilaterally in the direction of withdrawal or negation. A "positive" direction comes to blend with the negative one: the gradual acquisition of the *upāya*, the "compassionate means" needed to apply the negatively acquired wisdom and thereby to effectively help others. Thus, Kamalaśīla, wrote:

> He [the bodhisattva] should train himself not only in meditation which transcends the world, which goes without saying, but also in the arts and crafts of the world itself: for how else can he serve all the different aims of beings?...In brief then, the religious practice of a bodhisattva consists in wisdom and in means, and neither in wisdom alone nor in means alone. As we read in scripture: "Wisdom without means, and means without wisdom: these are a bodhisattva's bondage.[5]

And the *Daśabhūmika Sūtra*, for example, has in its fifth *bhūmi*: "He also acquires a knowledge of the arts and sciences like writing, arithmetic, medicine, etc."; and in the eighth *bhūmi*: "A bodhisattva especially cultivates the Perfection of Aspiration (*pranidhāna* or "vow") without neglecting the others, and he pervades the whole world with the feeling of friendliness."[6] At the same time, at least in some of the treatments (especially in the just quoted sūtra), the cultivation of the virtues or "perfections" is interwoven with the development of higher wisdom in the schedule of the bodhisattva aspirant. This reminds us that the *bodhisattva-bhūmi* are a more encompassing framework than the older *dhyāna*s, but also testifies to the consciousness, in Mahāyāna, of the necessity of these virtues for the contemplative. It is not

[5] Kamalaśīla, *Bhāvanākrama*, as quoted in S. Beyer, *The Buddhist Experience: Sources and Interpretations* (Encino, CA: Dickenson Publishing Co., 1974), 103.

[6] As quoted in Har Dayal, *The Bodhisattva Doctrine in Buddhist Sanskrit Literature* (Delhi: Motilal Banarsidass, 1975), 288, 290.

directly clear, however, how organically the three elements—contemplative life, virtues, and going out to others—are interconnected.

Let us next have a look at the decisive moments on the contemplative path. There is, first of all, the *terminus a quo* or point of departure. In Buddhism, this is presented as the decision to become a disciple of the Buddha, to "tread the path" (to become a "wayfarer"), or to "enter the stream"—all of which normally meant to "leave the household" and become a monk. In Mahāyāna, especially, the term *bodhicitta* looms large in this connection. It is the initial spirit whereby the bodhisattva (aspirant) tells himself: "I am going to become a Buddha," and pronounces the Four Great Vows, wherein he expresses his determination and makes his own liberation dependent on the attainment of buddhahood by all others:

> Sentient beings are numberless: I vow to save them all;
> The Passions are inexhaustible: I vow to destroy them all;
> The Dharma gates are numerous: I vow to enter them all;
> The Buddha's Path is unexcelled: I vow to walk it to the end.

It may be remarked that the terms used in Buddhism to denote the point of departure of the contemplative path appear to present it as an absolute beginning, while Christian views rather see it as an important but elective step in an ongoing Christian life, for instance, by using expressions like "the evolution of prayer life"—"prayer," or conscious dealing with God, covering both the mystical and non-mystical levels. Still, in the Buddhist scheme, one can make the decisive step only after one's karma has sufficiently ripened as a result of former good lives, and Buddhist hagiography often attaches great importance to the deep impressions of the impermanence of all worldly things received by the saints in their youth.

The *terminus ad quem*, the intended goal, is of course of utmost importance. It is in light of that goal, envisaged and aspired to in faith, that everything that happens on the path is judged as progress or drawback. I have sufficiently indicated already how the conception of the goal developed, in Buddhist history, from a limpid wisdom, whereby one is freed from all worldly delusion, passion, and suffering, to a buddhahood or bodhisattvahood, wherein wisdom is compounded with mercy, and rest with activity for others. But it may not be irrelevant to remark here that, in the former case, a peak is reached that completely transcends the path that led up to it and everything that was considered to be important in it (the famous "raft" that must be left behind once one reaches the other shore). In the latter case, however, a kind of survival of the path and its forms and virtues appears to be called for. Ruusbroec might have seen that evolution of Buddhism as an approximation of the Christian ideal. It should be remembered, however, that these diverging Buddhist conceptions have something very basic in com-

mon: the idea that the attainment of the contemplative goal is as such liberation or "salvation" itself—something that is alien to Christian mystical ideas.

Does Buddhism reckon with decisive "breakthroughs" along the way
between the point of departure and the goal? The answer is yes. Although
we may not find in Buddhism as clear a watershed as Ruusbroec presents in
his distinction between the Yearning or Inner Life and the God-contemplat-
ing life, the Buddhist path also shows important transitions. In the older
texts, the wayfarer reaches the important milestones of "nonretrogression"
(*avaivartaka*), "only one more rebirth," and "no more rebirths," and, as
already mentioned earlier, Theravāda reckons with the important moment
when the contemplative comes to "see" Nirvana, or wherein Nirvana
becomes more real for him than anything else. This is also called "the breakthrough to the Unconditioned." In the descriptions of the *bodhisattva-
bhūmi*s, too, decisive moments are indicated in a variety of ways and at
different stages. Also here the moment of nonretrogression (something that
"unfortunately" does not seem to exist in Christianity, where one can fall
from grace till the last moment!) is spoken of. Moreover, at a certain
moment, the bodhisattva obtains the "Eye of the Buddha," whereby he really grasps the *anātman* and the emptiness of all things, and, mostly on the
seventh stage, he reaches perfect wisdom, so that his further efforts can be
exclusively devoted to merciful activity. He is now a "celestial bodhisattva"
and is "to be honored like a Buddha." Here, too, the architectural scheme
appears to break down, since the question of whether he is now in Nirvana or
not cannot be answered.

When we turn to Zen, an altogether different world seems to open up.
Indeed, to speak of the path as an evolution in different stages denotes a
gradual approach to the goal, whereas, at least in its mainstream, Zen has
pronounced itself for "sudden enlightenment" over against all gradualism.
To put this in a somewhat broader context:

> Then again, some schools, particularly in East Asia, decried the tendency
> to divide the path into ever finer increments and insisted on the sudden-
> ness of the enlightenment experience. The Ch'an and Zen sects, for
> instance, virtually ignore the formal outline of the *bhūmi*s in their insis-
> tence that enlightenment is a sudden, radical break in consciousness.[7]

Zen therefore basically speaks of two decisive moments only: the moment of
entering the path, which is described in the usual Mahāyāna way, and the
moment of enlightenment. There is, it is true, a strenuous, sometimes short,
sometimes long, path of Zen training that in a sense prepares or leads up to

[7] Nakamura Hajime, "Bodhisattva Path," in M. Eliade, ed., *Encyclopedia of Religion* (New
York: Macmillan, 1988), 2:269.

enlightenment. But this may in no way be considered a cause of enlightenment. That path is then presented, especially in the Lin-chi or Rinzai tradition, in a totally negative way: all it does is lead the trainee to a dead end of all his faculties, a thorough impotence or despair—which is then often called "The Great Doubt" or even "The Great Death." It is from this point that enlightenment can break through as a Great Light, a Great Life, or Resurrection. H. Dumoulin, therefore, could write: "The Great Doubt, the Great Enlightenment, and the Great Joy—these three characterize the psychological process of the way of Zen."[8]

In the Zen chronicles, the enlightenment experience is mostly described only by the occasion that triggers its happening. That can be anything, from hearing a snowflake fall, being struck by a sunset, or hearing a Zen word, to, often enough, a sound slap from the master's hand—provided "the fruit is ripe to fall down all of a sudden." Sometimes, however, an attempt is made at describing how it feels to be enlightened, and then words like freedom, light, and joy certainly take center stage. In the following quotations, the dialectic of Great Doubt and Great Enlightenment comes to the fore especially clearly. The first one is from Zen master Yüan-wu (1063–1135).

> Putting your simple faith in this, discipline yourself accordingly; let your body and mind be turned into an inanimate object like a piece of stone or wood; when a state of perfect motionlessness and unawareness is obtained, all the signs of life will depart and also every trace of limitation will vanish. Not a single idea will disturb your consciousness when lo! all of a sudden you will come to realize a light abounding in full gladness. It is like coming across a light in thick darkness; it is like receiving treasure in poverty. The four elements and the five aggregates are no more felt as burdens; so light, so easy, so free you are. Your very existence has been freed from all limitations: you have become open, light and transparent.... Here is manifested the unsophisticated self which is the original face of your being; here is shown bare the most beautiful landscape of your birthplace.[9]

And Hakuin, who is more explicit in describing his experiences than most Zen masters, has the following to say:

> Never ask your teachers to explain. But when your activity of mind is exhausted and your capacity for feeling comes to a dead end, if something would take place not unlike the cat springing upon the mouse or

---

[8] H. Dumoulin, *Zen Buddhism: A History*, vol. 2 (New York: Macmillan, 1990), 382.

[9] As quoted in Thomas Merton, *Mystics and Zen Masters* (New York: Dell Publishing Co., 1980), 233.

the mother hen hatching her eggs, then a great flash of livingness surges up. This is the moment when the phoenix escapes from the golden net and when the crane breaks the bars of its cage.[10]

When a person faces the great doubt, before him there is in all directions only a vast and empty land without birth and without death, like a large plain of ice extending ten thousand miles. As though seated within a vase of lapis lazuli surrounded by absolute purity.... Within his heart there is not the slightest thought or emotion.... It is just as though he were standing in complete emptiness. At this time,...when he advances single-mindedly without retrogression, suddenly it will be as though a sheet of ice were broken or a jade tower had fallen. He will experience a great joy, one that never in forty years has he seen or heard.[11]

UNITY: COMPACT OR COMPLEX?

We are now left with the two important questions: How does Buddhism relate to, or again, what light can the Buddhist contemplative path throw on, Ruusbroec's mystical experience as a complex but integrated state, and as a union in love with the Other? These two questions are so inextricably interwoven as not to permit any separation. Still, for methodological reasons, I shall as much as possible reserve the element of love for the next section.

It is at this point that many rather abstract considerations made in the previous chapters should flow together to form two distinct "logics," or rather two concrete phenomenological shapes: a Buddhist and a Christian one. As to these "considerations," I am thinking here especially of the evocations of theistic clear transcendence over against Eastern "immanent transcendence," and of the own-being and value of the creatures in Christianity over against the illusory character of the multiplicity of things in Eastern speculation (chapter 4); and of the differences in evaluing the conative aspect of the human being, interpersonal relationships, and finally the unity in the All-One (chapter 6).

My use of "antagonistic language" here—A *over against* B—is not fortuitous. Indeed, we have found deep differences on all these points between the Buddhist and Christian conceptions, and it must be anticipated that they will build up into two profoundly diverging, possibly irreconcilable, paradigms of the mystical life. The light that they can throw on each other will then be, as said already before, mostly by contrast—somewhat like one being

[10] As quoted in Isshū Miura and R. F. Sasaki, *Zen Dust* (New York: Harcourt, Brace & World, 1966), 42.

[11] As quoted in Dumoulin, *Zen Buddhism: A History*, vol. 2, 381.

able really to know what peace means only by the experience of war. Furthermore, in this section I intend to play the role of the "devil's advocate" *over against* a too easy and uncritical acceptance, in much contemporary thinking, of the Buddhist paradigm as evidently superior to that of Ruusbroec, since the latter never reaches "pure unity" and remains in the personal sphere of love and encounter throughout.

Still, I would like to begin with two bits of evidence showing that the opposition between the two ideals of mystical life is not as stark as it might seem at first sight. First, there is the point already made in chapter 6 that, unlike the picture of a compact and undifferentiated unity mostly presented in Buddhist theory, the unity at work in Buddhism as a living reality, including its praxis or path and the symbiosis of Wisdom and Mercy in the bodhisattva path, is in fact a nuanced and complex one. Second, it can be said—although the formulation becomes very delicate here—that Ruusbroec shares with Buddhism (with the majority of Eastern speculation, and also with Eckhart) the ideal of total, undifferentiated, and "static" (eternal or "unborn") unity as the peak of mystical experience, and finds it realized in his own mystical path. Indeed, in Ruusbroec's description of the mystical state, we can discover all the elements of the "peak experience" that are stressed in Buddhism.

Let me illustrate this by selecting from the passages cited by Mommaers those expressions that show a distinct likeness to elements of the Buddhist ideal of unity:

> *no distinction or multiplicity:* "Above all this, the soul should rest in its beloved above all multiplicity."[12] "Where it [the spirit] is burnt up, it is onefold and there is no distinction left."[13] "And there it [the spirit] feels itself dead and lost and one with God without any difference."[14]
>
> *no forms or images:* "To rise above myself and above all particular forms and exercises to a state devoid of forms."[15] "We therefore always remain standing above reason in our very selfhood—imageless...."[16] "....the simple passing over into bareness and modelessness."[17]
>
> *non-ego:* About a lower stage Ruusbroec writes: "And even if they feel themselves raised up to God in a strong fire of love, they always keep

---

[12] *Spiritual Espousals. Opera omnia* III.a.813–14.

[13] *Sparkling Stone. Opera omnia* X.99–101.

[14] *Opera omnia,* X.772–3.

[15] *A Mirror,* Wiseman, 225.

[16] *A Mirror,* Wiseman, 240.

[17] *Sparkling Stone. Opera omnia* X.332.

their own self...."[18] "...the spirit sinks away from itself in enjoyment and floats away into God as in its eternal rest."[19]

a self-sufficient state: "...above all activity: a quieted rest in inactivity; above all holy living and practice of virtue: simple blessedness; and above hunger and thirst, love and longing for God: eternal satiety."[20]

This "perfect unity" is then further described, from Ruusbroec's standpoint with its focus on God, love, and encounter, in terms that may not be found as such in Buddhist texts, but that nevertheless fully correspond to the spirit of Buddhist unity. The idea of a timeless, preexistent unity ("unborn," "before the birth of your parents") becomes the existence in God before the creation. "...dying in love we shall pass away from all createdness into the superessential riches of God, and there we shall possess God in an eternal death to ourselves."[21] And further Ruusbroec speaks of "[beyond] clinging to God in love...[being] burnt up to nothing in the unity of love";[22] and "in a state of eternal enjoyment—that is, above works and virtues in a state of blessed emptiness, and above union with God in unity...."[23]

We may thus conclude, I believe, that Ruusbroec's mysticism, just like Buddhist mysticism, is animated by the same drive or urge for perfect unity, which in chapter 6 has been considered to be a characteristic of all mysticism, at least insofar as mysticism incorporates within itself, or combines with, the rational demand for the One and can thus be called, in a sense, "metaphysical mysticism." It will further appear, however, that this same drive for perfect unity occupies such a fundamentally different position in the respective mysticisms that, as concrete phenomenological "Gestalts," the two mysticisms stand in a sense at opposite poles, not only theologically, but also psychologically, anthropologically, and even "logically" or "metaphysically."

That basic difference, which we must now try to grasp as clearly as possible, has, of course, to do with the divergent nature of the two religions, their different metaphysical presuppositions, and the different role mysticism plays in each. At this point the basic difference between the two religions might be summarily characterized as follows: while Buddhism is a religion of liberation by unifying wisdom, Christianity is a religion of salvation by a believing and

---

[18] *Sparkling Stone. Opera omnia* X.336–7.

[19] *Spiritual Espousals. Opera omnia* III.b.1998–9.

[20] *Seven Enclosures. Opera omnia* II.615–18.

[21] *Sparkling Stone. Opera omnia* X.425–7. Note that Ruusbroec does not envisage a *simple* return to the pre-existent, uncreated state (the image or "exemplar" in God). For him, this state can only be reached after the image is realized in his created being, in his human existence.

[22] *Sparkling Stone. Opera omnia* X.326, 388.

[23] *A Mirror*, Wiseman, 246.

loving relationship with a transcendent and saving God. It merits repeating here that Ruusbroec is to be situated in the "mainstream" of Christian ("orthodox") mysticism—a mysticism that, like the religion itself, is centered on the conscious and intimate relationship with God, a mysticism of love. This point will be taken up again in the next section, but in the present context it needs to be stressed that Ruusbroec sees the love between the soul and its God as having its origin in the innermost life of God—starting from an original unity—and thus as representing the deepest ontological level. Thus, what Otto writes about Eckhart would equally apply to Ruusbroec:

> But Eckhart does not come like the emotional love mystics to an at-one-ment as an effect and as the summit of emotional conditions.... Rather, the at-one-ment is itself the condition and the first ground of the possibility of agapé.[24]

In other words, while being a mysticism of love, Ruusbroec's mysticism is at the same time a "metaphysical mysticism," but then of a metaphysics of love or of the interpersonal rather than of "being."[25] Furthermore, Ruusbroec considers this love as leading limitlessly to an ever more intimate union of the soul with God, while containing, at least at the peak of the contemplative life, the moment of perfect, undifferentiated, unity with God.

It is this latter trait that brings Ruusbroec's mysticism near enough to Buddhist mysticism to make a comparison meaningful: they both find the "peak" of mystical experience in complete unity. However, as intimated above, precisely in this common ground there appears most clearly the profound difference between Ruusbroec's vision and Buddhist contemplative theory. In a nutshell, this difference might be expressed as follows: in Buddhist theory, the peak of perfect unity is sufficient by itself and completely transcends and abrogates all that led up to it (and all that possibly comes after it); for Ruusbroec, this peak by itself is only an abstraction. It exists, is reached, and is maintained, not as the totality of any lived experience, but as

---

[24] R. Otto, *Mysticism East and West* (New York: Macmillan, 1932), 232. I believe, however, that Ruusbroec would not agree with the statement of Eckhart cited by Otto in this context: "Love does not unify; true, it unites in act but not in essence." For Ruusbroec, there is no deeper "essence" (or ontological level) beyond love, neither in the human nor in God.

[25] It should be noted here again that Ruusbroec's mystical ideas bring into question the sharp distinction that is often made between a "metaphysical" mysticism of essence and an "emotional" mysticism of love. The following remark by William James about the Spanish mystics certainly does not fit Ruusbroec's case, which makes one wonder whether it is any more suited to his Spanish counterparts: "They are with few exceptions non-metaphysical minds, for whom 'the category of personality' is absolute. The 'union' of man with God is for them much more like an occasional miracle than like an original identity." William James, *The Varieties of Religious Experience* (New York: The Modern Library, 1902), 416.

a pole—admittedly the highest one—of a more complex and living process of unity—a unity that does not leave the path behind but incorporates it within itself; a unity that involves not only the cognitive faculty but the whole person with all its faculties, a unity wherein rest and work unite; a unity that is better captured by the term "love" than by the word "unity" itself.

At first sight, of course, Ruusbroec seems to involve himself in a famous contradiction: how can he present perfect undifferentiated unity as the peak, and immediately afterward, or rather in the same breath, incorporate it in, and subordinate it to, a wider and this time complex unity? In a logic of being—or of nothingness, for that matter—this is certainly contradictory. That Ruusbroec himself is fully aware of that dilemma is sufficiently apparent from his frequent use of parallel sentences, wherein the "contraries" are brought together without any indication of a further synthesis of the two. But awareness alone does not solve the problem.

A first answer could be that Ruusbroec's texts are meant to describe a living experience, not to present a logical theory. This is true enough, but this does not appear to be the final answer in the case of a writer who proves himself to be an able dialectician and certainly not uninterested in theory. This contradiction must somehow have "made sense" to him. Could we possibly recapture some elements of that "sense?"

In our context—the reciprocal illumination of Ruusbroec's mysticism and Buddhist mysticism—it is extremely important to remark that Ruusbroec faced exactly the same dilemma as the Mahāyāna bodhisattva path: in the bodhisattva path too the highest peak of wisdom is de facto incorporated into a whole that is wider, complex, and in some sense higher. It could be said that the difference is only that Ruusbroec fully incorporated both horns of the dilemma into his mystical vision, while Buddhist mystical theory never fully did that. Let us first remind ourselves of how the dilemma appears in Buddhism. There can be no doubt that a wisdom of perfect undifferentiated unity was always seen as the peak of the Buddhist path. Huang Po, for instance, testifies to that in the following way:

> The very nature of the Great Way is voidness of opposition. Bodhidharma firmly believed in being one with the real "substance of the universe" in this life: Mind and that "substance" do not differ one jot—that "substance" is Mind.[26]

On the bodhisattva path, however, mercy—which recognizes the reality of beings with their differences and multiplicity—is, in fact, brought alongside wisdom at the peak of the path. H. Dayal summarizes that evolution:

[26] *The Zen Teaching of Huang Po*, trans. by John Blofeld (New York: Grove Weidenfeld, 1958), 70.

In the early Mahāyāna, Wisdom and Mercy are regarded as equally important.... [Still,] the glorification of Wisdom reaches its climax in the writings of the Mādhyamika school of philosophy [early Mahāyāna philosophy of emptiness].... *Prajñā* is extolled *ad nauseam*, while Mercy (*karunā*) is not discussed in detail. But the later Mahāyāna emphasizes Mercy more than Wisdom.[27]

Thus, Kamalaśīla, a representative of late Indian Mahāyāna, wrote:

He who wishes to gain omniscience [enlightenment] swiftly, must strive in three things: in compassion, in the thought of enlightenment, and in meditation. And he should practice compassion from the very outset, for we know that compassion alone is the first cause of all the qualities of Buddhahood. As we read in scripture: "...Blessed one, it is through compassion that the bodhisattva holds all the qualities of Buddhahood in the palm of his hand.... It is like life itself; only when there is life can the other faculties occur, and only when there is great compassion can the other qualities of a bodhisattva occur as well."[28]

Thereby, of course, the self-sufficiency of the peak of undifferentiating wisdom is, in fact, utterly done away with, in favor of a syzygy of two "opposing factors." And Buddhist literature shows an awareness of this. Thus, for instance, the bodhisattva is presented as a living synthesis of the two "contradictory" virtues of Wisdom and Mercy. Also, the question is asked: which is higher, a Buddha (a being who has achieved Nirvana at the peak of wisdom) or a bodhisattva (a being that stops before the peak, or "comes down" from it, in order to exercise mercy in this world), and the "logical" answer appears to be: the bodhisattva. And the notion arises of a kind of wisdom (*gotokuchi* in Japanese) that accrues to the peak of wisdom (and, in a sense completes and "enhances" it) and consists in the knowledge of compassionate means whereby the highest wisdom is applied in the service of mercy.

What therefore remains, for me, one of the "mysteries" of Buddhist history is the fact that, notwithstanding the profound evolution in Buddhism's religious ideal, the Buddhist metaphysico-mystical theory did not really change, never afforded Mercy a place comparable to that of Wisdom, always remained a logic of emptiness, and forever continued to see undifferentiated unity not only as the peak but also as the whole. This consideration prompts me, however, to formulate another, rather bold, statement: There is incompatibility between Ruusbroec's idea of unity-union with God and the prevailing Buddhist theory of mystical unity, which stops at emptiness as an

---

[27] H. Dayal, *The Bodhisattva Doctrine*, 44–5.

[28] Kamalaśīla, as quoted in S. Beyer, *The Buddhist Experience*, 99–100.

undifferentiated totality; but there is not necessarily incompatibility between Ruusbroec's vision and the bodhisattva path, when the latter is thought through to the end, with a right balance of Wisdom and Mercy, negation and affirmation, unity and otherness.[29]

The gist of my argument has thus been that Ruusbroec does not stand alone in his "logical contradiction" but is joined therein by the Buddhist bodhisattva path (even though Buddhist theory does not seem to recognize the dilemma and appears to keep one horn of the dilemma at arm's length). This might suggest that the contradiction is common to all concrete mystical paths that consider the experience of perfect unity with the absolute as a fact and as an integral element of mysticism. Could one argue that most Christian (and *a fortiori* Jewish) mystics do not lay claim to that perfect unity and are satisfied with a very intimate but still dual relationship with God? However this may be—and I certainly do not feel competent to come up with an answer to this question—the mere fact that Ruusbroec is not alone in having a problem does not suffice to explain it away. We are still faced with it and we must at least try to throw some further light on the question, even if we cannot answer it completely.

The problem could then be recast in the form of two questions. One, why does Ruusbroec consider the experience of complete unity as an integral (and, in a sense, the highest) part of the mystical experience? And what role does it play in his mystical path? And two, why is he convinced that one cannot stop at this peak, but must complement it by an equally important element, one that embraces duality, otherness, newness?

In Buddhism it appears to be taken for granted that the experience of undifferentiated unity is the decisive element, or even the totality, of true mysticism: it is not made into a theoretical problem, and it does not seem to be felt as problematic by individual contemplatives. Things are different, of course, in Christianity, where the very idea seems to militate against the first tenet of monotheism: the absolute transcendence of God. Ruusbroec—and also Eckhart, of course—must therefore have had very good reasons for incorporating it as an important element in the mystical path. Why is that element supposed to be there at all? Again, the first answer cannot but be that it is there, in Ruusbroec and Eckhart, because these mystics found it in the mystical experience they describe. Can we say anything more? Could it be that true, experiential recognition of God's absoluteness presupposes that

[29] Paul Swanson, author of *Foundations of T'ien-t'ai Philosophy* (Berkeley, California: Asian Humanities Press, 1989), has pointed out to me that T'ien-t'ai theory goes a long way—possibly the farthest of all Mahāyāna thought—in that direction, by virtue of the dynamic it introduces between emptiness and conventional existence. In other words, it stresses the necessity of going beyond a negative emptiness and reengaging oneself in the mundane world with bodhisattva-like compassion.

moment of total self-negation and absorption into God? If that could be said to be the significance and function of the moment of undifferentiated unity in Ruusbroec, this moment might be basically present, be it under other names, in all Christian mysticism, as, for instance, the following text suggests:

> The theology of Lady Julian [of Norwich] is a theology of the all-embracing totality and fullness of the divine love. This is, for her, the ultimate Reality, in the light of which all created beings and all the vicissitudes of life and of history fade into unimportance. Not that the world and time, the cosmos and history are unreal; but their reality is only a revelation of love.[30]

And could it be that this moment, wherein the soul and God disappear as it were in a higher unity, constitutes the experience of limitlessness, infinity, and total spiritual freedom? "Here a person is so possessed by love that he must forget himself and God, and he knows nothing but love."[31]

From the poverty of the above considerations it should be clear that I, as a non-mystic, find it hard to grasp exactly what the moment of perfect unity with God represents for a Christian mystic. I am even inclined to say that the positive image I have of that moment has its source rather in what I know of Eastern mysticism. For me, as a Christian, it is much easier to understand the second point: Ruusbroec's experience and conviction that one cannot stop at that perfect unity, that this kind of engagement with God could not by itself be called fully Christian, of course, but also would not even be fully religious or even fully human. Summarizing Ruusbroec's view, P. Mommaers is wont to say: "no union without unity; but equally no unity without union."[32] The following considerations may now help us to better understand the second part of that sentence, which makes Ruusbroec's idea of mystical union so different from the Buddhist one.

Ruusbroec's vision, it must be stressed again, is rooted in his mystical experience: an experience in the framework of a religion that from beginning to end is an engagement with a God who never ceases to be Other and who

---

[30] T. Merton, *Mystics and Zen Masters*, 141.

[31] *Spiritual Espousals. Opera omnia* III.b.1353–4.

[32] The parallelism of the parts of this sentence, and the presentation of the insufficiency of undifferentiated unity by itself is much clearer in Ruusbroec than in Eckhart, whose position on this point is rendered by R. Otto, for instance, in the following sentence: "Central for Eckhart also…is a simpler form of mysticism. It is the mysticism *not yet* of identity, but of indwelling, immanence, of a secret mutual relationship and interpenetration of God and the soul. These are *transitorial stages* to the more deeply mystical experiences of perfect unity, but are likewise their rivals, and often enough their equally important counterparts" (*Mysticism East and West*, 136–7). I have italicized the words that betray a subordination of the other pole under the moment of perfect unity, in contrast to Ruusbroec's coordination and simultaneity.

is believed to have created others besides himself rather than staying in the splendid isolation of self-sufficient unity. Being undifferentiatedly one with God, being totally "in God" (uncreated), which is undoubtedly the highest ideal a creature can think of, is then automatically taken up into the movement of self-communication whereby God "steps out of himself" toward the creatures. This view of the divine will later, in Hegel, give rise to the philosophical thesis that a unity *an sich* must "express" itself, that is, create the other of itself, in order to find a higher form of unity, unity *für sich*.

This philosophical thesis as such cannot be found in Ruusbroec, of course, but it is clear that for him a complex, living, and dynamic unity represents a higher form of unity than a "mere" compact unity. We may be reminded here of Saraha's opinion, cited earlier, to the effect that a break in symmetry is needed "to keep wholeness from stagnating."[33] And Ruusbroec would surely have appreciated the following words of a contemporary Christian writer:

> ...the uniform and undifferentiated One, the Identical without change or temporality, that is nothingness: nothing in it makes a sign, nothing makes itself manifest in it, nothing happens in it.
>
> [Creation and reconciliation in Christ constitute] the same renouncement of the quietude of the One-Identical, in order to rend oneself apart, to express oneself and to deliver oneself to the risk of the Other.[34]

All this is very far from the way mystical unity is spoken of in Buddhist theory. At the risk of oversimplifying and painting an overly black-and-white picture, let us try to analyze that difference a bit further by contrasting a few elements at work in the respective visions.

First of all, the Buddhist mystical peak stands by itself, completely transcending (and making abstraction from) the path that led up to it from the ordinary human situation, and not containing in itself (an inner motivation for) the return to that same human situation, the "way down from the mountain to the market place." Ruusbroec, on the contrary, insists that both the way up and the way down be included in the highest mystical life. Here it can be indicated, in passing, that the Buddhist position is open to the objection that the unity of the peak, although supposedly containing all intelligibility,

---

[33] H. Guenther, *Ecstatic Spontaneity* (Berkeley: Asian Humanities Press, 1993), 38. E. Lévinas speaks of "stopping the monotony of its identity." *Totalité et infini* (Paris: Kluwer Academic, n.d.), 340.

[34] B. Ibal, "Création, séparation et amour," *Revue des Sciences Religieuses* 66 (1992): 335, 341–2. This kind of conception is found in the Pure Land school of Buddhism, where absolute Buddhahood (in Japanese, 法身 *hosshin*) is said to divide itself into Buddhahood of essence and Buddhahood of expedient means, in order to reveal itself to and save all sentient beings.

cannot account for the existence of ordinary human life, fallen as it is in multiplicity. The French philosopher E. Lévinas points that out in the following words (although without reference to Buddhism):

> The positions which I just summarized gainsay the ancient privilege of unity which is found from Parmenides to Schopenhauer and Hegel. [From their standpoint] separation and interiority would be incomprehensible and irrational...[and] the factual separation out of which metaphysics originate would be the result of an illusion or a fault.... However, the philosophy of unity has never been able to say where that accidental illusion and fall, which are inconceivable in the Infinite, the Absolute and the Perfect, came from.[35]

Secondly, enlightenment in Buddhism appears as a "super-human" experience, transcending the working of all the human faculties and elevating the enlightened one to a very special status. Ruusbroec, on the other hand, presents the highest mystical experience as a human experience, wherein all the ordinary human faculties are involved (be it in a specifically unified condition), and whereby the mystic remains a "common human being." On this point, I found the following lines by Ruusbroec most impressive:

> And so we live completely in God, where we possess our bliss, and completely in ourselves, where we practice our love towards God.[36]

Finally, enlightenment is most often presented as basically "a finished product," a rounded totality as it were. For Ruusbroec, however, the mystical peak is infinitely open-ended, a unity as an ongoing process, forever enhanced by "further union" with a God who is not simply being but forever new life, a God who is eternally present and still forever coming anew.

As a kind of transition to our next section, the difference could also be expressed by saying that a different "image" of unity is at work in the two mysticisms. The Buddhist image of unity is that projected by reason; Ruusbroec's image of unity is rather that suggested by desire and love. It is a kind of unity that is only possible in persons, not in things; a unity that, rather than being destroyed by multiplicity and otherness, is enhanced by it. A rich sentence by P. Mommaers may sum it all up for us:

> Such complex beings as God and man are persons. They alone have the possibility of experiencing that which Ruusbroec regards as true oneness: not lifeless coincidence, nor restless absorption of one by the other, but rather an enjoyment of each other's "ground" in a perpetual meet-

---

[35] Lévinas, *Totalité et infini*, 105.

[36] *Sparkling Stone. Opera omnia* X.485–7.

ing.... In "being one," the fact of being other remains. The encounter goes on renewing itself in enjoyable possession.[37]

In the above, while not being able to take away the "logical contradiction" from Ruusbroec's conception of unity, I may have succeeded, up to a point, in presenting Ruusbroec's vision of unity—in all its difference from the conception of unity in Buddhist theory—as a coherent and existentially (and religiously) valuable one, and as one that is possibly not far removed from the more complex unity at work in Buddhist life.

MYSTICISM OF LOVE AND BUDDHIST MYSTICISM

In this final section, the analysis of the difference in phenomenological *Gestalt* between Ruusbroec's mysticism and Buddhist mysticism will be continued, but this time from a slightly different angle: while the previous section focused on the divergence in the vision of unity, here the difference will be considered more directly in the light of the rather current characterization: Buddhism's is a mysticism of wisdom and emptiness, Christianity's is a mysticism of love.

Here, as before, we want to see and circumscribe the difference as clearly as possible, while at the same time keeping an eye open for the possible common elements. In this section we are faced again with rather delicate problematics (most of which have been touched on above). Among the relevant questions the following might be paramount: How does Buddhist wisdom relate to love-mercy? In what sense does love intend unity? How far does love presuppose wisdom and emptiness? Are there no cases (or traces) of love mysticism in Buddhism?

At this juncture, we might first need clarification of a few points: whether and in what sense "all" Christian mysticism can be characterized as "mysticism of love"; what role the drive for unity plays in it; and what exactly Ruusbroec's place within Christian mysticism is. A (necessarily very brief) overview of Christian mysticism therefore appears called for at this point.

It has been said that unity or union (*unio mystica*) must not necessarily be seen as the defining common trait of mysticism in the Abrahamic religions:

> ...but it may be argued that union with God is not the most central category for understanding mysticism.... I have come to find the term "presence" a more central and more useful category for grasping the unifying note in the varieties of Christian mysticism.[38]

---

[37] P. Mommaers, "Introduction" to Ruusbroec's *Opera omnia* III, 19–20.

[38] Bernard McGinn, *The Foundations of Mysticism* (New York: Crossroad, 1991), xvii.

And the same author indicates that Gershom Sholem not only "refused to restrict mysticism to the experience of union with God," but went so far as to exclude "any kind of union from Jewish mysticism."[39] Sholem's conclusion may be questionable, but it is possible to maintain that, on the whole, the mysticism present in the monotheistic religions can be characterized as a mysticism of "relation" with God, rather than of unity with God, and most typically as a mysticism of love.

> All Western religions have produced mystics of love. Judaism, Christianity and Islam have known each its own kind of spiritual eros.[40]

It is significant, however, that a mysticism of unity or union is the oldest strand of mysticism at work in Christianity. It goes back at least to Origen (ca. 185–253), who discovered the primordial unity in the Biblical picture of the human being as the (ontological) image of God, and it underwent the influence of neo-Platonic mysticism, especially through pseudo-Dionysius (around 500 CE), for whom "the primordial union of the soul with God serves as the moving principle of the mystical ascent."[41] Sometime during the twelfth century, however,

> Christian spirituality underwent a basic change: its approach became more human and affective. Love had, of course, always been an essential ingredient. But now it became the whole thing.[42]

The typical Christian mysticism of love, in which personal love of God dominates, was born principally with Bernard of Clairvaux (1090–1153).[43] This does not mean that the drive for unity disappeared from Christian mysticism, but rather that the two propensities came to intertwine. Already in the twelfth century we see their synthesis in William of Saint Thierry, for whom "Amor ipse notitia est" (love itself is knowledge).[44] Eckhart (ca. 1260–1327) then appears to represent a revival of the more unilaterally metaphysical "mysticism of the image [of God]." He thereby carried this mysticism of unity of and with God to an extreme, where it becomes difficult to assign any positive role to difference or to discern any positive value in the self-nature of the creature. On the other hand, the mystical movement of the fourteenth and fifteenth centuries in Flanders, to which Ruusbroec belongs, together

---

[39] McGinn, *Foundations of Mysticism*, 335.

[40] Louis Dupré, "Mysticism," in M. Eliade, ed., *The Encyclopedia of Religion* 10:254. For this bird's-eye view of Christian mysticism, I rely heavily on this article.

[41] Dupré, "Mysticism," 252.

[42] Dupré, "Mysticism," 254.

[43] On Bernard of Clairvaux, see chapter 1, page 14 and note 2.

[44] On William of Saint Thierry, see chapter 3, page 52 and note 12.

with Hadewijch and others, clearly prolongs the line of William of Saint Thierry. Ruusbroec knew Eckhart's mystical writings and was influenced by them. But, as also indicated by the Yale theologian, Louis Dupré, he carefully corrected the "dangerous" tendencies in Eckhart, and brought both trends—the metaphysical one, based on image-unity, and the more affective one, centering on love-likeness—to an explicit and powerful synthesis.[45]

This all too summary overview of Christian mysticism up to Ruusbroec's time does not allow us, of course, to draw any definitive conclusions. It appears to point, however, in the following directions. First, the drive for unity and the dynamics of love are certainly not identical, but both appear to be at work in Christian mysticism, usually in a more or less close relationship, with sometimes the one and sometimes the other being the dominant ingredient. Second, Ruusbroec's mysticism, wherein the two are most intimately and very consciously drawn together, can be considered to be truly representative of Christian mysticism. Indeed, previous chapters have clearly shown, I believe, that the categories that pervade Ruusbroec's descriptions from beginning to end are "encounter" and "love." And, on the other hand, my previous section may have given a sufficiently clear indication of how strongly Ruusbroec's mysticism is directed at unity-union.

Next, we must have a look at Buddhist mysticism and its relationship to love-mercy. Here, we should remind ourselves of two points already made above:

1. Buddhism as a religion of Wisdom appears not to recognize the legitimacy of the conative or appetitive side of the human being; on the contrary, it appears to condemn it as "passion," to be eliminated by right thinking.[46]

2. Buddhist theory never came to assign a congruent place to Mercy-Love on the mystical path, even at the time when mercy had come to be considered, in the practice, as the final outcome of the Buddhist path.[47] The following considerations may be seen as elaborations on these two points.

Our problem finds a symbolic expression, as it were, in the fact that the term used to translate "love"—in expressions such as "God is love," "in Christianity love is central," etc.—into Chinese and Japanese is *ai* 愛, a term that in a Buddhist context (nearly) always carries the pejorative connotation of passion and attachment, the very things the Buddhist path is supposed to do away with. On the other hand, and on the level of "secondary virtues,"

---

[45] Dupré, "Mysticism," 253–4.

[46] See chapter 6, pages 125–6.

[47] See above, pages 132, 182–3, 191–2.

Buddhism has, from its very beginnings, recommended the "cultivation of the social emotions":[48] friendliness (*maitrī*), compassion (*karuṇā*), sympathetic joy (*muditā*), and impartiality or indifference (*upekṣā*). From these considerations "mercy" or "mercy-love" (indicated in Sino-Japanese by a combination of the first two virtues: 慈悲, *jihi* in the Japanese pronunciation) came to have a positive resonance in Buddhist parlance. It is significant, however, that already in this fourfold division, the first three "emotions" are supposed to be directed, by way of a total universalization, towards the final state of impartiality—which signifies the elimination of emotions that could be a hindrance on the path of wisdom. Thus, for instance, the Japanese Buddhist scholar Gadjin Nagao writes:

> ... "indifference" (*upekṣā*), getting rid of both love and hatred, means to be interested neither in happiness nor in suffering, neither in pleasure nor in sorrow [of oneself and of others]. It seems to be rather particular to Buddhism that such a neutral state is applauded as "good" and as a higher virtue.[49]

This will then grow into a veritable dilemma for Buddhist theory, because in Buddhist practice, especially in Mahāyāna Buddhism with its bodhisattva path, mercy will clearly rise to the rank of primary virtue and, in a sense, become the basic dynamic element of the Buddhist path. Two contrasting texts may bring this paradox to life for us:

> In one of the Hinayāna sects it was held that "there is no Mercy in the Buddha's heart," since Mercy was considered to be one of the passions.[50]

> Somebody asked Jōshū, "Buddha is the enlightened one and teacher of us all. He is naturally free of all the passions (*kleśa*), is he not?"
> Jōshū said, "No, he is the one who cherishes the greatest of all the passions."
> "How is this possible?"
> "His greatest passion is to save all beings!" Jōshū answered.[51]

[48] The expression, denoting the *brahma-vihāra* meditations, is taken from E. Conze, *Buddhist Thought in India* (Ann Arbor: University of Michigan Press, 1967), 80.

[49] Gadjin M. Nagao, "Tranquil Flow of Mind: An Interpretation of *Upekṣā*," *Indianisme et Bouddhisme: Mélanges offerts à Mgr. Etienne Lamotte* (Louvain-la-Neuve: Institut Orientaliste, 1980), 245.

[50] 木村泰賢 Kimura Taiken, 真空より妙有へ [From True Emptiness to Wondrous Being] (Tokyo: Kōshisha Shobō, 1929), 207.

[51] As quoted in Masao Abe, *Zen and Western Thought* (Honolulu: University of Hawaii Press, 1985), 79.

Indeed, for a doctrine that locates liberation in limpid Wisdom, in an emptiness beyond all oppositions and distinctions, love, even when provisionally
valued as Mercy, cannot but be a disturbing element, since it certainly is to be
reckoned among the emotions or passions and implies within itself desire,
and also because it involves the distinction of self and other. The time-
honored, and mostly routinely repeated, solution to this dilemma is a reduction of Mercy to Wisdom by a definition of Mercy as "the insight into the
non-duality of self and other" (自他不二 Jap., *jita funi*). In other words, it
appears to be general Mahāyāna doctrine that, in the I-Thou relationship, the
deepest and only real level is that of non-distinction, and that from the
insight into that non-distinction compassion is naturally born. In that vein
the noted Buddhist scholar Yamaguchi Susumu wrote:

> When non-discriminating wisdom turns to sentient beings...it is
> compassion.
> The more wisdom perfects its basic meaning, the more perfectly
> mercy manifests itself.
> Mercy can be defined as emptiness incessantly discovering being and
> emptying that being.[52]

When thus reduced to wisdom, mercy is not accorded any own reality or own
dynamism; and the notion of mercy-love is emptied of all alterity or otherness
and of all movement towards the other. The negation of otherness is, of
course, most striking when it is applied to the Mercy of the Buddha towards
sentient beings:

> Then where *can* there be Buddhas who deliver or sentient beings to be
> delivered? When the true nature of all things that "exist" is an identical
> thusness, how *can* such distinctions have any reality?[53]

On the other hand, mercy among sentient beings is mainly represented by
the first *pāramitā*: "giving" (*dāna*). Here Buddhism explains that for real
giving a threefold purity is required, with regard to the gift, the giver, and the
recipient:

> Pure giving is a selfless being and activity, on the basis of the negation
> first of all of the ego-consciousness of the giver.... It recognizes neither
> the giving I nor the receiving Thou.[54]

---

[52] 山口 益 Yamaguchi Susumu, 空の世界 [The World of Emptiness] (Tokyo: Risōsha, 1967),
33, 52, 113.

[53] *The Zen Teaching of Huang Po*, 109.

[54] Yamaguchi, *The World of Emptiness*, 100.

We must acknowledge the wisdom contained in these speculations. Indeed, true giving must imply the negation of the superiority of the self as giver and the negation of the other as fixated in a position of inferiority as recipient. The real question is, however, whether it implies negation of the existence of the other as having claims on me and calling me out of myself. There are in fact some Buddhist scholars who do not feel satisfied with the above "official" Mahāyāna doctrine on Mercy and, in particular, with the parallelism found therein between the negation of the self and the negation of the other. Let me first quote the man who is recognized as the "dean" of Buddhist studies in Japan, himself a devout Buddhist. After remarking that in Buddhism "mercy and equality constitute the identical practical principle," he concludes his considerations of mercy as follows:

> The practice of mercy lies in acting in the direction of the non-duality of self and other. This could also be said to mean: in each case to reject the self and to bring the other to life. If it meant only negating the self, it would amount to a nihilism. This has become nowadays an authoritative way of thinking, but in fact the ethics of non-duality aims at the overcoming of that standpoint.[55]

It rather looks to me as if Nakamura is trying in this text to have his cake and eat it too, but the main thing in my perspective is that he breaks through the equality or parallelism between (the negation of) I and Thou.[56]

My second example is taken from a scholar-preacher of the Pure Land school, that form of Buddhism that is totally centered on the saving mercy of Amida Buddha, but is strongly dependent for its "theology" on general Mahāyāna theory.

> Granted that it is one kind of erroneous view to see only the aspect of difference or differentiation, and to forget the infinite that is common to self and other, is not it also a mistake to see only the aspect of equality and identity?...Compassion arises because, while considering the commonality of self and other, one distinguishes in fact and at the same time between self and other.[57]

[55] 中村 元 Nakamura Hajime, 慈悲 [Mercy] (Kyoto: Heiryakuji Shoten, 1964), 136, 272.

[56] E. Lévinas expresses the asymmetrical relationship of I and Thou, for example, as follows: "What I permit myself to demand from myself cannot be compared to what I have a right to demand from the other. This moral experience, trivial as it is, points to a metaphysical asymmetry." *Totalité et infini*, 46.

[57] 曽我量深選集 [Selected Writings of Soga Ryōjin] (Tokyo: Yayoi Shobō, 1970) 1:254–5.

If one compares this for a moment with Christian speculation on the relationship of I and Thou, it looks quite possible that the aspect of equality is not sufficiently taken into consideration in the Christian reflection, while the latter aspect—that of otherness, distance, and movement between the two—gets all the limelight and is taken for granted. Let me cite two examples to illustrate that difference in outlook:

> The love project is neither egocentric closure on oneself, nor identification with the other, but an opening and gift of the self to the Other that respect its otherness.[58]

> Love can only exist in a world where there are genuinely different selves. When Jesus and the prophets teach that I should love my neighbor as myself, they do not mean to say that my neighbor *is* myself. Love is made both necessary and possible because my neighbor is not me.... Eastern psychologies, in their manifold variety, serve mainly to present the picture of how life can be lived if what we think are differences are really illusory. Since there is no real difference, love is redundant.[59]

With regard to the last sentence, it may be good to remark that, the theory notwithstanding, Buddhist praxis and preaching do not draw the conclusion that mercy is redundant.

If we then finally ask for the basis of the difficulty that Buddhist theory, with its mandatory resolution of all oppositions into emptiness, experiences in evaluating love, the following may be relevant. Buddhist theory locates the fundamental opposition that has to be overcome in the subject-object dichotomy that constitutes all ordinary consciousness. And I believe that it succeeds indeed in defending the non-duality of subject and object as data of consciousness. On that level, no real alterity or priority can be logically established. The theory seems to run into trouble, however, when it purports that the same procedure is valid also in the case of existential situations, especially the I-Thou relationship. Among Western philosophers it is probably E. Lévinas who most explicitly rejects that reduction of existential situations to the logical subject-object scheme, and vigorously defends the *sui generis* character of the I-Thou relationship, with its irreducible *altérité* and *extériorité*.

> The relationship with the Other does not have the same status as the relations offered to objectifying thought, wherein the distinction of the terms reflects at the same time their unity. The relation between me and the Other does not have the structure that formal logic discovers in all

[58] B. Ibal, "Création, séparation et amour," 341.

[59] Harvey Cox, "The Pool of Narcissus," *Cross Currents* 27/1 (1977): 25.

relations. The terms of the I-Thou relationship remain absolute notwithstanding the relation in which they find themselves.

...Exteriority is not a negation but a wonder.[60]

In the preceding we have mainly focused on one aspect of mercy-love that made it impossible for the Buddhist standpoint of non-differentiating wisdom to recognize mercy-love as anything more than a provisional reality: the differentiation or otherness mercy-love always implies. In the following we shall devote brief attention to a different, but of course not unrelated, aspect: the fact that love does not directly fall in line with wisdom, but belongs to the realm of the conative or appetitive, implies striving and desire. Mercy-love must therefore finally be negated and absorbed into the higher reality of wisdom, and cannot be trusted as the dynamics of the path to liberation.

At this point, it may be wise to widen our horizon by again having a look at India, that cradle of Buddhism. There it appears that, from rather early on—at least since the time of the *Bhagavadgītā*—three paths to salvation are being distinguished: action, knowledge, and devotion. The path of devotion (*bhakti*) is that of "loving faith," whereby one entrusts oneself to a personified deity. It is recognized as a path to unity, but is mostly seen as something to be finally subsumed under, or taken as a preparatory step for, the path of knowledge, which alone leads to perfect unity. Still, Rudolf Otto finds, in the figure of Prahlāda in the Vishnu-purāna, a mysticism of love or devotion that is not subordinated under wisdom—and that strikes one as showing surprising similarities to Ruusbroec's mysticism:

> [In Prahlāda's case], the mystical experience arises from a determined act of bhakti...the object seen consumes the seer.
>
> But without doubt this personal intercourse is here not something lower or of less value, which could be sacrificed to the mystical experience [*sic*]. One might say: the characteristic of this God is that he can be interchangeably present with the soul, either as blessed all-absorbing All, or as personal lover and friend of the soul.[61]

Coming back to Buddhism, there can be no doubt that the Buddhist position on the appetitive or desire, insofar as it is radically negative, is paradoxical and looks untenable. This paradox has been formulated, for instance, as follows:

[60] Lévinas, *Totalité et infini*, 197, 325.

[61] Otto, *Mysticism East and West*, 177, 178. I must object, of course, to Otto's restricting "mysticism" to one branch of it. The last part of the sentence may remind one of H. Bergson's urging philosophers "to understand how the love in which the mystics see the very essence of divinity can be both a person and a creative power." *The Two Sources of Morality and Religion* (Garden City, N.Y.: Doubleday, n.d.), 253.

> Desirelessness is ideal, yet one must cultivate one's desire to attain the ideal.... Although ultimately one strives to be free of all desires, the only way to accomplish this is by means of desire.[62]

In other words, since all motivation for human action rests on desire, the motivation for the practice of the Buddhist path also can only be found in desire. As to the question of what, in the Buddhist view, is wrong with desire, we must limit ourselves here to indicating its most obvious shortcomings: desire is after all a "passion" or emotion, and all desire is founded on a dualistic judgment that discriminates between good and bad, pleasurable and painful. A next question would then be: how have Buddhists been living with that paradox? Here again, two very rough indications will have to do. It appears that Theravāda Buddhism in fact works with a distinction between desire for lower goals, which is condemned, and the desire for the final goal, Nirvana, which is exempted from the general condemnation of desire.

> This implies that desire for the goal is [considered to be] a necessary part of the path to it, and also that these who desire anything other than nibbāna [Nirvana] do not qualify as Buddhist trainees.[63]

This might be considered to be very close to the position of Christian spirituality, which demands purification and unification of desire in the sole desire for God. Mahāyāna Buddhism, however, condemns that exemption of the desire for Nirvana or enlightenment as unfounded and illogical, and seems to direct the fire of its negation especially at that "higher desire." This Mahāyāna position shows many forms and ramifications, but its gist might succinctly be rendered by the following formula: All desire indeed belongs to a lower order, and anyway there is nothing in front of us to be desired or attained.

Still, whatever their philosophical theory, the Buddhist masters cannot avoid the recommendation of an ardent desire for enlightenment in their spiritual discourse. To cite only one example, the Japanese Zen Master Dōgen, who sternly forbids his disciples to see enlightenment as a result of practice, since "in the Buddha Dharma, practice and realization are identical,"[64] also tells them: "It is the one who arouses a serious striving who quickly attains enlightenment."[65]

---

[62] Grace G. Burford, "Theravāda Buddhist Soteriology and the Paradox of Desire," in R. E. Buswell and R. M. Gimello, eds., *Paths to Liberation* (Honolulu: University of Hawaii Press, 1992), 48.

[63] Burford, "Theravāda Buddhist Soteriology," 58.

[64] Dōgen, "Bendōwa," as translated by N. Waddell and Abe Masao in *The Eastern Buddhist* 4/2 (1971): 144.

[65] Dōgen, *Zuimonki*, iii, 14.

Can we draw any conclusions from all this? It seems hard to avoid the conclusion that the Buddhist exclusion of desire and love from the higher regions of spirituality is not well founded, since it is finally based on an a priori and exclusive appreciation of the cognitive component of the human being; and that the sweeping negation is untenable in practice. Still, we must admit that human desire is a tricky thing and that many of the Buddhist considerations on the necessity of "emptying" our desires are well taken and would have been subscribed to, I believe, by Ruusbroec. Buddhist speculation, for example, seems to suggest that religious dynamism should come from a *vis a tergo* (a power from behind) and not from a *vis a fronte* (a power in front): from an object put up in front of us. The reason is that in the latter case we are apt to clothe the object with forms born out of our lower desires. The distinction between these two kinds of force is not always easy, however. It could be argued that original Buddhism knew only a *vis a tergo*: the loathing of the *duhkha* (unsatisfactory condition) of the present world, *samsāra*, and no *vis a fronte*, since Nirvana was only defined as the negation of this world. In Mahāyāna, however, Nirvana came to be invested with four positive characteristics (permanence, bliss, self, and purity) and could thus function as an attracting *vis a fronte*.

This reminds one of Ruusbroec's use of the term "voreneempt." Therein Ruusbroec recognizes the need of a *vis a fronte*: in order to be intent on God, we must somehow represent God in names and images. Ruusbroec stresses, however, that it is necessary to transcend these images. The interesting thing for us here is that, in the explanation of the necessity of this transcendence Ruusbroec's presentation seems to be quite close to that of some Buddhists. In other words, the Flemish mystic argues that what is wrong with these images is that as one ascribes names to God, one takes or captures (*neempt*) God therein, and places him in front of (*vore*) one's mental eye.[66] Could this possibly be reworded as: the *vis a fronte* of the images must be replaced by the *vis a tergo* of the God one has already found before the seeking?

Finally, we must ask about the role of mercy-love in Buddhist religiosity. Above we have seen how *bhakti* or love-devotion to a personified religious object plays a big role in Hinduism. Would this *bhakti* element be absent from Buddhism? One certainly gets that impression from the reading of most histories of Buddhism, which mostly concentrate their attention on the evolution and different forms of Buddhist philosophy. When asked, however, whether these histories present a true picture of what really happened in the religious life of the Buddhist faithful, the answer can only be a resounding "No!" Taking a hint from the basic "creed" of all Buddhists: "I entrust myself to the Buddha, I entrust myself to the Dharma..."—notice that the

---

[66] See, for example, *Spiritual Espousals. Opera omnia* III.a.766–79.

205

Buddha always comes first—it could be said that these histories pay attention to the "path of the Dharma" and totally neglect the "path of the Buddha." That the entrusting to the Buddha, not an impersonal principle this time but a lovable person, plays an enormous role in Buddhist religiosity all through its history is attested to by the popularity of the *Jātaka Stories*, which tell us of the Buddha's former lives, by the veneration of the Buddha's relics (the so-called "stupa cult"), by the important place the Buddha's birthday plays in the Buddhist calendar of events, by the glory of the omnipresent Buddha images, by the recommended practice of meditation on the Buddha names, and so on.

It is true, however, that in Buddhist theory this devotion to the Buddha is most often presented as *upāya*, and is supposed to be overcome on the higher levels of the spiritual path, as Zen proclaims it in a lapidary way: "If you meet the Buddha, kill the Buddha." Thus, for instance, monks may be advised to leave the stupa cult to the lay believers in order to devote themselves exclusively to meditation. The question could be asked, however, whether this exclusion of mercy-love from the higher realms of mysticism is still guaranteed once the bodhisattva path has reached the point where it presents Mercy as the true outcome of the Buddhist path. "If compassion is the goal where discipline arrives, may it not be the initiative whence all things derive?"[67] And—a point which I have often made already—the final exclusion of *bhakti* in Buddhist theory does not prove that the element of personal devotion is not at work in Buddhist contemplatives, even of the highest attainment. Two perceptive and sympathetic Christian observers of Zen remark on that:

> There are in Zen certain suggestions of a higher and more spiritual personalism than one might at first sight suspect.[68]

> The religiously sensitive observer meets everywhere in Zen cipher-like signs of transcendence and personal relationship.[69]

---

[67] Kenneth Cragg, *The Christ and the Faiths* (Philadelphia: The Westminster Press, 1986), 312. A discussion has flared up recently in the Buddhist world on the question of whether the belief in a Buddha-nature, present in all sentient beings, is not a betrayal of the "original" Buddhist idea of emptiness. It is indeed difficult to decide whether these two ideas must be seen as contradictory or can be seen as complementary, but it is significant that, in the notion of Buddha-nature, Buddhist religiosity has come to unite principle and person, and to invest the basic reality of the universe with a very positive content and, as it were, with a "face."

[68] T. Merton, *Mystics and Zen Masters*, 17.

[69] H. Dumoulin, *Östliche Meditation und Christliche Mystik* (Freiburg/München: Karl Alber, 1966), 164–5.

If the *bhakti* element can be said to penetrate deeply all forms of Buddhism, it is in the Pure Land School or Amidism, which is rightly called a "Buddhism of devotion," that it comes fully into its own. Everything is concentrated here in the loving faith toward Amida who, as the ideal bodhisattva figure and out of mercy, vowed to save all sentient beings who entrust themselves to him by reciting his holy name. Obtaining enlightenment or liberation by the ordinary Buddhist mystical path (by one's "own effort") is here given up (as impossible, at least for 99% of all mortals). Instead, enlightenment will be obtained once one is reborn in the "Pure Land" prepared by Amida. It is significant that, in the doctrine of this school, desire becomes absolutely central. There is, on the one hand, as the pillar whereon everything rests, Amida's Primal Vow or "Aspiration" to save all beings, and, on the other, the basic appeal launched at all beings: "desire to be born in the Pure Land!" As a dynamic this appears to come very near to the dynamics found in Scripture, at least as presented in a text I recently read:

> Scripture...expresses most of all the theme of the covenant, that is, the theme of the march of two desires toward each other: first the desire-initiative of God to give himself to his human creature, and then the desire-response of the human creature to its God.[70]

[70] Henri Martin, "Désirs," C. Baumgartner ed., *Dictionnaire de spiritualité* 3 (Paris: Beauchesne, 1967), col. 608.

207

PART THREE

Natural Mysticism

10

Natural Mysticism: An Appreciation

No doubt dissenting tendencies in the idea and practice of the contemplative life at the time Ruusbroec was composing his major works had a major influence on his writing. We find reference in nearly all of his works to those who have "gone astray" by practicing what he calls "natural contemplation." Another indication of that influence is the prologue of Brother Gerard to Ruusbroec's *The Little Book of Clarification*, which dates from around 1350.[1] Considerable research has been done on the teachings of the various heretical groups, but I will pass over this except for a few facts relevant to the present context.

To begin with, let it be stated clearly that Ruusbroec did not invent adversaries, only the better to argue for his own position. What is more, scholarship has shown that his descriptions of the persons and practices he takes issue with are on the whole fair. If his language becomes strong—even crude—at times, it is because the matter was more than academic for Ruusbroec. He was abreast of the "lunatic fringe" of the new contemplative movements. But it was primarily

> the simple men and women, easily seducible, with whom Ruusbroec was concerned, as were his responsible contemporaries, to protect them from the harm which might come to them.... Few of them could read; and,

---

[1] See the Introduction to *The Little Book of Clarification*, in *Opera omnia* I.17, 24–2. *The Little Book* was composed in reply to criticisms leveled against his first work, *The Realm of Lovers*, just as later *The Sparkling Stone* would clarify the ideas in *The Spiritual Espousals*. Ruusbroec sought out his critics to discuss with them face to face. The most virulent criticism, however, only came a few decades after Ruusbroec's death from Gerson, the chancellor of the Sorbonne. Regarding Ruusbroec's own position on the authority of the Church and the ecclesiastical situation at the time, see pages 19–20 of the same Introduction. Let it suffice here to quote one expression of his spiritual confidence and freedom: "Of these things I have written often, but I surrender myself and submit to eternal truth and to the faith of Holy Christendom.... Yet what I experience, I experience. I cannot drive it from my spirit; even if it were a question of gaining the whole world, no one would ever be able to take from me the certitude and confidence that Jesus will not condemn me. When I hear otherwise, I prefer to keep silence" (*The Twelve Beguines*, in *Werken* IV.218:32–219:7).

once they had been rounded up and sentenced, what few books they owned were systematically destroyed."[2]

As for the doctrinal positions of his adversaries, Ruusbroec was acquainted with their popular and often more vulgar expressions. When he

> reports heretics as saying "I should be as glad for Christ to have been born of a common woman," or reproaches them, "You would as soon look at the wall as you would at the holy sacrament in the priest's hands," he is relaying to us the abusive language of the gutter, unlikely to have achieved any literary status higher than that of graffiti.[3]

A fair body of scholarship exists on Ruusbroec's knowledge and use of the dissenting literature itself and the way he reports it. We know that the adepts of "natural contemplation" he encountered drew from two main sources, one French, the other German.[4] Among the former was the fascinating beguine Marguerite Porete from northern France, who expounded the heresy of the "Free Spirit." Although the actual teaching and the story of its spread remain shrouded in mystery to this day,[5] we know that she died at the stake in Paris in 1310 and that her work, *Mirror of Simple Souls*, became very influential with contemplatives throughout Europe. We may also assume that Ruusbroec was well acquainted with the work, as was Eckhart.[6]

---

[2] E. Colledge and J. C. Marler, " 'Poverty of the Will': Ruusbroec, Eckhart and The Mirror of Simple Souls," in *Jan van Ruusbroec: The Sources, Content, and Sequels of his Mysticism*, ed. by P. Mommaers and N. De Paepe (Louvain: University Press, 1984), 44.

[3] Colledge and Marler, "Poverty of Will," 43.

[4] The first literary-doctrinal evidence was established in 1932, in J. Van Mierlo's pioneering article "Ruusbroec's bestrijding van de ketterij," *Ons Geestelijk Erf* 6 (1932): 304–46. It was pointed out then that in his earlier work Ruusbroec attacks the "quietism" of the beguines, whereas later—"systematically" in *The Twelve Beguines*—he aims at the "pantheism" of Eckhart and people who are influenced by his ideas. Van Mierlo still was in the belief that Ruusbroec probably knew Eckhart only "from hearsay."

[5] For a summary, see Wiseman, 5. In the description of the deviating contemplatives in *The Spiritual Espousals*, the word *free* appears several times with significant detail: "they maintain that they are free and united to God without intermediary"; "And they wish...to be free and to be obedient to no one, neither to pope nor to bishop nor to parish priest"; "for they wish to be free without the commandments of God and without virtues" (*Opera omnia* III.b.2078, 2098, 2161). The word *free* also figures importantly in Ruusbroec's own presentation of the correct contemplative way, where it points to the possibility of entering into a personal relationship with God. For instance, in *The Realm of Lovers*, he speaks of that relationship simply: "[People] will serve Him with free will in true obedience.... Because God has done all things out of free goodness." The freedom he has in mind is not a liberation from all sorts of human "intermediaries" but a liberation to "do all his works in freedom to God's glory" (*Werken* I.25.18–24).

[6] See P. Verdeyen, "Oordeel van Ruusbroec over de rechtgelovigheid van Margaretha Porete," *Ons Geestelijk Erf* 66 (1982): 88–96.

NATURAL MYSTICISM: AN APPRECIATION

From the Rhineland flowed different texts. First of all, there was Eckhart's Sermon 52, "Beati pauperes spiritu," which Ruusbroec seems to have known well. For example, when in the *Twelve Beguines* he

attacks the ancient Gnostic tenet of "poverty of the spirit" as a perversion of Gospel truths, the objects of his animosity, the places where he found this false "poverty" preached, were Eckhart's sermon and the analogues with his teaching which are in Margaret's *Mirouer*.

Ruusbroec's handling of the texts of the German Meister follows a pattern:

First, he makes several literal quotations from the sermon, and he then employs reductio ad absurdum. He takes some of Eckhart's most arresting paradoxes and shows what confusion they can produce in the minds of the unlearned, incapable of accepting them with the same theological subtlety in which they are advanced.[7]

The heretics Jan van Ruusbroec treats also drew inspiration from a number of minor German texts, which also originated in the circle around Eckhart and were already available in Middle Dutch by 1350. The most important among them is *Schwester Katrei* (Sister Catherine), a pamphlet of the beghards written in Strasbourg around 1320. The tract appears in the form of a dialogue between Catherine, the beguine, and her confessor, thought to be none other than Meister Eckhart himself. F.-J. Schweitzer points out how closely Ruusbroec's reference in *The Spiritual Espousals* to those who claim to "stand in a pure passivity…just like a loom" or "in a pure passivity without working" agrees with ideas that appear in the quietistic texts.[8]

Ruusbroec's reading of the texts of his adversaries redounds to his credit. This is especially true of his reading of Eckhart:

His theological mastery was seldom better displayed than by the deftness with which he isolated and analyzed what he considered erroneous in Eckhart's writings, and yet saluted what is good and true in his propagation of his cardinal theme, "the birth of the Word in the soul." In this, Ruusbroec showed himself more discriminating, perceptive and charita-

---

[7] Colledge and Marler, "Poverty of Will," 16. For examples of *verbatim* quotation by Ruusbroec from Sermon 52, see page 18. For further evidence of Ruusbroec's acquaintance with this sermon, see F.-J. Schweitzer, "Die 'Zweite' Ketzer 'Sorte' in Ruusbroecs 'Geistlicher Hochzeit': der Mensch als Gottes 'Werkzeug' und sein Verdienen," in *Ons Geestelijk Erf* 56 (1982): 132–5.

[8] F.-J. Schweitzer, "'Caritatem habe, et fac quod vis!' Die 'Freien Geister' in der Darstellung Jans van Ruusbroec und in Selbstzeugnissen," in *Jan van Ruusbroec* (see note 2), 54–8. Quotations from Ruusbroec can be found in his *Opera omnia* III.b.2083, 2128.

ble than most of Eckhart's contemporaries.[9]

The same is true of his handling of the teachings of the "Free Spirit":

> The presentation by Ruusbroec of the heresy appears, when one compares it with the testimonies of the "Free Spirits" themselves, on the whole as correct as far as the reproduction of the tenets goes.[10]

In his writings on natural contemplation, then, Ruusbroec does not take the position of the disinterested scholar; neither does he focus primarily on doctrinal contents. It is the life of his own people that is constantly on his mind. His aim is to open the eyes of those interested like him in the contemplative life to the theological and ethical consequences of their spiritual practices. That is to say, his primary audience was a practicing one, what we might call today "confirmed" believers. Most likely many of them were living in cloisters or were members of groups like the beguines and the beghards. The problem he addressed was not outside the Church but deep within its walls. Ruusbroec recognized that serious Christians of good will were praying in such a way that, unwittingly, they had fallen into heresy or were being lured in that direction. Thus in *The Spiritual Tabernacle* we find him accusing such persons of "liking to consort with the dead, that is, with those who are like them, in the sects."[11]

The picture this gives us of Ruusbroec is of one who embodies in his own person the ideal of Christian perfection. And indeed, in addition to being an eminent mystic and writer, he must have been a wise and holy man. (Official ecclesiastical approbation raised him to the status of Blessed but never went so far as to confer on him the title of Saint.) Still—and this is surely for the best—the wise and holy are far from perfect and never cease to be children of their time. In Ruusbroec's case, two faults are of particular interest to us here: his intolerance towards heretics and his bias against non-Christians.

As to the first, he tells us in *A Mirror of Eternal Blessedness* that "they should rightly be burned at the stake." This is enough to send shudders through the modern conscience, but the continuation of the passage leads one to question the depths of his compassion: "for in God's eyes they are damned and belong in the pit of hell, far beneath all the devils."[12] A knowledge of the context in which he was writing is some help here, but for the modern reader it does not entirely serve to justify his judgments.

---

[9] Colledge and Marler, "Poverty of Will," 14.

[10] F.-J. Schweitzer, "'Caritatem habe'," 67.

[11] *Werken* II.343:22–3.

[12] *A Mirror*, Wiseman, 231.

The same is true of what he has to say about non-Christians, though here the excusing circumstances are easier to accept. For Ruusbroec, as for the rest of his contemporaries in the Christian world, the non-Christian world was divided into two classes of people: the pagans and the Jews.[13] Within this pattern, bad Christians—that is, people who "publicly live in mortal sin"—are placed in the same category as the pagans who "do not follow the natural and rational law" and the Jews who "despise their law and the prophecies." Christians who have thus "turned away" from the faith are "worse" than those lawless pagans and Jews. The difference is that it is within their means to be converted, "for they are children and the others are aliens." Christian "unbelievers"—the heretics—are also classified as among the "damned," unless they choose to be converted. But Ruusbroec adds a strict qualification here: even those pagans who "live in natural justice" and those Jews who "live according to God's commandments" are damned. Worse still, the Jews are "more heavily" damned than the pagans, because "they despise the prophecies of their own law that speak of the coming of Christ and his passion."

Two points need to be made here if we are to advance beyond the surface tarnish that such statements give to the larger context of Ruusbroec's thought. First, Ruusbroec had the naïve belief that the Christian message is available for everyone throughout the world to accept, "for the name of Jesus Christ...has been preached and made known to all the ends of the world."[14] This means that each individual has the opportunity freely to "turn and convert" to its truth. Second, his image of God was of a divine being that offers his grace to everyone equally:

> All people, pagans and Jews, good and evil, have prevenient grace in common (*ghemeyne*). By means of His universal (*ghemeyne*) love which God has towards all, He has caused His name and the redemption of human nature to be preached and revealed to all the ends of the earth. Whoever wishes to turn can convert.... For God wishes to save all, and to lose none. For on the Day of Judgment, no one will be able to complain that too little was done for him, had he wished to be converted. Because of this, God is a universal (*ghemeyne*) radiance and a universal (*ghemeyne*) light which enlightens heaven and earth and each person according to his need and according to his worthiness.[15]

[13] I am summarizing here *The Realm of Lovers, Werken* I.17–19. For short parallels, see *A Mirror*, Wiseman, 229 and *The Little Book, Opera omnia* I.105–6.

[14] *The Realm of Lovers, Werken* I.19:10–3.

[15] *Opera omnia* III.a.65–75. On the importance of the "common," see chapter 8, pages 174–7.

THE PROBLEM OF NATURAL CONTEMPLATION

Before taking up the distinctions Ruusbroec draws between different kinds of contemplation, we need to be prepared for a certain linguistic oddity. Ruusbroec uses two almost synonymous expressions to refer to the contemplative way of his opponents: "contemplating naturally" (*natuerlijc scouwen*) and "turning inwards without grace" (*sonder gracie inkeeren*). The former has a positive ring, while the latter seems to suggest that those who follow nature's course are excluded from God's loving care. The wording suggests souls fallen from grace and exerting themselves in vain. To clarify, we need to look briefly at what Ruusbroec means by grace, the supernatural, and faith.[16]

Ruusbroec's presentation of divine grace follows the mainstream of Thomistic theology. Grace was the foundation of the experience of God and remained so up to the most elevated mystical states. If contemplative prayer entails an awareness of one's relationship with God, that relationship is initiated in a spiritual event prior to experiential awareness. Here Ruusbroec distinguishes, without separating, two elements in the appearance of grace. First, there is "prevenient grace," the stage at which one is prepared by events that give one pause to reflect on the human condition. One awakens as it were to the gap and the qualitative difference between the relative and the Absolute, between beings and the highest Being. And it is this natural awakening—not only to my limited essence but also to my unholy existence—that moves the individual to wonder if such a gap might be bridged and how. As *The Spiritual Espousals* has it:

> When the soul thus stands…in dread as to what it should do, considering God, itself, and its evil deeds, therefrom result a natural compunction for sin and a natural good will. This is the highest of that prevenient grace.[17]

In the longing to draw closer to what appears so strongly as Other, one comes to the acme of "natural" religiousness. This is where "nature" comes to the end of its tether. "God is so great, we are so small," Ruusbroec seems to suggest; "He is holy, we are sinners"—and that's that. How can one ever think of reaching beyond such clearly marked limits? It is as if one were to look out at a quiet landscape and long for it to open up into a smiling face. Exert oneself naturally as one will, the human being inevitably arrives at the edge of the separating abyss that only something "supernatural" would bridge.

This is where faith comes into the picture. To receive what is supernatural, people "have to bring nature to the highest that nature is able to accom-

---

[16] I am drawing here on two basic sources: *The Realm of Lovers*, Werken I.25:3–26:4; and *The Spiritual Espousals*, Opera omnia III.a.60–133.

[17] *Opera omnia* III.a.110–4.

plish." A desire emerges to enter into a new relationship with that Being the doctrine points at and whose supreme reality has been recognized in personal reflection. When nature brings this desire to its highest pitch of longing for a Thou, at that very point it fails. When nature "fails and can go no further," it realizes that the divine Being is also a person to relate to and as such is as "free" as human beings to desire what it wants to desire. There is no pre-established ground for a personal relationship. This is the point of entry into the supernatural. Only by accepting nature's failure in the face of God can the possibility of something new emerge. Ruusbroec describes this spiritual situation:

> God comes with supernatural light and enlightens the understanding, in such a way that a person believes and trusts more (*meer gheloeft ende ghetrouwet*) than one is able to describe.

An unforeseeable movement takes place. On the one hand, God "comes," breaking through the natural relationship to appear as a living God. This coming is not an apparition but a moving force, a "secret inworking" that provokes the human heart to correspond to its unexpected presence. God's coming is a power that also gives the power to react to it. On the other hand, one so touched by grace assumes an inner attitude typical of the personal relationship. One not only "believes and trusts" in the Other, but does so in a way that defies description—that is, unconditionally. "From this there springs forth a heartfelt love which, in freedom, unites him to God."

The above account summarizes how the human being "feels" when the natural resolve to struggle with ultimate questions opens one to the realm of the supernatural. One need not assent to the theoretical language in which it is couched to accept Ruusbroec's existential description of the plausibility of grace. As we have seen in chapter 7,[18] faith has an existential as well as a doctrinal aspect, and it is chiefly the former that Ruusbroec is accusing his contemplative opponents of having neglected.

But there is more than cool phenomenological description going on here. When Ruusbroec speaks of people who contemplate "without grace," he is thinking of Christians who deliberately choose *against* grace and who cling "stubbornly" to their own devices. At least in the case of the most educated of their ranks, he judges them to have fallen out of grace with God. And, we might add, had he known of Eastern contemplatives "turning inwards" in their own non-Christian way, he would likely have treated them on the same terms. The difference he points out at the experiential level corresponds to an objective distinction: pray in a certain way and certain consequences will follow.

[18] See page 145.

Perhaps this approach can still appeal to certain present-day readers. No doubt there are Christians who feel that somehow, somewhere, personal responsibility ought to be connected with God's grace. But for most of us that view has become problematic, if only because human beings, including those who hold the highest seats of religious authority, are so obviously incompetent when it comes to deciding how God's grace is meted out, on whom it is showered, and from whom withheld. In the Catholic tradition, the day has passed when peremptory statements about who "has" God's grace and who does not were dogmatically permissible. The Second Vatican Council not only repudiates any discrimination, it asks for an appreciative approach towards those who are "outside." In the case of non-Christian religions, the Council extends this concern beyond individuals to entire traditions as well.

But this still leaves us with the question of how to read the fourteenth-century author when he speaks of contemplation "without grace." The solution to the theological questions cannot lie in Ruusbroec's own writings. His books are not a Holy Writ that transcends the limits of the age in which they were written. But they do provide descriptive information on mystical experience, and this is how we shall continue to read them. Accordingly, we will read the terms *natural* and *without grace* in a phenomenological way. That is to say, we accept with Ruusbroec—but without any pretence of finding out who is favored by God and who not—that there exist two different kinds of contemplation or mysticism, both of which rely on a non-contemplative element that Ruusbroec calls "grace." Only then can we see what value his insights may still have for us today.

Indeed, Ruusbroec's point of departure for his appreciation of natural contemplation is his own portrait of mystical union, which we discussed earlier. He does not consider the experience of his opponents from any theoretical or dogmatic point of view, but contrasts it with the experience whose process he is himself familiar with. He does not judge it to be erroneous in view of some abstract teaching, but rather to be incomplete in view of the entirety of the mystical path. Thus his criticisms present alternative descriptions of ultimate reality or the awareness of God.[19]

To facilitate the reading of the texts—and so, alas, to weaken the suspense somewhat—we begin by marking off the main steps in Ruusbroec's discussion of natural contemplation. The error he is attacking comes to this: certain predominantly well-meaning Christians with a bent for contemplative prayer are striving for a kind of personal religious experience—for that "savor" or "taste"—that is dramatically lacking in the Church. They pray, or

[19] For clear instances of this approach, see *Opera omnia* III.b.1972; II.551–78; I.138–9.

rather they practice contemplation (the verb *to pray* is necessarily unsuited to them) in a natural way or without grace.

Remarkably, Ruusbroec does not reject this "natural" search for experience outright. On the contrary, he values it, and values it in a sincere and fundamental way that may well amaze his readers. Then why the attack? Because by opting for the natural way, one all but inevitably comes to reject a fundamental principle of the Christian religion. Natural contemplation implies that faith and grace, the basic supernatural gifts, disappear. But for Christian tradition it is precisely these gifts that are essential to the full relationship of the human being with God.

Faith and grace as such are not contemplative gifts. They do not require felt, mystical experience. They belong to us all in the form of the common and normally functioning spiritual ability to say yes or no to the Christian message. Ruusbroec censures the adepts of natural contemplation for deliberately eliminating from their spiritual lives the gifts that every "good person" is endowed with. In order to reach experiential union with God (or more accurately put, with the Absolute or Nothing, since for them the word God becomes meaningless), they must pass by these basic elements and concentrate all attention on experience.

Here we see the sharp edge of Ruusbroec's criticism as he confronts his opponents on their chosen ground. If, as the common human beings they are, they do not risk a personal relationship with the divine Other, then their particular spiritual experience is bound to be a limited one. Without the openness produced by faith and grace, their contemplation severely restricts itself. In Ruusbroec's striking phrase, "However high the eagle soars, it cannot fly above itself."[20]

Finally, let it be noted that Ruusbroec's writings on natural contemplation do not combine into a uniform corpus, but rather appear in one form or another in nearly all of his eleven treatises. Given the thirty years that elapsed between *The Realm of Lovers* and *The Twelve Beguines*, it is hardly surprising that Ruusbroec's views should have evolved. What is more, we see a shift in the object of his critique from the quietism of the beguines to the pantheism of certain of Eckhart's followers. The critical tone also strengthens as the years go on, as Ruusbroec's misgivings against the natural way of mysticism grow deeper and deeper. In his first work, his comments are rather tame: "But without the grace of God, seldom is it so nobly performed."[21] Later on, he no longer leaves much room for "noble" exceptions, as he dismisses the natural way of contemplation *tout court* as dehumanizing.

[20] *The Spiritual Tabernacle, Werken* II.336:36.

[21] *Werken* I.34.

Despite the great variety of comments and the contexts in which they are made, a single red thread seems to run through Ruusbroec's criticisms: all the deviations of the natural way ultimately result from the state of "idleness" or "rest" it encourages. In short, it makes good sense to read his passages collectively, rather than keep them fixed to their original works.

THE DESCRIPTION OF THE NATURAL WAY

To read Ruusbroec's presentation of the natural way of mysticism collectively does not give us license to skim through his writings uncritically. The literary style differs too much from one passage to the next. Description and interpretation are woven together; the focus shifts from questions of method to questions of results; and Ruusbroec's descriptions of the views of his opponents often alternate with his own views. Fairness to Ruusbroec, and indeed also to the question at hand, requires a rather attentive eye.

At the descriptive level Ruusbroec chiefly focuses on two subjects: the contemplative procedure of his opponents, and the experience it leads to.

The Method of "Turning Inwards"

Those who follow the natural way do so by "turning inwards" (*inkeer*). To start with, they acknowledge the impact of bodily posture on spiritual exercise. Inner exploration is tied to a particular position, as we see in the method of "sitting-still" in order to reach inner calm:

> But now consider the manner in which a person surrenders himself to this natural rest. It is a sitting-still (*een stille sitten*) without any practice within or without, in emptiness (*ledicheit*), so that rest may be found and may abide unhindered.[22]

In *The Four Temptations* we read something similar:

> The way of these people is to sit the body down quietly and without activity, its idle, imageless sensuality turned inward on itself.[23]

Yet it is not this awareness of the psychosomatic nature of contemplation that distinguishes the natural way. Ruusbroec himself, like the great majority of Christian mystics, is extremely sensitive on this point. He is consistent in viewing the human person as a single whole, but when he comes to explain to his readers how to go about praying, the body features strongly. In addition to his repeated defense of oral prayer, he advocates a number of

[22] *Opera omnia* III.b.1986–8.

[23] *Opera omnia* X.175–7.

physical positions.[24]

The reason Ruusbroec draws attention to the sitting position of those who practice natural contemplation now comes clear. In contrast to the traditional Christian practice that he follows, they restrict themselves to a single posture of prayer. Sitting in stillness evidently agrees with their inclination to "rest," and indeed prefigures their elevating "rest" to a position that surpasses and excludes all other forms of prayer.

But turning inwards goes further than the somatic. Note how Ruusbroec describes the method in its entirety. He begins with the general picture:

> The second way is a way of the natural light.... A person has to go this way by the lower faculties enriched with natural moral virtues, and by the higher faculties lifted up to idleness (*in ledicheden*), into the simple ground of the soul's essence (*inden eenvoldeghen gront des wesens der zielen*). [That ground] bears the image of God and is a natural realm of God.[25]

The reference to the essence of the soul, which recalls the portrait of the human treated in chapter 5, reminds us that those who would contemplate by the "natural light" are, like all of us, structured internally. In particular, the psyche is differentiated into three levels, each of which will have to be transgressed on the journey inwards.

After assuming the seated position, the next step on the natural way inward is to condition the sensory level of the psyche. In Ruusbroec's first work, *The Realm of Lovers*, moral purification through the exercise of the natural virtues is given as an integral part of natural contemplation. But in the following works, moral endeavor does not figure any longer. Ruusbroec's opponents appear to be interested only in eliminating all images. Their aim is to empty the senses, not to rehabilitate them. Reference to a state of being "unassailed by images" appears again and again in Ruusbroec's description of this stage:

> Now consider: when a person is bare and unassailed by images with respect to the senses, and empty, without activity (*ledich sonder werk*) with respect to his higher faculties, then he enters into rest by mere nature. All people can find and possess this rest in themselves in mere nature, without the grace of God, if only they can empty themselves of images and of all works.[26]

---

[24] See the final piece of *The Seven Enclosures*, *Opera omnia* II.922, 929–30.

[25] *Werken* I.12:23–30.

[26] *Opera omnia* III.b.1979–83.

The adepts of the natural way preferred sitting in stillness to any activity. Seen in terms of the first level of the psyche, they seem to be committed to a single interior exercise. Ruusbroec's aim of becoming "imageless" is something quite different. For him, the practice of emptying the senses always goes hand in hand with moral endeavor. The very first thing one must do when one has stepped "within" is to flee from

> impure imagination and images (*beelden*), so as not to dwell on them or keep them with delightful inclination. Thus we won't be filled with images (*verbeelt*).

Moreover, he has no intention of emptying the senses once and for all. There is always at least one image that remains. It may become transparent, but it can never be transcended absolutely:

> But we should turn to and in our Lord Jesus Christ and look at his suffering and death.... And then we practice what we have seen. Further, we impress and form this image (*beelde*) in our heart, in our senses, in soul and body and in our whole nature, like a seal is impressed and formed in the wax. Then Christ will take us with him into that lofty life where we are united with God.[27]

In *The Sparkling Stone* this matter of images is spelled out in these terms:

> But if this good man wants to become an inward, spiritual man.... If his heart is to be free of images (*onverbeelt van herten*), he should not possess anything with affection, nor should he willingly cling to anyone or deal with anyone. For all relationship and all affection which is not purely for the honor of God bring images in the heart of man (*verbeelt des menschen herte*).... If, therefore, a man wants to become spiritual, he must forego all fleshly affection and cling to God alone with desire and affection and possess him in that way. This will drive out all encumbrance from images (*verbeeltheit*).... And if he possesses God with affection, man will be freed of images inside (*van binnen onghebeelt*), since God is a spirit and no man can make a proper image of him (*ghebeelden*). Yet in his (spiritual) practice, man should concentrate on good images, such as the passion of our Lord and all things that may raise him to higher devotion. But when he possesses God, man must enter into a bare imagelessness which is God (*eene blote onghebeeltheit*).[28]

For Ruusbroec, becoming free of images is not an isolated goal. It is embedded inextricably in the broader question of what a person's affections and

---

[27] *Werken* III.228:30–229:11.

[28] *Opera omnia* X.25–41.

desire "cling to." And even if there is no way to "possess" God except as a "bare imagelessness," this does not mean that the images are simply to be rejected. For as we have seen, the active aspect of oneness with God demands that one "practice" and "concentrate on good images."

Ruusbroec's divergence from the view of his adversaries in this matter of images goes deeper still. To concentrate exclusively on images and their dismissal is not just a matter of secondary contemplative preference. It implies a suspense of interest in exercising the moral virtues. In other words, the natural way of contemplation leads to a questionable lifestyle. It forgets the very values that belong to simple humanity and to Christianity. In addition, there were certain disturbing facts that Ruusbroec found arresting. In the *Little Book of Clarification* he mentions one way of resolving the problem of being assailed by images:

> For they hold that the highest holiness is for man to follow his nature in every way and to live unrestrained so that he may dwell within in emptiness (*in ledicheit*)..., and turn outwards to follow every prompting of his body's desires and appease the flesh, in order that he may be speedily relieved of the image (*des beelds*) and return unhindered to the bare emptiness of his spirit.[29]

Now, Ruusbroec is clear about why the followers of the natural way tend to fall into an amoral lifestyle. To begin with, there is no doubt that one can succeed in emptying the lower faculties of images if one does not have to deal with the distractions of virtue and morality. If one is able to silence the voice of conscience, then the natural method of turning inwards is able to function on its own. As a passage from *The Spiritual Espousals* points out, this path towards inner rest is open to "all people":

> no matter how evil they may be, if they live in their sins without any reproof of conscience, and can empty themselves of images and of all activity.... In itself, this rest is no sin, for it is in all people by nature, if they could but empty themselves.[30]

The starting point of natural contemplation is therefore quite independent of a person's moral qualities. To turn inwards effectively, one has only to follow proper psychological procedure. But this jettisoning of conscience is

---

[29] *Opera omnia* I.125–30. The same procedure is followed by those who appear in *The Spiritual Espousals* (III.b.2112–9). And again, in *The Mirror* Ruusbroec mentions "some persons" who value the art of freeing themselves of all images so highly that they lose sight of morality: "they consider nothing to be either good or evil, since they are able to transcend images" (Wiseman, 235).

[30] *Opera omnia* III.b.2003–7.

hardly the norm for those who call themselves Christian. Rather, sin makes itself felt within and produces its own images:

> But sin constitutes such a great obstruction (*middel*) and darkness and unlikeness between faculties and being (*wesen*)—in which God lives— that the spirit cannot achieve union with its own being (*in sijn eyghen wesen*), which would be its own and its eternal resting place, were it not for sin.[31]

But it is not only at the start of the natural way inward that moral issues can be bracketed. Those who reach a level beyond the touch of images may also find themselves beyond the reach of temptation:

> They fly as high as nature can fly.... The enemy cannot tempt one who is unassailed by images (*in der onghebeeltheit*).

The problem with the contemplative so elevated beyond images and temporality is that at some point one must return to the ordinary human world. And then morality will have its revenge and show up the abstract nature of the one who follows the natural way: "But as he comes down, he is proud and cunning, intolerant and using wild words."[32]

The next stage on the natural way inwards brings us to the level of the spiritual faculties. A passage from the *The Realm of Lovers* offers further details:

> The highest stage of the natural way consists in the three highest powers being turned away from busyness and multiplicity and turned toward idleness in unity. The elevated mind [memory], turned in toward the bareness of its essence, becomes inactive in that simple essence. And the mind has a natural inclination to and lust for the simple ground of the mind.... It is turning inward from busyness and multiplicity into the bare essence of the soul, with a natural inclination toward [the essence] as to its origin and its natural rest. There the mind is present to the bare essence of the mind, and the essence is a natural richness for the mind.
>
> The second power is the intellect, which is turned in toward its essence and looks at the idleness of the ground. In this way the intellect becomes inactive by nature and rests in not-working. It is embraced by the simplicity of its essence....
>
> The third power is the will. It has embraced the mind and the intellect, which are then naturally inclined toward their origin.

31 *Opera omnia* III.b.1498–1502.

32 *Werken* II.336:16–29.

For, when the highest powers are unconcerned with temporal things and bodily enjoyments, and are lifted up into the unity of the mind, there results an enjoyable rest that pervades body and soul. Then the powers are pervaded by and transfigured into the unity of the mind, and the unity of mind into them.

The highest stage of the natural way is the essence of the soul that is suspended in God. It is immobile and is higher than the supreme heaven and deeper than the bottom of the sea and wider than the whole world...and it is a natural reign of God and the end of all the soul's activity. For no creature is able to act in its essence, but only God can act. For he is the essence of essences and the life of lives and the origin and support of all creatures.[33]

Once the lower powers of the soul have been emptied of all images of the outside world, the inward journey can carry on. Once the doors of sense perception have been shut and the production of images stopped, the supply of familiar objects to the higher powers is cut off. This means that they can be "turned away" from "busyness and multiplicity," and thus "unconcerned with temporal things and bodily enjoyments." At that moment, the contemplative becomes aware of the uncommon state to which the innate centripetal tendency of the faculties leads. This state is characterized as "idleness" (*leedicheyt*)—a key word for Ruusbroec, we recall, but one that is not easy to translate. It can refer to inactivity, and thus stand as a contrary to "busyness" (although the English word *idleness* has a pejorative ring that is not in the Flemish), but *leedicheit* may also mean the absence of objects or "emptiness." This ambiguity is well suited to describe what is going on in the higher faculties. Turned away from their accustomed domain, they find themselves without anything to cling to. They feel "empty" and, lacking anything to do, are condemned to "idleness."

The lack of anything for the spiritual powers to take hold of is also expressed in the term *bareness*. Thus memory is "turned in toward the bareness of its essence," and is "present to the bare essence of the mind." The term conveys well the inadequacy of ordinary modes of thought (as we shall see later in the term *wiselooes*, "without modes"). We are used to approaching the world about us with an intellectual grid that distinguishes things one from another, but now the "bareness" of the essence erases that grid and our usual way of organizing and controlling reality is no longer possible.

This cessation of ordinary spiritual and intellectual activity is suggested by two words we have already met: *werkeloes* ("without work") and *raste* ("rest"). Hence the intellect "rests in no-working" and the three powers

---

[33] *Werken* I.14:11–15:29. The paragraphing is my own.

together come to an "enjoyable rest."

Not surprisingly, the third and final stage on the way inwards has to do with one's "essence." It is a state of radical no-working. In the earlier stage of idleness, the spiritual powers could at least recognize their own impotence. Here even that simple activity is absent, for "this is the end of all the soul's activity." But for Ruusbroec this does not mean that life as such has come to an end. Rather, the contemplative is aware of an activity within, a kind of "life of lives" opening up a realm of human nature not accessible to even the highest activities of the psyche. Here one comes to the very core of being human, where "no creature is able to act in its essence, but only God can act."

This is as far as Ruusbroec's description of the contemplative's method in *The Realm of Lovers* takes us. By sitting still, letting go of all images and remaining idle, the person forfeits "all the soul's activity." Clearly we are beyond the mere question of methodology here. In addition to the particular state of consciousness, we are also told what the contemplative is conscious of. In a moment we will look more closely at the "object" of natural contemplation. Our point here has only been to show how in the end two things are present to the "idle" mind: the essence of the soul and its sense of being "suspended" in God.

AN APPRECIATION OF THE NATURAL WAY

Jan van Ruusbroec not only describes how his opponents go about living the spiritual life. He also shows his appreciation for the way they have chosen and the experience it leads to. His criticisms should never be allowed to eclipse this fact.

The Value of Turning Inwards

Surprising as it may sound, the basic reason Ruusbroec gives for appreciating the way of his opponents is its very naturalness. He considers their psychological method to correspond to an innate "inclination" in our nature. Before one ever takes up the practice of the way inward, there is a centripetal bent in our being whereby the lower and exterior is constantly drawn to what is higher and interior. Accordingly, when one turns inward with the conscious aim of experiencing "rest," one in effect actualizes this natural disposition towards centering:

> For all creatures are naturally inclined to rest, and therefore rest is sought by the good and by the evil in many a way.[34]

[34] *Opera omnia* III.b.1977–79.

226

Thus, as we have seen, when memory turns in to its own ground in contemplation, the contemplative is following a "natural inclination toward (the essence) as to its origin and its natural rest."[35] And if one should further touch on one's own essence experientially, then one would "feel the natural inclination the soul has to her origin."[36] In pursuing the natural way of contemplation, an individual awakens to an inborn human disposition:

> And mankind also has a natural fundamental inclination towards God because of the spark of the soul....[37]

We find in *The Little Book* a formulation of this that sums up nicely the psychological procedure of "plain simplicity" that is at work here:

> These men, remark, by their plain simplicity and natural inclination, have returned to the nakedness of their essence.[38]

Given his assessment of the way inwards as natural, it would also seem obvious that this way concurs with his conviction that mysticism is a matter of consciousness and therefore allows for a wide variety of forms, all within the realm of what is "natural" to the human being.

This attitude of Ruusbroec's comes out in the texts first of all in the parallel he draws between his own method and that of his opponents.[39] Psychologically speaking, he seems to follow the same way inward as they do, which implies that the contemplative prayer he stands for develops along the same line and passes through the same succession of states of consciousness as natural contemplation. On this question perhaps the most telling passage appears in *The Twelve Beguines*, where the two ways are summarized and set side by side. Of those who are "enlightened with the grace of God," it is said:

> In their turning inward above reason, into their own essence, there they find the reign of God in themselves and God in his reign.

On the other hand, those who do without grace

---

[35] *Werken* I.14:23.

[36] *Werken* I.62:5–6.

[37] *Opera omnia* III.a.103.

[38] *Opera omnia* I.68–9.

[39] Of course, in the case of the contemplative who goes inward "with grace," the word *method* should be used with caution. Insofar as it implies a technique that would "naturally" yield a contemplative experience of God, the term would be out of place here. In Ruusbroec's view, the psychological "method" of the contemplative should be carried by one's spiritual attitude as a person. In his words, "If we wish to see and find eternal life in ourselves, we must through love and faith raise ourselves up above reason to our simple eye" (Wiseman, 244).

are the ones who are freed of images from whatever things they come, and who by bare nature, without grace and without virtue, turn inward above reason into their own essence. There they find idleness, rest and imageless bareness.[40]

In both cases, the main part of the way inward is described in exactly the same words: *inkeere(n) boven redene, in haer eyghen wesen*. Still, a difference is suggested here between the two ways of contemplation, a difference that has to do with method. In the first case, Ruusbroec, significantly, omits mention of the first moment of turning: emptying the lower faculties of images. As has been pointed out already, the mystics "with grace" do not make such a radical break with images. Aside from this initial tactical difference, the entire procedure is the same in both cases. The real difference between the two ways lies rather in the outcome. The technique may be identical; the experience it leads to is not. We will return to this later.

This general similarity between natural and supernatural contemplation in the method of turning inwards may be further illustrated by certain points of convergence. After describing, in *The Spiritual Espousals*, how the person who goes the way inward *without grace* "enters into rest by mere nature," Ruusbroec draws a contrast with the "loving person" or the "inner person," that is, with the mystic *with grace*. The brunt of the comparison is that the latter cannot rest like the former:

> And all people can find and possess this rest in themselves in mere nature.... But the loving person cannot rest in this, for charity and the inward stirring of the grace of God do not lie still. And therefore, the inner person cannot long remain in himself in natural rest (*in hem selven in natuerlijcker rasten*).[41]

The references to rest here would seem to be a slip of the pen, unless we are prepared to accept that Ruusbroec sees his own contemplative path as passing through the same psychological state as his adversaries.

In any event, turning inwards is one way for the "natural light" to shine in a person's life. A passage in the final section of *The Realm of Lovers* is devoted to the "natural realm of God." The term refers to the divine presence in the outer world as well as in the inner world of the human spirit. On the one hand, it is said that "those who love"—that is, those with grace—come to know that realm:

> Furthermore, the realm of God is shown to those who love in the natural light, for neither grace nor glory extinguish the natural light but make

[40] *Werken* IV.40:1–28.
[41] *Opera omnia* III.b.1981–6.

it shine clearer. When [human] nature is not assailed by images of sin, one is able to know heaven and earth naturally.

On the other hand, it is the same natural light that illumines those who are without grace:

One is also able to know how the powers of the soul and the senses are ordered...and how all creatures are ordered. In this way the natural realm of God is shown to such a person, for one may know it without the grace of God.[42]

A further example of Ruusbroec's appreciation of the natural way deserves notice. In *The Realm* mention is made of a particular type of highly educated contemplatives without grace. They are said to be "deft in natural knowledge, often quite mannerly with respect to the exterior life, idle (*leedich*) and elevated by natural contemplation." As we will see in the next chapter, Ruusbroec poses sharp criticisms against this group of persons who are admired "on account of their subtleness and good manners exteriorly," and who prove indeed "of a high natural intelligence." But he also suggests that they might be converted to a life with grace. To do so, a change would be required, but not a rejection of the natural intellectual light and the natural moral endeavor. Rather, they will be required to maintain the gifts of nature.

They should maintain and possess in humility the clarity of their understanding. In this way the divine light will enlighten them further; by their idleness and detachment and lack of concern for earthly things they will come to the contemplative life. In true charity, generosity, and mercifulness, they should maintain the morality of the natural virtues in their relationship with God, other persons, and themselves. Out of this will emerge the active life.[43]

THE NATURAL WAY AND AUTHENTIC EXPERIENCE

According to Ruusbroec, those who take the way of turning inwards not only follow a method that is of value; they also achieve, without the intervention of divine grace, a genuine experience of God. Ruusbroec recognizes that these contemplatives do not end up with only an illusion. On the contrary, they actually come to experience what really is. This is why he never calls the

[42] *Werken* I.95:12–27.

[43] *Werken* I.23:15–24:28. Here again it is quite clear that "becoming worthy of grace" is not a matter of contemplation: "...in all their works and throughout their life, they need to intend (*meynen*) God's praise and honor with a humble heart" (24:15–8).

natural way "false," though he does often speak of a "false idleness." If there is any "deceit" in this mystical path, it lies in the decision to cling to rest and idleness. Or, as he puts it, to "possess rest" in a particular way, namely "in idleness."

What is it, then, that the contemplative without grace becomes aware of as the turning inward comes to term? One may speak of it as the ultimate in the sense that it is the wellspring of one's entire being and one's every action. At the same time, it is not the ultimate in that it is not a thing but a relationship. It is a "living life":

> There are some persons who, over and above all virtuous exercises, find and experience within themselves a living life (*een levende leven*), which joins together the created and the uncreated, both God and creatures.... This is a living life, which is in all of us essentially, in our bare nature.... This life is hidden in God and in the substance of our soul. Because it is in all of us by nature, some persons are able to perceive it apart from grace, faith and the practice of virtue. These are persons who have idly turned inward, above and beyond perceptible images, to the bare simplicity of their being.[44]

Ruusbroec's claim that turning inward without grace ends in awareness of one's essence is not surprising. More striking is the religious point he makes again and again: natural contemplation discovers the immanence or "indwelling" of God in the human. The *being* of the human appears as the *in-being* of God. Ruusbroec himself uses the term *in-wesen* or *in-sine*, literally "in-being." In *The Little Book* the same thing is expressed in the term already introduced, *in-hanghen*, "being suspended in":

> For they are so simple and so inactively united to the naked essence of their soul (*bloten wesene*) and to the indwelling of God in themselves (*den inwesene gods in hen*), that they have neither ardor nor devotion towards God, neither without nor within. For in the highest point in which they are turned, they feel nothing save the simplicity of their essence, hanging in the essence of God (*sempelheit haers wesens, hanghende in gods wesen*).[45]

A passage from *The Spiritual Tabernacle* recalls the comparison to the eagle mentioned earlier in this chapter:

> One who is able, by turning inward, to empty oneself of all images and forms, and of all consideration, who is able to elevate one's mind to a

---

[44] *A Mirror*, Wiseman, 235.

[45] *Opera omnia* I:78–83. Further on in the same work, it is said that they "have found within themselves in a natural manner the indwelling of God" (473).

bare emptiness, such a person is, so far as nature goes, a king among others, for there is no higher that human nature can soar. Making a nest and resting in the essence of the human, such a person gazes at the single truth that is always shining in one's own essence and in all beings.[46]

The passages cited here are only representative of many others in the same vein, but they show how seriously Ruusbroec values the object of natural contemplation. There is no doubt in his mind that those who delve into themselves not only touch on their own ontological foundations but also come in touch with the One who grounds all things. They experience the presence of the Creator.

Ruusbroec displays the same esteem for the object of natural contemplation as for its method. Again and again he asserts that this natural experience is integral to the supernatural way. An instance of this has already been cited at the start of this section.[47] Ruusbroec begins by pointing to "some persons" who experience the "living life." No doubt these are contemplatives *with grace*. He then ascribes that same experience to "some persons" who obviously make do *without grace*. And then, in the next page, he returns to the *supernatural way* only to offer the following description:

Now raise your eyes above reason and all virtuous exercises and with a loving spirit and fixed attention look at that living life which is the source and cause of all life and all holiness. It will be seen as a glorious abyss of God's riches and as a living spring in which we feel ourselves to be united with God.

Lying at the root of Ruusbroec's appreciation of natural mysticism is an assumption already taken up in chapter 5: the human being is by nature the image of the divine. This is why he can conclude that the mystic with grace "obtains and possesses supernaturally, in his essential being, all that the spirit ever received there naturally."[48]

---

[46] *Werken* II.336:12–20.

[47] See above, note 42 and corresponding text.

[48] *Opera omnia* III.b.1481–82. See the earlier discussion of this point on page 120 above.

11

Buddhism and Natural Mysticism

> People, driven by fear, go to many a refuge, to moun-
> tains and forests, to groves and sacred trees.
>   But that is not a safe refuge, that is not the last
> refuge....
>   One who takes refuge with Buddha, the Dharma, and
> the Sangha; one who, with clear understanding, sees the
> four holy truths....
>   That is the safe refuge, that is the best refuge; having
> gone to that refuge, one is delivered from all pain.
>
> —*Dhammapada*, nrs. 188–92.

Chapter 9 may have left the reader with the impression that Buddhist mysticism
and Christian mysticism differ so immensely from each other as to leave little
common ground. The present chapter may then send the pendulum back in
the opposite direction and perhaps convince us anew that the two are very
much on common ground, not only as to their aims and methods, but also
with regard to the hidden reefs they want to avoid on their voyage.

   At first sight, though, nothing may look more preposterous than to try
to involve Buddhism in a dispute which is, after all, basically a dispute with a
Christian context, and which has been defined in terms (natural v. supernatural) that would not seem to make any sense in a Buddhist context. If, then,
I wish to engage the reader in this adventure, my reasons must be very good
ones, indeed. Whether these reasons are good enough can only appear in the
course of our investigation and is, finally, a question for the reader to decide.
At the beginning of this chapter, I can only repeat the expectation that was
already mentioned in the Foreword: that the study of the "triangular relationship" between Ruusbroec's mysticism, the "natural contemplation"
Ruusbroec describes, and Buddhist mysticism will throw some additional,
and perhaps surprising, light both on Buddhism and on Ruusbroec's mysticism.

   To be a bit more specific at this point, I hope that our investigation will
clarify to what extent Ruusbroec's objections against natural mysticism derive

from his mystical experience itself and to what extent they find their origin in his "Catholic prejudice": the faith he cherishes and wants to defend against a very subtle enemy. On the other hand, our chapter should also make it clearer what we mean when we say that Buddhism is a religion. If up to now we have stressed that Buddhism is essentially mysticism, our emphasis now will instead be: Buddhism is (not only mysticism, but also) religion, even in its most mystical moments.

In our endeavor we cannot, it is true, make use of Ruusbroec's full definitions of "contemplation with grace" and "contemplation without grace," since that would involve us in unprofitable problematics. Ruusbroec may have been right when he diagnosed the attitude of his opponents as involving the refusal of a grace that was offered them in their faith. But, if there is any evident difference between the Christian natural contemplatives of Ruusbroec's time and Buddhist contemplatives, it is that in the case of the latter we certainly have no right to speak, from a Christian standpoint, of such a conscious refusal. Furthermore, as indicated earlier, present-day Christian theology can easily conceive of God's grace at work also in Buddhist contemplatives. We shall therefore feel free to leave that element of Ruusbroec's conception out of consideration, in the spirit of Eckhart:

> People try to find out whether it is "grace" or "nature" that saves us and they never reach a solution. How foolish of them! Let God rule within you, leave the work to Him. Do not trouble thyself whether He does it naturally or supernaturally. Both nature and grace are His! What does it concern thee how it suits Him to work in thee or in another? Let Him choose how or in what manner.[1]

We shall then have to work with a "definition" or, rather, delimitation of "natural contemplation" that is somewhat less inclusive than Ruusbroec's, one that focuses on the conscious attitude of the people in question. Such a delimitation does not alter Ruusbroec's fundamental appraisal of natural contemplation, while it might become more readily applicable to Buddhist contemplation.

But before getting to that delimitation, a word on the term "grace" may be in order. It is clear, I believe, that grace, in a strict sense, means "influence or help toward salvation or liberation from outside the person to be saved." In this strict sense, the term presupposes the existence of a personal, "divine" agent. Except perhaps for the Pure Land school or Amidism,[2] the term

---

[1] As quoted in Rudolf Otto, *Mysticism East and West: A Comparative Analysis of the Nature of Mysticism* (New York: Macmillan, 1932), 90.

[2] The "theology" of Pure Land Buddhism constitutes a rather delicate balancing act on this point. This is not the place to explain this in detail and I shall therefore limit myself to a rough

233

"grace" in this sense cannot be used in the Buddhist context. But "grace" can be understood in a larger sense also, and that in a twofold way: one positive, and one merely negative. With some (although vague) positive content, it can be used to denote a factor in the process of contemplation and liberation that is not reducible to the efforts of the individual person. Thus, the Indian mystic Śankara, who believed that his contemplation had to reach not only his own self (*ātman*) but the Brahman immanent in his self, could speak of grace in such a larger sense, to distinguish his position from that of the yogin, who "seeks salvation...apart from the one, eternal, Brahman and his blessedness."[3]

> Śankara cannot admit a "grace" [in the strict sense] of Brahman. Brahman as the higher or supreme Ātman, which is identical with every ātman (soul), cannot strictly speaking be gracious. But the fact that a man can achieve the highest state not in mere isolation like the yogin, but only in and through the attainment of Brahman, has indeed an analogy to the bhakta's "salvation by grace."[4]

In this larger sense, the term "grace" could also be used to indicate a "certain complicity" with the human efforts toward liberation in the universe or the general order of things. It appears to be something like what (some) Buddhists mean when they speak of "Dharma," for instance in the formula: "I seek refuge in the Dharma." In the purely negative way, finally, the term "grace" might be used to express the consciousness (encountered in many Buddhist texts) that enlightenment is certainly not the result of one's own efforts, while leaving the question open as to where it comes from.

Let me now try out my "delimitation" of "natural contemplation" by way of an enumeration of different elements that apparently were involved in the attitude of the people targeted by Ruusbroec, possibly in dosages and combinations that differed from person to person. By *natural contemplation* I would then understand a path of contemplation:

1. to which these contemplatives were not directly inspired by their Christian faith;
2. that they deliberately kept apart from their faith and its commandments;

sketch. Pure Land devotion implies the idea of a personal transcendent entity (Amida), by whose "grace" (called by them "Other-power") one is saved, but Pure Land doctrine, embedded as it is in Mahāyāna emptiness thinking, cannot straightforwardly speak of Amida as "other" or transcendent and of "grace" in this strong sense.

[3] Otto, *Mysticism East and West*, 165.

[4] *Mysticism East and West*, 165

3. in which they did not take up (or did not know how to take up) the content of their faith (the personal relationship with the Christian God and with Christ);

4. that they considered to be the highest reality and value for them, and of a higher level (humanly and religiously) than the "life of faith."

If we now return to Ruusbroec, we remember that, according to Ruusbroec, such an attitude not only shuts the contemplative off from the real source of salvation, which is not contemplation itself but rather the (supernatural) life of faith that they looked down on, it also at the same time prevents the contemplative from reaching the full blooming of contemplation, which can only be had by opening one's contemplation to the content of faith and the (supernatural) adventure with the personal God, and from attaining the highest unity with God.

Is not this an idiosyncratic Christian judgment, the kind of judgment no Hindu or Buddhist would ever make: asserting the superiority of one's own faith and contemplative path, and characterizing these as "supernatural" and lying far above the natural path of the opponent?

Not necessarily so. Rudolf Otto draws our attention to somewhat similar judgments, within Hinduism, about forms of contemplation that are considered to be truncated. The same Śankara, for instance, condemns those whose mysticism aims only at their deepest self, with disregard of Brahman, as follows:

> Those who practice yoga, who do not seek the Brahman, and wish to find the Ātman only, stand far below those who know Brahman, and are perilously far from salvation.[5]

And Hindu believers, who put the stress on personal devotion (*bhakti*) to the gods, appear to be even more severe in their judgment:

> The later Bhaktas condemned the Yogins with their Kaivalyam [the ātman in its blessed rest and sublime glory] and denied them the final capacity for redemption, which they allowed to every denizen of hell, so conscious were they of the wrong path upon which the Yogin is set.[6]

We find, thus, that even some Eastern religionists reckon with the dangers inherent in a contemplative path which, no matter how valuable in itself, is not well-directed: it leads to damnation.

Next we learn that Buddhism also has, from very early on, known a distinction that is strangely reminiscent of the natural *v.* supernatural one in Christianity. In chapter 2 we saw that the Sarvāstivādins taught that the path

---

[5] *Mysticism East and West*, 102.

[6] *Mysticism East and West*, 163.

of liberation consists of two elements: the (rational) knowledge of the Four Holy Truths (*darśana-mārga*) and the (contemplative) path of exercise (*bhāvana-mārga*), a progressive process of ridding oneself of the wrong affective attitudes. L. Schmithausen tells us, moreover, that these people characterized both these elements as "supramundane" (*lokottara*), and that they recognized a purely inner-worldly distancing process that is also possible for non-Buddhists. They maintained, however, that this inner-worldly path (*laukikamārga*) cannot be the final step to liberation, since it does not contain anything that can make the highest, most spiritual, form of worldly existence appear as still lacking something. That final step is, then, only possible in the supramundane Buddhist path that, through knowledge of the Four Holy Truths, can free us from that last bondage.[7] D. Ruegg makes the same point when he writes, for instance:

> According to Yaśomitra [Buddhist commentator of the 6th century CE (?)], Quieting (*śamatha*) is characteristic of this *laukikamārga*, full liberating knowledge (*ājñā*) being on the contrary a distinctive feature of the supreme supramundane Path.[8]

And Ruegg further mentions two states of "notionlessness" that "are in the Buddhist tradition clearly not thought of as characteristic of the Buddhist path"[9]—in other words, considered as a kind of natural and nonliberating contemplation.

The Mahāyāna Buddhist traditions appear to attach supreme importance to a distinction, which they constantly make, between the bodhisattva path or vehicle, which leads to perfect buddhahood, and the (Hīnayāna) paths of the *śrāvakas* (literally, "listeners") and the *pratyeka-buddhas* (people who obtain enlightenment by themselves)—paths that only lead to some kind of Nirvana. A modern reader may be inclined to ask what all the fuss is about, since both states appear highly mystical, with scarcely any difference between them. It is clear, however, that Mahāyāna doctrine holds that aiming at and reaching the other two states blocks one off, forever,[10] from reaching the highest peak of perfection possible to a human being, and considers that to be a misfortune on a par with eternal damnation. It must also be mentioned here that some of

[7] L. Schmithausen, "Zur Struktur der erlösenden Erfahrung im Indischen Buddhismus," in: G. Oberhammer ed., *Transzendenzerfahrung, Vollzugs-horizont des Heils* (Wien: Institut für Indologie der Universität Wien, 1978), 106.

[8] D. Ruegg, *Buddha-nature, Mind and the Problem of Gradualism in a Comparative Perspective* (London: School of Oriental and African Studies, 1989), 195–6.

[9] *Buddha-nature*, 197.

[10] It is considered to be an extraordinary and highly significant trait of the *Lotus Sūtra* that in it the Buddha declares that even *śrāvakas* and *pratyeka-buddhas* can "convert," that is, change their aim and direction to the bodhisattva path, and thereby reach full buddhahood.

the shortcomings ascribed to the other two paths by the Mahāyāna Buddhists show a distinct similarity to Ruusbroec's criticisms of natural contemplation. For a single example, we turn to Ruegg again:

> Buddhist tradition knows of a path which, independently and taken all by itself, leads exclusively to quietude (śamaikāyana).... In some places, however, the term śamaikāyana came to be used in connection with a class of persons who seek a more or less cataleptic calm, that is, with persons attached, in terms of the Three Vehicle (triyāna) theory, to the śrāvakagotra [the "family" or "clan" of the listeners] considered as a "genus" fundamentally different from the bodhisattvagotra. A Śrāvaka of this particular class would therefore be unable ever to attain the supreme awakening...of a Buddha.[11]

It is thus rather clear that "orthodox Mahāyānists" consider the other two (equally contemplative) Buddhist paths as "incomplete." Not so clear is the question of whether they also imply, in their rebuttal of the śrāvaka and pratyeka-buddha paths, that people on these paths have culpably refused or thrown away part of their true religious "vocation."

BUDDHISM IS MYSTICISM PLUS ALPHA

Above we have learned that Christian mysticism sees itself as carried by an act of faith that is not part of the contemplative praxis, and Christian life, even in its mystical peak, can never be "mysticism only." And H. Dumoulin appears to apply this to all sound mysticism when he writes: "The mystical experience must find its place within the totality of the spiritual life, for it to be able to bestow on the human being true enrichment of life and inner fullness."[12] The question now is, can this also be applied to all Buddhist contemplation? Let me say at once that I believe it can, *mutatis mutandis*. But since some people may object to associating Buddhism too closely with the term *faith*, it may be better to reformulate our proposition, perhaps in the following way: Buddhist contemplative praxis is supported by the particular and very rich religiosity of the Buddhist tradition, with its philosophical presuppositions, its religious doctrine (the four Holy Truths, the sūtras), its ethical precepts, its training in the virtues (*pāramitās*), its monastic institution, and, yes, its faith, together with its stress on love-mercy.

[11] Ruegg, *Buddha-nature*, 201.

[12] H. Dumoulin, *Östliche Meditation und Christliche Mystik* (Freiburg/München: Karl Alber, 1966), 97.

From our summary overview of Buddhist history we may remember that Buddhism never saw its path as exclusively *dhyāna*, and just now we have seen that (Hinduism and) Buddhism reckoned with a kind of "natural mysticism," a neutral and not necessarily religious method used to bring the hopeless tangle of ordinary consciousness to unity and rest and thus bring it into contact with its own deeper and original reality; and that Buddhism considered this as insufficient for, and even an extremely dangerous impediment to, full liberation or buddhahood. The moment may have come to bring things together and formulate a clear "thesis." Using a rather modern category not found in the Eastern traditions, we could say that Buddhism has always considered itself to be a "religion": not a purely natural, but a supramundane, path. Its mysticism, as embedded in that religion, can then be considered not to fall under the category of "natural mysticism." Speaking *a priori*, it seems probable that Buddhism, because of the centrality of the mystical element in it, has throughout its history been particularly vulnerable to, and thus has had to struggle with, some of the negative traits of natural mysticism that were pointed out by Ruusbroec. A discussion of just how far this has actually been the case will have to wait until chapter thirteen.

But since the first part of my thesis—namely, that Buddhism has always considered itself to be a religion—seems to contradict, rather blatantly, some ideas on Buddhism "imprinted" on the Western mind, it may not be superfluous to pay further attention to it before venturing any further. In chapter four the problem of simply labeling Buddhism as an atheism has been pointed out. The idea that Buddhism is atheistic in the sense of Western naturalist or rationalist atheism is only one aspect of a more general image of Buddhism painted by the early Western scholars of Buddhism, who came to know Buddhism not from its lived practice but from its most sober Pāli texts, and who wanted to impress on the minds of their Western contemporaries that "original" or "essential" Buddhism (unlike Christianity, and especially Catholicism), is a kind of no-nonsense sort of rational moralism and not at all a lot of "pagan rites and superstitious beliefs," as it had sometimes been portrayed by Christian missionaries.

Thus, for example, the famous translator into English of many old Buddhist texts, Rhys Davids, characterized Buddhism as "salvation merely by self-control and love without any of the rites, any of the ceremonies, any of the charms, any of the priestly powers, any of the gods, in which men love to trust."[13] Others stressed that, rather than being a religion, Buddhism is a kind of spiritual philosophy with an attitude to life "as cool and objective as that of the modern scientist." Edward Conze, a later and rather authoritative scholar

---

[13] C. A. Rhys Davids, *Buddhism* (London: SPCK, 1893), 41.

of Buddhism, describes that earlier trend as follows:

> In an effort to commend Buddhism to the present age, some propagandists have overstressed its rationality and its kinship with modern science.... [In fact] Buddhism resembles the other world religions much more than it resembles modern science.[14]

I am not contending that there is no truth at all in that earlier Western picture of Buddhism. While being a religion, Buddhism indeed carries within itself a strong "demythologizing" tendency. I only want to stress that the above picture is abstract and one-sided, and does not present Buddhism as it has come down in history up to this day. As the example of Conze shows, later scholars of Buddhism have recognized this for some time already, but that first picture seems to have stuck in the popular imagination.

That first image of Buddhism, imprinted on the Western mind in the late nineteenth century, has most probably been reinforced by all that has been written and said in the West about one particular form of Buddhism, namely, Zen, beginning with D. T. Suzuki and then by an ever-growing body of popularizers over the last thirty years. The impression is often given that, no matter what other Buddhist sects (less known in the West) may be teaching and practicing, at least Zen is the "pure thing": a natural (rational) form of contemplative praxis, not based on any religious worldview and free of all the usual but outmoded religious paraphernalia. In this view, Zen contemplative praxis can, therefore, be accommodated in any religious context, and, most importantly, used apart from all religion as a purely physio-psychological method for one's bodily and spiritual health and self-realization.

I am not going to enter here upon the questions of whether, in what sense, and under which conditions, Zen contemplative praxis (centered on *zazen*) can be adopted in the spiritual life of, for instance, a Christian, since these are not directly relevant to our theme. I can only remark in passing that the many experiments in that line made by Christian monks, nuns, and lay people are highly commendable. They, rather than *a priori* speculations, may lead to sound answers to the above questions in the not too distant future. What is really important in our context, however—also in view of the present infiltration of Zen into Western life, is the question of whether Zen can be considered to be, or at least can be used as, a non-religious ("natural") contemplative method.

---

[14] Edward Conze, *Buddhist Thought in India* (Ann Arbor: The University of Michigan Press, 1982), 26–7. Conze further writes: "There are, of course, a few modern writers, who make Buddhism quite rational by eliminating all metaphysics, reincarnation, all the gods and spirits, all miracles and supernatural powers. Theirs is not the Buddhism of the Buddhists" (29).

The Zen movement in Buddhism can be interpreted as a reaction (by the "practical" Chinese) against a Buddhist religious system that had become so top-heavy with intricate doctrine and an immense plethora of religious practices that it was easy to forget the one thing most necessary. And, at least in its language or "rhetoric," Zen might be considered the strongest "negative trend"—negative in the sense it has in "negative theology" —or, from a slightly different angle, as the most radically "secularizing" spiritual movement to be found anywhere in the world of religion. It is fond of sayings such as "Nothing Holy" or "When you meet the Buddha, kill the Buddha," and insists that the real expression of its spirit is not to be sought in religious forms but in everyday "nature"—"The willow is green, the flower is red"— and in profane culture, such as the "ways" (dō) of tea, of the sword, etc. Furthermore, the transmitted texts of the Zen patriarchs abound in sayings that seem to negate all "supernatural" elements and all and sundry religious practices outside objectless contemplation ("seeing into" your own nature or "Mind"), by reducing them allegorically to contemplation, or grading them down to the level of *upāya* (provisional expedients without intrinsic liberative value), or even presenting them as harmful to one's real spiritual development. A few examples of this:

> Priest Rinzai said: "You train in the Six Perfections [*pāramitā*, the cardinal virtues of Mahāyāna Buddhism] and the Ten Thousand Practices at the same time. As I see it, they all produce karma. To seek the Buddha and the dharma is to produce the karma of hell.... The Buddhas and patriarchs are men who do not seek for anything."[15]

> *Questioner:* "According to the sūtras, the World Honored One attained buddhahood after mastering the *Six Perfections.* How can this be called 'seeing into your own nature'?"
> Bassui responded: "All of these bring you fortune for which you can secure a life in the world of humans and heavenly creatures.... But one cannot expect to obtain buddhahood from them."[16]

> If you students of the Way do not awake to this Mind substance, you will overlay Mind with conceptual talk, you will seek Buddha outside yourselves, and you will remain attached to forms, pious practices and so on, all of which are harmful and not at all the way to supreme knowledge.[17]

[15] *Mud and Water: A Collection of Talks by Zen Master Bassui.* Trans. by Arthur Braverman (San Francisco: North Point Press, 1989), 58–9.

[16] *Mud and Water,* 8–9.

[17] *The Zen Teaching of Huang Po: On the Transmission of Mind.* Trans. by John Blofeld (New York: Grove Weidenfeld, 1958), 31.

And even the doctrine of the Buddha, as contained in the sūtras, does not seem to fare any better:

> The wisdom of the past, the present, and the future buddhas as well as the teachings of the twelve sections of the canon are immanent in our mind. ...those who enlighten themselves need no extraneous help. It is wrong to insist that without the advice of the pious and learned we cannot obtain liberation.[18]

> If you students of the way wish to become Buddha, you need study no doctrines.... It is obvious that mental concepts and external perceptions are equally misleading, and that the Way of the Buddhas is as dangerous to you as the way of demons.[19]

In these sayings of the Zen masters one can at least detect the following two convictions: (1) all religion is transcended in the mystical peak; and (2) when one goes for the highest mystical attainment, one had better leave aside all religious paraphernalia right from the beginning. Before jumping to conclusions, however, a few important points have to be made. First of all, just as negative theology is a negating movement *within* Christian theology, one that essentially gets its meaning from acting as a counterbalance to positive Christian theology, so Zen is a negative movement *within* the Buddhist religion, with which it shares the same basic presuppositions.

Moreover, we should not let ourselves be duped by the "rhetoric" of the Zen Masters. Already in chapter 6 a few lines were devoted to the very idiosyncratic use of language by Zen people: paradoxical and never negating without affirming, although not necessarily at the same time. Thus, the same Hui-neng [the famous "sixth patriarch"] who told his disciples that "they need not rely on scriptural authority, since they can make use of their own wisdom by constant practice of contemplation," also had the following to say:

> A bigoted believer in nihilism blasphemes against the sūtras on the ground that literature...is unnecessary.... You men should know that it is a serious offense to speak ill of the sūtras, for the consequence is grave indeed.[20]

And the following episode is recounted of the same Huang Po, who condemned all pious practices and any search for the Buddha outside oneself:

---

[18] *The Diamond Sūtra and the Sūtra of Hui-neng.* Trans. by A. F. Price and Wong Mou-lam (Boston: Shambala, 1990), 84.

[19] *The Zen Teaching of Huang Po,* 40, 75.

[20] *The Diamond Sūtra and the Sūtra of Hui-neng,* 83, 144.

241

Our master once attended an assembly...at which the emperor T'ai Chung was also present as a śramanera ["novice"]. The śramanera noticed our Master enter the hall of worship and make a triple prostration to the Buddha, whereupon he asked: "If we are to seek nothing from the Buddha, Dharma or Sangha, what does your Reverence seek by such prostrations?" "Though I seek not from the Buddha," replied our Master, "...it is my custom to show respect in this way." "But what purpose does it serve?" insisted the śramanera, whereupon he suddenly received a slap.[21]

Finally, Bassui, who used to make light of the precepts in many of his talks, also had this to say:

Never say that, though you break many precepts, diligent practice [of zazen] will prevent your being harmed by it. If this truly has not caused you any harm, why haven't you been awakened yet?[22]

It is not surprising, then, that recent Zen scholars insist that earlier studies of the Zen movement have relied too much on Zen texts, studied in isolation without paying sufficient attention to their context, the living Buddhist practice of the time. Gregory, for example, in a presentation of a little-known Zen text of the ninth century [late T'ang period] that describes many Zen rituals, writes the following:

Modern scholars have been drawn to it [late T'ang] as the formative period when a distinctly "Ch'an" [Zen] tradition emerged, a tradition supposedly characterized by a radical rejection of the ritual and devotional practices.... I believe that the study of this text will help relocate Ch'an within the mainstream of Chinese monastic practice, which is the proper context in which to evaluate its radical rhetoric.[23]

The many religious observances (worship of Buddha images, ceremonial recitation of the sūtras, prayers for the "hungry ghosts," etc.) practised in present-day Japanese Zen halls are therefore not indications of a syncretistic

[21] *The Zen Teaching of Huang Po*, 95–6. The episode may be legendary, but the message is conveyed in the authentic Zen way: while the negation was clearly expressed, the affirmation was not conceptualized but only "formulated" by a slap. At the end of the second leg of the "Spiritual Exchange Program" (in 1983), during which European Catholic monks had been sharing the life of the *unsui* (novices) in different Zen halls, a similar question was directed at Hirata Rōshi by the European monks, who had been struck by the deeply religious atmosphere and many devotional practices in the Zen halls. Asked: "What do you worship when you make these prostrations?" he answered: "My own deeper self and the Buddha without distinction."

[22] *Mud and Water*, 22.

[23] Peter N. Gregory, "Tsung-mi's Perfect Enlightenment Retreat: Ch'an Ritual during the T'ang Dynasty," *Cahiers d'Extrême-Asie* 7 (1993–1994), 119–20.

degeneration of the pure Zen spirit (which allegedly would have begun in the Sung period or even earlier) as has sometimes been maintained, even by some Zen masters themselves.[24] But H. Dumoulin reminds us that Zen contemplative praxis is not only surrounded in the Zen halls by practices that are clearly religious, it is itself intrinsically religious:

> Zen's enlightenment realizes in the immediate experience of the spiritual self a going beyond in the direction of transcendence. Although of a technical nature, the exercises that aim at the enlightenment experience are nurtured by a religious attitude.[25]

We are entitled, therefore, to include Zen within our general evaluation of Buddhism. Zen is not a case of "natural mysticism," even though it may be the form of Buddhism that, because of the radical priority it gives to contemplation (especially in its rhetoric), is most easily mistaken for, or abused as, a form of natural contemplation. Zen is, after all, Zen *Buddhism*; its contemplative praxis is supported by the Buddhist faith. It is inspired by that faith and continually accompanied by other expressions of that faith. "Faith" is, of course, a very ambiguous category, and the term cannot and should not be taken here in its full Christian or Pure Land Buddhist sense. What is meant by "faith" in the case of Zen might be tentatively defined as: stepping into a religious tradition; accepting its authoritative definition of the human predicament (*samsāra*, a totally unsatisfactory situation), of the desirable goal (enlightenment or Nirvana), and of the path to the goal (centrally, by contemplation); having confidence in the realizability of that goal and the validity of that path on the basis of the words and examples of the Buddha and his disciples throughout the ages; and the aspiration toward enlightenment awakened thereby. In his "Explanatory Notes on the Six Oxherding Pictures," Zen master Shibayama, for example, speaks of the "tether of faith":

> Faith means the aspiration for the joy of awakening in the Eternal and the Absolute, the happiness of losing the self in the Buddha. It is the single-minded longing for the Mind-Ox.... The tether is now fastened (a thought of faith is awakened), and for the first time the herdsman and the Mind-Ox are related through the tether. This is the first step toward the man and the ox finally becoming one....[26]

Faith may thus be said to play an essential role also in Zen. It must be remarked, however, that in Buddhism faith becomes superfluous at a certain

---

[24] Bassui for one; cf. *Mud and Water*, 58.

[25] Dumoulin, *Östliche Meditation*, 233.

[26] Abbot Zenkei Shibayama, *A Flower Does Not Talk: Zen Essays* (Tokyo: Charles E. Tuttle, 1970), 163–4.

moment, when one comes to "see" (the goal, true reality), and that, especially in Zen, faith exists as a function of the contemplative praxis from which, finally, liberation is expected.[27]

The question of whether or not Buddhism (including Zen) is essentially a religion may be approached from still another angle: a comparison with the "secularism" or "naturalism" found in the West. Elaborating these problematics is out of the question here, but a few remarks on the question may serve to round off our picture of Buddhism as essentially more than natural contemplation. "Naturalism," which is akin to scientism, took shape as a philosophical system in the United States, but as a frame of mind it is certainly widespread in other parts of the West as well. It has been defined as:

> a species of philosophical monism according to which whatever exists or happens is *natural* in the sense of being susceptible to explanation through methods which...[are] exemplified in the natural sciences.... Hence, naturalism is polemically defined as repudiating the view that there exists or could exist any entities or events which lie, in principle, beyond the scope of scientific explanation.[28]

Naturalism thus sees "nature" as a closed system, and the norm of everything. By comparison, notwithstanding a predilection for the word *natural* in the Buddhism of the Far East, Buddhism quite clearly is not a mere naturalism, but contains in its basic structure elements that transcend the natural. On a more superficial level, we could think of a belief in outer-worldly realms where "spiritual beings" live. This is represented in Buddhism by its doctrine on the different "worlds" of transmigration populated by gods, heavenly beings, etc. But much more central to Buddhism, and decisive for its supramundane quality, is the belief in Nirvana as the real "home" of all sentient beings. This tends to turn the meaning of the term "natural" upside down: it is not reason that is natural but a transcendental wisdom; it is not self-willed action that is natural but an activity that has its source in the all-one. Mahāyāna, it is true, strongly demythologizes Nirvana and insists that it is not a realm apart from this world but "identical with *samsāra* (this "natural" human world). Still, this identity bathes our human world in a light that is far from naturalistic or purely natural.

---

[27] That, at least, appears to be the most common Buddhist conception of faith, but Japan's "Zen genius," Dōgen (1200–53), who puts an enormous stress on "faith in the Way," thought differently. "Dōgen does not imply that faith precedes enlightenment or is eventually replaced by enlightenment. Throughout the ongoing advance in enlightenment..., faith and enlightenment, or believing and seeing, are twin companions of emptiness and Buddha-nature." Hee-jin Kim, *Dōgen Kigen: Mystical Realist* (Tucson: The University of Arizona Press, 1987), 62.

[28] The entry "naturalism" in: Paul Edwards, ed., *The Encyclopedia of Philosophy* (New York: Macmillan, 1967), 5:448.

There is, however, the fact that Zen rhetoric and theory often *sound* naturalistic. In the review article that has been mentioned already Langdon Gilkey expresses surprise at the, at first sight, strangely naturalistic character of Abe Masao's "Zen metaphysics," which appears to bring Abe's worldview close to the naturalism of a Santayana and a Dewey:

> Throughout his discussion Abe underlines in a variety of ways his denial that there is any "reality" transcendent to "the beings".... The beings as they are are all there is....
>
> Interestingly, this non-theistic...naturalism [of Santayana and Dewey] is, so it seems to me, despite its explicitly non-religious character, *metaphysically* much closer to Abe's Buddhism than are most of the alternative religious visions: Brahmanic pantheism, Christian or Sikh theism, or the finite theism of Process thought.[29]

But Gilkey then goes on to point out that, notwithstanding their theoretical nearness, Abe's Zen and Dewey's naturalism are in fact worlds apart, owing to a totally different existential appropriation of that worldview:

> What is fascinating in this comparison, therefore, is the near identity of these two metaphysical visions with regard to the *structures* of reality, and yet the utter disparity of their religious ways, of their piety.
>
> Compared to Hindu pantheism or Christian theism, this [Abe's Zen's] vision *is* naturalistic; but compared to the utter soullessness of modern scientific naturalism, this Buddhist vision seems laced with universal and effective "spiritual" structures.[30]

There is then a "metaphysical more," and especially a "religious more," that is not acknowledged in Abe's Zen theory as such. It may be good to reflect a moment longer on that "interesting," but baffling, phenomenon pointed out by Gilkey—although the little space available here will not permit me to elaborate on and undergird the rather strong conclusions I am going to draw.

Zen people like to stress that one cannot understand Zen unless one has experienced it, since Zen cannot be caught in concepts and words. This is, of course, exactly the claim all mysticism makes. That does not mean, however, that Zen people can or do keep quiet. Zen masters cannot avoid answering the questions of their disciples, at least not all the time, and in these cases mostly use the paradoxical sayings we have already seen. Moreover, to explain itself to outsiders and to prove its credentials as an authentic form of Mahāyāna Buddhism, Zen has produced a philosophical "Zen Theory," making use of the Mahāyāna logic of emptiness. Zen theoreticians ("theolo-

---

[29] Langdon Gilkey, "Masao Abe's *Zen and Western Thought*" [unpublished MS], 9, 8–9.

[30] Gilkey, "Masao Abe's *Zen and Western Thought*," 10, 12.

gians") thus claim that Zen is nothing but the radical putting into practice of the Mahāyāna philosophy of emptiness, which itself expresses the core of Buddhism and the original insight of the Buddha; and that, therefore, Zen represents a perfect unity of theory and practice—a "perfectly rounded circle," as I like to symbolize it. In that vein, H. Dumoulin has also spoken of "the closest connection imaginable between experience and doctrine in Zen Buddhism.... Metaphysical speculation, religious practice, and mystical experience are very closely knit together and grasped as a unity."[31]

All this is true enough if one understands Zen's sole "religious practice" as *zazen*, the imageless seated meditation. In this case, Zen's emptiness theory may be said to correspond perfectly to its religious practice. But the point I have been making is precisely that Zen Buddhism is not just *zazen* (if *zazen* is not interpreted in a "transcendental" way, as it is in Dōgen's case). The only conclusion is, then, that the full and true reality of Zen is not covered by its theory, and that this theory (as presented in nearly all books on Zen in the West), taken by itself without a concomitant study of the actual praxis, propagates a mistaken conception of what Zen is all about. There is, indeed, a close link among all the elements of Zen, but in an "organic" rather than a logical unity—the unity not of a homogeneous or empty circle, but rather of a tapestry or mosaic, wherein the different elements do not directly all point in the same direction but rather complement one another, often as mutually balancing polarities.

In the Introduction to a recent book on Buddhism, which they edited together, two prominent American Buddhist scholars strongly defend the thesis (about Buddhism in general, but specifically about Zen) that, if one really wants to know Buddhism, one must pay at least as much attention to its praxis or "path" (*mārga*) as to its theory—something that has not been sufficiently done in Buddhist studies of the past, since praxis and theory are not simply one but exist in mutual tension:

> At the very heart of every religious tradition are certain fertile antinomies.... In the case of Buddhism, one of the most profound of these life-giving antinomies is the creative and persistent tension between that religion's fundamental cognitive claims and its most characteristic conative injunctions..., the implicit tension between śūnyatā and mārga....[32]

After stating that an exclusively doctrinal approach is apt to produce "a truncated, asymmetrical, perhaps even eccentric Buddhism," they continue:

---

[31] Dumoulin, *Östliche Meditation*, 235.

[32] R. E. Buswell and R. M. Gimello eds., *Paths to Liberation: The Mārga and its Transformations in Buddhist Thought* (Honolulu: University of Hawaii Press, 1992), 24, 25.

An approach to Buddhism that gives mārga and Buddhism's conative import a value equal to that normally assigned to the cognitive message of śūnyatā and associated concepts...will reveal, we would propose, a Buddhism that is at once less alien from the world of ordinary human concerns and more sensitive to the presence of the transcendent in that world.[33]

But if all this is true and Zen is a truly religious and intrinsically Buddhist movement, what then about the secular uses of *zazen*, especially in the West, where Buddhism is not endemically present? The least that can be said is what Zen people themselves stress often enough: in these cases one cannot speak of true Zen. I submit that one thing more must be added: in these cases *zazen* can become a dangerous instrument, possibly producing warped personalities. The American theologian of "The Secular City" fame, Harvey Cox, diagnoses Western culture as "incurably obsessed with self and self-realization." He points at the possible, even probable, abuse of Eastern meditation in that setting, with the result being a still more "con-centric" or self-centered mode of being:

I think we can expect to see the growing use of meditation...to enhance the exploration and realization of the insatiable Western self. Self had already been made ultimate; and now the quest for the true self becomes the path to the Kingdom.[34]

With this indication of the non-authenticity and possible dangers of the secular uses of Zen's contemplative praxis, we are naturally led back to Ruusbroec's criticism of the defects and dangers of "natural contemplation." About these we must inquire more concretely in our final chapter. Does Buddhism fall within the scope of Ruusbroec's criticisms? Or, on the contrary, do Buddhist voices join Ruusbroec in leveling denunciations?

---

[33] Buswell and Gimello, *Paths to Liberation*, 27.

[34] Harvey Cox, "The Pool of Narcissus: The Psychologizing of Meditation," *Cross Currents* 27/1 (1977): 28, 18.

12

Natural Mysticism: A Critique

If Ruusbroec values the contemplative method of his adversaries and recognizes the experience it yields, it is because he does not find fault with natural contemplation as such. His critique, which is careful and discriminating, is aimed rather at the way it was practiced at the time. An accomplished contemplative himself, Ruusbroec focuses in the first place on the quality of the experience of those who follow the natural turn inwards. He is particularly struck by the way in which they "possess rest" and consequently overvalue it. He then seeks to identify the root cause of this preference for rest, which he finds in its apparent self-sufficiency. Next, he demonstrates that the range of the contemplative's experience is severely restricted by the natural way. Ruusbroec's critique also includes the way his opponents interpret their own quietistic experience, in particular the heretical aspect of their ontological statements about the human and the divine. Finally, Ruusbroec's critique aims at exposing the dehumanizing lifestyle that natural contemplation leads to. In this chapter, we shall consider each of these five points in turn.

THE OVERVALUING OF REST

Again and again Ruusbroec notes the exalted, even absolute, status that his opponents give to rest. This total devotion to quiet in the soul shows up in practice in the attempt to ward off all disturbances, both outward *and* inward. The aim of turning inwards is "that rest may be found and may abide unhindered,"[1] and to this end such persons even "regard all loving devotedness a hindrance."[2] In the end all good works are eliminated:

> For it seems to them that this emptiness (*ledicheit*) is so great that no one should hinder it by any works, however good they might be, for emptiness is nobler than all virtue.[3]

[1] *Opera omnia* III.b.1988.

[2] *Opera omnia* III.b.2011.

[3] *Opera omnia* III.b.2081–3.

Only a fanatical clinging to rest can account for this resistance to all interference. "When they find that rest in themselves...they want to possess it and hold on to it."[4]

There is reason for this fascination with rest, and it takes an experienced contemplative to recognize it. The fact is, this deep, "essential" quietude, free of the bustle of the faculties and of the inanity of ordinary busyness, produces an extraordinary and liberating delight. The satisfaction it brings to mind and body seems to justify itself. Rest is delightful (*ghenoechlijc*) to the point of being all that one needs (*ghenoecht*): "For they are lifted up in unknowing and modelessness and are satisfied with this (*hare ghenoecht*)...."[5] The outline of the natural way inward in *The Realm of Lovers*, which we discussed in the former chapter, makes the point:

> For, when the highest powers are unconcerned by temporal things and bodily enjoyments and are lifted up in the unity of the mind, there results an enjoyable rest that pervades body and soul.

And the eagle from *The Spiritual Tabernacle*, who soars "to the greatest heights nature is capable of," appears to be taken in by the same satisfaction. The awareness given him when he comes to "rest in his essence" is

> so satisfying for nature, that he despises and deems ignoble all consideration, discernment, and rational practice that hinders or assails by images his naked sight.[6]

It is little wonder that this same delight produces in the end a satisfaction that appears to the contemplative as "bliss":

> But they find their own essence: an imageless stilled idleness. And there they think they are eternally blissful.[7]

Thus do these contemplatives come to concentrate fully on their desire to "sustain rest."[8]

Ruusbroec's own picture of satisfaction produced in mystical union is one of a "felt well-being and a pervading savor"[9] that includes the whole person, body and soul. His familiarity with the experience of bliss is clear in his descriptions. For example, he notes that

---

[4] *The Four Temptations, Opera omnia* X.170–1.

[5] *Opera omnia* II.571–2.

[6] See note 29 of chapter 10 and its corresponding text, page 223.

[7] *Werken* II.366:22–5.

[8] *Werken* II.40:26–9.

[9] *Werken* I.62:19.

in this light the spirit sinks away from itself into enjoyable rest, for the rest is without mode and fathomless.[10]

Or again, he says that satisfaction leads one to "feel swallowed up in the groundless abyss of our eternal blessedness."[11]

It is in contrast to this that Ruusbroec relentlessly condemns the non-activity of the way of natural contemplation as "false" or "deceitful" or "devious" idleness.[12] A passage from *The Spiritual Espousals* gives us a good introduction to this crucial aspect of Ruusbroec's thought:

> When a person thus possesses this rest in emptiness (*dese raste in ledicheiden besit*) and regards all loving devotedness to be a hindrance, then he dwells within himself with rest (*blivet hi met rasten op hem selven*).[13]

The significant expression is the formula *raste in ledicheiden*, "rest in idleness." Before asking what this means in practice, it is worth noting the common juxtaposition of three words, interrelated but with quite distinct meanings. "Idleness" (*ledicheit*) is a methodological term that refers to a psychological state of turning inwards. "Rest" (*raste*) is a phenomenological term, which points to a particular aspect of the experience of being mystically one. And *wesen* (essence) is an anthropological term referring to the object of this experience. The relationship among them can be summarized simply: one needs to reach idleness in order to experience rest and to touch upon one's essence. If Ruusbroec does not always pause to draw the necessary distinctions, it is because he sees each one as entailing the others.[14]

When he does distinguish, it is for a purpose. In the summary passage from *The Spiritual Espousals* just quoted, for instance, Ruusbroec's purpose is to criticize the reduction of rest to mere idleness. They make rest solely the appanage of idleness on the assumption that being inactive is the sole and sufficient condition for being at rest. What they forget, as Ruusbroec sees it, is the relationship of rest with the other states of consciousness, and they gloat in a condition of being "unhindered." When rest is "nothing but an

---

[10] *Opera omnia* III.b.1894–5.

[11] *Opera omnia* III.b.1861–3.

[12] *Opera omnia* III.b.2187–8.

[13] *Opera omnia* III.b.2010–2. Further on in the same work (b.2021–2), we find the following parallel: "...when a person wishes to possess any rest in emptiness (*raste wilt besitten in ledicheiden*) without inner yearning devotedness to God, he has a propensity for all error." And in *The Four Temptations* Ruusbroec puts the same point in this way: "And because they are without practice and do not cling to God in love, they do not go beyond themselves (*en doerliden si hem selven niet*) but rest and idle in their own essence (*rasten in haers selfs wesen*)" (*Opera omnia* X.177–9).

[14] These distinctions can be found in the locus cited in note 8 above.

emptiness," one "falls" into a state of hebetude:

> But rest practiced in this way...produces blindness in a person, in igno-
> rance, and a sinking down into himself without activity. And this rest is
> nothing but an emptiness (*dese raste en es anders niet dan eene ledicheit*)
> into which a person falls and he forgets himself and God and everything,
> with respect to any activity.[15]

> For they lapse (*vallen*) into an idle blind emptiness....
> For they lapse into sleep and sink away from themselves in essential
> natural rest.

> They would press themselves into their essence with lostness and
> non-activity exteriorly as well as interiorly.[16]

Ruusbroec stresses again and again how wrong it is to see contemplation
as a self-incapacitation, especially when it comes to the capacity for love. In
choosing "not to cling to God in love," the followers of natural contemplation purge themselves of "loving devotedness," and "yearning devotedness"
altogether. Thus they

> stand in a pure passivity (*lidene*) without any activity upwards or down-
> wards, just like a loom...and this is why they are void of all virtue, and so
> empty that they wish neither to thank nor to praise God, and they have
> neither knowledge nor love, nor will nor prayer nor desire (*begeren*).[17]

In the context of a critique of the "lapse into idle blind emptiness" in
The Four Temptations, Ruusbroec goes on to complain that the deviating
mystics

> no longer pay attention to any good works, outer or inner. For they
> spurn all inner works, such as wanting, knowing, loving, desiring, and all
> works that join them with God.[18]

And thus it is that following the way inward without grace ultimately leads to
a static "pure passivity," "stillness," and "quietness," from which all the
dynamism and personalism he would attach to those terms has been drained.
His adversaries have become non-persons with no more life in them than "a
stick or a stone" and are consequently incapable of being "blessed."[19]

---

[15] *Opera omnia* III.b.1988–92.

[16] These three passages are taken from *The Four Temptations, Opera omnia* X.160, 169–70,
and from *Werken* I.62:8–10.

[17] *Opera omnia* III.b.2083–8.

[18] *Opera omnia* X.161–3.

[19] *Opera omnia* III.b.2184–5.

This last remark invites a closer look at the role of human consciousness in the highest mystical states. In *The Twelve Beguines*, Ruusbroec reacts as follows to those who say they are "nothing":

For if you do not exist, you do not seek. And then neither do you find.[20]

In the case of the person who "sinks away" into unity, shifting from exercising one's faculties to resting in one's essence "above and beyond reason," is there anything left to call "awareness"? For one whose spirit "feels itself dead and lost," should we not rather speak of a non-awareness or at least of a mere awareness of nothing? And if so, what possible relationship could this open to one's ordinary knowledge?

Standing on the dry land of reason, it is obviously no easy matter to draw conclusions about what it feels like to be adrift in the boundless sea of an empty consciousness. For his part, Ruusbroec does not tackle the question in an abstract manner. From his own contemplative experience, and with great personal stake in the matter, he tries to get at the experiential heart of the question. In gleaning Ruusbroec's remarks on the mystic's consciousness, one sees a basic argument emerge. Though somewhat lacking in sophistication, the conclusions are well-grounded in fact.

Basically, there are two points to Ruusbroec's argument. On the one hand, he insists that experience, however lofty, is always *someone's* experience. Behind the attributes "unsayable," "fathomless," and so forth there is always a concrete individual. On the other hand, he argues that it is not given to human consciousness to enter an *absolute* state, utterly detached from everything that went before it. Not even the most advanced consciousness of the mystic is something miraculously new, a self-contained, immanent science that breaks with all natural modes of awareness. Mystical consciousness is always a natural consciousness. Let it be expanded and refined in the most exceptional degree, consciousness does not add one whit to its original capacity for awareness. Nor does it diminish in the least its awareness of what is going on within it.

Mystical experience, then, remains the experience of the human subject who has come to it. If the praying subject were to be annihilated, there would be no knowing going on any more, no consciousness:

And if our being were annihilated (*ghinghe oec onse wesen te niete*), we would neither know nor love nor be blessed.[21]

But a person is not only *wesen* but also *crachte*, faculties. These faculties may have to "idle" for the contemplative to enjoy unity, but this does not mean

[20] *Werken* IV.51:9–10.
[21] Wiseman, 247.

that they have to be annihilated:

> And therefore, when we are raised up in our highest feeling, all our faculties stand [idle] (*staen ledich*) in an essential enjoyment, but they are not reduced to nothing (*en werden niet te nieute*), for then we would lose our being as creatures.[22]

Furthermore, Ruusbroec sees mystical consciousness as an expansion of ordinary consciousness by speaking of it as "above reason and without reason" (*boven redene ende sonder redene*):

> There, however, we are above reason and also without reason in a state of clear knowing, in which we feel no difference between ourselves and God.[23]

The distinction between "above" reason and "without" reason may be stated summarily:

> *boven redene*: → *redene* perceives but cannot comprehend.
>
> *sonder redene*: → *redene* perceives nothing.[24]

Let us begin with two passages regarding the mystic's consciousness as it extends above reason:

> And we feel this touch in the unification of our higher faculties, above reason, yet not without reason, for we perceive (*vernemen*) that we are touched. But if we wish to know what it is or whence it comes, then reason and all creaturely work fall short,... all creaturely activity which operates with distinction must fall short.[25]

And a few lines from *The Mirror*, cited earlier, merit repeating here:

> Although we are above reason, we are not without reason and therefore feel (*ghevoelen*) that we are both touching and being touched, loving and being loved, and always being renewed and returning to ourselves. We feel ourselves coming and going like lightning in the heavens.... We therefore remain always standing above reason in our very selfhood—imageless, gazing, and striving in incomprehensible richness.[26]

---

[22] *The Sparkling Stone, Opera omnia* X.576–9.

[23] Wiseman, 246.

[24] *Opera omnia* II, 275.

[25] *Opera omnia* III.b.1823–6. See also b.1273–7.

[26] Wiseman, 240.

Chief among the traits Ruusbroec attributes to mystical consciousness are two. First is the difference between perceiving and grasping that holds true at every stage of contemplative knowing. The higher one goes, the more inward one turns, the more does awareness exceed the grasp of comprehension.[27] The distinctions of reason grow ever more inadequate as the mystical "touch" becomes present. This does not mean that the spiritual faculties and senses are anesthetized. As Ruusbroec says, throughout "we perceive (*vernemen*) that we are touched" and "we feel (*ghevoelen*) we are both touching and being touched." Reason does not go numb: "Nevertheless, the spirit is ever anew compelled and aroused by God and by itself to sound the depths of this touch...." Being unable to say "what it is" does not prevent one from knowing "that it is."[28]

Secondly, the different forms of knowing in mystical consciousness are interconnected and react with each other. And since Ruusbroec teaches that "God works in us from within outwards," higher states of awareness always affect the lower. Each experience heightens what went before it, like a series of inner eyes at each of whose openings the earlier eyes are further dilated, and leaves one with the sense that there is "too much" to experience. Thus Ruusbroec can speak of the mystic's reason as "open-eyed in the dark, that is, in unfathomable unknowing."[29] Ruusbroec speaks further of the opening of a "simple eye":

> This resplendence of God which we see in ourselves has no beginning nor end, no time or place, no way or path, no form, no figure, or color. It has wholly embraced, grasped and pervaded us and opened the eye of our simple vision so widely that this eye must remain open forever, for we cannot close it.[30]

Finally, the simple eye is filled with God's own light, as if in a "gazing at the light with the light in the light." But even here, when "God is apprehended and seen with God," it is still the human person who does the knowing:

> And therefore, the eyes with which the spirit contemplates and gazes upon its Bridegroom are so widely dilated that they will never again be closed. For the gazing and contemplation of the spirit remain eternally (fixed) on the hidden revelation of God.[31]

[27] On the graphic quality of this word, see chapter 3, page 56.

[28] *Opera omnia* III.b.1292–1301 and b. 2118–28. See note 16 of chapter 3, page 54, and its accompanying citation.

[29] *Opera omnia* X:520–1.

[30] Wiseman, 244. See chapter 3, page 62 and note 32.

[31] *Opera Omnia* III.c.88–91.

As for the "bliss" of the experience, it would seem that its heightened enjoyment should be unhindered by any other awareness dragging it back into the realm of the ordinary. As we have seen, Ruusbroec continually underscores the difference between work and rest, so much so that the latter is not conditioned by any spiritual acts.[32] He takes his place with the most daring mystical authors by claiming that the highest satisfaction of the contemplative is a sinking away from oneself without return—or what he calls *salicheit*, blessedness.[33] This is one of Ruusbroec's most important ideas. On the final page of *The Mirror*, "the highest that anyone can express in words" is called "a dying life and living death, in which we go out of our own being into our superessential [blessedness]." There, God's "Spirit absorbs our love, swallowing it up into himself in [enjoyment and in one blessedness] with himself."

In this context he also makes use of the corresponding adjective, *salich*, blessed. Thus in the concluding paragraph of *The Mirror* we read:

> If, then, we live in love, we are blessed in our very being (*salegh in onse wesen*); and if we die to ourselves in love and in the enjoyment of God, then we are blessedness itself in God's being (*salegheit in Gods wesen*).

A masterly simple passage in *The Sparkling Stone* brings out the relationship between *salicheit* and *salich* well, showing how in mystical consciousness we are conscious of the "unfathomable feeling" being experienced as our very own (*onse eyghen es*). Ruusbroec has been speaking of "unity" and ends with the statement that "we are unwrought from ourselves and wrought by God until we are immersed in love, where we possess bliss and are one with God." He then goes on to describe the experience of bliss:

> When we are united with God in that way, there remains a living knowledge (*levende weten*) and an active loving in us, for without our knowledge we cannot possess God, and without our practice of loving we cannot be united with God, nor remain united with him. For if we could find bliss without knowing (*salich sijn sonder onse weten*), a stone, which has no knowing, could also find bliss. If I were lord of all the earth and did not know it, what would I stand to gain? And therefore we shall always know and feel ourselves tasting and possessing (*ons emmermeer weten ende ghevoelen smakende ende besittende*).[34]

To conclude our treatment of Ruusbroec's critique against the overvaluing of rest, it is worth noting how the very manner in which he address-

---

[32] See chapter 8, note 2, pages 156–7, and its accompanying citation.

[33] See chapter 8, page 166.

[34] *Opera Omnia* X.524–33.

es his opponents implies that mystical experience is always part of the consciousness of a particular individual. For instance, when in *The Spiritual Espousals* he speaks of the "natural rest" that is common to all people, he adopts an impersonal tone in talking of those he would criticize:

> In this emptiness, the rest is delightful and great. In itself this rest is no sin, for it is in all people by nature, if they could (but) empty themselves.

But then his manner changes abruptly and he becomes personal:

> But when one wishes to practice and possess this rest without acts of virtue..., when a person thus possesses this rest in emptiness and regards all loving devotedness to be a hindrance, then he swells within himself with rest.[35]

By shifting the focus to the subject of the desire who comes to "possess" this rest, Ruusbroec directs a noncontemplative question at his opponents: If the height of the way inwards is stillness, then just *whose* stillness is it? Is the highest experience like a grin without a cat, a woman's smile without the woman? Does not the whole process take place from start to finish for a particular person, or is there some self-fulfilling method at work that makes the individual dispensable? Those who could champion detached contemplative experience have fallen into abstraction, forgetting who it was that set out on the way inward, who brought the lower faculties to dispense with images and to exercise virtue, who turned the higher faculties into their ground, and finally who achieved rest. For Ruusbroec there is no question that *someone* possesses that rest, only of *how* it is possessed.

In short, the difference between himself and his opponents is that, for him, the contemplative makes use of idleness to *possess rest*, while for the latter the contemplative sinks away into idleness and *is possessed by* rest.

THE SELF-SUFFICIENCY OF THE TURN INWARDS

Ruusbroec finds the root cause of the seduction of rest and the loss of personality to lie on this side of mystical experience, in a problem that can be stated in noncontemplative terms. With almost obsessive regularity, he repeats the point in his writings on natural contemplation: turning inwards goes wrong when it is seen as independent of everything else in the psyche, including the relationship of the person with the divine Other. He therefore asks his opponents to consider what is the object of their intention (*meynen*) on the way, and in so doing applies the same standard to them as to all ordi-

---

[35] *Opera Omnia* III.b.2005–12.

nary "good people." By laying the stress on personal intention (*meyninghe*) rather than on privileged experience, Ruusbroec the mystic demystifies mysticism. He puts the mystics in what he feels is their proper place by facing them with the fundamental question of whether they are living their lives with or without grace.

Ruusbroec addresses the quietistic experience of his opponents by referring them to its latent assumptions. First, a practical observation from *The Four Temptations* for those who "find that rest in themselves without love or practice of virtue":

> And all those who come to this are simple people or young people unpractised in virtue, or people who have not died to themselves, even if they have practised great penance for a long time, but without the right intention and the love of God.[36]

Next, consider the following remarks concerning those who are "idle and elevated by natural contemplation":

> They always stick to their own will. Their pride gives them an uplifted heart; they always want to be, and presume they already are, superior because of their special way of life.... Because of the idleness of natural contemplation and because they are not driven by God's grace, they often fail to reach out to fellow humans in need. Charity never fails, but nature is unjust insofar as it turns its intentions on itself in contemplation. They value contemplation more than any work of charity, which is not right, for we have been commanded to works of charity, and contemplation without works of charity, however supernatural, will come to naught.[37]

Ruusbroec characterizes the "elevated" contemplatives by deliberately using the same expressions about self-will and self-centered intentions applied to those who ride less spiritual vehicles. As for the question of whether high mysticism does not transcend these questions by detaching the mind from the lower levels of the psyche and opening one up to the Unknown, Ruusbroec is firm in his rejection of any privilege: "nature...intends itself in contemplation." Contemplation can never touch God if one does not have one's intentions fixed on God. Like all other natural activities, it is linked to personal will. *Scouwen* is in itself good; still, it is not the source of the relationship of the human being with God. Contemplation is only a means by which a person intends God; it never constitutes that relationship itself.

[36] *Opera Omnia* X.172–5.

[37] *Werken* I.23:18–24:8. It is interesting to compare these remarks with another passage from *The Realm of Lovers, Werken* I.61:30–62:22.

Ruusbroec goes on to point out that the sublime work of contemplation—be it natural or supernatural—is always subordinate to the other, ordinary task of charity. Many sources in mystical literature stress the struggle of the contemplative with concrete works of charity that seem to hinder mystical experience. Ruusbroec is firm in his insistence that contemplatives always consider themselves embodied and social beings, not ethereal spiritual essences. If not, all contemplation is in vain.

Natural contemplation, then, is a "work," but only one out of many works that can bring the human closer to the divine Other. This is why Ruusbroec is so insistent that his opponents take note of their intentions. *Meyninghe* determines the sense and the scope of *scouwen*. If one is only intent on oneself, contemplation is private. If one is always intent on the Other, it is a means to reach "the One we intend and love." And without the divine grace to reorient one's intention from self to Other, there is no mystical encounter, no rising above oneself.

THE EAGLE DOES NOT FLY ABOVE ITSELF

At this point we may return to the question of the range of experience of those who contemplate without grace. Basically, Ruusbroec's argument is that such persons arrive at a limited, broken, incomplete experience. At best, they end up in heightened self-awareness. We recall the phrase from *The Spiritual Espousals* quoted earlier that sounds the keynote of Ruusbroec's critique of natural contemplation:

> When a person thus possesses this rest in emptiness...then he dwells within himself with rest (*blivet hi met rasten op hem selven*).[38]

A little later in the same work we find a passage that strikes out forcefully against the underlying personal attitude (the term *hem selven*, himself, is repeated no less than six times). As to the question of what happens to one so "turned back upon oneself," Ruusbroec says that such a one "desires consolation."[39] Unlike the contemplative who is touched by grace and looks for a Thou, the contemplative without grace waits only to be consoled by further experience. Experience does come, and it is not unauthentic. But since there is no Other on the horizon, the circle closes about the person and all experience is finally reduced to self-awareness. One cannot experience something

---

[38] *Opera omnia* III.b.2010–12.

[39] Here Ruusbroec is clearly speaking from his own experience as a contemplative. A few lines further he adds: "And a little consolation can greatly gladden them, for they do not know what they are missing." The implication is that his experience is richer and more complete than that of his opponents.

without first assuming it to exist. The passage ends with a frightening expression, summarizing Ruusbroec's view of those who have not, by divine grace, opened up to God:

> when a person wishes to possess any rest in emptiness without yearning devotedness to God.... For he is turned away from God and is inclined towards himself with natural love, and he seeks and desires consolation.... For in all his work he is turned back upon himself, and he seeks and is intent upon his rest and his profit more than the honor of God. The person who lives this way in mere natural love always possesses his own proper self undetached from self-will.... For they are proud and untouched and unenlightened by God, and this is why they remain within themselves. And a little consolation can greatly gladden them, for they do not know what they are missing.... These people live entirely contrary to charity and to the loving inward-turning in which a person—whom nothing but an incomprehensible good, namely, God alone, may appease or satisfy—offers himself with all that he can possibly do, for the honor and the love of God. For charity is a love-bond which carries us away and in which we renounce ourselves and are united with God and God with us. But natural love turns back upon itself and upon its ease, and always remains alone.[40]

The Little Book of Clarification underscores this resultant solitariness and explains its cause:

> For above the essential repose which they possess they feel neither God nor otherness (*anderheit*).... For the divine light has not shown in their darkness and that is because they have not sought it with active love and supernatural freedom.[41]

Once again the eagle from *The Tabernacle*, soaring high and nesting in its essence, makes its appearance:

> For it wants to know and not to believe, to have without hoping, to possess without loving. Therefore, however high the eagle flies, it cannot fly above itself.... Grace and charity, however, do carry one above oneself into God, there to make one's nest, for God becomes one's dwelling and one's rest.... Behold, the bird that nature forbids us is the most prized in grace.[42]

[40] *Opera omnia* III.b.2021–50.
[41] *Opera omnia* I:120–3.
[42] *Werken* II:336:34–337:17.

The problem with natural contemplation is that one is deceived into expecting too much of one's own feathers. When Ruusbroec uses the term *person*, we recall,[43] he means something that "subsists in itself":

> Further, we are someone different from God (*een ander van gode*) and cannot become one; we remain in otherness (*in anderheit*). That is where we subsist in ourselves, each in one's own person.[44]

Thus the metaphor of the eagle's flight suggests that the spiritual core of man—one's "person" where one is oneself—cannot be changed by contemplative practice. What may happen is that one becomes aware of changes going on, but one cannot actually bring those changes about. For this the spirit must open itself to "otherness." The flight into one's essence does not lift one above and beyond oneself.

Ruusbroec uses the metaphor of another bird, the owl, to represent the limitations of natural contemplation, and he does so with a touch of irony. It is the contemplative feathers that "burden the spirit." Only a new set of feathers can set it free:

> The owl teaches us that some persons fly in the night, that is, by means of the natural light, without God's grace. Their flight, carried along by a spirit that is free of images, brings them into the bareness of their essence (*in bloetheit haers wesens*). These are the feathers with which nature flies into a simple rest (*eenvoldegher rasten*). But these feathers burden the spirit, so that it is not able to fly above its nature.... Where the spirit is imageless, it should be informed with God's goodness. And where sight is empty and barren, there reason should be enlightened with the divine truth. In so doing, one would love and know beyond nature and desire God's honor in all one's works. With such feathers one could fly above one's created essence and enjoy God in eternity.[45]

It should now be clear that for Ruusbroec resting in the Other is altogether different from resting in oneself. It is a matter of distance and movement. One is more "lost" as one sinks away into a being different from one's own. For the contemplative with grace the divine Abyss, not the human ground, becomes the locus of rest. This is the point of the metaphor of the eagle's flight. Without grace, the contemplative "makes his nest and finds his rest in his essence." With grace, it is in God that "he makes his nest, for God himself is his dwelling and his rest."[46] This rest he speaks of is qualitatively different:

---

[43] See chapter 5, pages 107–11.

[44] See chapter 5, page 110, note 27, and its accompanying citation.

[45] *Werken* II.343:2–16.

[46] *Werken* II.336:17–18, 337:3.

This (natural) rest is contrary to the supernatural rest which one possesses in God, for that is a loving transport (*ontvlotentheit*), with a simple inner beholding (*insiene*), into incomprehensible brightness. This rest in God is always sought actively with inner yearning and is found in enjoyable inclination, and is possessed eternally in the transport of love (*in ontvlotentheiden*), and when it is possessed, it is nevertheless being sought: this rest is exalted above natural rest, as high as God is exalted above all creatures.[47]

Three points merit mention here. First, the distinctive mark of supernatural rest is that it occurs "in God"—that is, not in one's own limited self but in an unfathomable Other. Second, it is a "transport" that allows the contemplative to "see in" an "incomprehensible brightness."[48] This grasp of the incomprehensible, not from a distance but by being permeated with it, belongs to the rest that comes from taking the turn inwards "with grace." In the third place, these two elements make it possible to specify the experience of rest as incessantly self-renewing: each time it is found and possessed, it calls forth a new search.

ERRONEOUS INTERPRETATIONS

Ruusbroec's opponents did not confine themselves to the experiential level. They used their experience of "rest" as a basis for ontological statements about God and humans. For Ruusbroec, it would be more surprising if they had *not* done so, given the human tendency to make sense of experiences. He does not fault his opponents for making such statements, but for being too simplistic about it. In a word, they go no further than identifying their experience with reality. They do not submit their ideas to any kind of objective or outside criteria, but rather force the words passed on to them by tradition into a mold of their own making.[49]

This slackening of the usual tension between experience and words is clear, for instance, in the word *God*. Instead of asking themselves, as mystics have done through the centuries, "Is what I have experienced God?", they leap at once to the conclusion, "This is God!" But *what* they have experi-

---

[47] *Opera omnia* III.b.1992–8.

[48] *Ontvlotentheit* is one of Ruusbroec's typical suggestive terms. The prefix *ont-* indicates that the rest of which he speaks draws one out of oneself. We see this, for instance, in *The Sparkling Stone*: "We shall be able to sink into love forever and sink away from ourselves in those unfathomable depths (*ontsinken ons selven in die grondelose diepheit*)" (*Opera omnia* X.108–9).

[49] To use the language we met in Ruusbroec's portrait of the human in chapter 5, once the natural mystics have reached their essence, they wipe out the proper activity and contributions of the spiritual faculties, especially of the intellect.

enced is, for Ruusbroec, no more than their own essence. Granted this essence is vastly different from everything else in consciousness; and to enter it is to enter "the wild and barren desert," where one must "wander about without mode or manner."[50] But the contemplatives without grace

> are lifted up in unknowing and modelessness (*onwisen*) and are satisfied with this, and this modelessness (*die onwise*) they take for God.[51]

What is more, the self-satisfied enjoyment of the bliss of rest eliminates awareness of any intermediary between the human and the divine. Union with God is immediate, unqualified, and self-justifying:

> They have united themselves to the blind, dark emptiness of their own being; and there they believe themselves to be one with God and they take that to be their eternal beatitude.[52]

Ruusbroec does not doubt that they have touched on the divine within themselves, on that same in-being (*inwesen*) of God in human being (*wesen*) that he himself stresses. Their error, as the following passage from *The Little Book* sums up succinctly, is this:

> For in the highest point in which they are turned, they feel nothing save the simplicity of their essence (*haers wesens*) hanging in the essence of God (*gods wesen*). This absolute simplicity which they possess they regard as being God because there they find a natural repose. This is why they consider themselves as being God in the ground of their simplicity, for they lack real faith, hope, and love.[53]

Time and again Ruusbroec points to this absence of spiritual activity—no faith, no hope, no love—as the reason why these contemplatives so easily identify their essence with God. Once rest is only possessed in idleness, all distance necessarily disappears and one feels as if one has become God:

> These are the ones who...experience modelessness (*onwise*) and possess it without the love of God. And so they consider themselves to be God.[54]

> ...through their vacant imagelessness...they have found within themselves in a natural manner the indwelling of God (*inwesen gods*) and pretend to be one with God without the grace of God.[55]

[50] *Mirror*, Wiseman, 247.
[51] *Opera omnia* II.571–2.
[52] *Opera omnia* I.115–7.
[53] *Opera omnia* I.81–6.
[54] *Opera omnia* II.563–5.
[55] *Opera omnia* I.473–5.

According to Ruusbroec, his opponents end up simply idolizing their own essence. When contemplative experience is the only true faith, a person is bound to be charmed by a shining self-awareness.

> ...they do not go beyond themselves but rest and idle in their essence. And so their essence is their idol for they think they have and are one essence with God, and that is impossible.[56]

Once the contemplatives have taken to molding God and themselves on their "rest in idleness," there appear, in addition to the basic statement "I am God," a number of secondary truth claims. On the whole, Ruusbroec argues that they contradict, and even work against, fundamental Christian tenets. He mentions several such heretical ideas and takes issue with them, but the basis for his disputation is ever and again the same: experience appears as the sole principle, rest as the uncontested starting point. Several steps seem to appear consistently in the process.

In the first place, the experience of rest leads to the conception "I am nothing." A group of deviant contemplatives characterized in *The Spiritual Espousals* claims, thus,

> that they have given their spirit to God in rest and emptiness, and that they are one with God and annihilated to themselves (*te niete ane hemselven*).[57]

In *The Twelve Beguines* he has his opponents say "that they are so idle it is as if they did not exist," and a few pages on, "that the essence of the soul is nothing and that the essence of God is also nothing for the idle soul."[58]

Obviously, these people have a paradoxical way of substantializing experience, namely by inferring "I do not exist" from idleness. And this first statement about their own unreality leads them to a similar statement about God, who is then also conceived of as "nothing." Perhaps the most telling passage appears in *The Twelve Beguines*, where the context is Eckhartian. The opponents are introduced as people who "disdain modes as well as modelessness." And this is their path of thinking:

> They go beyond themselves and all that is created, beyond God and Godhead, and say: "God is nothing and they are nothing as well. Nothing is neither blissful nor unholy, neither working nor idle, neither God nor creature, neither good nor bad." Behold how in this way they forfeit their created being and become nothing, in the same way as God

---

[56] *The Four Temptations, Opera omnia* X.178–80.

[57] *Opera omnia* III.b.2109–11.

[58] *Werken* IV.41:11; 52:15–16.

in their imagination has become nothing. Heaven and earth and everything God has made has existence and being. But these unbelieving people say: "We are nothing and our God is nothing."[59]

The remarks about their disdain of modes and modelessness refers to their total absorption in idle emptiness. Even the crucial and awesome transition every contemplative makes upon entering into his essence, from what has mode to what has no mode, has been obliterated.

The word *nothing* brings us to a third typical step in the train of thought that Ruusbroec is criticizing. The original *niet* is a substantive: God is *a* nothing, which accords well with the paradoxical manner these mystics have of substantializing what they experience as something undefinable. In this context, however, it is clear that *nothing* is not to be understood in its usual, absolute sense. God is still a reality, but that sort of reality that is diminished by any attribute we might apply to it. Contemplatives who "disdain modes as well as modelessness" and who strive ever more to "go beyond" naturally end up thinking of God as a non-differentiated no-thing. And as a result, all distinction between creatures and among creatures vanishes as well.[60]

Passages illustrating this view abound. Note the following from *The Mirror*:

They have discovered within themselves a formless state above reason (*onwise boven redene*) and therefore think in their folly that on the Last Day all rational creatures—both the good and the wicked, both angels and devils—will become a single formless being (*een wiselooes wesen*). That being, they claim, will be God, blessed in nature and having no knowledge nor will.[61]

A bit further along in the text, those who "live in a formless way above all forms" are said to believe that

both good persons and wicked persons will all become a single, simple divine substance, in which they will all be but one essential beatitude without any knowledge or love of God. Consequently, according to them, God will neither will, know, nor love any creature.[62]

From their individual experience, then, the natural contemplative infers an ontology of "all rational beings" and a theology of the "single formless

[59] *Werken* IV.50:23–32.

[60] In chapter 8, page 159, we have seen Ruusbroec stressing the persistence of this differentiation even in the highest bliss.

[61] Wiseman, 229–30.

[62] Wiseman, 231.

being." The divine being is thus granted the features of the "formless state" of the contemplative: natural blessedness accompanied by immobile inactivity. In *The Seven Enclosures* Ruusbroec refers to this image of God as "purely existing being":

> and this modelessness they take for God.... They imagine that all ordering of life or of reward or of distinction shall disappear in eternity, and that nothing will survive but an eternal purely existing being (*een ewich istich wesen*) without personal distinction (*persoenlec ondersceet*) either in God or in creatures.[63]

The most spirited passage on this subject appears in *The Little Book*, where Ruusbroec attacks the idea of an ultimate Being devoid of activity and distinctions as contrary to the doctrine of the Christian Trinity:

> These men...have returned to the nakedness of their essence, so that it seems to them that life eternal shall be nothing other than an impersonally existing blessed entity (*een istech salech wesen*) without distinction of rank, of saints, or of reward. Yes, and some are so insane as to state that the Persons will disappear into the Divinity and that, there, nothing else will remain in eternity but the essential substance of Divinity; and that all the blessed spirits with God will have returned to the essential beatitude (*weseleke salecheit*), so simply that, beyond this, nothing else will remain, neither will nor activity nor distinct knowledge of any creature.[64]

Ruusbroec's own idea of being mystically one with God allows for order and distinction in reality. Against the view that God is a lifeless something (*een istich wesen*), Ruusbroec proposes the idea of "a living eternal something" (*een levende eewich yet*):

> The prophet tells us that the fools say: "There is no God." This is what has happened to you, when you say that God is nothing, and that in that nothingness you find everything. This is a patent lie. For if you did not exist and you were not seeking, neither would you find. And if neither you nor God exist, then no creatures exist. For God is a living support of all that he has created; he lives in us and we in him. He is a living eternal worker. He gives us his grace and demands of us eternal living works, that we should confess, know, and love him, that we should thank and praise him. These are eternal living works which he works in us and with us, for they begin in him and by him they are brought to perfection. Above these works there is nothing except the enjoyment of him, and with him,

[63] *Opera omnia* II.572–6.

[64] *Opera omnia* I.68–76.

in eternal blessedness. For he is our life, all that we need and desire in time and in eternity. He is a living eternal something, higher and deeper, longer and wider than everything he has created or might create.[65]

DEHUMANIZING EFFECTS

We may distinguish two sides to Ruusbroec's description of how the natural way affects the lives of its followers. First, it affects one's interiority as a "person"; second, it affects one's outer activity. Together they spell a devastation of what is characteristically human, as the contemplative becomes progressively depersonalized and desocialized. We have seen Ruusbroec complain often of those who lose their nature by "non-activity exteriorly as well as interiorly" that they "often fail their fellow-humans in their need," because they "value contemplation more than any work of charity."[66] In one of his last works he makes the same point:

> This error...disdains working, contemplating, desiring, loving, learning, knowing, having. It disdains the worship of Holy Church and all the sacraments, the commandments and the counsels, the whole holy Gospel, the teaching of Christ and his life, his holy suffering, his passion and his death.[67]

As for their exterior activity, these contemplatives appear to give up the most common Christian practices first:

> They disdain and attach no importance to the rules and customs of the Holy Church and to all that the saints have written, whereas they consider the lack of regulations of their evil sects, which they themselves have invented, to be holy and great.[68]

---

[65] *Werken* II.51:5–23.

[66] *Werken* I.62:9–10; 24:2–6. Ruusbroec's own point of view shows up clearly in *The Mirror* when he notes that "persons in religious orders, however advanced they may be in contemplation," should, if they are asked to, take up an office "even if during their periods of recollection and prayer they feel hindered and distracted because of the things which have been entrusted to their care" (Wiseman, 226).

[67] *Werken* II.50:14–9. In *The Seven Enclosures* the same rejection of the common, "exterior" Christian way of life is expressed as follows: "All the sacraments and practices of Holy Church, such as fasting, keeping vigil, praying, chanting and reading, order and law, all the Holy Scriptures and all that the saints practiced from the beginning of the world they consider as minimal and altogether worthless. For they are lifted up in unknowing and modelessness..." (*Opera omnia* II.567–71).

[68] *A Mirror*, Wiseman, 229.

266

The people Ruusbroec is describing not only brush aside Christian customs; they give free rein to individualism and slip into a moral laxity as if into the "nobility of nature." *The Little Book* paints the following picture:

By means of the bare emptiness which they feel and possess they are, so they say, without knowledge, loveless, and quit of all virtues. And as a consequence they endeavor to live without awareness of what evil they do, neglecting all the sacraments and all the virtues and all the practices of the Holy Church, for they think they have no need of them.... For what pagans, Jews, and bad Christians, both learned and unlearned, find and understand by natural reason, these wretched men can neither attain nor wish to.... They are self-willed and subject to none; and this is what they call spiritual liberty. They practice the freedom of the flesh by giving the body what it lusts after; and they consider that to be nobility of nature.... they think themselves above the law and above God's commandments and those of the Holy Church.... For they hold that the highest holiness is for man to follow his nature in every way and to live unrestrained so that he may dwell within in emptiness, with inclined spirit, and turn outwards to follow every prompting of the body's desires and appease the flesh, in order that he may be speedily relieved of the image and return unhindered to the bare emptiness of his spirit.[69]

[69] *Opera omnia* I.86–130.

13

Buddhism and the Critique of Natural Mysticism

So far, this book has taken the form of an investigation into the relationships among three sides of a triangle: Ruusbroec's mysticism, "natural contemplation," and Buddhism. The questions treated come into especially sharp relief in this final chapter, where we must bring into the picture the relationship of Buddhism to those aspects of natural contemplation that Ruusbroec has singled out for criticism. Do these elements correspond to traits of Buddhism? Or does Buddhism fundamentally side with Ruusbroec in his critique?

REST AS THE DOMINATING EXPERIENCE

> We must be still and still moving
> Into another intensity
> For a further union, a deeper communion.[1]

We have heard Ruusbroec, on the one hand, describe "rest in God" as the highest peak of the contemplative path and, on the other hand, criticize the "natural contemplatives" of his time for turning the enjoyable rest in idleness and emptiness into an absolute and the only thing that counts. It may be worth our while to summarize here Ruusbroec's objections against that attitude, since it may be interesting to see whether and how far these same themes are also at work in the Buddhist statements about the problem. Ruusbroec's denunciation of "false idleness," then, appears to contain the following elements:

1. Rest is taken by itself and detached from all preceding and concomitant states;
2. Rest is seen as the result of staving off all disturbances from the outside and stopping all interior motion—thus, as motionlessness and the end of all activity;

[1] T. S. Eliot, as cited in W. Johnston, *The Still Point* (New York: Fordham University Press, 1970), 113.

3. Rest is clung to for its highly enjoyable character and, therefore, taken as the absolute terminal, beyond which there is nothing to strive for;
4. In such a rest one does not go beyond the self: there is no otherness in it;
5. Such a rest "depersonalizes": reduces to the state of "a stick or a stone."

The problem of contemplation *versus* activity is not peculiar, of course, to Ruusbroec or even to Christian mysticism (with its "Mary and Martha" paradigm and its preoccupation with the commandment of active love). A quick look at Chinese Taoism or at the Indian *Bhagavadgītā* suffices to convince one of that. And even Ruusbroec's basic position of the unity of rest and activity appears to be prefigured in the Hindu classic. When the hero of the Gītā tale, Arjuna, asks the god Kṛṣṇa whether he should engage in action (which in his case meant going to war) or pursue contemplation, Kṛṣṇa answers, in substance, that both cannot be separated; that there must be a unity of renunciation-rest and action. The mental and bodily faculties must be at work while the self remains motionless.

How is it, then, with Buddhism? In a nutshell, these problematics are strongly present in all of Buddhist history—which is not surprising in view of Buddhism's pronounced contemplative character. Because of this, Buddhism (and especially Zen) has always been particularly prone to the "quietist temptation," but Buddhism has valiantly fought and successfully overcome this temptation, again and again—at least in its praxis, if maybe not clearly in its theory. Since I do not have the space, nor the competence, to present a full overview of Buddhist history seen from this perspective, a few highlights and some representative texts will have to suffice here.

The idea that, on the path to buddhahood, rest is never sufficient by itself is clearly represented in the older Buddhism, and is still so represented in Theravāda, by the stress on the cultivation of the ethical life and on the necessity of quieting meditation (*śamatha*) going hand in hand with a growing insight into the Buddha's doctrine (*vipaśyanā*). It is possible, however, that the very idea of Nirvana as the ideal state, and the idea of the Arhat (the hero who has stilled all inner movement and is impervious to the outer environment) as the ideal person, carry within themselves the tendency to esteem rest without activity. In reaction to this, the Mahāyāna (which, however, as we have seen, tends to put less stress on ethics and discursive thinking) came to characterize the ideal state as "non-abiding (in) Nirvana": the Nirvana'ed person returns to the world to *work* for others. "Paradoxically put, the spiritual insight here is that to renounce Nirvana for oneself, in love for others, is to find oneself in Nirvana, in its real sense"[2] (which is then not mere rest).

---

[2] E. A. Burtt, *The Teachings of the Compassionate Buddha* (New York: New American Library, 1955), 162.

Also the figure of the Arhat is criticized from early on as the embodiment, as it were, of a self-centered quietism: the Arhat is a person who thinks only of his own liberation without being moved by the plight of others; a person "intoxicated with the happiness that comes from the attainment of perfect tranquillisation." Instead, the ideal person then became the bodhisattva, a person "kept away by the power of all the Buddhas from [being intoxicated by] the bliss of the *samādhi*, and who thereby will not enter into Nirvana,"[3] but will instead engage in activity for others. That the bodhisattvas do not sink into the quietude of Nirvana or into Nirvana as merely quietude is attributed here simply to the power of all the Buddhas. In other texts it is said to be the result of the altruistic intention they expressed in their "bodhisattva vow" at the beginning of their career: "I shall not enter Nirvana before I have carried all others to the other shore."

It thus appears to be the growing emphasis put on merciful action for others that kept Mahāyāna from turning into quietism. On the other hand, several ideas came to the fore in this same movement that, by themselves, seem rather conducive to seeing the stoppage of all activity as the ideal. The reduced emphasis on ethical action and rational thinking is, indeed, compounded by ideas that present both action and thinking as detrimental to liberation. Since liberation consists in overcoming karma, and all actions (even good ones) produce karma, liberation can only be the result of the cessation of all action. And since it now became customary to see this-worldly reasoning as totally incapable of reaching the transmundane saving truth, the natural conclusion drawn was that all natural thinking must be stopped (thoughtlessness or non-mentation was necessary) to open the way for a grasp of the truth on a higher level of consciousness.

Probably more influential still, and more important in our context, was the belief that "Buddha-nature" was innate in all sentient beings—a belief that originated in later Mahāyāna and became a basic tenet in all East Asian Buddhism. From this belief it is easy to conclude that one is originally pure and "complete," and that *bodhi* (enlightenment, the "fruit") is not to be obtained by action but only to be awakened to in one's own "ground," in a sudden flash of insight. We shall see all these ideas, only summarily listed here, at work in the episodes and texts of Mahāyāna history, and to these we now turn.

---

[3] Both expressions are from the *Laṅkāvatāra Sūtra*, as translated in Burtt, *The Teachings of the Compassionate Buddha*, 165. One notices that the paradoxical situation of the bodhisattva is expressed in at least three ways: as not entering Nirvana to stay in the world, as coming back to the world after having entered Nirvana, or as entering a Nirvana that does not remove him from this world.

The most dramatic clash in Buddhist history between the quietist and opposing tendencies took place in what has been called the "Council of Lhasa." Very simply (and uncritically) put, this was a debate that took place in eighth-century Tibet at the invitation of the king, between representatives of Chinese Buddhism—later known in the Tibetan tradition as "the teaching of Hva śan" and branded as "quietist"—and representatives of a more action-oriented Indian Buddhism, led by Kamalaśīla. The outcome was that the Chinese tendency was defeated, and Tibetan Buddhism from that time on set its course by the Indian "pole star." What was at stake in this debate is formulated by D. Ruegg in a way that links it with themes we have already encountered:

> the expression "teaching of the Hva śan" has served, in the Tibetan historical and doctrinal texts, as a model and exemplar of a theory considered to have unduly stressed that form of quietism which excludes ethical and intellectual effort or that form of understanding that focuses non-analytically on the Empty alone, in contravention of the Buddhist principle that Quiet (*śamatha*) and Insight (*vipaśyanā*)...are co-ordinate and have to be cultivated together either in alternation or in unison as a fully integrated syzygy.[4]

> As for the doctrine of Hva śan Mahāyāna..., what was at issue was clearly not only quietism in the sense of the abandonment of praxis and of the first four perfections (*pāramitā*) [expressing the ethical endeavor]—though it was this too—but also the *dṛṣṭikaṣāya* of taking pleasure in emptiness—that is, in a frozen and more or less cataleptic fixation in the empty.[5]

> In the *Bhāvanākrama*...Kamalaśīla also cites the thesis [of the opponents] that the Six Perfections (*pāramitā*) are contained in Dhyāna [the fifth Perfection: meditation], so that through the cultivation...of the latter all the Perfections are cultivated, whereas generosity (*dāna*) [the first Perfection] and the others should not be cultivated separately.... It is only in respect to foolish people that salutary conduct consisting in generosity and the like has been indicated.[6]

It comes as no surprise that the themes mentioned in the Lhasa controversy are all to be found also in Zen texts.[7] Indeed, in its extreme emphasis on

---

[4] D. Ruegg, *Buddha-nature, Mind and the Problem of Gradualism in a Comparative Perspective* (London: School of Oriental and African Studies, 1989), 5–6.

[5] *Buddha-nature*, 110.

[6] *Buddha-nature*, 95, 93.

[7] There are other realms in Buddhism besides Zen where our problematics are at work in a

dhyāna, Zen evinces clear quietistic tendencies. The history of Zen, however, also contains vigorous reactions against these tendencies, and although there may not have been any clashes as dramatic as the "Council of Lhasa," the ever-present tension between the two tendencies at times comes to a climax in Zen as well. We could mention, among others, the early struggles between Southern and Northern Ch'an, the controversies around the "Ch'an of silent enlightenment" (*mo-chao Ch'an*) in the Sung Dynasty, and, in Japan, the battle of Hakuin against the quietist degeneration of his sect. Since there can be no question here of treating that history in any systematic form, I shall, in the following, simply assemble some Zen texts selected at random that attest to the presence of quietist tendencies and of the struggle against them.

> It [the question of liberation] simply resolves itself into not reacting to anything which occurs and to not (allowing) the mind (to dwell) anywhere whatsoever. Those who have attained to this will have entered Nirvana.... This may be called reaching the highest state of contemplation at a single stroke.[8]
>
> ...the Great Void is perfection wherein is neither lack nor superfluity, a uniform quiescence in which all activity is stilled.... I advise you to remain uniformly quiescent and above all activity.[9]
>
> If...you rest tranquilly in nothingness—then you are indeed following the Way of the Buddhas.[10]
>
> As to performing the six paramitas and vast numbers of similar practices, ...since you are fundamentally complete in every respect, you should not try to supplement that perfection by such meaningless practices.[11]
>
> As long as students of the Way haven't eradicated their conscious minds, all their activities and words are the deeds of karmic consciousness; they are not in accord with the Way.[12]

very pronounced form. There is, for example, the larger controversy in Japanese Buddhism concerning "original enlightenment" (*hongaku*) *versus* "beginning enlightenment" (*shikaku*). On this, see the special issue of the *Japanese Journal of Religious Studies* on "Tendai Buddhism in Japan," 14/2–3 (1987).

[8] Hui-hai's *The Path of Sudden Attainment* in C. Humphreys, *The Wisdom of Buddhism* (London/Dublin: Curzon Press, 1979), 202.

[9] *The Zen Teaching of Huang Po: On the Transmission of Mind.* Trans. by John Blofeld (New York: Grove Weidenfeld, 1958), 75.

[10] *The Teaching of Huang Po*, 88.

[11] *The Teaching of Huang Po*, 30. Ruusbroec counters this way of thinking with the idea of becoming ever more "like" God by the practice of virtue, while already "one" with God.

[12] *Mud and Water: A Collection of Talks by Zen Master Bassui.* Trans. by Arthur Braverman (San Francisco: North Point Press, 1989), 95.

> Thus when your mind is deluded, you are breaking all the precepts, and when you see into your own nature, you are at once keeping all the precepts.[13]

These few texts—especially when taken together with those already cited in chapter 11—suffice to illustrate that Zen Buddhism is, as it were, walking on the edge of the precipice of quietism, and that it has many characteristics in common with the party criticized at the "Council of Lhasa." This does not prove, however, that the Zen tradition as such would be a protagonist of quietism; it only intimates what will become clearer still from the later quotations: that Zen succeeded in remaining a sound contemplative tradition only at the cost of an ever-renewed battle against this in-built tendency. That Zen is no quietism is vigorously asserted, for example, by Thomas Merton:

> Zen is not a mysticism of introversion and withdrawal. It is neither quietism nor Hesychasm.... In other words, Zen, as properly understood, refuses to countenance the deliberate cultivation of a state of inner emptiness from which one might exclude all images and all concepts in order to experience oneself in a well-defined condition of silence, tranquillity and peace.[14]

And Paul Demiéville wrote:

> Faced with the old Chinese dilemma of motion and rest, of activity and passivity, the school of Hui-neng [the Southern sixth patriarch]...resolutely takes the side of activity; or, rather, of a "coincidence" of activity and passivity, of a "middle way" that reconciles the two. It does not cease denouncing the Northern School, that of Shen-hsiu..., the followers of which remained "sitting in immobility," engaged in "viewing their mind" and "observing their inner purity."[15]

Let us now view a few texts that testify to the ongoing struggle. We begin with a quotation from the "Fives Gates of Tao-hsin" [the fourth patriarch]:

> Maintaining unity without going astray—dwelling at once in movement and rest, we can see the Buddha-nature clearly and enter the gate of *samādhi*.[16]

---

[13] *Mud and Water*, 19–20.

[14] Thomas Merton, *Mystics and Zen Masters* (New York: Dell Publishing Co., 1980), 21, 221–2.

[15] P. Demiéville, *Le Concile de Lhasa* (Paris: Collège de France, Institut des hautes études chinoises, 1987), 126, note 1.

[16] As cited in H. Dumoulin, *Zen Buddhism: A History*, vol. 1 (New York: Macmillan, 1988), 100.

The sixth patriarch, Hui-neng, is especially outspoken in his criticism of quietism:

> Learned audience, when you hear me talk about the void, do not at once fall into the idea of vacuity.... It is of the utmost importance that we should not fall into this idea, because when a man sits quietly and keeps his mind blank, he will abide in a state of voidness of indifference.[17]

> To obtain liberation is...thoughtlessness.... Thoughtlessness is to see and to know all dharmas [things] with a mind free of attachment.... But to refrain from thinking of anything, so that all thoughts are suppressed, is to be dharma-ridden, and this is an erroneous view.[18]

> In our system of meditation, we neither dwell upon the mind...nor upon purity. Nor do we approve of non-activity.[19]

> When our mind clings to neither good nor evil we should take care not to dwell upon vacuity or remain in a state of inertia.[20]

Later, Zen master Yung-ming (904–975) will advocate the adoption of the Nenbutsu practice (reciting the name of Amida Buddha) into the Zen life, as a remedy against quietism. To defend his position, he quotes, for example, the following text from the *Awakening of Mahāyāna Faith*, a very influential Mahāyāna text of the 5th century or later:

> If people only cultivate tranquillity, the mind stays in a state of lethargy. They become indolent, do not seek virtue and become separated from great compassion.... Whether walking, standing, lying or sitting, one should simultaneously practice "tranquillity" and "insight."[21]

When turning to Japan, we first encounter Dōgen (1200–1253). The reconciliation of rest and activity, enlightenment and practice, was maybe *the* fundamental problem this profound thinker struggled with, till he came to his very original synthesis of activity and rest. He strongly criticized what he called "stopping thought in abysmal quietude" (息慮凝寂, *sokuryo-gyōjaku*) and admonished his disciples as follows:

---

[17] *The Diamond Sūtra and the Sūtra of Hui-neng*. Trans. by A. F. Price and Wong Mou-lam (Boston: Shambala, 1990), 80.

[18] *The Diamond Sūtra and the Sūtra of Hui-neng*, 85.

[19] *The Diamond Sūtra and the Sūtra of Hui-neng*, 98.

[20] *The Diamond Sūtra and the Sūtra of Hui-neng.*, 100–1.

[21] Yung-ming, *Treatise on the Unification of Myriad Goods*, in Heng-ching Shih, *The Syncretism of Ch'an and Pure Land Buddhism* (New York: Peter Lang, 1992), 231.

Students of the Way, even if you attain enlightenment, do not think that this is now the ultimate and thus abandon your practice of the Way. The Way is endless. Even when enlightened, you should still practice the Way.[22]

And Abbot Obara, a twentieth-century disciple of Dōgen, renders his master's spirit as follows:

In the Genjokoan book of Shobogenzo [Dōgen's main work] it is written: "In the feeling of inadequacy of body and mind the dharma is fulfilled; know also that in the feeling that the dharma has been fulfilled, there is yet something lacking." When we come to know of Buddhism, to feel that it is well, that all is at peace, to set ourselves down in a state of so-called satori, means there is as yet no real understanding of Buddhism. If we are really receptive to Buddhism, there is always the feeling of not enough, not enough; limitless endeavor and striving age after age, that must be the spirit of Mahayana. There is no feeling of completion.[23]

Of the later Japanese Zen Masters we need mention only two. The older one, Bassui (1327–1387), produces a list of Zen people with wrong attitudes and mentions among them: "And still others...sink deeply into a shell of tranquillity."[24] And he further warns:

Bassui spoke reprovingly: "Don't spend your life sitting in a ghost cave."[25]

Becoming settled and quiet while the mind exists is the heretical Zen of silent illumination. Meditation in complete stillness is an activity of the devil.[26]

Finally, for Hakuin (1685–1768), the great reformer of Japan's Rinzai Zen, *the* sworn enemy of true Zen was "sitting in silent enlightenment like tree stumps." Of him H. Dumoulin writes:

His [the usually tolerant Hakuin's] vehement polemics were aimed exclusively at Zen monks who sat in their monasteries and enjoyed a deceptive tranquillity.... As he says, they "foolishly take the dead teach-

---

[22] Dōgen, *Record of Things Heard.* Trans. by Thomas Cleary (Boulder: Prajna Press, 1980), 119.

[23] Trevor Leggett, *The Tiger's Cave* (London: Routledge & Kegan Paul, 1977), 64.

[24] Bassui, *Mud and Water*, 86.

[25] *Mud and Water*, 102.

[26] *Mud and Water*, 97.

ings of no-thought and no-mind, where the mind is like dead ashes with wisdom obliterated, and make these into the essential doctrines of Zen. They practice silent, dead sitting as though they were incense burners in some old mausoleum...."[27]

When we review what has been said, we can conclude, I believe, that Buddhism in its history has been scarcely less severe than Ruusbroec in its condemnation of the attachment to the bliss of silent sitting in mere rest. We can also remark that several of Ruusbroec's objections against that attitude are also present in the Buddhist denunciations. If there is any difference, it may be on the following two points. First, Buddhism does not seem to stress as clearly as Ruusbroec does the need for the restful contemplative peak to be linked organically with preceding and concomitant personal states. Second, Mahāyāna in general recognizes the need of "going beyond the self" in an outgoing mercy for the other, but that "need of the other" for the highest human experience is not apparent in the considerations of the Zen masters.

THE TURN INWARDS AND ONTOLOGICAL CONCLUSIONS

I have just stressed that, in its history, the Buddhist path, as a practice based on experience, has mostly succeeded in overcoming the pitfalls of "blissful quietude" that Ruusbroec accused the "natural contemplatives" of his time of falling into. The remainder of this chapter may, on the contrary, suggest that Buddhist theory or philosophical speculation succumbed to these same temptations, which indeed are "inherent" in Buddhism as a mystical religion.

As indicated in the Foreword, one of the things that triggered the writing of this book was our surprise at finding that the theories of the medieval natural contemplatives, as recorded by Ruusbroec, are so strongly reminiscent of Eastern, particularly Buddhist, mystical speculation. Ruusbroec's criticisms, therefore, also appear to bear on some aspects of Buddhist theory. Only these medieval Westerners labored under a triple disadvantage as compared with their Eastern "counterparts." First, in the culture in which they lived, these natural contemplatives did not have a long tradition of open discussions that could have refined their thinking and removed some of the excesses. Second, they did not have the benefit of guidance based on long experience and numerous precedents. Third, their experience, as they interpreted it, brought them into conflict with the doctrines and practices of the religion of their societies to which most of them still officially belonged.

[27] H. Dumoulin, *Zen Buddhism: A History*, vol. 2 (New York: Macmillan, 1990), 384. The quotation is from Hakuin's *Yabukōji* 薮柑子.

The question as it is phrased now, namely, whether Buddhists too are prone to consider the turn inwards—in Buddhist language, *dhyāna, śamatha,* etc.—as self-sufficient, appears to call for a nuanced answer. In chapter 11, I have endeavored to show that the Buddhist path in its totality is not only a mystical venture but also a full-fledged religion wherein the turn inwards is at the same time motivated and relativized. Buddhist living praxis thus has withstood the absolutization of the turn inwards and of its peak experience, blissful rest. But what about Buddhist theory? Here we have a different story, I believe, and since this may be important for the dialogue between Christian mysticism and Buddhist mysticism, I want to give this story a moment's attention.

No matter how much similarity we can detect between these two mysticisms, it is clear that their basic views of reality (their "ontologies") are fundamentally different. To use again a formulation by P. Mommaers that I have cited earlier: to the question, "What must be considered to be *the* Reality?" Buddhism (especially Mahāyāna) answers: "being [or rather nothingness] that reduces all to the same," and Christianity answers: "love that does not cease provoking difference." Or to phrase the problem somewhat differently, Ruusbroec's conviction appears to be that the turn inwards naturally leads one to an experience of, or an encounter with, (the personal) God, unless, that is, one arbitrarily stops the movement on the way (as the natural contemplatives are doing). The decisive value here lies in the otherness of God, which draws the mystic out of and above her or himself. For the Buddhist, on the contrary, the idea appears to be that the turn inwards naturally leads to the experience of undifferentiated or empty oneness, unless one stops the movement halfway (as the Christian mystics, with the possible exception of Eckhart, are doing). Here, the decisive value might be said to lie in the freedom from, or absence of hindrance by, any multiplicity or otherness.

Which is right and which is wrong? It would seem that, although both convictions are subjectively not unrelated to their respective mystical experiences, an appeal to mystical experience as such is not able to cut this Gordian knot. On this point, we must probably abide by William James's verdict, even though his formulations may not be the best possible ones:

> The fact is that the mystical feeling of enlargement, union, and emancipation has no specific intellectual content whatever of its own. It is capable of forming matrimonial alliances with material furnished by the most diverse philosophies and theologies.... We have no right, therefore, to invoke its prestige as distinctly in favor of any special belief.[28]

[28] William James, *The Varieties of Religious Experience* (New York: The Modern Library, 1929), 416–17.

It might also be said that the mystical experience is too rich in content to be captured in any rational concept, and that therefore the temptation is great to single out one striking feature of its conceptual formulation. Still, to the mystics themselves who have just reached an ecstatic peak of experience, it must seem as if they finally have seen reality as it really and truly is, and it is therefore rather natural for them to draw ontological conclusions from their mystical experience. The criticism that Ruusbroec directs at the natural contemplatives, that they "mold the Absolute and themselves on their rest in idleness," has therefore a ring of truth to it. And we can assume that Ruusbroec's intention was to say that this experience by itself, no matter how real and impressive, could not be trusted to render a full and definitive picture of reality, since it was after all a moment in a complex process of experience, and thus "abstract" by itself.

Here I must confess that Ruusbroec's critique dovetails perfectly with the misgivings I have felt for a long time about the way the Mahāyāna philosophy of emptiness or "All-One" is defended with an appeal to mystical experience, especially in Zen. On this point H. Dumoulin wrote, for instance:

> Zen-satori means the experience of the All-One. All descriptions of Zen masters flow into the monistic-cosmotheistic Mahāyāna metaphysics.
>
> This doctrinal formulation goes beyond the experience and interprets the experience in the sense of a monistic philosophy. The experience never offers anything more than the entrance of one's own self into absolute reality.[29]

It has seemed to me that in this Mahāyāna discourse the peak experience of undifferentiated unity and quietude has been totally privileged as a revealer of truth, with complete disregard of the possibilities for truth of the preceding path up the mountain and the ensuing descent from the mountain, back to the market place. This has naturally evoked the Shakespearean reaction, "There are more things in heaven and earth, Horatio, than are dreamt of in your philosophy." Closer to home, this means: your philosophy does not account for your own Buddhist path as a path, makes the moment of transition from modes to modelessness unthinkable, and cannot provide any real motivation for coming down again to the level of merciful activity for the others, which you yourself aver to be necessary even for true wisdom.

It could then further be argued that a doctrine like this, which makes ontological affirmations and negations—for example, with regard to the existence of a personal God—runs counter to the intentions of the Buddha who,

---

[29] H. Dumoulin, *Östliche Meditation und Christliche Mystik* (Freiburg/München: Karl Alber, 1966), 221, 108–9.

as the supreme pragmatist, wanted his disciples to stay away from all meta-physical views and only insisted on a way of thinking that is conducive to a spiritually liberating attitude. Sakyamuni, moreover, warned against "attach-ments to certain 'altered states of consciousness' or 'mystical experiences' that are common among advanced practitioners of *jhāna* [*dhyāna*] meditation," and specifically against a form of attachment that he called "lust for formless-ness."

> The *jhāna* attainments were highly pleasurable, he elaborated, and if one became attached to them they became a fetter to further spiritual growth. Moreover, such mystical experiences were likely to be misinter-preted, leading to erroneous beliefs (*micchādiṭṭhi*) which were themselves fetters, as he taught in the Brahmajāla Sutta (*Dīgha Nikāya*, sutta 1).[30]

Steven Collins, on the other hand, discovers in Theravāda Buddhism a "style of teaching which is concerned less with the content of views and theories than with the psychological state of those who hold them."[31] Without un-duly generalizing this finding, one might consider the possibility that Theravāda Buddhism has been more faithful here to the Buddha's intentions than Mahāyāna has.

I cannot pursue the possible relationships between mystical experience and metaphysical theory any further, but I believe I have already indicated sufficiently my conviction that Mahāyāna theory cannot be considered to have developed unilaterally from Buddhist mystical experience or to be a straightforward objectification of that experience. The historical background certainly shows a much more complicated pattern. One has to take into account, for example, the general "monistic" climate of Indian speculation, with which this metaphysics shows a family resemblance, notwithstanding its negation of the *ātman* and *Brahman* ideas. It may not be amiss, therefore, if we want to consider once more the difference in vision between Buddhist mysticism and Christian mysticism, to rely this time on a rather famous char-acterization by a great admirer of Indian *advaita* (non-dual) spirituality, Bede Griffiths:

> Hinduism conceives of the divinity as *Saccidananda*, a being perfectly aware of itself in an absolute beatitude. The Christian doctrine of the Trinity adds to this a further dimension, by conceiving of the divinity as essentially a communion of love. The highest being is not only pure con-sciousness reflecting itself in eternal wisdom, namely, the Word. It is also

---

[30] Nathan Katz, "Perfection without God: A View from the Pāli Canon," *Studies in Formative Spirituality* 14/1 (1993): 20, note 11.

[31] Steven Collins, *Selfless Persons* (Cambridge: Cambridge University Press, 1982), 129.

pure love communicating itself, overflowing beyond itself, in the power of the Spirit. The divine is the fullness of love, i. e., of personal relationships.[32]

ON BEING BEYOND ONESELF IN MYSTICAL EXPERIENCE

The term "ecstasis," which precisely denotes being beyond oneself, tends to appear in almost all descriptions of mysticism, and certainly is not out of place in the conceptions of mysticism of both Buddhism and Ruusbroec. The content of the term would differ considerably, however, in each case.

Ruusbroec's thinking on this point might be summarized as follows: mystical union is the complexity of being in oneself (centrally in one's "essence," but concomitantly in one's faculties) and, at the same time, being beyond oneself, in God. The "beyond oneself" alone would leave no human person, no consciousness, nothing one could call a mystical "experience"; the "in oneself" alone would not free one from the self. Moreover, true being beyond oneself can only be obtained in the Other: in God and in neighbor, in an ec-centric way, in love.

Buddhist mystical thinking, on the other hand, appears to envisage mystical union as the simplicity of being beyond oneself—a beyond oneself that does not imply, this time, a being in an Other, but that is described as a pure getting rid of the self in egolessness (in older texts) or as being beyond the everyday conscious self in one's "true self," which knows no borders of self and other and thus implies unity with all, with the universe, or with the cosmic Buddha(-nature) (in Mahāyāna texts, especially East Asian ones).

Once again it appears that a criticism that Ruusbroec levels at the natural contemplatives is also applicable to Buddhist mystical thinking. The criticism this time is twofold: a simple turn inwards or "concentric move" towards one's own depths cannot by itself raise one beyond oneself ("the eagle does not fly above itself"); and, a so-called "mystical state" that breaks completely with the natural modes of consciousness cannot be called someone's mystical experience.

As to the first criticism, it looks as if nothing for or against it can be said from the mystical experience itself. It is remarkable, however—as we have already had occasion to point out—that in older Buddhism a comparable conviction was at work: the idea, namely, that the last thread that binds one to the ego cannot be cut by the mere turn inwards or *śamatha*, and a supplementary force is needed to effectuate that. I have not been able to spot that valuable element in Mahāyāna thinking as yet. Could it be that in fact—but

---

[32] Bede Griffiths, "Le Christianisme à la lumière de l'Orient," *Bulletin de l'A.M.I* 49 (1990): 75.

without recognition in the theory, except perhaps in the T'ien-t'ai dynamic between emptiness and conventional existence—the Mercy element had taken over this role?

What, then, of Ruusbroec's objection that an undifferentiated consciousness, totally cut off from the ordinary working of the human faculties, cannot constitute a human experience? It is true, I believe, that in Buddhism, too, there is a strong tendency to present the highest mystical experience, enlightenment, as completely transcending the conditions of ordinary consciousness and, as remarked earlier, to consider the enlightened one as not belonging any more to the class of ordinary mortals. I shall limit myself here to three short remarks.

First, it does not seem to be the case that Ruusbroec would not appreciate the beauty of that mystical ideal of a "pure" consciousness, free from all human debilitating conditionings. However, supreme realist that he is, he sees this state as an "impossible ideal" by itself and therefore as having reality only as a moment in a more complex and truly human state—wherein one "feels oneself coming and going." A similar awareness of that at once "ideal" and "impossible" status of such a consciousness seems to have existed in Indian speculation on the subject, as attested to by the following text:

> The *Māṇḍūkya Upaniṣad* anticipates the later, radical expressions in its description of the highest state of consciousness as one beyond dreamless sleep.... The deeper self (*ātman*), thus discovered, tolerates no subject-object opposition. If taken literally, this state would eliminate consciousness itself and with it the very possibility of a "mystical" state. Yet such a total elimination of personal consciousness remains an asymptotic ideal never to be reached but to be approached ever more closely.[33]

Second, the question of the possibility of such a "pure consciousness" or "pure experience" is being discussed anew at present in Religious Studies circles, mainly in connection with the Buddhist (and especially Zen) claims on this point. The meaning of the term has been analysed variously as either "non-dualistic consciousness," "contentless (non-intentional) consciousness," or "a state of consciousness unmediated by concepts taken from the world of everyday experience." The crux of the question in this contemporary debate appears to be whether or not a human experience, not mediated by socially constituted conceptual and linguistic schemes, is possible.[34]

[33] Louis Dupré, "Mysticism," in: Mircea Eliade, ed., *The Encyclopedia of Religion* (New York: Macmillan, 1988), 10: 248.

[34] Cf., for example, Robert K. C. Forman, *The Problem of Pure Consciousness: Mysticism and Philosophy* (Oxford: Oxford University Press, 1990), and D. Barbiedo's review in *Philosophy East and West*, 43/4 (1993): 766-7. The analysis of the term goes back to Paul Griffiths.

Third, Ruusbroec's insistence on the human ingredient in even the highest mystical experience can also be seen in the light of the Christian conviction that the God, who granted the creature a self-nature or "own-being" beyond God himself, forever respects that "own-being," even in the moments of his strongest merciful in-working on his creature. Thus it is considered that God cannot save a human being against its will, and that the act of faith, no matter how much it is a gift of God, must be an act of the human subject. In this respect, it is instructive to see how these ideas fare in Pure Land Buddhism, which, like Christianity, attributes salvation to the working of an "Other-power," but, on the other hand, lives in the sphere of Mahāyāna (mystical) ideas. In Pure Land Buddhism, then, the possibility of a conflict between Amida's saving will and the human will does not seem to be seriously considered, and the act of faith, necessary for salvation, is presented (at least in Shinran) as having Amida as its subject. We might see therein a tendency toward total transcendence of the human subject and its faculties, analogous to the way in which enlightenment is presented in other Buddhist circles.

DEHUMANIZING EFFECTS OF BUDDHIST MYSTICISM?

Finally we come to the question of whether Ruusbroec's allegation that the path of natural contemplation has dehumanizing effects on its practitioners—narrowing their consciousness, making them look down on the human, especially social, virtues, and so on—would have any bearing on Buddhism. The answer, as I see it, could be summarized in the following three points:

1. This criticism certainly does not apply to the Buddhist path lived in its fullness—a path that, as argued earlier, cannot be called a "natural mysticism."
2. The Buddhist path, like every particular path (the Christian one included), has its in-built limitations—limitations that, in the Buddhist case, are connected with the centrality of the turn inwards in it.
3. When reduced to the turn inwards alone, the Buddhist path is indeed prone to the deviations indicated by Ruusbroec.

The first point does not, I think, need much belaboring. History is there to show that, on the whole, Buddhism has had a very humanizing effect on the peoples in which it took roots, and is at the least co-responsible for that special kind of irenic humaneness that one encounters in Asian peoples and that has sometimes been called "Eastern humanism." Furthermore, there can be no doubt about the important role that the monks, those Buddhist contemplatives, have played in that process. History, however, is not the only witness. Anybody who has had the benefit of a long acquaintance with

Buddhist monks and lay people can testify to an encounter with personalities of high, and sometimes extraordinary, human quality among them.

If then we speak of in-built limitations with regard to Buddhism, it must be in the awareness that *all* religions, no matter how "supernatural," are human endeavors and therefore imperfect and prone to lopsidedness, and with due regard for the fact that these limitations are, in a sense, only the shadowsides of Buddhist strengths. If I want to speak of them at all at this juncture, it is because, in a roundabout way, they appear to illustrate and confirm the misgivings Ruusbroec had about natural contemplation.

In the ongoing Buddhist-Christian dialogue an oft-recurring theme—and one on which a broad consensus appears to exist on both sides—is the observation that, while Christianity is prone to lose sight of the inner, "experiential," side of religion in its overly great preoccupation with outer doctrine and action, Buddhism, on the other hand, in its heavy stress on the turn inwards, finds it hard to come to grips with the outer, especially social, realities of human life. This consideration is not really a novel one; it has induced scholars of religion in the past to classify Christianity (together with Judaism and Islam) as a "prophetic religion," and Buddhism (together with most Oriental religions) as a "mystical religion." The only new note may be that, in the present dialogue, both Christians and Buddhists are looking for ways to overcome the traditional one-sidedness of their own religion by learning from the other.

I have had occasion earlier to comment on the resolute focus on the subject or "inner man" found in Buddhism,[35] and we might also remind ourselves of Kenneth Cragg's characterization of the Buddha's concern as exclusively directed at the individual in its "existential frailty."[36] Two concrete illustrations may now suffice to make my point. Above we have paid attention to the Buddhist analysis of the virtue of giving (*dāna*).[37] We may now remark that the conditions stipulated there all have to do with attitudes of the giving subject, while the objective need of the receiving "object" does not enter the picture at all. This has prompted me to remark on occasion, albeit half in jest: if the good Samaritan had paid heed to these injunctions, he might have left the robbed and wounded Jew lying by the wayside.

Another indication of the Buddhist propensity to consider the outer, material, world as not religiously relevant can be found in a habit of speech (at first sight, innocent) that appears to be general in Japanese Buddhist discourse. As true Mahāyānists, Japanese monks, in their sermons and treatises, duly stress the importance of mercy. A word mostly used in that context is

[35] See chapter 6, page 134.

[36] See chapter 6, page 122.

[37] See chapter 9, pages 200–1.

rita 利他 (benefiting others). So far so good, but, nearly automatically and as if the two were equivalents, *rita* is then qualified by *kyōke* 教化. This latter term literally means "imparting the Buddha's doctrine" or, in a broader sense, "leading the other toward enlightenment." By that identification, the whole realm of the material needs of one's neighbor is excluded from the scope of the virtue of mercy. This is, unfortunately, not a simple question of words; it betrays an inner attitude.

One way in which Ruusbroec criticized people given to natural contemplation was: "they often fail their fellow humans in their need, because they value contemplation more than any work of charity." It would be unjust to say that Buddhism as such falls within the scope of that criticism, but it can be said that the very nature of the Buddhist religion as basically a path of inwardness can easily lead practitioners in that direction, if they neglect the counterbalancing elements that are also found in Buddhism. Or, to say the same thing from a slightly different angle, Buddhism is admirably suited—better, probably, than Christianity—to leading the practitioner to spiritual freedom, but not so directly geared—and less so than Christianity—to encouraging commitment to the "good causes" of humanity.

This leads us then to phenomena in Buddhism, or on the fringes of Buddhism, wherein the counterbalancing elements are neglected and that, as a result, fall directly within the scope of Ruusbroec's "dehumanizing effects" criticism. Above I have a few times and rather brazenly expressed my conviction that a theory of emptiness that does not account for everyday life and does not give mercy its real due is a prime example of this imbalance. Religious theory does not by itself constitute religious attitude, of course, but it may sway the religious attitude in its direction, and it would not be an exaggeration to say that this particular theory, put literally into praxis, would lead to a less than human life.

As to the praxis, we must turn a last time to Zen, that school of Buddhism in which the turn inwards tends to be most central and exclusive. We can, then, first say with confidence that Zen Buddhism, lived according to its true tradition and in its monastic setting, is not conducive to the dehumanizing effects of which Ruusbroec speaks, but, on the contrary, is able to produce personalities of very high human quality. Earlier, however, I have said that Zen is "walking on the brink" of quietism. In the same vein I could now say that the conditions for authentic Zen are very strict, and that, if these conditions are not fulfilled—if what I have been calling the "counterbalancing elements" are not fully at work—the result is apt to be a kind of "wild Zen" that shows all the dehumanizing effects of which Ruusbroec accused the natural contemplatives of his time: disdain for religious practices; moral abuses; abnormal growth of the ego until it becomes the sole judge of everything; asocial behavior; and so on. Illustrations of this could easily be

284

found even in Japan, the country in which the Zen tradition is strongest; but, not surprisingly, Zen practice is most exposed to these dangers in the countries of the West, where the Zen tradition is not as yet well established. We can recall here the scandals, sexual and otherwise, that have threatened the reputation of several Zen masters and Zen halls in America in recent years.

In connection with a Zen master who had been abusing several of his disciples sexually, the question has been asked: "How is it possible that an enlightened person does such a thing?" We could consider this question a concrete, contemporary formulation of the whole problem of the human and religious value of natural contemplation. A stab at an answer may, therefore, serve to round off our considerations on this problem. Two opposing answers to the question have been given by Zen people: one, "Such immoral behavior proves that the man is not really enlightened"; two, "Enlightenment has nothing to do with moral behavior." This seems to indicate that two different conceptions of the nature of enlightenment exist in Zen circles. The first, which cannot conceive of an immoral enlightened person, sees enlightenment as the desired outcome of the Zen Buddhist life, and thus as the attainment of the Buddhist ideal of perfection. In a Zen perspective, Buddhist perfection certainly has deep contemplative states as its centerpiece, but for these people it naturally implies the idea of "holiness," a mastery of the desires and passions that is at one and the same time a condition and a result of the mystical attainment.

The second conception appears to consider enlightenment in much the same way as Ruusbroec's natural contemplatives conceived of their mystical state of perfect rest: something absolute by itself, the only constituent and norm of human perfection. The attainment of enlightenment solely depends on the implementation of its intrinsic, technical or psychological, rules. It is not dependent on the moral qualities of the person and need not prove itself in a morally impeccable life or in what otherwise might be considered to be the signs of human excellence.

The question of whether Zen practice is supposed to make its practitioners morally upstanding human beings can be extended to other human qualities that are deemed desirable. It then becomes, for example: Are Zen practitioners supposed to develop into persons actively engaged in the service of their fellow human beings? Or again: Is the enlightened one supposed to be a person who is not swayed by the collective passions of his group, such as nationalism? These questions, too, have actually been asked in the recent Buddhist-Christian dialogue, and they have received the same twofold answer given above.

I submit that all this sufficiently proves that what is at stake in Ruusbroec's dispute with the natural contemplatives of his time is not simply a parochially Christian matter and equally not merely a thing of the past. I also fancy that, to the question that has been haunting me throughout the writing of my part of the present book—Can Ruusbroec's mysticism and Buddhist contemplation really illumine one another?—it provides a final nudge in the direction of a positive answer.

Afterword

Paul Mommaers

Home again after a second extended stay at the Nanzan Institute, I was delighted to tell my friends and colleagues how well Ruusbroec had been received. Both in formal seminars and in countless informal exchanges of ideas, scholars working in Buddhist sources or in the borderlands between Buddhist and Christian thought had taken a keen interest in the medieval mystic who has been the object of my own affections and academic interest these past many years. I was moved to see their attention to the accuracy and complexity of Ruusbroec's descriptions and their eagerness to grapple with the problem of "natural contemplation." Then one day, a colleague teased me with the obvious question, "But did *you* learn anything?"

Now that our project has come to an end, the answer is clearer to me than it was in the thick of the work: At first, I was skeptical of what the Buddhist tradition might add to my understanding of Christian mysticism; then I became skeptical of my own skepticism; now I am fascinated by the possibilities. What once appeared to me purely scholarly questions have deepened into the same kind of mystery that I have found in Ruusbroec and other mystics. Only by meeting with persons who search the texts of the Buddhist tradition in order not only to clarify their deliverances but to be touched by them was this possible.

Not that I was disinterested in the spirituality of the East, but it always seemed to be veiled in a fluttering gossamer of esotericism that made my interest stop short at mere curiosity. As a Western Christian living in the age of interreligious dialogue and encouraged by the openness to other religions of the Second Vatican Council, I knew better. The problem was that I could not bring myself to *feel* better about letting Buddhism affect my own beliefs. Meantime, I had read enough of the books an educated person is supposed to read, and was not coming at Buddhism blind. But I did my reading with a more than passing empathy for the Enlightenment notion that all the world's religions can be distilled rationally down to a single common essence.

This was the pair of lenses I brought with me when I set off for Japan. In the course of the project, I found myself often slipping the glasses off and learning to trust the same naked eye I need to work with sources closer to my own experience and education.

And just where is this interreligious mystery? For me, it lies in a conjunction of two facts. On the one hand, Buddhism and Christianity are poles apart in their conception of reality. They view the Absolute in sharply different if not outright incompatible ways, and this in turn leads to distinct ways of valuing the human and the world of nature. The admonition of the *Dhammapada*, "Look upon the world as a bubble, look upon it as a mirage" flies in the face of Christian faith for which the world is not only very real but a gift from and a sign pointing back to the Absolute.

On the other hand, there is the fact that Buddhism and Christianity share an unmistakable commonality of spiritual experience and insights. I found this to be true on a number of large questions, such as the belief that "the ego with its self-isolating self-centeredness is enemy number one of all moral and spiritual life" (136). I also found it to apply to numerous points of fine detail. To put it bluntly enough to amount to a break from my former Christian-Western perspective, Buddhism shows definite spiritual views which I had assumed were the apanage of Christianity and could not take true root in so alien a religious and philosophical soil.

The paradox is informative. The basic approach of Christianity to reality is that all things rest on a single, ultimate foundation. This "ground" that underlies the things that make up reality is not merely some primal material or order, but an original source. Ruusbroec puts it neatly: far from being "a purely existing *being*," this Absolute is "a living eternal *something*." It is not some formless stuff but a differentiated, active presence. This is what Christianity understands by referring to the Absolute as Creator and Providence. I see no way to iron this element out of the Christian tradition. But neither do I see Buddhism able to dispense with its faith in an Absolute as an ultimate nothingness or emptiness into which all differentiated beings eventually dissolve. This contrast at the ontological level also reverberates throughout the existential outlooks of the two traditions. Where the fundamental Christian "feel" for life is one of presence and dynamism, for the Buddhist the central experience is of vanishing into a stillpoint. Where the Buddhist strives to see all things in steadied insight, the Christian is moved by an insatiable desire to taste all things on its way to savoring the Ultimate.

This difference of perspective exhibits its sharp edges in the contrasting views of the human. To be sure, the reality of the *I* has become increasingly problematic to Western reflection and Buddhist anthropology is not cut of a single cloth. Still, the fact is that the idea of *anatta* or *anātman* that is the cornerstone of the Buddhist view of the human remains a stumbling block to the Christian.

Certain factors soften the opposition. I have been struck by Buddhism's deconstruction of the illusory unity and continuity of the *I* as a matter of what Jan Van Bragt calls "spiritual policy" (134). And of course the fact that the interpretation of no-self as the ontological nonexistence of the ego may be more a fruit of later speculation than of Sakyamuni's own teaching. Such nuances, however, do not erase the disparity between the human being seen as a no-self and the human being seen as a person. For when all is said and done, the Christian view of the human being as created by God implies two correlative elements. On the one hand, the human individual is "suspended in God" as Ruusbroec puts it, and thus in no way an isolated, substantial ego. But on the other, the individual is a *created* individual, different from the Creator, something "subsisting in itself" and endowed with the capacity to use the being it is continuously receiving and indeed with the responsibility to do so. No amount of empathy or comparison of similarities can sail us around these rocky straits. It is hard for me to understand how a Buddhist can appreciate fully, given the doctrine of no-self, those features of the Christian experience that imply personhood and personal encounter with the divine Other. The idea of God as one who provokes a personal reaction and of faith as developing that stimulus into a life of yearning to "meet" God, ideas we have seen central to the mystical path, seem to be precluded by belief in *anatta*. However successful the Enlightenment heritage was at blending the colors and blearing the edges, there seems to be something intrinsic to the respective traditions that resists the effort.

In the initial stages of this project, I expected Buddhism to fall *tout court* under the weight of Ruusbroec's critique of "natural mysticism." I knew full well, of course, that the spiritual tradition stemming from Sakyamuni the Buddha towers high above the dissenting movement of the fourteenth century that Ruusbroec had taken as his foil. Still, I imagined that Buddhist mystics, lacking the awareness of "grace and faith," were bound to pinnacle experience at the expense of the noncontemplative aspects of the spiritual life. I anticipated—and everything I had read disposed me to anticipate—that Buddhism would finally land itself in the sort of quietism and social apathy that the best tradition of Christian mysticism has always railed against. I am sure my co-author smiled one of his inscrutable smiles when I first set forth my hypothesis, but I am just as sure that it was lost on me. In any case, the focal point of our efforts took shape around this question. What I learned, as I am confident the reader who has worked through the thirteen chapters of this book has also learned, is that Buddhism rather takes sides with Ruusbroec against the limitation of natural mysticism. On this score, to paraphrase Ruusbroec, my eyes may have opened too wide to close again. Suffice it here to mention only a few of the main points.

In the first place, I understand that the spiritual heirs of the Buddha do not detach experience from its attendant noncontemplative acts and attitudes. If in fact "Buddhism is (not only mysticism, but also) religion, even in its most mystical moments" (233), and given the qualifications Van Bragt himself makes in this regard, the conclusion is enough to make a Christian sit up and take notice. In other words, *grace*—by whatever name—has a part to play in Buddhist contemplation as well. There is consciousness of "a factor in the process of contemplation and liberation that is not reducible to the efforts of the individual person" and at the same time there is a conviction that "enlightenment is certainly not the result of one's own efforts" (234). In other words, Buddhist contemplatives are not unaware of the *supernatural*, as is evidenced in their concern with "natural and nonliberating contemplation" (236). Likewise, *faith* makes an appearance in Buddhist contemplative practice. Even when, as a Christian, I take due note that this word is used here in the broader sense of "religion" and that faith is not without its own ambiguities and qualifications, I cannot ignore the unmistakable presence in the Buddhist contemplative life of an attitude that intimates the "act of faith" with which I am familiar. I do not hesitate to state that in reading and rereading Zen master Shibayama's text on the "tether of faith," I am moved in the same way that the Gospel and Ruusbroec move me.

A second point at which Buddhist contemplative doctrine caught my attention has to do with its critical aspect. After pointing to the presence of grace, the supernatural, and faith, Van Bragt goes on to claim: "Buddhism (and especially Zen) has always been particularly prone to the 'quietist temptation,' but Buddhism has valiantly fought and successfully overcome this temptation, again and again" (269). This is a crucial statement, and a very suggestive one. The student of Western mysticism in general, and Ruusbroec in particular, cannot but be encouraged to hear voices as different as Kamalśila, Dōgen, and Hakuin join chorus with their Christian counterparts. Among the many citations, I would single out two that I found particularly suggestive. In the first, from the *Laṅkāvatāra Sūtra*, the bodhisattva is described as a person who is "kept away by the power of all the Buddhas from [being intoxicated by] the bliss of the samādhi, and who thereby will not enter into Nirvana" (270). I take this to imply that it takes the "supernatural" intervention of "all the Buddhas" for a contemplative to reach a healthy relativization of mystical bliss. When such a person is said to renounce Nirvana only to "instead engage in activity for others," I cannot but hear familiar echoes. I think of Saint Paul who wrote of his wish "to depart and be with Christ; that is better by far; but for your sake there is greater need for me to stay in the body" (Phil 1:23–5). I think, too, of Ruusbroec, for whom the ideal contemplative was the "commoner." Indeed, the second text attracts me precisely because the filigree of this commoner is embossed so clearly in it. I refer to Paul Démieville's characterization of the school of Hui-neng as "resolutely taking the side of activity; or, rather, of a 'coincidence' of activity and passivity" (273).

Our project is over. In some ways the results are simpler than either of us expected. In others, we are more than ever aware of the richness and surprises that await to be uncovered. Given the age and circumstances in which Ruusbroec lived, the mystical experience he brings to the fore is bound intimately and exclusively to the Christian faith. If our efforts have shown anything, it is that these bonds are not a confinement. Important elements of his spiritual doctrine appear outside their own confessional framework and can in turn be enhanced by contact with sources Ruusbroec could not even have imagined. As was pointed out frequently, lived Buddhist praxis shows closer affinities to Ruusbroec's mystical teaching than Buddhist theory does. I take this to mean also that Buddhism opens up a liberating space between experience and speculation that seems to give the Christian mystic free and easy access to an otherwise very different body of doctrine. I am convinced that further exploration of this space can only redound to the benefit of both traditions. To enter it, one needs more than the tools of the scholar. One needs to trust in the hopeful words of Jesus: "The wind blows where it wills; you hear the sound of it but you do not know where it comes from, or where it is going" (John 3:8). Of that, too, I am convinced.

Index

Abe Masao 阿部正雄, 128, 199, 204, 245
Abhidharma, 135
Abhishiktananda, 41
Abhūmika, 182
Absence, of activity in the subject, 91; of objects, 225; of personal presence, 146, 151; of spiritual activity, 262
Absorption, 35, 37, 44; in God, 193, 195; in idle emptiness, 264. *See also dhyāna, śamatha*
Abundance of God, 54, 163, 169
Abyss, 66, 106, 110, 114, 149, 151, 154, 169, 172, 231, 250, 260
Advaita, 78, 279
Affective, 32–3, 197–8, 236; mysticism, 18–9; prayer, 151,157
Agapé, 116, 126, 189
Aggregates, 185
Ājñā, 236
Ai 愛, 131, 192, 198, 242, 281
All-one, 34, 124, 186, 244, 278
Altérité, 202
Amida, 31, 34, 201, 207, 234, 274, 282
Amidism, 92, 207, 233
Anātman, 102, 123, 136, 184, 288
Anatta, 102, 123, 288–9
Anderheit, 110, 159, 170, 259–60
Anew, 54, 154, 157, 160, 171, 195, 254
Annihilation, 24, 66–9, 95–6, 140, 163, 173, 252–3, 263–4
Antinomy, 87, 180, 246
Apophatic, 33, 148
Appetitive, 30, 114–17, 125, 138, 198, 203. *See also* conative
Aquinas, Thomas, 20, 70, 105, 129, 216
Arhat, 38, 269–70
Arjuna, 269

Ascent, 52, 79, 132, 144, 149, 197
Asia, Asian, 30, 34, 37, 93, 128–9, 184, 270, 280, 282
Aspiration, 83, 145–6, 182, 207, 243
Asymmetry, 201, 246
Atheism, 70–2, 75, 79–80, 238
Ātman, 77–8, 102, 123–4, 136–8, 184, 234–5, 279, 281, 288
Augustine, 61, 63, 67, 100, 103–5, 113, 116, 118, 123, 125, 134–5, 137
Avaivartaka, 184
Avidyā, 40, 80
Awakening of Mahāyāna Faith, 274

Baker, Augustine, 15, 66, 69
Balthasar, Hans Urs von, 30
Bareness, 59, 67, 151, 154, 158–9, 187, 224–5, 228, 260
Barth, Karl, 82
Bassui Tokushō 抜隊得勝, 240, 242–3, 272, 275
Beatitude, 168, 262, 264–5, 279
Beelde, 118, 222
Beghards, 213–14
Begheren, 114–15
Beguines, 2, 22, 62, 110, 119, 164, 170, 211–14, 219, 227, 252, 263
Beloved, 19, 25, 48–9, 56–7, 60, 147, 160, 165, 169, 174, 187
Bendōwa. See Shōbōgenzō
Bergson, Henri, 89, 126, 203
Bernard of Clairvaux, 14, 52, 61, 117, 196–7
Bhagavadgītā, 203
Bhakta, 75, 234–5
Bhakti, 78, 127, 129, 203, 205–7, 235
Bhāvana-mārga, 136
Bhūmi, 182, 184

293

Blessedness, 57, 72, 104, 106, 119, 157, 166–9, 175, 188, 203, 234, 250–2, 255, 265–6.

Bliss, 57, 106, 143, 149–50, 157–8, 168–9, 175, 195, 205, 249, 255, 262–4, 270, 276–7, 290

Bodhi, 34–5, 37, 182, 207, 270

Bodhicitta, 183

Bodhidharma, 190

Bodhisattva, 38, 76, 78, 88–9, 93, 132, 182–4, 187, 190–2, 199, 206, 236, 270, 290

Body, integral with soul, 13, 20, 36, 87, 104–6, 147, 157, 175, 181, 185, 220, 222, 249; distinguished from soul, 64, 223, 225, 239, 249, 267, 269, 275

Brahmabhāva, 75

Brahman, 75, 77–8, 137, 234–5, 279

Breakthrough, 91, 95, 178, 180, 184

Bridegroom, 17, 21, 51, 53, 64, 146–8, 151–2, 254

Buddha, 122–4, 135–7, 278–9, 283, 289; as model, 35, 86, 183, 199; and the self, 74–5, 87–8, 91–4, 130, 240–3; devotion to, 38, 76, 78, 85, 96, 205–7, 232, 242; doctrine of, 40–1, 88, 90, 236, 240–1, 246, 269, 284; *pratyeka-buddha*, 237; silence of, 88

Buddha-nature, 37–8, 82, 87, 89, 92–3, 123, 125, 131–3, 206, 236–7, 244, 270–1, 273

Buddha-womb, 87, 89. *See also* *Tathāgata-garbha*

Buddhahood, 183, 191, 194, 236, 238, 240, 269

Buddhist-Christian, 3, 28–30, 127, 283, 285. *See also* dialogue

Burning, 144, 152, 159, 164, 167, 171–2

Burnt, 21, 67, 143–4, 159, 164, 187–8

Buswell, Robert E., 92, 204, 246–7

Busyness, 112, 145, 224–5, 249

Cartesianism, 16, 101–2, 103, 110, 123–4, 137. *See also* Descartes

Cessation, 79, 181–2, 225, 270

Chapman, John, 59

Charity, 39, 42, 51, 117, 150, 175, 228–9, 257–9, 266, 284

China, Chinese, 34, 37, 131, 240, 242, 269, 271, 273

Christ, the awakened, 41; the bride-groom, 17, 49, 51, 60, 146, 147, 151–2; comings of, 21, 146–8, 151–2, 215; as object of desire, 116, 145, 147, 148, 290; overcoming of in mysticism, 96, 112, 145, 212, 222, 235, 266

Clinging 56, 67, 79, 132, 158–9, 170, 188, 249, 274

Cobb, John, 83, 124

Cognitive, 30, 43, 62, 125–6, 128, 136, 179–80, 190, 205, 246–7

Commitment 222, 284

Commoner, 111, 174, 176, 290

Community, 2, 61, 83, 86, 116

Compassion, 38, 88, 132–3, 182, 191–2, 199–201, 206, 274

Complexity, 131, 133, 147, 173, 175, 186–7, 189–90, 194–6, 278, 280–1, 287

Comprehend, 55–6, 61, 70, 139, 150, 152, 253

Conative, 125–6, 186, 198, 203, 246–7

Concentric, 106, 247, 280

Contradiction, 38, 85, 92, 110, 129, 132, 143–4, 190–2, 196, 206

Conversion, 14, 52, 56, 215, 229, 236

Conze, Edward, 129, 181, 199, 238–9

Council of Lhasa, 271–3

Cragg, Kenneth, 122, 126, 206, 283

Creator, 63, 79, 106, 118, 161, 163, 231, 288–9; God as, 79–80

Creation, creatures, 83–5; mysticism of, 85; mystical knowledge of, 229, 263–5; as image and likeness, 118–20, 161, 188; detachment from, 15, 24, 69, 74–5, 83–5, 148, 188, 222, 225, 229; negation of, 80, 83–5, 129, 186,

193–4, 197–8, 282, 289; reality and value of, 80, 83–5, 109–11, 129, 175, 186, 193–4, 197–8, 253, 263–6, 282, 289; relation of to God, 18, 74–5, 104–7, 109–11 119–120, 125, 153, 161, 175, 188, 193–4, 197, 209, 225–6, 230, 253, 261, 263–6, 282, 289

Dāna, 200, 271, 283

Darśana-mārga, 236

Dayal, Har, 182, 190–1

Death, in Buddhism, 72, 122, 138; Great D., 93, 185; to oneself, 188, 255; of Christ, 35, 147, 222

Deconstruction, 102, 123, 134, 137, 144, 180–1, 288

Dehumanizing, 219, 248, 266–7, 282–6

Demiéville, Paul, 92, 273

Depersonalizing, 266, 269. *See also* dehumanizing

Descartes, René, 101, 103. *See also* Cartesianism

Descent, 33, 79, 114, 132, 134, 148–9, 278

Desire, of the body, 223, 267, 285; for God, 14, 50–1, 53–4, 59, 114–7, 145, 147, 153, 163, 217, 222–3, 266–7; for non-being, 69, 125–6; going beyond, 167, 203–5, 251, 260; religion of D., 28, 30, 114–17, 147–53, 157, 171–2, 195, 203–5, 207, 217, 288

Desirelessness, 204

Desocialized, 266

Detached, 252, 256–68

Devotion, devotional, 2, 19, 38, 75–6, 78, 85, 127, 203–7, 222, 234–5, 242. *See also* love mysticism

Dhammapada, 74, 83, 133–4, 232, 288

Dharma, 38, 72, 74, 87–8, 90, 92, 124, 131, 134, 183, 204–6, 232, 234, 240, 242, 275

Dhyāna, 35, 40, 44, 181, 238, 271–2, 277, 279

Dialogue, Buddhist-Christian, 3–5, 27–30, 32, 72, 77, 127–8, 213, 277, 283, 285, 287

Diamond Sūtra, 43, 87–8, 93, 130, 181, 241, 274

Dichotomy, 70–1, 75, 79, 86, 116, 138, 202

Differentiation, 133, 147, 168, 201, 264

Dionysius, 62, 197

Discipline(s), 29, 35, 50, 53, 144, 185, 206

Discriminating, discrimination, 34, 38, 125, 248

Discrimination, discriminatory, 38, 91, 175, 218

Divinity, 50, 148, 203, 265, 279

Dōgen 道元, 92, 204, 244, 246, 274–5, 290

Dualism, 16, 32, 71, 74, 79, 86, 126–7, 129, 134, 156, 158–9, 161, 192, 204

Duhkha, 205

Dumoulin, Heinrich, 29, 31, 34, 37, 81–2, 91, 185–6, 206, 237, 243, 246, 273, 275–6, 278

Dupré, Louis, 3, 7, 40, 81, 85, 126, 197–8, 281

Durt, Hubert, 44

Dynamic(s) 93, 104–5, 107, 116, 118–9, 125, 134, 149–51, 158, 162, 170, 175, 192, 194, 198–9, 203, 207, 281

East, Easterners, 5, 28, 34, 38, 73, 77, 83, 93, 129, 184, 244, 270, 280, 287

Eckhart, Meister, 1, 20, 29–31, 66, 75, 84–5, 107, 129, 187, 189, 192–3, 197–8, 212–14, 219, 233, 277

Eenicheit, 158–60, 167, 170

Eeninghe, 157–60, 170–1

Ego, 46, 101–2, 113, 125, 131, 136–7, 280, 284, 288–9

Egocentric, 116, 161, 202

Eliade, Mircea, 33, 40, 81, 184, 197

Emotions, 16, 18–9, 60, 125–6, 136, 186, 189, 199–200, 204

Emptiness, 130–1; as negativity, 73; as ideal, 30, 37, 184, 196, 199–200, 202, 206, 234, 246, 288; overcoming, 38, 94, 126, 131–3, 186, 191–2, 246, 271, 273, 278, 281, 284; in Christianity, 24, 53, 77, 115, 188, 220, 223, 225, 231, 248, 250–1, 256, 258–9, 262–4, 267, 268. *See also* *śūnyatā*

Encounter, 4, 12, 27, 54, 59, 103, 136, 139, 146–7, 159, 161, 165, 178–9, 187–8, 196, 198, 258, 277, 283, 289

Enjoyment, 18–9, 25–6, 112, 120, 143–4, 149, 153, 161–2, 166–7, 188, 253, 255, 262, 265

Enlightenment, 13, 21, 28, 35, 39–44, 52, 54, 64–5, 78, 84, 86–9, 90–6, 123, 131–2, 135, 152–4, 176, 180, 184–5, 191, 195, 199, 204, 207, 227, 234, 236, 243–4, 270, 272, 274–5, 281–2, 284–5, 290

Ethics, 19, 36, 38–9, 72, 79, 126, 136, 201, 214, 237, 269–71. *See also* morality

Everyday, 12, 33, 42–3, 46–8, 73, 80, 86, 91, 101, 131, 240, 280–1, 284

Evil, 36, 38–9, 79, 104, 119, 215–16, 223, 226, 266–7, 274

Exercise, 14, 103, 111, 144, 176, 187, 191, 220–2, 230–1, 243, 256

Exteriority, 203

Eye, 25, 54, 117; of the soul, 61–2, 150, 152, 205, 227, 254; of the Buddha, 184

Eyghendo(e)m, 67, 108–9, 119, 167

Eyghenheit, 67–8, 159

Eysschen, 160, 162

Failure, 53, 55, 149–50, 170, 217

Faith, and mysticism, 4, 13–15, 31, 40, 42, 53, 59, 82–3, 90, 94, 128–9, 145–6, 148, 203, 211, 219, 227, 230, 233–5, 262–3; in Buddhism, 76, 85, 183, 185, 207, 237–8, 243–4, 282, 290

Falieren, 164

Fathomless, 156, 160, 162, 169, 171, 173, 250, 252

Formless(ness), 91, 94, 168, 171, 181, 264–5, 279, 288

Freedom, 47, 58, 74, 80, 93, 185, 193, 211–12, 217, 259, 267, 277, 284

Genjōkōan. See Shōbōgenzō

Ghebreken, 143, 149, 162

Ghebruken, 143, 166, 168–9, 175

Ghelijc, 159–61

Ghelijckenisse, 118, 160

Ghemeyne, 105, 175, 215

Ghenoechlijc, 249

Gherenen, 147, 165, 171

Gherinen, 60–1, 65, 152, 158, 166

Gift, 13–14, 17, 22, 50, 69, 83, 90, 110, 112, 137, 150, 152, 165, 200–2, 282–3, 288

Gilkey, Langdon, 128, 245

Gimello, Robert M., 92, 204, 246–7

Giver, 147–8, 200–1. *See also* gift

Godhead, 114, 149, 151, 263

Godless(ness), 70–2, 81

Gotokuchi 後得智, 191

Grace, 52, 75, 84, 120, 145, 152–3, 161–2, 165–6, 184, 215–9, 265, 289–90; mysticism without, 4, 145, 216–21, 227–31, 233, 251, 258–62; condition of full mysticism, 69, 145, 172, 217, 258–61; mysticism as awareness of, 14, 31, 53, 94; mystics not sole possessors of, 86–7, 257; and Buddhism, 31, 93, 233–4, 290. *See also* supernatural

Griffiths, Bede, 279–80

Griffiths, Paul, 281

Guenther, Herbert V., 133–4, 138, 194

Haas, Alois M., 30, 43, 82

Hadewijch, 8, 19, 22, 50–2, 55–8, 61, 63–5, 149–51, 198

Hakuin 白隠, 185, 272, 275–6, 290

Hartshorne, Charles, 78, 80

Hegel, G.W.F., 101, 194–5

Hélyot, Marie, 24

Hilton, Walter, 1, 14

Hīnayāna 35, 234, 236; schools, 36–44.

Hinduism, 4, 39, 41, 78, 83, 86, 123–4, 137, 205, 235, 238, 245, 269, 279

Hisamatsu Shin'ichi 久松真一, 87

Holiness, 43, 81, 119, 167–8, 223, 231, 267, 285

Hongaku 本覚, 272

Huang Po Hsi-yüan 黄檗希運, 43, 71, 79, 88, 92, 130–1, 134, 138, 190, 200, 240–2, 272

Hui-hai, *see* Ta-chu Hui-hai

Hui-neng 慧能, 43, 87–8, 93, 130, 181, 241, 273–4, 290

Humanity, 17, 50, 71, 109, 122–3, 139–41, 148, 176, 223, 284

Humphreys, Christmas, 92, 132, 272

Hva śan, 271

Ibal, Bernard, 194, 202

Idleness, 143, 167–8, 220–1, 224–6, 228–30, 249–50, 256–7, 262–3, 268, 278

Ignorance, 25, 80, 88, 135–6, 251

Im-mediacy, 44, 49, 55–6, 60, 94, 99

Imageless(ness), 21, 55, 58–9, 67, 94, 158–9, 187, 220, 222–3, 228, 246, 249, 253, 260, 262

Immanence, 42, 75, 81–2, 85, 107, 186, 193, 230, 234, 241, 252; immanent transcendence, 75, 84, 186. *See also* transcendence

Immediacy, 42–4, 48–9, 55–61, 94, 99, 140, 243, 262

Impersonal, 38, 77–8, 206, 256

Inactivity, 54, 162, 166, 188, 225

India, Indian, 36, 74–5, 77–8, 81, 92, 125, 129, 131, 135, 191, 199, 203, 234, 269, 271, 279, 281

Indifference, 79, 199, 274

Individual, Individuality, 72, 77, 95, 104, 106, 118, 124, 130, 133–5, 216, 234, 252, 256, 283, 289–90

Individualism, 267

Indwelling, 74, 76, 107, 154, 193, 230, 262

Inkeeren, 114, 216, 220

Inner man, 134, 283

Integrated, 174, 178, 186, 271

Intellect, 40, 62, 64, 91, 104, 111, 114–15, 125–6, 145, 149, 152, 224–5, 261

Interdependence, 74, 181

Intermediary, 55, 60, 67, 108, 139, 142, 148, 153–4, 158–9, 174, 212, 262

Interpersonal, 76, 126, 128, 186, 189

Intersubjectivity, 79, 126

Introversion, 28, 101, 125, 151, 153, 273

Inwardness, 94, 102, 166, 284

Inward-turning, 153, 259. *See also* turning inwards

Inwesen, 230, 262

Inworking, 145, 151–2, 157, 160, 217, 282

Islam, 31, 197, 283

Istech, istich, 265

I-Thou, 126, 200, 202–3

James, William, 16, 22–3, 34, 46, 189, 277

Japan, Japanese, 3, 6, 27, 30–1, 37–8, 74, 80, 83, 87, 92, 137, 191, 194, 198–9, 201, 204, 242, 244, 274–5, 283–5

Jātaka, 206

Jesus, 35, 63, 109, 112, 115–6, 145, 148, 202, 211, 215, 222, 291

Jhāna, 279

Jihi 慈悲, 199

Jita 自他, 200

John of the Cross, 18, 30, 60, 63, 127, 151

Johnston, William, 28–9, 34, 39, 82, 127, 268

Judaeo-Christian, 45, 70–1, 79

Judaism, 80, 197, 283

Kamalaśīla, 131, 182, 191, 271

Karma, 38, 72, 82, 183, 240, 270

Karmic, 72, 272

Karunā, 191, 199

King, Winston L., 42, 70, 83, 115, 231, 271

Kleśa, 199

Kṛṣṇa, 269

Lamotte, Étienne, 129, 199

Laṅkāvatāra Sūtra, 270, 290

Laukikamārga, 136

Lavelle, Louis, 126–7

Le(e)dicheit, 220, 223, 225, 248, 250–1

Leggett, Trevor, 35, 76, 275

Le Saux, Henri, 41

Lévinas, Emmanuel, 194–5, 201–3

Lhasa, 92, 271–3

Liberating, 36, 73, 90, 236, 249, 279, 291

Likeness, 17, 118–20, 160–1, 173–4, 178, 187

Linchi. *See* Rinzai

Logic, 14, 23, 76, 79, 83, 101, 126, 130–3, 142, 180, 188, 190–2, 196, 202, 246

Lokottara, 35, 236

Lotus Sūtra, 236

Love, as ultimate, 78–9, 189, 198, 277, 279–80; in Buddhism, 78–9, 93, 126–7, 132, 190–1, 195–207, 237, 269–70; and desire, 114, 115–17, 126–7, 148–9, 171–2, 199–200, 203, 217, 251; and duality, 56, 78, 126–7, 143, 158–9, 161–72, 179, 193–4, 200–3, 252, 255, 260, 264; and mysticism, 18–19, 22, 25–6, 48–9, 67, 106, 126–7, 139, 141, 149–53, 158–76, 178–9, 195–200, 257–8; and wisdom (knowledge), 30, 52, 55, 63–5, 106, 132, 149–50, 152, 187–8, 191, 196–8, 200, 205, 227–9, 277

Love-mercy, 196, 198, 237. *See also* mercy-love

Love mysticism, 14, 18, 19, 22, 25–6. *See also* mysticism of love

Mahāyāna, 33, 35, 37–40, 87, 91, 94, 180–4, 190–2, 199–201, 204–5, 234, 236–7, 240, 244–6, 269–71, 274, 276–82

Maitrī, 199

Marcel, Gabriel, 46

Mārga, 246–7

Maritain, Jacques, 38, 84–5, 179

Māyā, 83–4, 129

McGinn, Bernard, 196–7

Meditation, 4, 28–9, 35–6, 50, 91, 181–2, 191, 206, 237, 243, 246–7, 269, 271, 274–5, 279

Meeting, 72, 139–55, 157–8

Mercy-love, 34, 38, 78, 126, 198–200, 203, 205–6

Merton, Thomas, 28–9, 33, 41, 77, 84, 92–5, 185, 193, 206, 273

Metaphysical mysticism, 30, 188–9, 197

Method, 11–12, 14, 16, 139, 220–1, 223, 226–9, 231, 238–9, 248, 256

Meyninghe, 257–8

Micchādiṭṭhi, 279

Minne, 19, 22, 114, 163–6, 168, 171–2

Minne-mystiek, 19

Modeless(ness), 21, 159, 163, 173, 187, 249, 262–6, 278

Modes, 11, 15, 21, 33, 52, 61, 64, 111, 131, 146, 161, 163, 173–4, 225, 252, 263–4, 278, 280

Mommaers, Paul, 3–7, 41, 56, 82, 127, 132, 174, 187, 193, 195–6, 212, 277, 287

Monk(s), 28, 90, 183, 206, 239, 242, 275, 282–3

Morality, 20, 50–2, 102, 136, 160, 162, 201, 221–4, 229, 267, 284–5, 288. *See also* ethics

Moralism, 160, 162, 238

Movement, inner, 19, 50, 147, 151, 153, 200, 202, 269, 273; Buddhist, 36, 38, 86; by God, 151, 194; between God and soul, 162, 165, 217, 260

Muditā, 199

Multiplicity, 80, 91, 112–13, 127, 129–30, 133, 137, 145, 147–8, 152, 186–7, 190, 195, 224–5, 277

Murdoch, Iris, 102

Musil, Robert, 48, 57–8, 68

Musō 無想, 42

Musō Soseki 夢窓疎石, 88

Myōkōnin 妙好人, 31

Mystical religion, 39, 41, 81, 85, 276, 283

Mysticism of Love, 189, 196–7, 203. *See also* love mysticism

Nāgārjuna, 130, 132

Nagao Gadjin 長尾雅人, 199

Nakamura Hajime 中村 元, 184, 201

Naturalness, 104–5, 107, 117, 119–20, 160, 199–200, 216, 224, 226–7, 229, 231, 233, 264, 277

Nibbāna, 204. *See also* Nirvana

Niet, 68, 109, 250–1, 253, 264

Nieuwlant, 56–8

Nirvana, 35–8, 72, 74, 80, 123, 132, 134, 181–2, 184, 191, 204–5, 236, 243–4, 269–70, 272, 290

Nishida Kitarō 西田幾多郎, 83, 92

Nishitani Keiji 西谷啓治, 31, 42, 137–8

Non-activity, 93, 250–1, 266, 274

Non-contemplative, 218, 256, 289

Non-duality, 33, 75, 78, 81, 92, 126, 131, 200–2, 279, 281

Nonretrogression, 184

Nothingness, 15, 66, 73, 104, 107, 124, 137, 151, 154, 190, 194, 265, 272, 277, 288

Nuwe, 114, 157, 171

Ōbaku Kiun, *see* Huang Po Hsi-yüan

Obara, 35, 76, 78, 275

Oberhammer, Gerhard, 30, 37, 78, 82, 129, 236

O'Leary, Joseph S., 72, 77

Oneness, 105, 108, 119, 129–30, 148, 195, 223, 277

Onghebeelt, 55, 222, 224

Onghemiddelt, 55

Ontbliven, 162

Ontmoet(e), 146, 159

Ontological, 34, 37, 84, 106, 109–10, 135–6, 189, 197, 231, 248, 261, 276, 280

Onwise, 262, 264

Oriental, 94, 123, 125, 283

Otherness, 34, 54, 56, 75, 82, 93, 95–6, 110, 143, 159, 164, 170, 192, 195, 200, 202–3, 259–60, 269, 277

Other-Power, 92, 234, 282

Otto, Rudolf, 29, 75, 77–8, 84, 129, 189, 193, 203, 233–5

Outdoing oneself, 54, 162–3, 167

Own-being, 130, 186, 282

Oxherding, 132, 243

Pāramitā, 37, 39–40, 200, 237, 240, 271–2

Parfit, Derek, 102

Paradox, 3, 288; in Buddhism, 37, 180–1, 199, 203–4, 241, 245, 270; in Western mysticism, 16, 52, 106, 213, 263–4

Passion, 36, 38–9, 80, 87–9, 91, 116, 125, 135, 145, 179, 183, 198–200, 204, 215, 222, 266, 285

Passivity, 49–55, 57, 60, 66, 90–4, 118–9, 140, 152, 162

Peak, 86, 127, 132–3, 178, 180, 183, 187, 189–95, 236–7, 241, 268, 276–8

Perceiving, 50, 57, 64, 150, 168, 230, 253–4

Perfection(s) 50, 57, 75, 77, 127, 132, 182, 214, 236, 240, 265, 271–2, 285. *See also pāramitā*

Persoenlec, persoenlijc(k), 108–9, 112, 119, 265

Persoenlecheit, persoenlijcheit, 109, 119

Persona, 76

Personalism, 78, 206, 251

Personality, personhood, 47, 68, 77, 79, 119, 174, 189, 256, 289

Persone, 110, 119, 143

Petyt, Maria, 56–7

Plotinus, 49, 61, 150

Porete, Marguerite, 127, 212

Positivity, 35, 54, 56, 73, 80, 83, 93, 115, 129, 135, 140, 150, 159, 182, 197, 199, 205–6, 216, 234, 241

Possession, 49, 56–7, 60–1, 67–9, 104, 106–7, 109–10, 112, 118, 120, 137, 146, 166–7, 169, 172–4, 196, 222, 231, 250, 255–6, 258

Prajñā, 35, 37, 40, 44, 87, 181, 191

Pratītya-samutpāda, 74, 76, 124, 130

Precepts, 87, 237, 242, 273

Pre-mystical, 50–1, 54, 140

Process, 14, 33, 58, 65, 68, 71, 91, 118, 133, 144, 157–8, 167, 178, 181–2, 185, 189, 195, 218, 234, 236, 245, 256, 263, 278, 290

Proust, Marcel, 46–7, 49–50, 60

Pseudo-Dionysius. *See* Dionysius

Psychosomatic, 63, 151, 220

Pudgaladṛṣṭi, 132

Quiescent, 272

Quietism, 44, 49, 52, 92, 212–3, 219, 248, 257, 269–74, 284, 289–90

Quietude, 194, 237, 249, 270, 274, 276, 278

Quine, Willard van Orman, 102

Rast(e), 143, 166, 174, 225, 250–1

Rasten, 156, 166, 169, 228, 250, 258, 260. *See also* resting

Reaction, 5, 44, 66, 77, 120, 131, 140, 151, 157, 160, 173, 240, 269, 278, 289

Rebirth, 72, 86, 184

Redene(n), 162–3, 228, 253, 264

Relation, relationality, 71, 75–6, 106–7, 118–9, 125, 127, 130, 137–8, 147, 164, 197, 202–3

Renewal, 158–9, 171–2, 174–5, 196, 253

Resting, 47, 146–7, 166–74, 224, 231, 252, 260. *See also* rast(en)

Rinzai 臨済, 185, 240, 275

Rita 利他, 284

Ruegg, David S., 92, 131–3, 236–7, 271

Sacraments, 168–9, 266–7

Sacred, 42, 79, 129, 232

Sad, 68

Sadheit, satheit, 166

Sakyamuni, 35, 74, 86, 88, 122, 135, 279, 289. *See also* Buddha

Salech, salegh, salich, 167, 169, 255, 265

Salecheit, salegheit, salicheit, 166, 168–9, 175, 255, 265. *See also* blessedness

Samādhi, 270, 273, 290

Saṃsāra, 38, 86, 132, 135, 205, 243–4

Śamatha, 37, 133, 236, 269, 271, 277, 280

Sangha, 38, 86, 89–90, 232, 242

Saraha, 132–3, 194

Sarvāstivādin, 36

Saux, *See* Le Saux

Schmithausen, Lambert, 36, 236

Schoonenberg, Piet, 78, 86, 129

Seeing, 16–17, 23–5, 38, 57, 61–3, 68, 83–4, 94, 100, 119, 146, 148, 153–5, 159, 232, 240, 244, 253

Self-annihilation, 68

Self-awareness, 67, 102, 258, 263

Self-centeredness, 123, 136–8, 288

Self-conscious, 67–8, 158–9

Self-consciousness, 67–8, 95, 105, 164

Self-founding, 103

Selflessness, 53, 136, 200

Self-presence, 67, 95, 112–13

Senses, language of the, 12–13, 16, 61, 94; going beyond, 49, 55, 64, 91, 123, 151–2, 221–2; and the soul, 104, 145–6, 171, 222, 229, 254

Shakespeare, William, 48

Shikaku 始覚, 272

Shinran, 282

Shōbōgenzō 正法眼蔵, 275; *S. Genjōkōan* 現成公案, 275; *S. Bendōwa* 辨道話, 92, 204; *S. Zuimonki* 隨聞記, 204

Sin, 14, 75, 136, 166, 215–6, 223–4, 229, 256

Sitting, 44, 131, 221–2, 226, 273–6

Skandha, 135

Social, 12, 41, 78–9, 100, 122, 199, 258, 282–4, 289

Soga Ryōjin 曾我景深, 31, 201

Sokuryo-gyōjaku, 274

Spirituality, 3–4, 24, 70–1, 80–1, 85, 133, 136, 197, 204–5, 287

Śrāvaka, 236–7

Stages, 59–60, 62–3, 89, 144, 150, 171–2, 178, 180, 184, 193

Stillness, 43, 221–2, 249, 251, 256, 269, 272, 275

Stirring, 151–3, 157, 171–2, 228

Striving, 81, 133, 159, 171, 191, 203–4, 218, 253, 264, 269, 275, 288

Subitism, 44, 92

Subject-object, 126, 202, 281

Subsistence, 104, 108–11, 260, 289

Substance, 18, 103–4, 125, 137, 190, 230, 240, 264–5

Substance-substrate, 110

Substantialization, 74, 77, 138, 263–4

Sudden(ness), 12, 37, 44, 46, 49, 91–2, 184–5, 270, 272

Śūnyatā, 130–2, 246–7

Śūnyatādṛṣṭi, 132

Supernatural, grace, 17, 120, 145, 161, 216–7, 219, 228, 233, 290; as opposed to natural, 17, 116–7, 120, 145, 161, 216–7, 219, 228, 231–3, 235, 239–40, 257–9, 261, 283, 290. *See also* grace

Suspended, 24, 105, 107, 110–11, 225–6, 230, 289

Suzuki D. T. 鈴木大拙, 28–9, 31–3, 42–3, 77, 80, 95, 239

Syzygy, 131, 191, 271

Sūtras, 33, 35, 40, 86, 93, 132, 136, 181, 237, 240–2

Ta-chu Hui-hai 大珠慧海, 272

Tanabe Hajime 田辺元, 38, 83

Taoism, 34, 93, 269

Tathāgata-garbha, 89. *See also* Buddha-womb

Teresa of Avila, 12, 30

Theism, 70–84, 186, 245

Theravāda, 36–7, 184, 204, 269, 279

Thomas Gallus, 62

Thomas à Kempis, 2

Thomism. *See* Aquinas

Thoughtlessness, 270, 274

Tibet, 37, 92, 271

Tibetan, 135, 27

Touch, Divine, 12–4, 18, 54, 60–1, 64–5, 67, 106, 149, 152–3, 157–9, 163, 165–6, 171, 231, 253–4, 257; absence of in experience, 24, 93, 224; and Nirvana, 181; of one's own essence, 227, 231, 250

Tracy, David, 28, 83, 124

Transcendence, God's, 56, 85, 148, 161, 192; of the self, 206, 243; immanence and, 75, 81–2, 94–5, 186; of everything, 35, 46–7, 83, 85, 127, 194–5, 244, 282; of forms, 29, 94, 137, 148, 168, 205, 222–3, 241; of ordinary knowledge, 33–5, 94, 181, 194–5, 281

Transformation, 35, 39, 46, 62, 64–6, 127, 132, 139, 154, 160, 164

Trinity, 30, 66, 76, 96, 109, 119, 126, 153, 176, 265, 279

Turning inwards, 101, 151, 155, 176, 178, 181, 216–17, 220–1, 223, 226, 228–30, 248, 250, 256. *See also* inward turning

Ueda Shizuteru 上田閑照, 31, 42

Unborn, 35, 187–8

Uncreated, 18, 153, 188, 194, 230

Undifferentiated, 133, 180, 187, 189–94, 277–8, 281

Union, mystical, 19, 63, 66, 79, 94–5, 106, 149, 156, 196, 218, 249, 277, 280; and unity, 30, 167, 170–2,

188–9, 191, 193, 195; as likeness, 161; as unification, 94–5, 157–60; in love, 25, 127, 186; with God, 101, 108, 117–8, 120, 157, 159, 197, 219, 262; with Christ, 146; living, 159, 268

Unitive, 56–7, 63, 94–5, 140

Unity, in the human being, 104–113, 118–9, 121, 123, 134–5, 151, 163, 224–5, 238, 249; in Christian mysticism, 15, 21, 41, 49, 59, 60, 65, 82, 83, 99, 127, 129, 154, 160–8, 170–3, 186–98, 255; of love, 67, 126, 159, 165–7, 170–4; mysticism of, 30, 136; original, 94, 107–8, 110, 118–119, 125, 189; compact, 30, 38, 44, 81, 96, 127130, 133, 180, 186–96, 198–202, 280–1, 288; complex, 127, 130–1, 133, 139, 159–63, 170–3, 186–96, 278, 280–1, 288

Upāya, 78, 88, 127, 131, 182, 206, 240

Upekṣā, 199

Utewerken, 162–3, 167

Value, 115, 223, 240; of the conative, 247; of contemplation, 257, 266, 284–5; of mystical consciousness, 17, 218, 223, 226–9, 235, 257; of personal God, 203, 277; of the world, 80, 83, 186, 197

Van Bragt, Jan, 128, 288–90

Verbeelt, 60, 222

Verber(r)en, 143, 164, 172

Vernuwen, 158, 171–2, 174

Vipaśyanā, 37, 44, 133, 269, 271

Virtue, 18, 23, 48, 50–1, 53, 58, 119, 144, 166–7, 169, 188, 192, 199, 223, 228, 230, 248, 251, 256–7, 272, 274, 283–4

Vis a fronte, 205

Vis a tergo, 205

Vision, 13, 62–3, 65, 73, 254

Vonke, 107

Waldenfels, Hans, 29, 73, 77

Weil, Simone, 39, 48–9, 51, 58, 60

Wer(c)kele(e)k, wer(c)kelijc(k), 108, 119, 143, 159, 163, 172, 174

Wesele(e)c, weselijc(k), 105, 108, 119, 163–4, 168, 265

Wesen, 105–6, 108, 114, 119, 137, 143, 167, 221, 224, 228, 230, 250, 252, 255, 260, 262, 264–5

Wholeness, 128, 132–3, 194

William of Saint Thierry, 52, 63, 150, 197–8

Wisdom, 30, 136, 276; Buddhism as a religion of, 28, 40, 125–7, 181–8, 196, 198–207; impersonal, 38, 78; transcendent, 37–8, 40, 87–8, 90–6, 181–6, 241, 244; and compassion, 88, 126, 132, 181–4, 187–8, 190–2, 198–207, 278–80

Wiselo(o)es, 161, 168, 225, 264

Wittgenstein, Ludwig, 101–2

Woolf, Virginia, 15–16, 46–7, 60, 68

Working, 31, 38, 62, 64, 133, 144–5, 151, 156, 166, 171, 176, 195, 213, 263, 266, 281–2

Yabukōji 薮柑子, 276

Yamaguchi Susumu 山口 益, 200

Yaśomitra, 236

Yearning, 53, 114–15, 144, 148, 151, 184, 250–1, 259, 261, 289

Yoga, 234–5

Yogācāra, 135

Yung-ming Yen-shou 永明延壽, 274

Zaehner R. C., 46–7

Zazen 坐禅, 91–2, 239, 242, 246–7

Zuimonki. See Shōbōgenzō